THE ROUGH GUIDE TO

Psychology

Dr Christian Jarrett

www.roughguides.com

Credits

The Rough Guide to Psychology

Editing & picture research: Joe Staines
Typesetting: Pradeep Thapliyal
Diagrams: Katie Lloyd-Jones
Proofreading: Neil Foxlee
Production: Rebecca Short

Rough Guides Reference

Editors: Kate Berens, Tom Cabot,
Tracy Hopkins, Matthew Milton,
Joe Staines, Ruth Tidball
Director: Andrew Lockett

Publishing Information

Published April 2011 by
Rough Guides Ltd, 80 Strand, London WC2R 0RL
345 Hudson St, 4th Floor, New York 10014, USA
Email: mail@roughguides.com

Distributed by the Penguin Group:
Penguin Books Ltd, 80 Strand, London WC2R 0RL
Penguin Group (USA), 375 Hudson Street, NY 10014, USA
Penguin Group (Australia), 250 Camberwell Road, Camberwell, Victoria 3124, Australia
Penguin Group (New Zealand), 67 Apollo Drive, Mairangi Bay, Aukland 1310, New Zealand

Rough Guides is represented in Canada by Tourmaline Editions Inc.,
662 King Street West, Suite 304, Toronto, Ontario, M5V 1M7

Printed in Singapore by Toppan Security Printing Pte. Ltd.

376 pages; includes index

A catalogue record for this book is available from the British Library

ISBN: 978-1-84836-460-8

1 3 5 7 9 8 6 4 2

Contents

Part V: Psychology at large

Part VI: Psychological problems

Part VII: Resources

Preface

As this book goes to print, the UK government has just announced plans to start measuring the happiness of the country's citizens. Together with frequent brain-based science breakthroughs and endless media comment on mental health, work stress and celebrity breakdowns, it's yet another sign of how psychological issues are higher up the public agenda than ever before.

Psychology is about turning the objective scientific approach inwards to study ourselves and why we behave the way we do. Conjecture and intuition are put to one side and potential explanations are tested with experiments, just as they are in more traditional sciences.

Psychology isn't perfect. Most of its experiments are conducted with participants from the industrialized West, often with small sample sizes and findings too rarely followed up over time. That doesn't mean we should reject it as a pseudoscience. On the contrary, by recognizing the value of quality psychological research and providing the discipline with adequate funding and resources, we all gain – whether through reducing prejudice or improving treatments for mental health, or by finding more effective ways to combat global problems such as climate change.

How this book works

The Rough Guide to Psychology brings you up to speed with the very latest findings from hundreds of psychology experiments. It tells you about the discipline's history as well as the latest interpretations of classic experiments, such as Stanley Milgram's controversial research into obedience, and famous case studies, like that of Phineas Gage, the nineteenth-century railway worker who survived an iron rod passing through his brain.

This is not a textbook and the material isn't always arranged by sub-discipline, the way psychology tends to be studied in schools and universities. Instead, it starts with you, the reader, working outwards to your personal relationships and then on to society at large. Later sections deal with the way psychology is applied to the real world, for example in politics, business and education. Finally, the focus shifts to psychological problems, including depression, anxiety and schizophrenia, and to therapeutic approaches, from psychoanalysis to Cognitive Behavioural Therapy.

The book contains frequent references to experiments and case studies, and, wherever possible, names and dates are provided to help you track down the original research online. By the end, you'll have discovered that many psychological findings are humbling – we're far more flawed and error-prone than we like to think. You'll also have discovered how psychology can be used to navigate these weaknesses, exploit our strengths and improve people's lives, not just through therapy but in every sphere of contemporary life – in industry, in schools and in hospitals. There is so much more to learn, and the book ends with a list of useful resources – from websites and blogs to books and organizations.

Acknowlededgments

Many thanks to Ruth Tidball and Joe Staines at Rough Guides: Ruth for proposing the book and her warm encouragement in the early months; Joe for his diligent editing and many constructive suggestions.

I'd like to thank the British Psychological Society and in particular my editor there, Jon Sutton, for the opportunities given to me. Much of my knowledge of psychology research and trends is derived from the work that I'm lucky enough to do for them.

I'm grateful to Klaus Scherer at the Centre for Affective Sciences for permission to adapt some text on emotion that I wrote previously for the Centre's website. Thanks also to Tom Stafford whose conference presentation provided the inspiration for the box on page 59, and to Vaughan Bell whose writing and links on the Mind Hacks blog are an endlessly valuable resource.

I read many books in preparation for writing this guide and I'd like to acknowledge several of the authors whose writing I found particularly informative and inspiring. These include: Steven Pinker, Dan Ariely, Matt Ridley, James Surowiecki and Alison Gopnik.

I'm grateful too to the authors of countless articles published in *The Psychologist*, *New Scientist*, *The APS Observer* and *Scientific American Mind*, from which I learned so much. I'd also like to recognize the hard work and ingenuity of the many psychologists whose research and ideas are discussed in these pages.

Thanks to my mother, Linda, for encouraging me on the path to writing many years ago. And most of all, thank you to my beloved wife Jude: I couldn't have done it without you!

Christian Jarrett, 2010

The Rough Guide to

Psychology

Introduction: What is psychology?

Take a seat in a bustling bar or café and you'll doubtless hear energetic discussions about who did what to whom and why. That's because we're all psychologists at heart. Rare is the person who doesn't wish to understand him or herself better. Who isn't interested in improving their relationships with the people they live and work with? Visit a school and see an ink-stained teacher struggling to engage a class of recalcitrant children. Listen as a nurse urges a heart-attack survivor to stop smoking. Gatecrash a tense board meeting where managers are persuading overworked staff to go the extra mile. Marvel as hoards head herd-like for the beach on a scorching summer's day. Psychology, literally "the study of the mind", is about all this and much more. It's the science of why we think and behave the way we do, alone and in our relationships, and its findings are relevant to every aspect of our lives.

Psychology – science or common sense?

The difference between professional psychologists and the rest of us is that they know what they *don't* know. They are the ultimate sceptics. From the café to the boardroom, you're likely to find people using intuition – their gut instincts – in their attempts to understand or influence other people. Psychologists, by contrast, strive to be objective about the subjective. They measure, test, observe, report, verify and repeat. They propose dispassionate hypotheses for why people behave the way they do, and then perform experiments, gathering evidence to test whether those hypotheses stand up to scrutiny.

Anatomy of a psychology experiment

An important experiment by Harvard University psychologist Ellen Langer and her colleague Judith Rodin conducted in the 1970s found that elderly nursing home residents given more responsibilities and choices went on to live longer and enjoyed better health. This study provides a useful way of exploring the basic anatomy of a typical psychology experiment. The residents who were given the chance to care for a houseplant, to choose where to receive visitors, and which films to watch were the **experimental group**. The residents who didn't receive these benefits (they were given a houseplant but told the staff would care for it) became the **control group**, with which the experimental group could be compared.

The residents who took part in the study were known as **participants**, referred to collectively as the **study sample**. Ideally, the residents should have been selected at random (to avoid experimenter **bias**) and if the findings were to generalize to all nursing home residents (the **population** of interest), they should have been representative of that broader group.

Psychology experiments usually involve measuring something and in this case both groups of residents completed tests of their health,

mood and alertness before the intervention began (at **baseline**) and then again at the study end – the **outcome**. Many studies also repeat their **measures** at several subsequent **time points**, known as the six-month, one-year (or whatever the delay is) follow-up. Studies that take repeated measures over time are known as **longitudinal**, whereas those that take an isolated snapshot are **cross-sectional**. The former are considered superior because they can establish that a change in a given factor at one time point has led to a change in another factor later on. Cross-sectional studies, by contrast, are unable to demonstrate the direction of causality between factors.

To judge whether any differences between baseline and outcome measures, or between experimental and control groups, are significant, psychologists use **statistical tests**. Generally these show the possibility of the current outcome (or one even more extreme) being observed if the null hypothesis were true. The **null hypothesis** is the opposite of the **hypothesis**. In Langer and Rodin's study, the hypothesis would have been something like: "greater responsibilities and freedoms are good for nursing home residents' mental and physical health" whereas the null hypothesis would have been something like: "greater responsibilities and freedoms make no difference to nursing home residents' mental and physical health."

Psychologists typically consider an observed difference to be **statistically significant** if there is a less than five percent chance that it, or an even more extreme outcome, could have occurred if the null hypothesis were true. Increasingly, researchers in psychology believe it is also important to provide some measure of the size of the difference that is observed, not just whether the difference is statistically significant or not. This is known as the **effect size**, and in Langer and Rodin's study it could influence whether the difference in outcomes between the experimental and control groups was **clinically significant** (that is big enough to make the difference between a person meeting the criteria, or not, for a diagnosis, such as for depression) or practically meaningful, in terms of quality of life and increased longevity.

Finally, when Langer and Rodin came to publish their results they would have had to submit them to a **peer-reviewed** academic journal (they chose the *Journal of Personality and Social Psychology*). Peer-review involves anonymous experts in the field scrutinizing the study's methodology and statistics to ensure the conclusions are justified, and that there is enough information for other scientists to replicate or extend the study should they wish to. Peer-reviewers can reject or accept a paper, and in either case they will usually provide useful feedback to the study authors. Nearly all the experiments referred to throughout this book have been published in peer-reviewed journals.

In the teachers' common room, the new recruit struggling with a boisterous class seeks the advice of an older colleague. "Punish any trouble-makers and show them who's boss", the veteran teacher says. Anecdotally, such an approach may have seemed effective for this particular teacher, but is that really what works? Perhaps the novice teacher isn't giving enough praise, or doesn't talk enough to the pupils. A psychologist won't just take anyone's word for it. They'll directly test the effects of different teaching styles. They might allocate different kinds of teachers

Isn't it all just obvious?

When people encounter reports of new psychological research in the media, a common reaction is to think "I could have told them that". In some ways this is understandable. For a start, the subject matter of psychology is people – something we're all extremely familiar with. Research has shown that such familiarity gives people false confidence in a topic: for example, it's been shown that we overestimate our understanding of mundane technologies like zips and flush toilets simply because we encounter them every day.

Secondly, a "folk psychology" has built up over tens of thousands of years leading to a rich body of cultural wisdom. This can mean that whatever psychological science uncovers, it's easy to feel that we already know about it. But folk psychology is contradictory. On finding a like-minded romantic interest, for example, we might find it encouraging that such unions have a proven history as reflected in the saying "birds of a feather flock together". And yet we could just as easily have fallen for an outlandish character and found the explanation for our attraction in the adage "opposites attract". So with some psychology findings – whatever the result – with the benefit of hindsight it's easy to feel that the outcome was obvious and easy to explain.

In reality, some psychological findings turn out just the way we'd expect while others are truly surprising. And of course, we can't possibly know in advance which will be which. Imagine psychological experiments had confirmed the benefits of debriefing people after a trauma, rather like a form of psychological first aid. That might seem obvious, but actually it's wrong. And it's a good job that such research really has been conducted because it turns out that routine, immediate psychological debriefing after a trauma can actually harm victims – interrupting natural recovery processes, inducing re-traumatization and in some cases provoking symptoms through the power of suggestion! In fact it's possible to dine out on all sorts of surprising psychological findings (did you know that wiggling your eyes from side to side can boost your memory performance?), but to do so is to miss the point that the value of a psychological finding shouldn't rest on how surprising it is.

to different classrooms and compare outcomes. Or perhaps they'll seek out schools with alternative approaches and collect as much evidence as they can for what kind of approach works best. Chapter 21 looks at what research in this area has found.

Or consider that nurse trying to convince the stubborn patient that he mustn't smoke any longer. She might aim to shock him with statistics about just how many people are falling victim to smoking-related illnesses. But perhaps she's using the wrong tactic – she might have had more luck if she told him about the legions of people who are giving up smoking, and how much better they're feeling for it.

Because psychology is about people, it's often seen wrongly as a soft science. One reason for this is the familiarity of psychology's subject matter to us all. Most of us will happily trust the judgement of an astrophysicist who advocates String Theory. But if a psychologist were to tell an experienced teacher that their lifetime approach is sub-optimal – well, you can imagine the reaction. Most people harbour strong beliefs about why we and other people act like they do. This is known as folk psychology and it can sometimes clash with scientific psychology. If psychological scientists report a finding that is consistent with widely held beliefs, then they tend to be ridiculed for wasting funding on discovering the blindingly obvious (see box opposite). On the other hand, counter-intuitive findings, especially ones that contradict age-old ways of doing things, can provoke a hostile reaction. Few of us like to be told that our intuition is wrong.

But far from being a soft or easy science, psychology is, at its best, the epitome of the sceptical scientific approach. Because people and their lives and relationships are so complicated, and because we all – including psychologists – hold so many preconceptions, the science of psychology must be watertight. Psychologists by necessity are ingenious when it comes to devising ways to test their assumptions. They're eagle-eyed at spotting and skilful at controlling the extraneous factors that could interfere with their results.

A brief history of psychology

People have been asking psychological questions and proposing psychological ideas since time immemorial. It's human nature to do so. Some of the earliest recorded psychological ideas are found in the writings of

Wilhelm Maximilian Wundt (1832–1920) is seen by many as the grandfather of Psychology. In a remarkable career spanning 68 years, he trained more than 180 doctoral students, many in the new science of psychology, and published more than 50,000 pages of books and articles. Several of Wundt's students would go on to form famous psychology laboratories of their own.

the Ancient Greek philosophers. Consider Epicurus's advice that a circle of close friends is one of the most important ingredients for a happy life. Similar examples could be taken just as easily from ancient civilizations in China, India or Egypt. Or fast-forward to the seventeenth century and examine the writings of philosopher John Locke on the "tabula rasa" – the idea that a baby's mind is like a blank slate waiting to be filled by education and sensory experience. But crucially, these were psychological musings, not psychological science. The application of the scientific approach to psychological questions occurred only relatively recently, with psychology's birth usually traced to the establishment of **Wilhelm Wundt's** laboratory at the University of Leipzig in 1879. In the United States, the leading pioneer in psychology's early years was **William James**.

Wundt had stated his intention to form a new science of psychology in his 1874 book *Principles of Physiological Psychology* in which he argued that the same experimental rigour deployed in physiology, such as in Hermann von Helmholtz's measures of the speed of nerve transduction, could similarly be brought to bear on our inner experiences of the outside world. In his experimental psychology laboratory, Wundt, along with his students and colleagues, would carefully record people's subjective experiences of different sensory stimuli – an approach known today as "introspection" or "experimental self-observation". Later in life, Wundt also wrote ten volumes on *Völkerpsychologie*, which trans-

William James (1842–1910)

William James, the brother of novelist Henry James and diarist Alice James, is most famous for his peerless two-volume, 1400-page book *The Principles of Psychology*, a hybrid of textbook, self-help manual and confessional memoir, published in 1890. His *Varieties of Religious Experience* (1902) is also considered a classic.

James's remarkably lucid insights into the human condition remain as fresh and relevant as ever, and contemporary students continue to benefit from his clear descriptions of key psychological phenomena ("Everyone knows what attention is. It is the taking possession by the mind, in clear and vivid form, of one out of what seem several simultaneously possible objects or trains of thought."). James's gift was likely forged in the flames of his own turmoil – he struggled to settle on a career path, studying medicine, art and philosophy before taking up psychology, and he suffered a breakdown of depression and anxiety in his early twenties.

James was offered a place at Harvard in 1873 where he taught the first ever course on experimental psychology. There's debate over whether he, a medic by training, also founded the first US psychological laboratory in 1875 at Harvard, or if the honour should go instead to his doctoral student G. Stanley Hall who established a laboratory at Johns Hopkins University in 1883. Supporters for the latter argue that James's lab was mostly for demonstration rather than original research. Such controversies aside, it's difficult to exaggerate his influence and today James is usually referred to as the father of American Psychology.

Although James conducted little actual psychology research of his own, his writings – especially on such topics as consciousness, free will, attention, the self and emotions – anticipated many later psychological findings. In a sense James's psychology was self-taught, although he did study briefly under Helmholtz during one of his many visits to Europe, and also met other European psychology and physiology pioneers, including Carl Ludwig, Carl Stumpf and even Wilhelm Wundt. James was also heavily influenced by Charles Darwin, as revealed by his writings on the possible adaptive functions of human consciousness.

James served as president of the American Psychological Association in 1904 and his former student Mary Whiton Calkins would become the first female president of the Association the following year. As scientific psychology sought to distance itself from the practices of mediums, mesmerists and other charlatans, James's continued interest and involvement in the paranormal became an enduring embarrassment to his psychologist peers. In turn, James became progressively disillusioned with experimental psychology as it began to shun introspection in favour of an exclusive focus on outwardly observable behaviours. The year before James died he met Carl Jung and Sigmund Freud at Clark University, reportedly describing the latter as a man obsessed by fixed ideas.

Indolence and Drunkennefs.

An illustration from the English translation of Lavater's *Essays on Physiognomy*. The Swiss clergyman Johann Kaspar Lavater (1741–1801) was a key figure in the revival of interest in physiognomy, the belief that you could read a person's character from his or her face.

lates awkwardly as cultural or ethnic psychology. Here Wundt argued that it is not enough for psychology to study individual minds, it must also dig deeper into cultural history and the evolution of local legends, mores and language. Often ignored and rarely translated, some historians say the series laid the foundation for many aspects of contemporary psychology.

The science of psychology faced many battles in its early years. Psychological pioneers encountered resistance from academics in the field of mental philosophy – the branch of that discipline concerned with topics such as consciousness, free will and the relation between the mind and the body – and provoked scepticism from physical scientists who felt that inner experiences were beyond the reach of the scientific approach. At the same time, the public's perception of psychology was misinformed by the popularity of pseudoscientific practices such as **phrenology** (inferring character traits by the feeling of bumps on the head), **physiognomy** (inferring character traits from facial features) and spiritualism. The advocates of these beliefs often mislabelled themselves as psychologists and many also offered questionable advice on mental ills and marital strife.

The earliest scientific psychologists like Wundt were inspired by research in physiology that showed the possibility of quantifying people's experiences of physical stimuli, such as light and sound. The physiologist Ernst Weber had shown, for example, that people's sensitivity to a change in pressure on their skin isn't fixed, but varies in proportion to the pressure currently being applied. This is known as the Weber-Fechner Law and it also applies to other senses (see p.56).

So the earliest psychology laboratories tended to focus on sensory phenomena, and psychology's scientific reputation gradually began to grow. By 1900 there were over forty psychology laboratories in North America, a large number of them set up by students of Wundt. The first major British psychology lab was opened at University College London (UCL) in 1898 by **James Sully**, with a little help from the scientist and polymath **Francis Galton** (Charles Darwin's cousin), while the first in the southern hemisphere was established in 1908 in New Zealand.

As scientific psychology grew, its pioneers began to organize themselves. The **American Psychological Association** was founded in 1892 by a group that included **G. Stanley Hall**, its first president. The **British Psychological Society** started life as The Psychological Society in 1901 at UCL, with ten founder members including James Sully and **W.H.R. Rivers** (famous for his treatment of soldiers during World War I). The current name was adopted in 1906 to distinguish it from a separate "unacademic" organization that shared the original name. Psychology's first official journals were also established during this era, including the **American Journal of Psychology**, founded by G. Stanley Hall in 1887, and the **British Journal of Psychology**, created by James Ward and W.H.R. Rivers in 1904.

The development of psychology at the end of the nineteenth century and the beginning of the twentieth can be divided broadly between the **structuralists**, led by another of Wundt's students, **Edward Titchener**, and the more diverse **functionalists**, who didn't really have a leader as such. Both schools were particularly focused on the scientific study of consciousness, but structuralists were concerned with breaking it down into its constituent parts, largely through introspection (reflecting on one's own mental experiences), whereas the functionalists (inspired by Darwin) were more interested in how consciousness works and what adaptive purposes it serves. Another distinction is that the structuralists were concerned with purely scientific questions whereas the functionalists led the way in applying psychology to real life.

Another powerful influence on psychology near the start of the twentieth century was the emergence of **Sigmund Freud**'s psychoanalysis (see p.342). In many ways this was a blow to the new science of psychology. Although Freud began his career as a hard-nosed scientist, his later psychoanalytic ideas were based more on case studies and conjecture than on experimentation. Scientific psychologists were largely unimpressed, but psychoanalysis would capture the imagination of the public, especially in the US, and proved particularly influential in psychiatry and clinical psychology. Freud also inspired a small army of followers, including **Carl Jung** and **Alfred Adler**, who developed their own influential versions of psychoanalysis. To this day, many people confuse psychology with psychoanalysis and you're likely to discover Freudian literature in the psychology section of many a bookshop.

As the early twentieth century progressed, the techniques and focus of the early scientific psychologists gave way to a new, powerful movement in psychology known as **behaviourism**. Inspired by ground-breaking animal research into learning and conditioning by **Ivan Pavlov**, **Edward Thorndike** and others, behaviourism turned the focus of psychology to that which is outwardly observable. Consciousness and mental states were no longer seen as valid topics of inquiry and all links with philosophy were broken. Initially championed by **John Watson**, of Little Albert fame (see p.110), behaviourism would come to dominate American psychology for nearly fifty years, reaching its zenith in the teachings of **B.F. Skinner** (see p.14).

However, it is important to note that during a similar period, Germany saw the rise of **Gestalt psychology**, which was specifically concerned with the holistic contents of consciousness. Gestalt psychologists, like **Max Wertheimer**, focused on understanding mental experiences in their entirety, as they occurred – recognizing that mental experience is often distinct from, or more than, the sum of its parts. A good example is

the well-known image that can be perceived either as two faces looking at each other in profile or as a vase, depending on which elements are seen as the foreground and which as the background. Gestalt psychologists would go on to make early break-throughs in memory, learning and perception, in many ways anticipating the cognitive movement that was to emerge in psychology from the 1950s.

Two heads facing each other in profile or a vase? This famous illusion was devised by the Danish psychologist Edgar John Rubin in 1915.

COGNITIVE REVOLUTION

Inspired in part by developments in computer technology and artificial intelligence, the second half of the twentieth century saw a new dawn in psychology as more and more researchers began to study the mental processes that behaviourism had outlawed. Some historians have even described this change as a **cognitive revolution**. Cognitive psychology pioneers include British psychologist **Frederic Bartlett**, who performed ground-breaking work on memory; **Noam Chomsky**, famous for his work on language acquisition and the idea that there is a universal grammar; and **Ulric Neisser**, whose 1967 book *Cognitive Psychology* is credited by some for giving a name to this new and exciting field.

Cognitive psychology is all about the mental activities that go on in our brains, as we process and store incoming sensory information and plan and execute bodily movements. Many of its models are based on flow diagrams of boxes and arrows, rather like the input and output schematics of a computer. Today, cognitive psychology is the dominant approach in **experimental psychology** and researchers in other fields often adopt a cognitive perspective. Social cognition, for example, is a popular and influential branch of social psychology, which recognizes that in order to understand social behaviour it is important to consider how people think about themselves and others. And perhaps the fastest moving and most well-funded area of psychology at the beginning of the twenty-first century is **cognitive neuroscience**, which aims to understand the relationship between our mental processes and the wet tissue housed in our skulls.

A taxonomy of psychology and psychologists

Broadly speaking there are two kinds of psychologist – researchers or **psychological scientists** who perform experiments, and **practitioners** who apply the findings of psychology in real world settings. Many psychologists do both, but for simplicity's sake let's start with psychological researchers. Like a city, psychology has been prone to sprawl, so today we find psychologists conducting research in an astonishing multitude of areas, with new avenues of investigation appearing all the time. In the same psychology department, you're likely to find a social psychologist analysing the use of language in newspaper coverage,

The behaviourists: John Watson and B.F. Skinner

John Broadus Watson (1878–1958) burst onto the psychology scene in 1913, age 34, when he delivered an iconoclastic lecture at Columbia University, slamming the nascent science for its past failures and arguing for a new exclusive focus on the prediction and control of outwardly observable behaviour – what became known as behaviourism. Watson had started his postgraduate studies at the University of Chicago studying philosophy under John Dewey but, unimpressed, he changed supervisors and ended up completing his doctoral thesis on the brain changes associated with learning in rats.

By the time Watson delivered his controversial address at Columbia University, he was already head of the psychology department at Johns Hopkins University, having joined the school just five years earlier. His address was published a few weeks later as an article in the journal *Psychology Review*, entitled "Psychology as the Behaviourist Views it". Known by many as the "Behaviourist Manifesto", this article would come to signify the birth of behaviourism.

Watson's reputation continued to rise and two years later he was duly elected president of the American Psychological Association. However, everything changed in 1920 when it was discovered that he had been having an affair with his student Rosalie Rayner. Forced to resign, Watson subsequently married Rayner, and she acted as his co-author on what has become his most famous and controversial research – the conditioning of a baby known forever in psychological mythology as "Little Albert" (see p.110). Although Watson continued writing about psychology for the general public, he followed his departure from Johns Hopkins University with a career in advertising in New York City at J. Walter Thompson, becoming vice-president, and a millionaire in the process.

Burrhus Frederic Skinner (1904–90) took Watson's ideas and ran with them, establishing what would become known as radical behaviourism. At one time probably the most famous scientist on the planet, Skinner actually started out his post-grad days with a brief stint as a writer and poet, but the works of Pavlov and Watson turned him onto psychology. Eventually he became a professor at Harvard University, and his name would become associated in psychological mythology with the eponymous Skinner box, a chamber for training rats.

Skinner's radical behaviourism argued that human and animal actions can be understood entirely in terms of reinforcement schedules – in other words, whether past behaviours had been followed by rewarding or punishing consequences. Among Skinner's most famous works are his first book *The Behaviour of Organisms* (1938); *Verbal Behaviour* (1957), which drew scorn from the celebrated linguist

Noam Chomsky; and the controversial, bestselling *Beyond Freedom and Dignity* (1971), which argued that much of human behaviour is controlled by the environment. Skinner's research and writings became influential in many areas of public life, including education and criminal rehabilitation. To this day, there's a commune in Mexico called Los Horocones that lives according to the principles of Skinner's behaviourism.

As well as inventing the Skinner box, Skinner also created a pigeon-guided missile system during World War II (it apparently worked but was never used) and a glass, temperature-controlled "Air Crib" for babies. A *Life* magazine article published in the 1950s about the crib provoked allegations that he experimented on his own daughter, some of which rumble on to this day.

B.F. Skinner invented the baby tender or Air Crib in order to provide infants with a clean, safe environment in which to develop. He tested it on his own daughter Deborah, seen here with her mother Yvonne Skinner.

a **developmental psychologist** watching the way babies respond to smiles, and a cognitive psychologist scanning participants' brains while they remember lists of words. Indeed, consider any aspect of how we behave and you can be fairly sure that there is a psychologist somewhere in the world investigating that topic.

One way to think about psychology research is on a continuum from the big picture to the tiniest detail. You can identify psychologists by their position on this spectrum. **Social psychologists** tend to study people from the outside – crowds, friends, relationships. **Cognitive psychologists**, by contrast, tend to lift up the bonnet and investigate how memory and perception work. Some **biological psychologists** zoom in even closer, studying individual brain cells. They also study aspects of behaviour like stress and sleeping. It's as if these different psychologists are working on different floors of the same office building. Like company colleagues, they're all working towards the same end – understanding human thought and behaviour – but day-to-day, they probably won't have that much to do with each other.

Another way to characterize psychologists is by their theoretical orientation. **Evolutionary psychologists**, for example, seek to understand the way people behave in the context of our evolutionary origins. Some evolutionary psychology has been criticized for working backwards – looking at a given behaviour and dreaming up an ad hoc explanation, such as that language evolved because hand gestures wouldn't be seen across the long grass of the savannah. Quality evolutionary psychology, however, provides novel, testable insights. Russell Jackson and Lawrence Cormack's "evolved navigation theory", for example, accurately predicted that people will perceive a vertical distance as greater when viewed from above compared with below, based on the rationale that a drop is far more likely to lead to harm.

Another important field of psychology that's grounded in a particular theoretical orientation is **positive psychology**. Founded by Martin Seligman at the University of Pennsylvania, positive psychology is an antidote to the traditional focus of psychology on people's problems, and seeks instead to study people's strengths and how to nurture them.

One further important way to distinguish psychology researchers is between those who measure and those who identify themes and ideas. Formally, this is the difference between quantitative and qualitative research. A **quantitative** researcher would go about investigating mood by devising a scale and rating people according to how many items they agreed with on that scale, thus resulting in a mood score. A **qualitative** researcher, by contrast, would interview people about how they were feeling. They'd transcribe those interviews and look for recurring themes and ideas in the way people talked about their mood. Many psychologists perform both types of research, and qualitative research can help lay the groundwork for quantitative research. Interviewing people about their mood, for example, could help identify the kinds of questions that a mood scale should include.

APPLIED PSYCHOLOGY

Categorizing psychologists is easier when it comes to those professionals who apply the findings of psychology to the real world. When most people think of a psychologist, they probably imagine a therapist working with clients who have mental health issues. Such psychologists are known as **clinical** and **counselling** psychologists and they do indeed form the largest grouping of applied psychologists. In case you're wondering, **psychiatrists** are different. Although the two professions often work together closely, psychiatrists are medical doctors who have chosen to specialize in mental health. Traditionally, psychiatrists followed a medical model and were concerned principally with formal diagnosis and with prescribing treatments, especially drugs. By contrast, clinical and counselling psychologists tend to avoid diagnostic labels and instead construct formulations – this is a "big picture" approach, which considers the biological, social and psychological factors affecting a client. As you'd expect, psychologists also advocate and deliver "talking therapies" rather than drugs. Today there is a blurring of these approaches and many psychiatrists will adopt a psychological perspective. Another change from the past is that whereas psychiatrists used to always be the lead professional in a given service, psychologists are increasing in their influence and authority. In 2010 in the UK, for example, four psychologists were for the first time granted "approved clinician" status, giving them overall responsibility for patients detained for treatment and testing under the Mental Health Act.

There are also **health psychologists** who work in hospitals and people's homes, finding ways to improve the quality of life of patients, helping them recover from and adapt to illness. On a larger scale, health psychologists also often advise government authorities on how to improve public health, for example by devising and running obesity-reduction programmes or anti-smoking campaigns.

Organizational or **business** psychologists go into companies and use findings from psychology to improve the way teams work together, optimizing recruitment, office structure and staff training. **Educational psychologists** work in schools and local authorities, helping and assessing children with special educational needs and advising on school policies and practices. There are also **sports psychologists** working with individual athletes and teams, helping improve training, boosting team cohesion and guiding positive thinking.

Of course there are also **forensic** or **criminal** psychologists, made famous through fictional dramas like the UK television series *Cracker*. Most forensic psychologists work in prisons or other secure institutions,

What is cognitive archaeology?

Like many academic disciplines, psychology is forever fragmenting into ever finer and newer specialisms. An apt example is the emerging field of cognitive archaeology – a marriage between psychology and neuroscience on the one hand and archaeology on the other. This new field is founded on the idea that archaeological artefacts can shed light on how the human mind evolved. Cave drawings reveal evidence of symbolic thought, while ever more intricate tools are a physical manifestation of early humans' evolving ability to plan ahead and share technological advances.

As an example of cognitive archaeological research, consider a recent study by Dietrich Stout at the Institute of Archaeology and Thierry Chaminade at the Wellcome Trust Centre for Neuroimaging in London. They and their colleagues scanned the brains of three archaeologists with the rare ability to perform two types of early Stone Age tool-making, dating from between 2.6 and 0.25 million years ago: the creation of Oldowan stone chips and the crafting of more complex Acheulean cutting tools. As the archaeologists performed their dextrous skills in the brain scanner, a raft of visuo-motor regions were activated, with the Acheulean technique exercising a more extensive network than the Oldowan. Crucially, both techniques activated areas that overlap with language-related brain regions, leading the researchers to conclude that increasingly skill-intensive tool use may have co-evolved with language in a mutually reinforcing way.

One issue at the heart of cognitive archaeology is what's known as the "sapient paradox". This is the observation that our genetic make-up has remained virtually unchanged for the last sixty thousand years even while the human mind appears to have evolved rapidly in terms of cultural practices, and the use of numbers and written language. This turns on its head the traditional idea that biological evolution drove the progress of human culture, and instead suggests that cultural and technical innovations unleashed the potential of the human brain.

helping clients there who have mental health problems, and running rehabilitation programmes. A small minority also advise police on so-called psychological profiling – using clues from a crime scene and patterns of behaviour to infer the characteristics of the perpetrator and the way they're likely to behave next.

The future of psychology

Psychology is thriving. Students are queuing in ever greater numbers to study the subject. New technologies are offering undreamt of opportunities. The world over, from President Obama's White House appointments (for example, Cass R. Sunstein) to the French prime minister's creation of a brain and behaviour research unit to inform public policy, there are signs that political leaders are recognizing the value to be gained from this burgeoning young science.

And yet it would be remiss not to mention the challenges facing the discipline. Perhaps most worryingly of all, commentators have noticed that an extraordinarily high percentage of experimental participants in psychology are WEIRD – that is, from Western, Educated, Industrialized, Rich and Democratic countries.

Writing in *The American Psychologist* in 2008, Jeffrey Arnett analysed leading psychology journals and found that 68 percent of participants were based in the US, and 96 percent were from rich, Western countries. In a separate 2004 analysis in *The Psychologist* magazine, Hugh Foot and Alison Sanford found that up to 90 percent of participants in American research on perception and cognition were university students. These figures suggest that many findings from psychology are grounded on a seriously biased sample. What's true of the average white, youthful, middle-class student may well not apply to an elderly farmer in West Africa.

This argument was made most loudly in a 2010 article by Joseph Henrich of the University of British Columbia and his colleagues. They dug out rare research featuring diverse samples to show that there are cross-cultural differences in various aspects of human psychology, including visual perception, memory, morality and the heritability of intelligence. In fact, according to Henrich's team, "WEIRD participants" often perform unusually compared to people from other cultures, making them a particularly inappropriate subject group to study. "...[T]hese empirical patterns suggest that we need to be less cavalier in addressing questions of human nature on the basis of data drawn from this particularly thin, and rather unusual, slice of humanity", they wrote.

Another challenge for contemporary psychology researchers is to conduct experiments that are deemed to be ethically acceptable. Many of the classic experiments in psychology, such as the willingness of participants to follow orders and punish a person with an electric shock, simply wouldn't be allowed today, on ethical grounds. That isn't to say that psychologists aren't proving ingenious when it comes to finding ways round such problems, for example by replicating classic research on obedience using virtual reality.

While offering exciting opportunities, technological advances are also posing new problems. Functional brain imaging, for example, generates a bewildering amount of complex data and it can seem at times as though psychology is struggling to keep up. In 2009, the brain imaging community was rocked by the "Voodoo Correlations" controversy, in which many respected researchers were accused of analysing their findings inappropriately (see p.45).

It's also worth remembering that psychology is a young science. There are few taken-for-granted facts and many contradictory findings. When biologists refer to genes or chemists refer to the elements, there's a consensus about what these things are and what they mean. But when books are written about psychology, there's a tendency to back up any factual claims with reference to specific experiments – a tradition that is continued throughout this book.

The applied professions of psychology aren't without their problems either. In 2008 and 2009, for example, the American Psychological Association found itself repeatedly on the defensive over the role of psychologists in interrogation practices conducted at Guantánamo Bay and elsewhere during the Bush era. In the UK, meanwhile, it wasn't until 2009 that the government finally put into law the statutory regulation of psychologists. Up until then, anyone could legally call themselves a psychologist, a situation little changed from the nineteenth century.

Part I

Welcome to you

1 How you see yourself

Let's start the story of psychology with you and what you know about yourself. You've known you your whole life. In fact, you spend every waking minute with yourself, so you'd think that by now you'd have a pretty accurate picture of the kind of person you are. Actually, I'm afraid to say, you probably don't. Research shows consistently that our view of ourselves is subject to such an overwhelming array of distortions and delusions it's amazing we even recognize ourselves in the mirror each morning. Most of us seem to have an uncanny inability to predict what we will and won't enjoy. And, with the exception of those who are depressed or suffering chronic low self-esteem, we exhibit a ludicrously inflated sense of our own abilities. No doubt these positive distortions serve an adaptive evolutionary purpose, equipping us with a psychological suit of armour with which to face the dog-eat-dog world.

The Lake Wobegon Effect

Would you say you're among the best drivers on the road? Research shows that most people think so, although logic dictates we can't all be better than most. In one oft-quoted study, for example, Ola Svenson found that 88 percent of US student participants and 77 percent of Swedish students rated themselves as among the top 50 percent of their peers for driving safety. Ninety-three percent and 63 percent, respectively, rated themselves as among the most skilful. Even more damning though is a study by Caroline Preston and Stanley Harris published in 1965. They interviewed fifty drivers who were in hospital following a car crash. Despite the fact that 35 of these calamitous characters were deemed by police as responsible for the crash, they nonetheless rated their own driving just as highly as did 50 comparison drivers who'd never had an accident.

Most drivers regard themselves as being among the best on the road, even when faced with evidence to the contrary.

Our immodesty when it comes to driving isn't the exception; it's the rule. Similar positive biases affect people's judgements of many aspects of themselves, from their high morality to their good looks and popularity. A study by Ezra Zuckerman and John Jost at Stanford University found that 36 percent of student participants reported having more friends than the average student, whereas just 24 percent reported having fewer friends than average. These suspicious statistics suggest that quite a few students were overegging their popularity.

What's more, in a surprising twist, the researchers found that even more students exaggerated their popularity when asked to measure themselves against their friends, rather than against a "typical other". In this case, three times as many students said they had more friends than their friends, as those who said they had fewer friends than their friends. Ironically, the objective, rather sobering truth is that on average most of us actually have fewer friends than our friends – a statistical quirk known as the "friendship paradox".

Sociologist Scott Feld described the friendship paradox in a paper published in 1991 called "Why Your Friends Have More Friends Than You Do". The crux of it is that we're far more likely to be friends with someone who has say, fifty friends, than with someone who has just one friend. Indeed, fifty people will be in the position of having this friend who has fifty friends. By contrast, just one person will be in a position of having the one-friended friend as their friend. In other words, popular people get counted in lots of people's tallies of how many friends their friends have, whereas unpopular people get counted only very rarely. All this conspires to make it a statistical fact, in Feld's words, that "most people have fewer friends than their friends have". The same logic applies to sexual relations. People are often upset to discover their partner's prolific sexual history and yet, on average, you're far more likely to be sleeping with someone who has had numerous sexual partners than you are to be sleeping with someone more chaste.

Even psychologists aren't immune from habitual self-aggrandizement. Investigations of therapy outcomes show that, on average, approximately ten percent of clients will get worse following therapy. But far from being aware of their fallibility, a survey by Charles Boisvert and colleagues of 181 practising psychologists across the United States found that an alarming 28 percent were completely ignorant of there being any

You don't know your own head size

You're not as big-headed as you think. It's not that you're modest – far from it, as the main text makes clear. No, literally, the size of your head is probably smaller than you think it is. Ivana Bianchi at the University of Macerata asked students to draw the outline of their own heads as accurately as possible. The students overestimated their own headsize by 42 percent, on average, from memory and by 8 percent with the help of a mirror. By contrast, overestimates of other people's headsizes were 24 percent from memory and 10 percent with the head in view. When the students used a measuring tape to indicate the height of their heads, the estimates overshot by 18 percent, compared with 13 percent for other people's heads. So, whether drawing or using the measuring tape, participants' estimates for their own head sizes tended to be larger than their estimates for other people's heads.

It's unlikely this heady distortion is a recently acquired form of self-ignorance. The researchers also compared head size in classic portraits and self-portraits dating from the fifteenth to twentieth century. You guessed it, head size was bigger in the self-portraits. Bianchi's team confessed to not really knowing why people overestimate their head size, although they're now researching the possibility that it reduces the risk that we will get our head stuck in a hole!

such thing as negative outcomes in psychotherapy. This blindspot was further exposed in a striking study by Michael Lambert and colleagues. They asked forty clinicians to predict which of their collective pool of five hundred patients would deteriorate in therapy. Even though the researchers warned the clinicians that a fairly typical proportion would be eight percent, the clinicians predicted stubbornly that virtually no patients would be worse off after therapy. The stark reality was that forty subsequently deteriorated.

Indeed, our tendency to delusional self-glorification is now so widely supported by psychological findings that the phenomenon has attracted its own name – the "Lake Wobegon Effect", after the broadcaster Garrison Keillor's fictional town where "the women are strong, the men are good-looking, and all the children are above average".

Rose-tinted spectacles

All this self-adoration is well and good, and perhaps a select few have been blessed and are actually as wonderful as they think they are. But for the rest of us it surely leaves a question begging: how on earth do we continue to hold ourselves in such high esteem in the face of our inevitably slow, and at times painful, progress through life, from lost jobs to romantic rejections? It turns out that our inflated egos are supported by a highly selective and manipulative memory. It's as if each of us has our very own memory spin doctor, on hand to present us to ourselves in the best possible light.

Take people's memories of the grades they achieved at school. When Harry Bahrick and colleagues asked 99 students to recall their grades, the majority of errors were in the direction of grade inflation. Can't remember whether you scored an A or B in that exam? It was bound to be an A, or so your memory spin doctor tells you.

Or consider people's recollections of past health checks. Robert Croyle and his collaborators asked hundreds of participants to recall their cholesterol test results from several months earlier. Guess who was most likely to deflate their cholesterol score? That's right, participants with higher, more unhealthy, cholesterol ratings were more likely to distort their scores downwards.

According to the social psychologists Carol Tavris and Elliot Aronson, authors of the book *Mistakes Were Made (but not by me)*, there's an almost limitless supply of research providing similar examples. Studies have apparently shown people's tendency to overestimate how

Simply the best? In our memories of past exam results, the tendency is to over- rather than underestimate our successes.

much money they've given to charity; to recall voting, when they didn't; to remember using a condom when their own diary records show the opposite to be true; and to say their children walked and talked earlier than they really did. Such distortions help reduce what psychologists call "cognitive dissonance", the uncomfortable feeling of holding two conflicting thoughts simultaneously, in this case the mismatch between our benevolent view of ourselves and the reality of how we actually conduct our lives.

In fact, so keen are we to protect our positive self-image that, according to Tavris and Aronson, we also change the part we played in former events. Whereas we tend to attribute our past successes to our own abilities, we blame our former failures (if we remember them at all) on circumstances beyond our control. Yet when it comes to assessing other people's performances, we apply the opposite rule. No wonder we end up feeling so superior.

Somewhat paradoxically, even though we employ many mental tricks to sweeten our self-image, research suggests that most of us find it uncomfortable when other people have what we feel to be an unrealistically negative or positive perception of our abilities. Indeed, there is a distressing complex, identified by the US psychologists Pauline Clance and Suzanne Imes in the 1960s, known as the **Impostor Syndrome**, in which a person believes they are a fraud – that their achievements are down to luck and that their abilities overrated by others. Originally it was thought that women were particularly prone, but more recent research suggests that men are just as susceptible. Psychologists aren't immune either. In 1984 Margaret Gibbs of Fairleigh Dickinson University reported that 69 percent of the US psychologists she surveyed reported having these feelings

Taken altogether these studies seem to suggest that, far from being based on reality, our knowledge of ourselves is positively skewed. On any given dimension, from driving ability to popularity, we display an astonishing tendency to see ourselves as better than most. Helping maintain this rose-tinted view is a creative memory system that's happy to rewrite significant chapters of our past to create an account that fits

How culture can influence your view of yourself

The way you see yourself could be influenced, in part, by the kind of cultural background that you're from. Angela Leung at Singapore Management University and Dov Cohen at the University of Illinois proposed this in a 2007 study in which they asked American partici-pants with different ethnic backgrounds to imagine travelling in a skyscraper lift to meet a friend on the top floor, while that same friend was simultaneously travelling downwards to the skyscraper foyer. The idea was that participants' performance in the next stage of the task would be affected by whether they'd imagined that skyscraper scenario from their own or the friend's perspective. That's exactly what seemed to happen. When the participants were subsequently given a map showing the city "Jackson" and asked to mark the location of a second city, "Jamestown", which they were told, ambiguously, was the "next" city "after" Jackson on the north-south highway, those with a Euro-American heritage tended to mark Jamestown as being north of Jackson, consistent with their having imagined the skyscraper scenario from their own perspective (going up in the lift prompting them to think of north). By contrast, participants with an Asian heritage tended to locate Jamestown south of Jackson, consistent with their having imagined the skyscraper scenario from the perspective of their friend travelling down in the lift. Leung and Cohen concluded that this and other findings show how our cultural values are embodied in the way we see ourselves in the world. Americans with an Asian heritage place more value on how their actions will look to others and so view themselves from the outside, the researchers argued, whereas Americans with a European heritage place more emphasis on knowing what you want, and so view situations from their own perspective.

with our idealistic self-concept. Oh and by the way, layered on top of these distortions is our tendency to think that other people are more prone to self-bias than we ourselves are – the so-called "bias blindspot".

Affective forecasting

So far we've seen how little accurate knowledge we have about our current selves and even our past selves. This self-ignorance also extends into the future, as it appears we're close to clueless when it comes to anticipating our emotional reaction to future circumstances – a skill psychologists call "affective forecasting". Research in this area helps explain why we gladly arrange to visit a cantankerous relative on the other side of the country, and yet, as the meeting draws ever nearer, it begins to loom darkly, more like a visit to the dentist than a pleasure trip. We find ourselves soul-searching: "What was I thinking? Why, oh why, did the me of 21 February think it would be a remotely sensible idea to arrange for myself to hike across the country in the middle of summer to see an aunt who I can't stand?"

What answers does psychology have? First of all, research shows that we overestimate the emotional impact of future events – a habit that helps explain the irrational dread as the aunt visit looms. The London-based psychologists Nick Sevdalis and Nigel Harvey investigated this tendency by tricking participants into thinking they were playing a financial game with a stranger in another room. Participants had to choose how much of £10 to split with the stranger, knowing that if she turned down their offer, then they'd end up with nothing. The participants also had to predict how bad they'd feel if this happened. In reality, there was no stranger and the researchers made it so that all 47 participants ended up losing the £10. Crucially, the amount of disappointment participants actually reported feeling afterwards was far less than they had predicted. A follow-up experiment with students showed that they similarly over-estimated how good an unexpectedly high coursework mark made them feel. In other words, bad events don't hurt as much as we think they will and positive outcomes don't feel nearly as good.

These examples may seem trivial, but other research has shown that major life events like winning the lottery or developing a chronic illness also have far less of an impact than we might imagine. For example, people asked to imagine how they'll feel after developing a chronic illness say its impact will be devastating, yet research with patients

Waiting for the train. It's not always as bad as you remember.

suffering from end-stage renal disease showed their mood was just as positive as the mood among a group of healthy people.

Research is beginning to provide clues as to why we are so poor at predicting how we'll feel. One common mistake, it seems, is that we tend to imagine the worst or best possible scenario to help us predict our reaction to future situations. Carey Morewedge and colleagues showed this by approaching people at a railway station and asking them to recall a time their train had been delayed and how this made them feel. A twist was that half the participants were asked to recall *any* time this had happened whereas the other half were asked to recall the *worst* ever occasion. Despite these contrasting instructions, the participants asked to recall any occasion remembered a past travel nightmare that was just as negative as did the participants specifically instructed to remember their worst ever train delay.

It is a similar story when it comes to imagining positive events. Football fans asked to imagine any time that their team had won tended to recall an occasion just as wonderful and euphoric as fans specifically asked to remember their team's best ever victory.

Another clue for why we're so useless at predicting our future feelings comes from a study by Dan Gilbert, the author of *Stumbling on Happiness*, in which he asked a group of people to imagine how much they'd enjoy eating crisps if they had first eaten either sardines or chocolate. These participants tended to overestimate or underestimate, respectively, their enjoyment of the crisps relative to a second group of participants

You can't read your own body language

If our self-knowledge is somewhat limited then perhaps we could gain a truer picture by watching video footage of ourselves and analysing our own body language. Sadly, it seems that this is not the case. Whereas observers can watch that same video and make insights into our personality, we appear to have a persistent egocentric blindspot.

Wilhelm Hofmann at the University of Würzburg and colleagues made this finding after asking dozens of undergraduate students to rate how much of an extravert they were, using both explicit and implicit measures. The explicit measure simply required them to say how talkative they were, how shy and so on. The implicit measure was the Implicit Association Test (IAT), which allocates categories to different response keys on a keyboard. The idea is that we'll be quicker to respond if two categories that we associate in our minds, such as words relating to the self and words related to socializing, share the same key. The IAT was used as a way to tap subconscious self-knowledge. As typically happens in this kind of research, there was a mismatch between the participants' explicit and implicit judgements of their own personalities – they might describe themselves as outgoing while their IAT responses suggested they saw themselves as more of an introvert (see also p.177).

Next, the participants were tasked with recording a one-minute television commercial for a beauty product. The participants then watched back the video of themselves, having been guided on how to use non-verbal cues to judge how extraverted or introverted a person is. Having seen themselves on video, the participants then rated their own personalities again, using the explicit measure.

To cut a long story short – the participants weren't able to use the videos to improve their self-understanding. The participants' extraversion scores on the implicit test still showed no association with their post-film explicit ratings, and there was no evidence either that they'd used their non-verbal behaviours (such as amount of eye contact with the camera) to inform their self-ratings.

In striking contrast, outside observers who watched the videos made ratings of the participants' personalities that did correlate with those same participants' implicit personality scores, and it was clear that the observers had used the participants' non-verbal behaviours to help them make these personality judgements.

Why can't we use a video to improve the accuracy of our self-perception? Cognitive dissonance – our discomfort at holding inconsistent beliefs about ourselves – could once again be to blame. People may well be extremely reluctant to revise their self-perceptions, even in the face of powerful objective evidence.

who really did get to eat either sardines or chocolate followed by crisps (without first having to imagine what it would be like).

According to Gilbert, this is because the first group of participants couldn't help but compare the anticipated pleasure of the crisps against the imagined experience of eating sardines or chocolate, whereas the participants who simply did the eating enjoyed the crisps for what they were, regardless of what they'd eaten first. Gilbert believes this is exactly what we do in real life. When thinking about that visit to our aunt we compare the anticipated experience unfavourably against the potential joy of going to the football that weekend, or of going to the movies with a friend or partner. The reality when it comes to a given scenario – be that eating crisps or visiting the aunt – is that we're usually so engrossed in the moment that we just experience the situation for what it is, rather than comparing it against other possibilities.

MAKING BETTER PREDICTIONS

Fortunately, there are things we can do to help improve our ability to predict our future feelings. One tactic derives from the study discussed earlier in which a group of rail passengers was asked to recall any delayed journey and another group their worst delayed journey. Both remembered equally dire experiences. Differences between the groups only emerged when they were asked to predict how they'd feel if they were delayed that day. In this case, the people previously asked to recall their worst ever journey made far less dramatic predictions. It's as if their awareness that they had recalled an extreme example from their past made them realize a delay that day probably wouldn't be so bad. The lesson, it seems, is that we may not be able to prevent ourselves from invoking extreme memories, but recognizing that we do this could help us form more realistic emotional forecasts.

There's another simple way we can improve our emotional foresight – ask a friend. In another study by Dan Gilbert, female undergraduates were asked to predict how much they'd enjoy a five-minute speed date with a man. They had one of two kinds of information available to help them: a written profile of the man or a personal account from one of their peers who had dated the same man. Before the date, but after their prediction, the women got to see whichever information they'd so far missed out on, just to keep things equal once the date took place. After the date, the women rated how the experience actually went, and this was compared to their earlier predictions. What transpired was that the predictions based on a friend's experience were far more accurate. It seems that by finding out how someone similar to ourselves enjoyed a given experience we can bypass the shortcomings in our own affective forecasting.

There's one catch here, which you might have seen coming: people nearly always think they know better themselves. At the end of Gilbert's study, the majority of the women, even those who'd just experienced first-hand how useless the profile information about the man had been, still said they'd prefer to have personal information about a future potential date rather than feedback about another woman's experience. In other words, Gilbert says, when it comes to predicting our future enjoyment, we find it difficult to believe that a friend's experience could possibly be more insightful than our own best guess.

Let's return one last time to that visit to our grumpy aunt. We've hopefully explained the exaggerated sense of dread as the visit approaches, but what about our decision to plan the visit in the first place? Decision making will be covered in more detail later in the book (Chapter 5), but in the meantime, an article published by psychologist Paul Bloom in 2008, entitled "First Person Plural" may shed some light on this issue. According to Bloom: "Many researchers now believe, to varying degrees, that each of us is a community of competing selves, with the happiness of one often causing the misery of another."

Bloom provides some familiar examples, such as the you that rises in the morning cursing the you of the previous night who decided not to bother to set up the coffee machine. Or the cunning you who buys an alarm clock that jumps about so that the sleepy you of the mornings will have to get out of bed to turn it off. When it comes to your aunt there is a dutiful you, who finds it rewarding to be the kind of person who takes time out to see their relatives. The hedonist you might not be too happy about this when the weekend arrives, but then if you always heeded the calls of your inner hedonist you'd probably never go to work or put the rubbish out. So, when you find yourself in an unwelcome situation of your own making, remember that community of competing selves, and console yourself that one of you might well be finding the experience rewarding.

Your brain

You are your brain. Without it you wouldn't exist. Finding out how these three pounds of greyish-pink, spongy tissue give rise to you remains one of science's greatest challenges. Some clues reside in the brain's sheer physical complexity. Superlatives are hard to resist when it comes to an organ boasting more brain cell connections than there are stars in the galaxy. For technophiles who like to marvel at the full specifications, that's around one hundred billion neurons forming five hundred trillion connections (a five, with fourteen zeroes after it). And we shouldn't forget the brain's housekeeping cells, the glia, of which there are upwards of one hundred trillion. All this hardware comes at a price. The brain accounts for just two percent of our body mass and yet consumes a whopping twenty percent of our energy.

> "... at every level of brain organization, from regions and circuits to cells and molecules, the brain is an inelegant and inefficient agglomeration of stuff, which nonetheless works surprisingly well."
>
> David Linden, *The Accidental Mind* (2007)

But let's not be too reverential. As David Linden points out in his book *The Accidental Mind*, it's an organ built out of yesterday's parts. Like the car engine with its irrationally sized components and other oddities, the brain is what engineers would call a "kluge". It's a clumsy design, inelegantly constructed, that nonetheless gets the job done. The reason the brain is a kluge is that it never had a designer. It emerged piecemeal as a result of evolution by natural selection. It's why we find brain areas associated with human-like thought plonked atop of more primitive regions also found in many animals, and why we find many parallel systems and "redundancy" – that is, the same or similar functions fulfilled by more than one brain region or system.

A guided tour

As a general rule, the brain is rather like the body in its symmetry. Most structures are duplicated, with one instance on each side of the midline. The brain (and spine) also has its own shock absorption system. It's surrounded by a layer of **cerebrospinal fluid**, and also contains several large fluid-filled reservoirs known as ventricles. This system helps give the brain buoyancy and provides some protection if we suffer a blow to the head, or we're violently thrown about.

The images of the brain that we're used to seeing show only the wrinkled outer structure – the giant hemispheres of the **cerebral cortex**, placed together like two halves of a walnut. This six-layered, undulating formation is the human brain's most distinguishing feature, as it is so enlarged compared with the cortices of most other animals. The wrinkled look comes from the fact that the cortex is intricately folded, possibly a side effect of the space constraints imposed by the skull. The parts that bulge out are known as the **gyri** and the valleys are known as **sulci**. Psychologists use these features to help navigate the brain. Pick up an academic article on the brain and you'll find it littered with references to these landmarks – the post-central sulcus, say, or the inferior temporal gyrus.

The cerebral cortex supports what's often termed "higher" mental functioning: conscious thought, planning and memory. More than any other animal, we also have large swathes of so-called "association cortex"

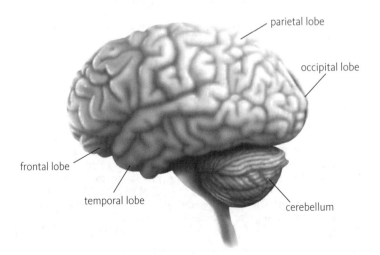

parietal lobe

occipital lobe

frontal lobe

temporal lobe

cerebellum

that isn't dedicated to processing any one type of information. Moving from front to back across the cortex, we find the **frontal lobes** beginning above the eyes (including the anterior cingulate cortex characterized by some as part of the "oh shit!" circuit of error monitoring), followed by the **parietal cortex** near the crown of the head, and then the **occipital cortex** at the back of the head. On either side of your ears we find the **temporal lobes**. If you unfolded the cortex and laid it out on a table, it would cover an area about 1m^2 and about 2 to 5mm deep.

Also visible from the outside of the brain, roughly level with the nape of your neck, is the cauliflower-like **cerebellum**, which plays an important role in movement and learning. It almost looks like a mini-version of the brain, with its own two hemispheres and, amazingly, although it only accounts for ten percent of the brain's volume, it contains more neurons than the rest of the brain put together. In relative terms, the cerebellum is particularly large in organisms like fish, which depend on agility for survival.

Some myths about the brain

❑ **The ten percent myth**. The most enduring and ubiquitous brain myth must surely be the idea that we use only ten percent of our brains. Sadly, this is far from true as the suffering and disability experienced by many a stroke sufferer surely illustrates. Even the tiniest area of brain damage can have devastating consequences. It's true the brain has an impressive ability to adapt to damage. But this doesn't mean that under normal circumstances all our healthy nervous tissue isn't put to good use. This can be seen to dramatic effect in brain scanner images, which show the whole organ pulsing with activity.

❑ **Left brain vs. right brain**. This is perhaps more of a simplification than a myth – the popular idea that the left side of the brain is cold and logical while the right-hand side is creative and intuitive. It's true that we have two brain hemispheres that appear to be differentially activated by different kinds of task. The most obvious example is language functions, which in most people are predominantly localized to the left hemisphere. But the reality is rather more complex than the myth suggests. For example, while the left hemisphere is dominant for language, the right hemisphere is involved in language processing too, especially when it comes to understanding the gist of what's said. In reality, our two hemispheres work together, so it's unwise to think of the brain as comprising two separate specialist systems.

To discover the inner regions of the brain, we need to slice the two hemispheres apart, which requires cutting through a massive bundle of connecting nerve fibres known as the **corpus callosum** – described by the fictional doctor Dr Gregory House as the "George Washington Bridge" of the brain. This great connector has around two hundred million neurons passing through it and is responsible for most of the cross-talk between the two hemispheres.

A curious feature of the corpus callosum is how much it varies in size between one person and another, with some people having up to three times as many connecting fibres as others. It used to be thought that this variation was associated with gender and handedness but hundreds of studies have failed to turn up any consistent evidence for this. Another important factor could be "hemispheric dominance" – that is, whether it is the left or right side of your brain that is the more dominant.

Two Hawaii-based researchers, Bruce Morton and Stein Rafto, tested this idea in a paper published in 2006. They first established the hemi-

❏ **The brain is grey**. People will often talk about grey matter or their grey cells. There is more than a grain of truth in this. Much of the brain is indeed grey in colour. In reality, however, a lot of it is also white, thanks to the fatty insulation that covers many of our brain cells, and much of it is also red or pink because of all the circulating blood. So if you saw a real, living brain in all its glory it would probably appear greyish pink. Preserved brains have a more pronounced dull grey appearance because of the fixatives used to stop them from decaying.

❏ **Adult brains can't grow new cells**. A myth that used to be supported by the best scientific evidence. Neuroscientists believed that we are born with all the brain cells we'll ever have. Research conducted over the last couple of decades, however, has shown that this simply isn't the case. Adult brains can and do grow new brain cells, a process that's known as "adult neurogenesis". The most fertile brain region when it comes to new cells is the hippocampus, a structure involved in memory. In fact, thousands of new brain cells are created in the hippocampus every day. Intriguing new research suggests that stress inhibits the creation of new brain cells, while learning, exercise and anti-depressants all seem to boost cell birth.

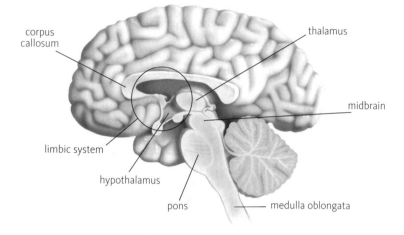

spheric dominance of 113 participants by asking them to mark the midpoint of a horizontal line. A left-ward bias in this task is a sign of a dominant right hemisphere. Subsequent brain scans of the participants showed that those with a more dominant right hemisphere, whether male or female or right- or left-handed, tended to have a ten percent thicker callosum, on average, than participants with a more dominant left hemisphere.

With the brain sliced in half, other regions buried beneath the cerebral cortex become visible. Starting from the brain stem and working upwards, we find regions like the **pons** and **medulla**, which regulate basic survival functions, including breathing and heart rate, as well as reflexes like sneezing and being sick. Next is the **mid-brain**, which includes basic sensory centres such as the **superior colliculi**. For many animals, this is the hub of their visual processing, whereas we have evolved additional cortical visual pathways. However, one of our visual pathways is still relayed straight to the superior colliculi for rapid, subconscious processing, and one day its speed might save your life. If I hurled a ball in your direction and you amazed yourself and me by catching it before you'd even consciously registered what was happening, then you can be pretty sure that feat was thanks to your superior colliculi.

Upwards and forwards, we find the **thalamus** – the brain's great relay station – and the **hypothalamus**, which is involved in releasing hormones, sexual urges, aggression and maintaining your body's temperature, hydration and satiety. Many scientists are busy trying to find ways to alter hypothalamus function for various medical ends, such as to help obese people lose weight. Either side of the thalamus are a group of subcortical structures, known collectively as the **basal ganglia**, which are involved in emotions and the control of movement.

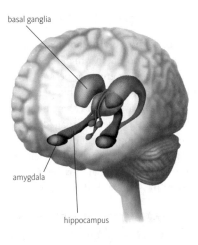

basal ganglia

amygdala

hippocampus

Last up on this whistle-stop tour, but definitely not least, are some important structures that may not be visible even with the brain sliced in half. Buried in the temporal lobes is the **hippocampus**, which plays a vital role in memory. The name means seahorse in Greek, which is what early anatomists thought the curvy structure resembled. Also deeply buried are two almond-shaped structures known as the **amygdala**, which are involved in emotional memory, including learned fears. Together with parts of the cortex and the olfactory bulb (involved in our sense of smell), the hippocampus and amygdala form what's known as the **limbic system**, which plays a key role in many of our emotions.

Investigating the brain

Our current knowledge of the workings of the brain comes from a diverse range of sources, including animal experiments, brain imaging and observation of patients with brain damage or neurological illnesses. During research with non-human primates, investigators use electrodes inserted directly into the animal's brain to record from single cells as the animal performs a certain behaviour – a procedure that usually isn't possible with humans because it is too dangerous and invasive. To this day, much of what we know about brain cells comes from these kinds of studies.

THE ROUGH GUIDE TO PSYCHOLOGY

LEARNING FROM WHEN THINGS GO WRONG

Research with brain-damaged patients uses a kind of reverse engineering approach, in which the functional role of a brain area is inferred from what happens to a person when that area has been damaged. In the nineteenth century this generally involved observing changes to a patient's behaviour and then, after they died, looking to see which part of the brain had been damaged. One of the most famous case studies in neuropsychology is that of Phineas Gage, a railway worker whose personality changed after an accident sent a tamping iron straight through the front of his brain (see box below). Today we don't have to wait until a patient has died to find out which part of their brain is damaged because

The truth about Phineas Gage

Phineas Gage, the nineteenth-century railway worker who survived after his frontal lobes were shot clean through by a tamping iron, is one of psychology's most famous case studies, with his story having become something of a popular legend. Films, plays, poems, even Youtube sketches, have all been inspired by this tale about a man whose personality was supposedly changed forever by his brain damage.

Before the accident, so the story goes, Gage was a hard-working, popular, friendly man, but post-injury he transformed into an aimless, disinhibited, aggressive bully. The case of Phineas Gage is generally used by textbooks and authors to demonstrate the localization of specific behaviours and personality traits to the frontal lobes, and the apparent permanence of changes brought about by damage to those lobes. In recent years, however, the historian Malcolm Macmillan has exposed just how little evidence Gage's story is based on. For example, no autopsy was performed on Gage and by the time his body was exhumed, nothing was left of his brain.

Macmillan has also uncovered evidence that casts doubt on the version of the Gage story as it is popularly told. Far from his injury permanently changing him into an aggressive waster, Macmillan says that Gage worked for several years post-injury as a stagecoach driver – a demanding job that would have required intact social and cognitive skills. Two recently discovered photographs of Gage appear to support Macmillan's arguments. Gage is seen as a smartly dressed, proud and handsome man holding the tamping iron that made him famous. Macmillan says his revised account of the Gage story fits with modern evidence showing the possibilities of rehabilitation even after serious long-standing brain injury.

Phineas Gage poses proudly with the tamping iron that shot through his brain.

we can use brain imaging to get a good idea while they are still alive.

To chart the localization of function in the brain, neuropsychologists look for what they call "dissociations", which is when damage to one part of the brain has specific functional consequences, whereas damage to another region does not, thus implying some kind of functional independence between the two areas. The holy grail for this kind of work is the "double dissociation" which is when one patient has damage to one area, another patient has damage to a different area, and each patient exhibits distinct patterns of behavioural impairment.

Probably the best known example of a double dissociation was uncovered in the nineteenth century by the French surgeon Paul Broca and the German neurologist Carl Wernicke. Broca described a patient who suffered damage to the rear of his left frontal lobe. His comprehension was unaffected but he was subsequently only able to utter the syllable "tan", hence his nickname Tan Tan. By contrast, Wernicke worked with a patient who, after suffering damage to the temporal lobe, seemed to have lost the ability to understand speech. Wernicke's patient could still utter words, but because his comprehension was destroyed, his speech was garbled nonsense. Today, these regions of the brain are still referred to as Broca's and Wernicke's areas, respectively, although the functional distinction is seen as being between syntax (Broca's area) on the one hand, and semantics or meaning (Wernicke's area) on the other, rather than between production and comprehension.

Further clues about brain function were provided by a series of studies conducted in the 1960s, 70s and 80s on so-called "split brain" patients, who'd had their corpus callosums severed in an attempt to help relieve intractable epilepsy. Michael Gazzaniga and colleagues presented words and images to one hemisphere of these patients but not the other, to see what would happen. This is possible by getting a participant to stare

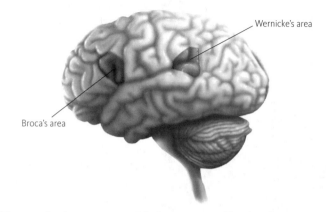

Wernicke's area

Broca's area

These two key language areas of the brain are joined by a bundle of nerve fibres called the arcuate fasciculus. A parallel, more circuitous, connection was discovered in 2004 and named Geshwind's territory.

straight ahead, with the result that anything then presented to the right of this point will be processed by their left hemisphere, and anything presented to the left will be processed by the right hemisphere.

Gazzaniga's team found that if they presented one of these epilepsy patients with a picture of an apple to their right hemisphere, the patient couldn't say what it was because in most people the right hemisphere doesn't have the capacity to produce speech. Meanwhile, the left hemisphere, which can produce speech, couldn't see the apple. But if the patient were next presented with a bag of objects including an apple, they'd reach with their left hand (controlled by the right hemisphere) and pick out the apple, thus indicating that they had seen the earlier picture. It gets odder. So long as the researchers made sure the held apple was out of view of the left hemisphere, the participant when asked wouldn't be able to say what he was holding, because that information was confined to the right hemisphere. Most of us have a sense of wholeness and unity, a feeling that we're one person with one stream of consciousness. The split-brain studies suggest our unified selves can be divided in two by the slice of a surgeon's scalpel.

WATCHING THE BRAIN IN ACTION

While studies of brain damaged patients continue to be fruitful, research into brain function has been revolutionized over the last few decades by technological advances in imaging. Using techniques like functional magnetic resonance imaging (fMRI) and positron emission tomography (PET) researchers can now pinpoint changing patterns of brain activity while participants, healthy or otherwise, lie in a scanner performing different tasks.

Psychologists of the past couldn't possibly have dreamed of tools like this. Thousands of brain imaging studies are now performed every year, many of them published in the world's most respected scientific journals. Their findings also draw attention from the popular press, usually prompting dubious headlines such as "scientists locate brain's love centre", alongside eye-catching images of colourful blobs on the brain.

So what does fMRI really measure, and what do those blobs mean? When a region of your brain is more active, it uses up more oxygen. In response, the brain sends along more oxygenated blood and it is the relative concentration of oxygen-rich and oxygen-light blood that is measured by fMRI – what scientists call the Blood Oxygenation Level Dependent Contrast or BOLD response. Similarly, PET tracks blood flow changes via the injection of a radioactive substance that collects in greater concentrations where the brain is more active. In other words, brain imaging does measure changing activity levels, but it is an indirect, imperfect measure. The scanner isn't actually recording the firing of individual brain cells.

When we read about people's brains being scanned while they are shopping or falling in love, we must remember too that in reality they were strapped prostrate inside a noisy (in the case of fMRI) metal tube, their head held still with cushioned clamps, while they viewed shopping or romantic images through goggles or an intricate system of mirrors. Around twenty percent of participants bail out of these experiments because they find the conditions too claustrophobic.

Despite the promise of brain imaging technology and the undeniable contribution it has already made to our understanding of brain function, there has, in recent years, been something of a backlash. Critics have begun to doubt the value of all these imaging experiments and to reminisce with fondness about the old-school days of creative, carefully controlled behavioural experiments. What, after all, they ask, does it mean to localize a particular function to a precise part of the brain? Some critics have even branded the brain imaging project as nothing more than a form of modern-day phrenology – the nineteenth-century "science" that linked personality traits to the shape of the skull (see box overleaf). To paraphrase the scepticism of philosopher Jerry Fodor: we

Phrenology

Invented by the German anatomist Franz Josef Gall in the eighteenth century, phrenology was the study of the shape of the skull as a means of discovering a person's underlying traits. Like modern-day psychologists, the phrenologists believed that the mind is rooted in the brain, but contrary to contemporary views, they held that entire personality traits and aptitudes are localized to specific brain areas, as betrayed by the pattern of bumps on the skull. In the United States in the nineteenth century, the Fowler brothers – Orson and Lorenzo – spawned an entire phrenological industry, in the form of books, magazines and phrenology heads. The latter remain popular ornaments to this day, many still bearing the Fowler trademark.

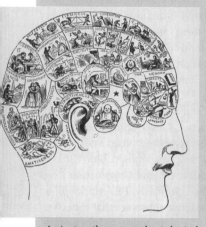

A nineteenth-century phrenological chart of the human faculties.

always knew there was a difference between verbs and nouns, but once somebody showed they were associated with activity in different brain areas, well then we knew they were different "scientifically".

Fodor could well be right that the allure of brain images is related to our tendency to believe things more if they're seen to be neuroscientific or brain-based. In a 2007 study Deena Weisberg and her colleagues at Yale found that scientifically naïve participants and neuroscience students – but not neuroscience experts – were more satisfied by poor explanations of psychological phenomena if those explanations were accompanied by gratuitous neuroscience jargon.

The brain imaging field probably slumped to its nadir in 2009 when a team of American psychologists, led by Ed Vul at the Massachusetts Institute of Technology, identified what they claimed was a series of serious statistical errors in many of the most high profile, recently published brain imaging studies in social neuroscience. These were studies that had linked social emotions with brain activity and spawned a thousand headlines in the process. Vul's paper originally had the provocative title: "Voodoo Correlations in Social Neuroscience" (later changed to a more conservative title by nervous journal editors) and was leaked on the Internet ahead of publication, subsequently causing a storm in the blogosphere and other scientific outlets.

Many of the accused researchers later published robust rebuttals, but the damage had been done. The saga left a lingering sense that the new technology was producing data of unprecedented complexity, and the sophistication of the researchers' analysis simply couldn't keep up. After all, these papers were mostly published by psychologists, not statistics professors. In research presented at the 2009 Human Brain Mapping conference, Craig Bennett at the University of California, Santa Barbara provided a further graphic demonstration of the folly of conducting brain imaging research without the necessary statistical checks and balances in place. Bennett's team scanned the brain of a dead Atlantic salmon while it was presented with emotional photographs versus "at rest". Using substandard statistical tests of the kind used by a significant portion of published brain imaging studies, the group found an area of the salmon's brain that was more active during the photo condition compared with at rest – an obviously spurious result with a message for any researchers who are lax with their statistical methods.

Ultimately, though, the Voodoo affair and dead salmon study will surely have strengthened the field, flushing out bad practice and generating healthy debate about just how to handle research hardware that generates a blizzard of complex data every second. Most psychologists today recognize that while some crude localization of function is possible, the brain is best understood as being made up of functional networks or systems. Most tasks, however simple, activate a whole swathe of interconnected brain regions that work together in concert. When leading psychologist Steven Pinker was asked to summarize brain function in five words, he said "brain cells fire in patterns", and it is uncovering the ways that different regions of our brains work together, in patterns of fluctuating activity, that is the foremost goal of modern cognitive neuropsychology.

The plastic brain

A key characteristic of the brain is its "plasticity" – the ability to change its structure and function in response to task demands. Probably the most famous demonstration of neuroplasticity was the London taxi driver study published in 2000 by Eleanor Maguire and her colleagues at University College London. Maguire scanned the brains of taxi drivers who'd passed "the Knowledge" – a test of their memory of over three hundred of the city's routes, which takes about two years to master. The scans showed that the posterior hippocampus of the taxi drivers was enlarged compared to a control group of participants. By contrast, the drivers' anterior hippocampus was smaller. What's more, the longer a person had been a taxi driver on London's streets, the more exaggerated the structural differences. The findings appear to show that the brain's structure changes to meet the demands placed on it. In this case, the posterior of the hippocampus – a structure known to be involved in representing space – had grown at the expense of the anterior hippocampus.

Just consider for a moment what this means. If you spent the next few weeks learning to juggle, your new skills would be reflected in functional reorganization and restructuring in your brain. Learn a language, learn an instrument or start playing tennis. However you choose to use your brain it will adapt and change in response. A 2007 study suggested these changes can even occur over incredibly short time scales. Inspired by research showing that in blind people the redundant visual cortex can be farmed out for use by the senses of touch and hearing, Jorg Lewald and his team at the Ruhr-Universität investigated the effects of blindfolding a sighted person for just ninety minutes. Amazingly, after this short

In 2003 the Thai government imposed a night-time curfew on all local online computer games in order to curb the apparent addiction among young people to a game called Ragnarok Online.

spell in darkness, the sighted participants' ability to loca~~
space was significantly improved. Other research has sh~~
minutes in the dark similarly improves tactile acuity. Eve~~
hour to the next, the brain is morphing and rewiring itself so as
mize performance.

IS NEW TECHNOLOGY CHANGING OUR BRAINS?

In recent years, experts and non-experts alike have begun to wonder whether our minds are being fundamentally altered by the prolonged time many of us spend on the Internet, watching TV or playing video games – a sensible question given what we know about the brain's malleability. Unfortunately, in providing a commentary on this issue, the mainstream media have tended to latch onto doom-merchants whose pronouncements are often based on conjecture rather than evidence.

For instance, Professor Susan Greenfield, the Oxford University neuroscientist and former director of the Royal Institution, predicted in an article for the *Daily Mail* that "if we were to scan the brains of young people who spend a lot of time playing computer games and in chatrooms, we would find that the prefrontal cortex is damaged, under-developed or underactive – just as it is in gamblers, schizophrenics or the obese." In a 2008 article for *The Atlantic* (since expanded into a book, *The Shallows: What the Internet is Doing to Our Brains*), the writer Nicholas Carr described the changes he's experienced: "My mind now expects to take in information the way the net distributes it: in a swiftly moving stream of particles. Once I was a scuba diver in the sea of words. Now I zip along the surface like a guy on a Jet Ski."

Everything changes our brains, so there's no doubt that time spent browsing the web or playing video games is doing something to our grey matter. The evidence for whether these effects are positive or negative is, however, far more nuanced than Greenfield, Carr and their ilk would have us believe. Consider children's TV: although some shows, such as the *Teletubbies*, have been linked with adverse effects, others, like *Sesame Street*, are seen to have benefits including improved literacy. So in this case, it's not the medium that's important, it's the content.

It's a similar story in relation to video games. Yes, violent games do appear to increase aggressive thoughts and actions to a modest degree. But action-themed games have been linked with a raft of mental bene-

Five ways to boost your brain power

1. **Eat breakfast** One of the simplest things you can do to boost your brain power is to make sure that you eat a healthy meal in the morning. In a 2005 literature review, nutritionist Gail Rampersaud looked at the results of 22 studies and found that children and adolescents who ate breakfast subsequently showed better memory performance and/or test grades than their classmates who skipped breakfast. But make sure you choose one of the less sugary cereals with a low glycaemic index (GI). Psychologist Keith Wesnes tracked the mental performance of children through the morning and found that those who'd eaten the low GI All Bran, rather than the high GI Coco Pops, showed less decline as the day wore on.

2. **Use smart drugs** Research is uncovering a number of smart drugs or "cognitive enhancers" that seem to boost the mental performance of healthy people, without having serious adverse effects. One such drug is Modafinil, which was originally used to treat excessive sleepiness. In a 2003 study, for example, Danielle Turner and colleagues at the University of Cambridge found the average memory performance and reaction times of forty healthy people given modafinil were improved compared with twenty people given a placebo. Of course there are always risks associated with taking drugs, and in 2007, the psychologists Barbara Sahakian and Sharon Morein-Zamir – concerned about the use of the drugs to fight jet lag or to boost productivity – called for a debate on the regulation of cognitive enhancers.

3. **Exercise** Physical exercise is good for your mind, not just your body. It has been shown to improve mood and to aid mental performance, probably because it increases blood flow to the brain. What's more, Nicola Lautenschlager and colleagues showed that it's never too late to start. They studied older adults with mild memory problems and

fits, including better motor control, superior task switching and better visual short-term memory. The puzzle game Tetris is also associated with benefits, including improved neural efficiency and increased grey matter volume.

What about the Internet? Relevant evidence is thin on the ground. On the one hand, a 2009 study by Stanford University researchers found that so-called "media multitaskers" (students who tended to use several media at once, such as browsing the web and listening to the radio) were more easily distracted by irrelevant information and found it more difficult to switch tasks. On the other hand, University of California researchers published a study that same year showing that when experienced Internet users performed Google searches, activity in their found that those allocated to a six-month home exercise programme (at least three fifty-minute sessions per week of moderate physical activity, such as walking) subsequently showed modestly improved mental performance over an eighteen-month follow-up period compared with control participants who weren't enrolled on the programme.

4. **Meditate** Meditation can give you more control over your brain's limited resources. Usually, if you present people with a stream of letters and ask them to watch out for two numbers embedded in that stream, they'll spot the first, but if the second number comes too soon after the first, they'll completely miss it. This is called the "attentional blink" and it occurs because for a brief period – the "blink" – people allocate all their attention to the first number. In 2007, the cognitive neuroscientist Heleen Slagter, and her colleagues, showed that the attentional blink was reduced among participants who'd been on a three-month meditation retreat. They'd practised Vipassana meditation, which teaches people non-reactive awareness or "bare" attention.

5. **Play video games** It's the perfect excuse for an afternoon on the video games console. Research has shown that habitual game players have superior mental abilities, including enhanced visual attention, when compared with non-players. It's not just that people with certain cognitive skills choose to play games. In their 2003 study, Shawn Green and Daphne Bavelier recruited non-game players, and showed that ten days spent playing an action video game (*Medal of Honor*) boosted their visual attention skills relative to a group of control participants who spent the same time playing the puzzle game Tetris.

dorsolateral prefrontal cortices (DLPFC) increased substantially more than when they read passages of text laid out like a book. The DLPFC brain region is associated with sustained attention and thoughtful analysis – so increased activity here is hardly what you'd expect for an activity that some say is making us stupid.

The conscious brain

How does the physical brain give rise to the subjective experience of consciousness? This question is at the very frontier of psychology and neuroscience and is usually seen as consisting of two separate problems, one more difficult than the other. The easier problem concerns working out the cognitive processes that underlie consciousness. For example, there are obvious links between attention and consciousness whereby we tend to be conscious of those things that we pay attention to. Related to this are the neural correlates of consciousness. We can study brain damaged patients to find out which brain areas and biological systems are necessary for a person to remain conscious. From this we've learned that consciousness doesn't reside in any one particular brain structure but instead reflects distributed activity across the brain. A network involving the thalamus and the cortex seems to be particularly important.

The so-called "hard problem" of consciousness, by contrast, refers to the puzzle of how the brain can give rise to first-person experiences such as what it feels like to stroke a dog, or why red has that redness about it. From this flow all sorts of philosophical problems – for example, how do we know that anyone else truly has these phenomenological experiences? Perhaps they go through the motions of responding to incoming sensory information and expressing their thoughts and feelings but, like zombies, don't actually experience that subjective essence of being. The attitude of most leading researchers in this field is that by untangling the cognitive and neural mechanisms underlying consciousness we might find that the "hard problem" evaporates.

An exciting breakthrough in recent years has been the use of brain imaging to detect signs of consciousness in patients diagnosed as being in a persistent vegetative state (PVS), a form of waking coma in which consciousness is presumed to be absent. In 2010, Martin Monti and colleagues communicated with a PVS patient by asking him simple questions, such as "is your father's name Alexander?", and instructing him to visualize playing tennis to indicate yes, or imagine walking around his house to indicate no. These two mental tasks triggered contrasting patterns of brain activity, and scans of the patient's brain suggested he was following the instructions and answering the questions correctly. It's hoped this approach could in the future be used to aid diagnosis and help find out patients' needs.

The brain on stand-by

In the early 1990s, the pioneering neurologist Marcus Raichle and his colleagues identified one of the most intriguing functional networks in the brain – a suite of regions (parts of the prefrontal cortex, the midline and the parietal and temporal lobes) that grew more activated the less a person was requested to do. By contrast, attending to an external task, no matter what it involved, appeared to put this same network to sleep. Raichle's team dubbed this the "default mode network". In an interview for *The Psychologist* magazine Raichle recalled being troubled by the fact that "even if you just had somebody lying in the scanner with their eyes open or closed and they weren't doing anything other than being awake and then you asked them to do something demanding, not only did the areas that you might expect light up, but areas went down – that was the opening for us."

What do we know about what the default network is actually for? One theory is that the network comes alive when we're mind-wandering, thinking about the past and possible futures. The psychologist Malia Mason and colleagues tested this idea directly with a study published in 2007. They invited participants into a brain scanner and asked them to perform either novel or highly practised memory tasks. Earlier on they'd established that the participants' minds were, as you'd expect, more likely to wander during the highly practised tasks, which had become rather boring. The key finding was that the default mode network was significantly more active during the practised tasks compared with the novel tasks. What's more, this was particularly the case among the participants who reported being more prone to mind-wandering.

The brain asleep

If mind-wandering is what the brain does on stand-by then you might think that sleep is what happens when the brain is fully shut down. On the contrary, ground-breaking research in the 1950s showed that the brain is highly active during sleep as it completes a series of ninety-minute cycles drifting back and forth between deep, slow-wave sleep and rapid eye-movement, or "REM", sleep. If you were to record the surface electrical activity of a person's brain while they enjoyed forty winks of REM sleep, you'd not see much difference from the kind of activity their brain displays while it's awake. Today, a continuous stream of new findings is uncovering just how important this sleepy activity is to memory consolidation, filtering and creativity.

An important study of rats, published in the 1990s, showed that sleep reactivates patterns of brain cell firing that occur during wakefulness, thus consolidating the memories represented in those patterns. Matthew Wilson and Bruce McNaughton, then at the University of Arizona, recorded the brain activity of rats performing a spatial task that involved finding food. Neurons in the hippocampus that fired together during the foraging task also fired together as the rats slept, as if the rodents were rehearsing their earlier discoveries.

But the sleeping brain doesn't just store away all your memories, it seems to judiciously select and preserve those that are most important. Consider a study published in 2008 by Jessica Payne and her colleagues at Harvard University. They tested students' memories for neutral objects (such as a car) and emotional ones (a crashed car) set against neutral backgrounds (for example a street scene). Consistent with past research, they found that emotional objects were remembered better than neutral objects – in both cases at the expense of memory of the neutral backgrounds. But after a twelve-hour delay spent awake, although the advantage for emotional objects over the neutral backgrounds remained, the memory for both declined significantly. However, it was a different story after a twelve-hour delay spent asleep. In this case, memory for the emotional objects, but not the backgrounds, remained entirely preserved. In other words, sleep seems to consolidate emotional information far more than neutral material.

As the evidence has accumulated showing how important sleep is for memories, the search has turned towards finding a way to boost these natural processes. The first success was reported late in 2009 by John Rudoy and colleagues at Northwestern University. They had students learn the locations of fifty objects on a computer screen. As the objects appeared they were accompanied by an appropriate sound – a cat with a meow, a kettle with a whistle. Next the students slept and the sounds of some of the objects were replayed. Re-tested upon waking, the students performed much better for the objects cued during sleep than for un-cued objects, even though their pre-sleep performance for the two groups of objects had been the same. The noise cuing had no such benefit when the exercise was repeated with the students just sitting quietly rather than sleeping, thus suggesting the researchers really had tapped into sleep-based memory processing. Look out for the appearance of commercial versions of these kinds of memory-boosting exercises sometime soon!

WHEN SLEEP GOES WRONG

Like everything else, sleep sometimes goes wrong. Perhaps the most striking example of this is what's known as "sleep-related automatism" – a form of sleepwalking disorder. Usually when we're asleep and deeply involved in our latest dreamy adventure there's a kind of paralysis mechanism that makes sure we don't accidentally get up to any real-life mischief. It does this by blocking the signals that go from the brain to our muscles (there are a few exceptions – such as those used for breathing and the signal that leads to early-morning erections!). But this paralysis mechanism can go awry, occasionally with tragic consequences.

The meaning of dreams

Contrary to popular wisdom, dreams occur during both REM and non-REM sleep but in the latter case they are usually shorter, and less vivid and intricate. When we're in a dream, we usually think it's real. On rare occasions we have a "lucid dream", which is when we're in a dream and we know it, in some cases with the ability to deliberately control the fantasy that unfolds.

Science still hasn't solved the mystery of why we dream. Psychologists are divided between those who see dreaming as a meaningless side effect of sleep and those who believe dreams are connected to our waking lives in some meaningful way. In line with common experience, research has confirmed that what we get up to when we're awake can affect the content of our dreams – what Freud dubbed "day-residue".

What's more contentious is whether the content of your dreams reveals anything significant about you and your desires that would remain hidden if it weren't for the dream. Freud, rather famously, believed that dreams provide the "royal road to the unconscious" and that decoding the symbolism in dreams can reveal a person's hidden wishes. By contrast, some contemporary experts have proposed that dreams occur when the brainstem randomly stimulates memories and that these stirrings are translated into a semi-coherent narrative by the cortex. By this account, dreams are the subjective consequence of haphazard physiological events and any attempts to extract deeper meaning from them amounts to little more than wishful thinking on the part of the interpreter.

Henry Fuseli's *The Nightmare* (c.1790).

In 2009, for example, the British man Brian Thomas strangled his wife to death in their holiday caravan. He was cleared of murder late in 2009 after psychologists for the defence and prosecution agreed that he had been asleep and not in control of his own actions.

Another way that sleep goes wrong is when it remains stubbornly elusive. Around 33 percent of Americans are said to suffer from insomnia – either difficulty falling off to sleep or waking early without being able to return to slumber, or both. The condition can become self-perpetuating as sufferers grow increasingly anxious about their lack of sleep. In fact there's evidence to suggest insomniacs get more sleep than they realize. In a 2004 study, Nicole Yang and Alison Harvey kitted out forty insomniac university students in Oxford with an actigraph – a watch-like gadget that records nocturnal tosses and turns. This allowed the researchers to compare how long the students had really taken to fall asleep with how long the students thought it had taken them. When the data was used to show the students that they were falling asleep quicker than they realized, their estimates on subsequent nights grew more accurate and they became less anxious about their sleep patterns.

Tackling this sleep-related anxiety is particularly important because other research has shown the worry about not having enough sleep can be more debilitating than the lack of sleep itself. Christina Semler and Alison Harvey, also based at Oxford University, showed this by tricking insomniac students with false actigraph feedback into thinking they'd had less sleep than they really had. This caused the students to have more negative thoughts (for example, "I can't cope today"), to feel more sleepy, to perform more sleep-related monitoring (noticing aching muscles and sore eyes), and to resort to more compensatory behaviours (such as taking a daytime nap). All this despite the fact that the actual quality of their sleep was the same on the days they were given false negative feedback as it was on days that they were given positive feedback.

Your sense of the world and movement within it

It feels as though we experience the world raw, directly and as it really is. But that is to underestimate the almighty storm of information raging outside of us. If our brains processed all this, we'd go into meltdown. So our perception of the world is heavily edited, filtered through various sensory pathways. At the same time, our brains compensate by filling in missing information and always striving to predict what will happen next. The result is that we sense things that aren't there, and miss an awful lot that is.

Part of this selective view of the world arises because of our limited attentional resources. Like a spotlight, the brain focuses on some sensory information at the expense of the rest. You can experience this by suddenly paying attention to the contact of the seat on your back and buttocks (if you're sitting), or to the pressure of the ground on the soles of your feet. That sensory information was always available, but it's only when you tune into it that it reaches the level of conscious awareness.

As we move about in the world, we're constantly flicking our attention back and forth, from one object of interest to another, forever zooming in and out with varying degrees of intensity. We do this within each sensory domain and also across the senses. But our attention is a finite resource. So the more we invest in processing one thing, the less we have left over for others. There are some exceptions to this rule: for example, there's evidence that our mental performance can be enhanced when we're walking or cycling, probably because of the benefit of increased arousal.

Not paying attention

This idea of attention as a limited resource is demonstrated by a well-known phenomenon in psychology: the **attentional blink**. If you ask a person to look out for a letter, say "X", embedded in a stream of successively presented numbers, you'll find that their ability to detect any other stimuli immediately after that "X" will be severely compromised. Related to this is a phenomenon known as **change blindness** or "inattentional blindness". The fact that we can only fully attend to so much at once means that a surprising amount in a scene can change without us realizing it. There are several videos on the Internet that dramatically demonstrate just how much we can miss of what's going on. Two of the best are the "colour changing card trick" (tinyurl.com/39qlbl) by psychologist Richard Wiseman, and the "gorilla in our midst" test (tinyurl.com/2d29jw3), based on one of the most famous experiments in modern psychology, conducted by Christopher Chabris and Daniel Simons. Watch the gorilla test before reading on, if you want to

Weber-Fechner Law

The founding psychologists of the nineteenth century showed how it is possible to apply the objectivity of science to the subjectivity of sensory perception. The Weber-Fechner Law, named after the nineteenth-century German physiologist **Ernst Weber** and his compatriot, physicist and psychologist **Gustav Fechner**, provides an apt example. It describes how much of an increase in a sensory stimulus is needed for us to detect a change. It turns out that the size of change needed is not an absolute amount. Rather, the amount needed for a perceptible change varies relative to the size of the initial stimulus – usually an increase of about three percent.

If you consider this for a moment, you'll see that it tallies with your everyday experience. Imagine that you're hauling a huge suitcase to the airport. Adding a book to the front-zip compartment won't make a discernible change to the weight, even though you'd easily notice the weight of the book if it were the only thing you were holding.

Psychologists have had fun over the years comparing the Weber-Fechner law across the senses – it turns out, for example, that we're more sensitive to changes in brightness than loudness. Other studies have compared the law across a life span, showing that the amount of percentage change needed to provoke a change in perception actually increases as we get older – as we gradually lose our sensitivity.

experience the effect for yourself. This film instructs viewers to count the number of times a basketball is thrown between players dressed in white, while ignoring passes made by players in black. Most people who watch the clip are so engrossed by the task that they fail to notice a person in a gorilla suit walk right across the screen!

So our experience of the world is heavily edited, partly because of the attentional **bottleneck**. But another reason why our experience of the world is incomplete is because we can only process the world via the sensory tools at our disposal. Evolution has equipped us with a whole range of sophisticated sensory equipment, from light-sensitive cells, to temperature-sensitive touch receptors, but like a thermometer that only measures from 100°C down to minus -5°C, these biological sensory tools have their limits. It's well known, for example, that dogs can hear high-pitched sounds that we're oblivious to. And of course, there is a lot of information and material we simply don't have the tools to detect and experience directly, for example X-rays and infrared light.

So, rather than feeling that you have an unhindered, flawless view of what's out there in the world, it would be more accurate for you to imagine your perception as a best guess – one that's based on inferential processes in your brain that are forever crunching away, mostly beneath the level of conscious awareness. In the language of science, these processes are considered by many to operate according to **Bayesian principles**, after the English mathematician Reverend Thomas Bayes (1702–61), in which fresh evidence from the senses is considered against existing beliefs derived from past experience. According to the neuropsychologist Chris Frith, this understanding of perception helps explain the hallucinations experienced by people with schizophrenia. Such hallucinations are perceptual beliefs like any other, except for the fact they are less constrained by past evidence and current sensory information.

Yet another impediment to the accuracy of our sensory experience is delay. We feel as though we're experiencing the world as it is right now. But it takes time for incoming sensory signals to be conducted down nerve pathways, to be processed, and to give rise to conscious experience. The moment you experience a sensation it's already out of date. The brain knows this and to compensate it spends a lot of effort predicting what the world is probably like now given how it was just a moment ago, all the while taking into account complicating factors such as whether you've moved. These predictive processes are extremely useful, but they're yet another reason why your experience of the world isn't raw, real or, as psychologists say, "veridical". Often what you see or feel isn't what's really there, but what your brain predicted would be there. A powerful example of this is provided by the "hollow-mask" illusion, of which there are many examples on the Internet (see tinyurl.com/laxzx). Our expectation that a face will protrude outwards is so strong that we usually perceive hollowed-out faces as if they are convex rather than concave.

The message from all this is that while you experience the world as seamless, immediate and complete, the truth is that it's delayed, selective, filtered and constructed. That our mental movie of the world feels so convincing, so smooth and fluid is a testament to the engineering of the brain. Exactly how it all comes together so successfully is an enduring mystery that psychologists are still busy attempting to solve.

Vision

For many people, sight feels like our dominant sense. This is reflected in the fact that around fifty percent of the brain is involved to some degree in vision. Sight is also the sense that has been studied most extensively by psychologists.

Seeing begins as light lands on your retina, stimulating the rods and cones – your photo-receptors – which are arranged in a cup shape across the back of each eye. The image that arrives here has been focused and reversed (left to right, and up and down) by the cornea, the transparent film at the front of the eye, which acts like a lens. The rods and cones translate the light signal into an electrical wave of activity that travels down the optic nerve towards the brain's main relay centre – the thalamus – from where it is routed to the **visual cortex** at the back of

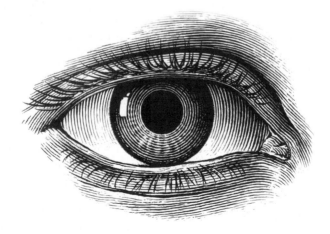

How to visit the toilet in the dark

Learning how vision works can have its advantages. Take the process of light adaptation. This is the way that our vision gradually adjusts to the dark. But does this adaptation occur in the eyes, or later on in the visual pathway, in the brain? You can test this by sitting in a dark room and adjusting both your eyes to the darkness. Next, cover one of your eyes with your hand, and then turn the lights back on full. Wait a minute or so, so that adaptation occurs through your open eye. Now you need to turn the lights off again and switch your hands around, so that you're now covering the eye that was exposed to the light. If adaptation occurs centrally in the brain, you should be blinded by the darkness. After all, you spent a minute or so with light entering your brain via your one open eye. However, hopefully you'll find that you can see just fine in the dark with the eye that you kept covered. That's because light adaptation doesn't occur in the brain, it occurs locally in each eye. You can use this technique when visiting the toilet in the night. When you get to the toilet and turn the light on, keep one eye closed. When it's time to return back to bed, simply close your light-adjusted eye and navigate your way with the eye that you kept dark adjusted. Hey presto – no more tripping up in the night!

your brain. Another branch, instead of going to the thalamus, routes direct to a sub-cortical structure known as the superior colliculus – this is an evolutionarily old visual pathway that allows you to respond rapidly without engaging the thinking parts of the brain.

The bulk of visual processing goes on in the visual cortex where there is a hierarchical division of labour – early regions process the most basic aspects of the incoming signal, such as line orientation, while later regions focus on characteristics like colour and motion. A famous case study, first described in the early 1980s, involved a German woman, known as L.M., who suffered damage to the part of the visual cortex specifically devoted to processing motion, following a stroke. Though she could still recognize things, she could no longer see them move. Water poured from a kettle appeared frozen like an iceberg and crossing roads became a serious hazard.

After the visual cortex, the visual pathway branches in two. One branch travels over to the temporal cortex, near the ears, is involved in object recognition and similar processes, and is known as the "what pathway". The other branch takes the high road to the parietal cortex, near the crown of the head. This branch is involved in processing spatial information and is known as the "where pathway". This dual-pathway account of visual processing has been supported by the study of brain-damaged patients. For example, there's a condition known as **optic ataxia**, associated with damage to the "where" pathway. These patients can recognize what things are, but can't reach for them appropriately. By contrast, patients with damage to the "what" pathway show the opposite deficit. For example, they won't be able to tell you which way a post-box slot is oriented, but give them a letter and they'll post it at just the right angle.

We tend to think that we either can or cannot see something. Another form of brain damage shows how this is an oversimplification. **Blindsight** has been studied extensively by the psychologist Larry Weiskrantz and is associated with damage to the primary visual cortex. Patients with this problem report that there is a whole part of their visual field that is effectively blind – they feel as if they can't see anything there. Curiously, however, when forced to make a decision about whether there is, say, a square or circle, in that part of their vision, they will perform better than if they were simply guessing. Quite how they do this isn't fully understood. However, it's likely that the subcortical pathway to the superior colliculus plays a role. There may also be islands of intact functioning in the part of their visual cortex that is damaged. What the syndrome shows is that it's possible to be consciously blind while still being able to "see".

VISUAL ILLUSIONS

Illusions, especially of the visual variety, have proven extremely useful to psychologists because they expose the short cuts and assumptions used by our brains to create as accurate a representation of the world as possible. One of the best known is the **Kanizsa triangle**, named

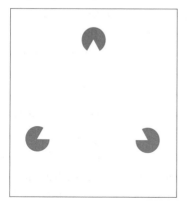

after the Italian Gestalt psychologist Gaetano Kanizsa. The observer perceives a triangle with edges that don't really exist. The illusion occurs because of the way the brain uses statistical probabilities to deduce what's out there in the world. In this case it calculates that it's more likely that there is a white triangle occluding the three circles than that there happen to be three circles with the exact same triangular chunks taken out of them. This assumption also leads to an illusory perception that the occluding triangle is brighter than the white background.

Another well-known visual trick is the **Ebbinghaus illusion**. This shows how context affects our perception. In this case, a central circle surrounded by larger circles appears smaller than a central circle surrounded by tiny circles, even though both the central circles are really the same size. There is an added twist to this illusion. In an influential study, involving cut-out discs, Salvatore Aglioti and colleagues showed that, although

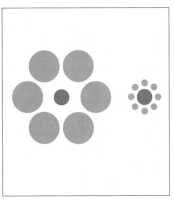

the two inner circles appear to be of different size, when we reach for them with forefinger and thumb, we actually form the same size grip for both. Aglioti's team interpreted this as further evidence for the dual pathway account of visual processing. In this case, it seems that the more conscious "what" pathway is tricked by the illusion, whereas the more automatic "where" pathway, used for reaching, is somewhat immune.

As well as being useful research tools for studying perception, visual illusions have started to be exploited for practical benefit. A great real-life example is found on a dangerous stretch of Lake Shore Drive in Chicago. The city authorities have altered the spacing of white lines on the road so that they become progressively closer together on the approach to a risky bend at Oak Street. The lines create the sensation of speeding up, thus prompting drivers to slow down before the bend.

Other applications are at a more experimental stage. David Elliott and colleagues published a study in 2009 in which they used an illusion to make a step look higher than it really was. Recordings from an eight-camera motion-capture system showed that students gave a step with vertical lines on its forward face approximately 5mm greater clearance than a step decorated with horizontal lines. The students also estimated that the step with vertical lines was taller than the step with horizontal lines. The increased clearance doesn't sound like much, but it could be enough to prevent people tripping – an accident that can be fatal to elderly people. Two thousand elderly people die in the UK every year following a fall, with the majority of these falls happening on stairs.

Hearing

Sound ripples through the air, causing three tiny bones inside your ears to vibrate. From here, the sound is passed to your hair-lined inner ear – known as the cochlear – which translates the signal into neural activity. This neural signal then travels to the brain stem, onwards to the thalamus before reaching the **auditory cortex**. To localize sounds, your brain compares information arriving at the two ears in terms of loudness and timing. A sound originating from straight ahead, for example, will arrive at the two ears at the same time, whereas a sound coming from the left side of space would obviously reach your left ear first and would be perceived as louder in that ear compared with the right ear.

The auditory channel provides another powerful demonstration of how our perceptual experiences are based not just on what is served up by our senses, but also on what our brains bring to the table. Listen to an excerpt of music played backwards (Led Zeppelin's "Stairway to Heaven" is available on a website run by Jeff Milner: www.jeffmilner.com/back-masking.htm) and it will sound like nonsense. However, if you're then told which words to listen out for in the backward music (the website provides them) and you hear the song again, the words immediately become clear. In fact, once you've been told the backward lyrics, you can't unhear them – the incoming sounds are permanently filtered through your "top-down" expectations.

Although the situation is not as well understood as it is for vision, it's looking increasingly likely that, as with visual information, the auditory pathway is divided along two parallel branches – one for "what" the sound is and the other for "where" it is. Animal lovers should look away now, because the most compelling evidence to date for this dual-pathway account of auditory processing actually comes from a rather invasive study with cats. In 2008 Stephen Lomber and Shveta Malhotra inserted ultra-cold tubes into the brains of cats to selectively freeze brain-activity in either the rear or frontal regions of their auditory cortex, which is the part of the brain, near the ears, that processes sounds. Crucially, the researchers found that when they froze activity in the frontal part of the auditory cortex, the cats lost their ability to localize sounds, but they could still discriminate between sounds. By contrast, the opposite pattern of impairment was found when the researchers froze the rear part of the cats' auditory cortex. Cats are mammals, and if they have

Human echo-location

We usually think of humans as having five major senses – sight, hearing, touch, taste and smell. Some psychologists might also add proprioception to that list, which is the sense of where our limbs are positioned in space, and perhaps also the vestibular senses (housed in the inner ear and involving balance and orientation in space). However, it's probable that only a few people know about human echo-location. This is the ability to detect, bat-like, where things are by emitting sounds, for example by making a clicking noise with the mouth, and listening for how those sounds echo back. In 2009 in *Psychology Today* magazine, psychologist Lawrence Rosenblum documented a remarkable group of blind mountain-bikers – called Team Bat – who use echo-location to detect obstacles as they are riding along, albeit slowly and with a few wobbles (see the videos section at www.worldaccessfortheblind.org). Also in 2009, in the first systematic investigation of its kind, a research team led by Juan Antonio Martínez confirmed that the palate clicks used by Daniel Kish, leader of Team Bat, are the most effective sounds to use for echo-location. The researchers added that anyone is capable of developing echo-location skills and that after two hours practice a day for two weeks, you should be able to detect blindfolded whether you have an object in front of you or not.

separate "what" and "where" pathways for auditory processing, then it's very likely that we do too.

One obvious difference between hearing and vision is that we can close our eyes but we can't close our ears. This has psychological implications, with recent research showing that exposure to too much noise can be bad for your health, presumably because unwanted noise is so stressful. For example, a Swedish epidemiological study led by Jenny Selander, involving thousands of people, found evidence of a link between exposure to traffic noise and the risk of having a heart attack – even after taking account of the potentially contributory role played by air pollution.

At this point, as we go through the different senses, you might be getting the impression that each sense functions entirely separately from the others. The reality is that there is plenty of crosstalk between the senses, even among the majority of us who don't have synaesthesia (see p.71). This is demonstrated dramatically in an illusion called the **McGurk effect**, named after the psychologist Harry McGurk. It plays off the fact that people's lip movements influence what we hear. If you watch a video of a person saying the sound "GA" but with the soundtrack altered to play the sound "BA", what you'll actually hear is the sound "DA". This is because the auditory centres of your brain are influenced by information coming from your eyes about the lip movements of the person in the video. The result is that you experience a sound that reflects a merging of information from both the senses. If you want to try it out, there are plenty of examples on the Internet (for example, at tinyurl.com/4rgzyn).

Smell

We sense a smell when chemicals bind to receptors in our noses, initiating a nerve signal that travels to what's known as the **olfactory bulb** (olfaction is the scientific name for smell), housed on the underside of the front of the brain. Traditionally, humans have been thought of as having a rather inferior sense of smell compared with many of our mammalian cousins. However, an amusing study conducted in 2006 suggested we might have underestimated our sniffing skills. Jess Porter and colleagues asked participants to drop to all fours to track the scent of chocolate through grass. Just like a dog, 21 out of 32 participants were able to track the 10-metre trail. What's more, the researchers chose four of these successful trackers and showed that three hours' practice a day for three days substantially improved their sniffing skills, such that they became twice as fast at tracking. "Our sense of smell is less keen partly because we put less demand on it", said Porter at the time, "but if people practice sniffing smells, they can get really good at it".

Porter's team didn't stop there. They also wanted to see if humans locate smells by comparing the input to our two nostrils, much as we locate sounds by contrasting the information arriving at our two ears. The researchers found that participants' tracking accuracy dropped to 36 percent with one nostril taped up compared with tracking with both nostrils clear, suggesting that we do indeed gain useful information about the location of smells by comparing between our nostrils. This finding was consistent with an earlier study, conducted by the same research team, in which a piece of breathing apparatus was used to deliver smells selectively to just one nostril or the other. The participants' task in this case was simply to indicate which nostril the scent had arrived through, which they did with 75 percent accuracy – far better than if they had simply been guessing. This suggests that some neurons in the part of the brain that processes smells are selective for just one nostril or the other, again confirming the idea that our sense of smell is more sophisticated than had previously been thought.

The most salient thing about smells is probably whether they are pleasant, disgusting, or somewhere in-between. It used to be thought that much of this emotional reaction was acquired throughout our lives, based on association and cultural connotations. However, a surprising study published in 2009 suggests many of our preferences for smells may be hard-wired, and that they can be predicted by those smells that are liked by mice!

Nathalie Mandairon asked thirty participants to rate their preference for a range of odours including geraniol, which has a floral smell, and guaiacol, which has a smoky whiff about it. The researchers were careful to use smells that weren't biologically significant – for example, signalling danger or rotten food. Despite the apparently random nature of the odours, the ones the participants said they favoured, such as geraniol, tended to be the same as those that thirty mice spent the longest time sniffing. Similarly, the odours that the humans liked least, such as guaiacol, tended to be the ones the mice were least interested in. The researchers weren't sure what distinguishes a preferred smell from a disliked one, but the difference must reside ultimately in the chemical structure of the substances, and this experiment suggests we are born to prefer some over others.

Taste

Related to smell is our sense of taste. The flavour of food comes from these two senses being combined, which is why food doesn't seem as enjoyable when you've got a cold and your nose is blocked. The perception of taste arises from receptors located on your tongue, particularly along the edges. Scientists usually talk about there being four "primary tastes": sweet, sour, salty and bitter. A possible fourth is "umami" which is triggered by monosodium glutamate, a chemical that's commonly used in snack foods. Compared with vision, we have few words for describing flavours. Without actually mentioning the food you're eating, have a go at describing the taste of your latest meal to a friend and you'll see what I mean. Many of us even get confused between two of the main taste categories of sour and bitter – the first being like a lemon and the second like tonic water or onion juice.

From a psychologist's perspective, one of the most interesting things about taste is just how susceptible it is to suggestion and expectation. For example, Jack Nitschke and his collaborators at the University of Wisconsin trained students to associate a range of flavoured water-

solutions with various symbols. Water mixed with quinine (making it bitter), for example, was repeatedly paired with the minus symbol. Later the students had their brains scanned while they sampled the various solutions. This time the researchers flashed up misleading signals – for example, the bitterest water was tasted alongside a crossed-out minus sign, which had earlier been paired with a milder drink. These contradictory signs not only affected the students' perceptions of the water – in the latter case making the water taste less bitter – they also dampened the brain's response to the bitter drink.

The effect of expectations on taste can even lead to increased enjoyment of a wine, just because we think it's more expensive. Hilke Plassman at INSEAD and colleagues provided a striking demonstration of this in 2008 when they asked twenty participants to taste five wines, ostensibly as part of an investigation into whether it matters to enjoyment how long you spend sloshing a wine around your mouth. Each wine was presented with its name and usual price and, perhaps unsurprisingly, the participants said they preferred the taste of the more expensive bottles. But they'd been duped. There were really only three wines – two of which were offered twice with a different price-tag. One was presented as costing $5 and $45, the other $10 and $90. In each case, the participants gave the same wine a better rating when it was labelled as more expensive. Moreover, brain scans taken during the experiment showed that pleasure-related regions were more active when participants drank what they thought was a more expensive bottle. When it comes to wine, it seems you really do get what you pay for.

Touch

We speak of touch as if it's just one sense, but our skin is packed with a variety of receptors that are actually sensitive to many different types of stimulation, including mechanical pressure, temperature change, pain and itch. Once these receptors are activated, the signal is passed to the spinal cord. From here, the message can either zip straight to a motor neuron that originates in the spinal cord, thus inducing a rapid reflex response (such as when we withdraw a hand from a flame), or the message can be routed up to the sensory centres in the brain for further analysis, and ultimately for the conscious sensation of touch.

Inside our brains there is a kind of mini-version of ourselves – a **homunculus** – where each part of the body is represented in neural tissue. This homunculus, which forms a horizontal strip across part of the parietal cortex, isn't to scale, but rather, the more sensitive a part of the body, then the more tissue is given over to representing it. A clay model of the sensory homunculus would therefore be a hideous-looking figure with huge hands, lips and genitals. What's more, the sensory homunculus in the brain isn't actually arranged as our physical bodies are arranged. For example, the brain tissue representing your feet is nestled next to the cells that represent your genitals!

There's a simple way to measure the sensitivity of a given part of your skin, called the **two-point discrimination test**. Look away while a friend places two drawing pins onto the palm of your hand. As they bring the two points closer together there will come a distance beyond which it feels to you as if they are using just one pin. Now do the same thing but with the points applied to your back, and you should find that the merging sensation happens much earlier, when the pins are still further apart. That's because fewer brain cells are given over to representing the skin on your back compared with the skin on your palms.

Movement

All this sensory information evolved to serve one key purpose – to enable us to move appropriately so that we could hunt down food, flee from danger and chase potential mates. But having the right sensory information is just the beginning. Moving smoothly and accurately is an engineering task of epic proportions. First, substantial transmission delays must be overcome. What you see now happened a moment ago, and there will be a further delay before a command to move reaches your limbs. This is overcome via endless **prediction** and **anticipation**, using cues to guess where things will be by the time you get round to responding. Second, how much force is applied to a muscle depends on the current length of that muscle, which is controlled by the relevant limb's position. So your central nervous system – your brain and

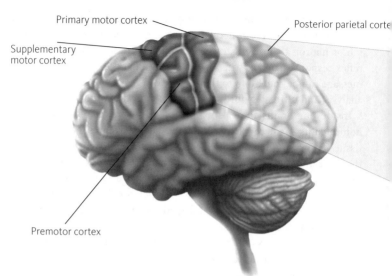

Primary motor cortex

Posterior parietal corte

Supplementary
motor cortex

Premotor cortex

spinal cord – also needs to know the current position of all your limbs. This is achieved via feedback from special receptors known as **muscle spindles**. Finally, all your muscles needs to be coordinated. Bending your arm, for example, means simultaneously relaxing the muscle used to straighten it. Simply twisting your torso will have massive ramifications for any manual movements you're currently engaged in. In fact, any movement you make will probably have implications for the control of any other part of your body. It's not entirely clear how the brain manages this degree of complexity, but it seems likely that movements are launched according to best estimates and then they're monitored and corrected "online".

It's because of the predictive processes that the brain uses to overcome transmission delays that we're unable to tickle ourselves. One such predictive process is to anticipate in advance what the consequences will be of our own actions. So when we perform a movement, any expected consequences are predicted and cancelled out. When it comes to tickling yourself, this means the sensory consequences of your own tickling are predicted and removed. Supporting this account, psychologist Sarah Jayne-Blakemore found she could reinstate people's ability to tickle themselves by providing them with control of a foam-covered robotic interface with a built-in delay. The effect of the delay was to make it seem as if someone else was performing the tickling.

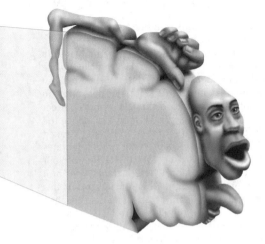

In front of the strip of tissue containing a sensory map of the body is a second strip, the "primary motor cortex", in which distinct areas are responsible for sending commands to different body parts. Other cortical regions involved in motor control are also shown.

Another way that transmission delays are overcome is by delegating control of many movements to automatic systems. In fact, all of our motor control is really a delicate balance between our internally generated, "wilful" control and reflexive, environmentally triggered movements. We take this for granted most of the time, but there is at least one situation where your brain's autopilot can be made suddenly noticeable. It's been dubbed the **broken-escalator phenomenon** and it

Man doing forward gymnastics flip. Illustration from Eadweard Muybridge's *Animal Locomotion* (1887).

Rubber-arm illusion

For this illusion, you need one of those rubber arms that you can buy from a joke shop – alternatively a stuffed rubber glove might do the trick. Put the fake arm on a table in front of you, in a plausible position that could correspond to one of your real arms. Next, place your corresponding real arm under the table, out of view. Now you need a friend to stroke your real arm with a feather or pen, and you must watch as they simultaneously stroke the fake arm in perfect synchrony with your real arm. Hopefully, you'll soon experience the strange sensation that you can feel the rubber arm being stroked as if it were your own! This happens because your brain integrates the sight of the rubber arm being stroked with the feeling of your real arm being stroked, thus remapping where it thinks your arm is located in space. Attempts have recently been made to put this illusion to practical use. In 2009, a team of researchers in Sweden reported that they were able to use the illusion to help amputees experience a feeling of touch in a prosthetic arm. Henrik Ehrsson and colleagues stroked the stump of an amputee and stroked their prosthesis in synchrony. Many amputees struggle to develop any sense of ownership of a prosthetic limb, and the researchers hope that the illusion could be used to help counter this.

often occurs when we walk onto a broken-down escalator of the kind that used to seem irritatingly common on the London Underground. The brain learns through experience that it needs to perform certain adjustments to compensate for the movement of the escalator, to stop you plunging head over heels. For many people, these adjustments become so automatic that they occur inappropriately even when the escalator is broken. So when you first step onto the defunct escalator, you'll probably find you experience an involuntary body-wobble, creating an odd sensation.

WHO'S IN CHARGE?

Never mind brief moments on autopilot, a famous study by Benjamin Libet in the early 1980s challenged the idea that "you" are ever really in control of your movements. Libet exploited the fact that whenever we make a voluntary movement our brains exhibit a spike of preparatory electrical activity that can be recorded by electrodes placed on the scalp. Libet asked participants to move one of their fingers and to also watch the second-hand (actually a rotating dot) on a clock, and to note the moment that they had made the decision to move. His surprising discovery was that preparatory activity in the brain actually preceded by about half a second the moment when participants said they had made their decision. This result suggests that the feeling of ownership we have over our voluntary movements is something of an illusion, apparently undermining the idea that we have free will.

Some commentators have criticised Libet's methods. For example, at the instant a decision is made, the time perceived on the clock will actually be the time from several moments earlier, because of the delays inherent in neural transmission. Of course this would actually lead to an underestimation of the extent to which preparatory brain activity had preceded the conscious will to move. Another criticism is whether we're actually capable of detecting when we've made a conscious decision. In a 2008 paper, William Banks and Eve Isham at Pomona College in Canada claimed to show that people infer the timing of their conscious decision indirectly, using feedback from the body movement in question – a strategy the researchers were able to exploit with delayed video feedback, thus leading their participants to make skewed claims about their decision times.

These criticisms notwithstanding, another study using brain imaging, published in 2008, appeared to replicate and extend Libet's results. Chun Siong Soon and colleagues scanned the brains of participants while they decided to move either their right or left index-finger. Around ten seconds prior to the instant that the participants said they had made their conscious decision, Soon's team observed patterns of brain activity in two areas which not only revealed that a movement was about to be made, but also revealed whether the movement would be with the left or right hand.

Mixed messages

Most of us experience our five senses as if they're completely separate, but for a minority of people it's as if their neural wires have got crossed. These individuals have a heritable condition called **synaesthesia**, which means they experience a mixing of two or more of their senses. One of the most common forms is so-called "grapheme-colour synaesthesia", in which letters and numbers reliably trigger the sensation of certain colours.

There are many other forms of synaesthesia: lexical-gustatory synaesthetes, for example, experience a particular taste whenever they hear certain words (there's a report of one man who had to dream up nicknames for some of his friends, because their real names triggered unpleasant tastes). Hearing-motion synaesthetes, meanwhile, hear beeps, whirring or tapping whenever they see movement or flashes. Indeed, new forms of the condition are being documented all the time. In 2008, neuroscientist V.S. Ramachandran and his colleague David Brang described the first-ever cases of "touch-emotion synaesthesia", in which people experience specific emotions whenever they touch certain textures or surfaces. For example, one participant experienced strong disgust whenever she felt denim, while another person described feeling perfect contentment and happiness at the feel of silk.

Synaesthesia was first described by the polymath Francis Galton in the nineteenth century, and for a long while, much research effort was expended on establishing whether the condition was genuine. There's now strong evidence that the subjective reports of synaesthetes are real. For example, synaesthetes who say that the letter A triggers the colour red are quicker at identifying the letter A when it is written in red ink, rather than blue ink, just as you'd expect if their synaesthetic experience was real. Hearing-motion synaesthetes, meanwhile, are better than normal people at judging whether two streams of visual flashes are identical, just as you'd expect if they were able to use accompanying sounds to help them make their judgements.

More recently, research has moved on to investigating how synaesthesia occurs, how prevalent it is, and what the condition can tell us about the way all our minds work. A recent study of some British schoolchildren suggests the condition may be far more prevalent than was previously thought. When psychologist Julia Simner and her colleagues tested 615 children aged 6 to 7 years in 21 UK schools, their conservative estimate was that 1.3 percent of the children had grapheme-colour synaesthesia. They reached this conclusion by testing the consistency with which the children associated letters and colours. The children classified as synaesthetes were more consistent over a year than the other children were over ten seconds! Based on their findings, the researchers estimated that the average primary school in England and Scotland contains two children with grapheme-colour synaesthesia.

A popular theory for synaesthesia explains the condition in terms of excess wiring between parts of the brain involved in processing the different senses. This makes intuitive sense but was challenged by a study in 2008 by Roi Kadosh of University College London, which involved hypnotizing suggestible students to make them perceive certain numbers in certain colours. Not only did the students report experiencing synaesthetic-like sensations, they also had difficulty perceiving a number when it was presented against a background that matched the colour they'd associated with it (just as you'd expect to happen with a true synaesthete). Kadosh's team concluded that they had induced synaesthesia, and that extra neural connections couldn't possibly have developed in that time, so there must some other explanation for the condition. One possibility, they argued, is that normal brains inhibit many of the connections between sensory areas, with this suppression being missing in people with synaesthesia and those under hypnosis. An alternative argument is that the wiring account of synaesthesia is accurate, and that hypnotic synaesthesia, though it leads to a similar effect to true synaesthesia, is induced via a completely different neural mechanism.

Another recent discovery in the field of synaesthesia research is that the condition may have as much to do with concepts as with the senses. In a study by Julia Simner and her colleague Jamie Ward, tip-of-the-tongue states were induced in a group of people with lexical-gustatory synaesthesia by showing them pictures of obscure objects. Focusing on those instances when the participants said they knew what the object was but just couldn't quite think of its name, the researchers discovered that when the participants had a word on the tip of their tongues ("castanets", for example), it triggered the same taste (for example, of tuna) as when they were told the actual word. It was as if the concept of a castanet, rather than the word itself, triggered the associated taste.

4 Your memories

Everybody has a story to tell. For most of us, it's the places we've been, the people we've known and the experiences we've had that make us who we are. This sense of ourselves, as a character at the heart of an unfolding narrative, would be impossible without memory. In biological terms, memory is reflected in the endlessly changing patterns and strengths of connectivity between brain cells. One of psychology's most important contributions in this field has been to catalogue and define the different types of memory and the way they function.

Defining memories

The story of our lives depends on **autobiographical memory** (also known as episodic memory), a form of long-term storage that provides a coherent record of where we've been, what we've done and who we've known. Another kind of long-term memory is called **semantic memory**, which stores all the facts we know about the world, such as the name of the capital of France. Yet another form relates to the skills we've learned, such as riding a bike or driving a car, and this is known as **procedural memory**.

Then there is our short-term memory, one form of which is usually described as **working memory**, reflecting the fact that it's involved in processing, not just storage. Working memory allows us to keep a mental note while we perform a calculation or task, such as remembering a phone number just before we dial, or keeping our choice in mind before giving an order to the waiter. Working memory is usually thought of as having three parts: a visual component, rather like the note pad you keep by the phone; a sound component, which is like a limited-storage dictaphone; and a central executive, which supervises and delegates to the first two components.

A classic psychology study from the 1950s by George Miller established that most people's short-term storage capacity is limited to seven items, "plus or minus two". This limit applies to chunks of information, so

Is there a limit to how much we can memorize?

It's hard to say for sure, and the answer will obviously vary from one person to another, but what we do know is that human memory capacity is massive and far larger than most experts had previously realized. In a 2008 study, a team led by Timothy Brady (an MIT graduate student at the time) sat fourteen participants down for five and a half hours and presented them with pictures of 2,500 mundane objects, each shown for three seconds (view the task at cvcl.mit.edu/MM/). Ten minutes after this marathon session had ended, the researchers presented the participants with three hundred pairs of pictures, and for each pair they had to say which object was among the original sample of objects they'd watched earlier.

Remarkably, the participants picked out the correct object around ninety percent of the time. Research from the 1970s had similarly shown that people were able to perform feats like this, but in these studies, earlier objects were paired with completely different pictures, thus prompting critics to argue that it was only gist memory (see p.76) that had such a large capacity. Brady's test, by contrast, was much more difficult, showing that we have a huge capacity for detailed, "photographic" memories. Objects seen earlier were paired with three different kinds of previously unseen stimuli: an object from an entirely novel category; a physically similar object from a previously seen object category; and finally, an object identical to one seen earlier but presented in a different state or pose (for example, a side-cabinet with one of its doors open rather than closed). Even in the latter, most difficult condition, participants answered with an average accuracy of 87 percent. Brady's team felt they were able to "...raise only the lower bound of what is possible", and that the upper limit of human memory storage was yet to be identified.

whereas you can only store around five random letters, you should find you can store many more if they are arranged in the form of meaningful words or acronyms.

There are several further ways to distinguish between types of memory. The first relates to the fact that all of what we know is not actually available to our conscious minds. In other words, we have many **implicit memories**. For example, if you're more than, say, 25 years old, I doubt whether you can recall every member of your final class at school, and yet if you were shown a class photo, memories of most of your classmates would probably come flooding back. Similarly, there's no way that you could remember every song you've ever enjoyed, and yet if you heard one of these songs, you'd recognize it straight away. In a sense, procedural memories for skills are a kind of implicit memory too – these are abilities you've memorized but which you would have a hard time articulating. In contrast, **explicit memories** are those that you can call to mind at will and talk about.

Related to this is the distinction between **verbatim** and **gist** memory. The former describes a precise, highly accurate memory for what happened or what was said. Verbatim memory usually fades rapidly, leaving behind a memory of the gist of what happened – its meaning and implications.

Another distinction in memory research is between **recognition** and **recall**, which overlaps somewhat with the distinction made earlier between implicit and explicit memory. Imagine that you are given a list of words to remember and that your memory is then tested the next day. Asking you to report as many of the words as possible that had been on the list would be a test of recall, whereas asking you to distinguish between the words on the original list and words added to it would be a recognition test. Recognition is often easier, although it can be prone to error if the new items are similar in meaning to the old.

False and dynamic memories

Experts used to think of memory as akin to a video recording of what's happened, fixed as an indelible trace in the brain. It's now recognized that memory is in fact a creative, reconstructive process. Rather than pulling out a dusty old file from the archives, your brain recreates past experiences based on the gist of what happened. This is why we're so prone to false memories.

You can experience a false memory by attempting to memorize the following list of fifteen words with just one read through: volley, return, ball, court, serve, umpire, backhand, racket, line, Wimbledon, shot, forehand, net, lob. After you've read them, put the book down, wait five minutes and then look at this next list (try to keep the earlier list covered up). Your task is to identify which words are new and which are from the original list: lob, umpire, tree, crocodile, lamp, tennis, car, bottle, serve, restaurant, volley, court, computer, garden, chimney. Now check how well you did against the original list. If you wrongly identified the word "tennis" as being in the original list then you've experienced a false memory caused by the human tendency to store the gist of things rather than a verbatim record. Most of the time, gist memory serves us well, but its vulnerability to generating false memories can cause problems, especially when it comes to witness testimony in court (see p.256).

As well as being creative and constructive, many of our memories are also dynamic, a phenomenon psychologists have dubbed "representational momentum". Imagine you see a photograph of a man falling from a tall building. Research has shown that your memory of this picture will evolve in the direction of the implied motion, as if playing out the man's fate in your mind. Because of this, if I showed you a second picture with the man slightly further along the trajectory of his fall and asked you whether the photo was the same or different from the first, you'd be likely to mistakenly say that it was the same picture. By contrast you'd be far less likely to make this error if I showed you a comparison picture of the man higher up, earlier in his trajectory. A neat study by psychologist Carl Senior showed that representational momentum is stopped or reduced when a magnet is used to temporarily disrupt the part of the visual brain that usually processes movement, thus demonstrating the ongoing links between memory and sensory processing.

Related to representational momentum is a phenomenon known as "boundary extension". This is the way that our memory for a scene expands beyond its original border. Imagine you've just looked at a scene in a holiday snap. You might think that your memory for the scene will stay faithful to the edges of the photo, but in fact your memory spills out over the edges, effectively expanding the scene beyond its original borders. This effect may sound odd, but it probably occurs as a result of the fact that our vision is only high acuity in the centre of our gaze. Although we actually

Glance at this photo, then take a quick look at the photo overleaf.

Boundary extension: this photo may seem identical to the one on the previous page but in fact it's an expanded version.

perceive the world via a series of discrete snapshots, we nonetheless enjoy a smooth, borderless visual experience because our brains are constantly anticipating what's beyond the borders of each glimpse and glance.

Amnesia

For a memory to graduate from short-term storage into episodic memory appears to depend on a brain structure called the hippocampus (see p.39). When this structure is damaged, either through injury or illness, the result is amnesia. An amnesic will usually be able to tell you about their life story prior to their illness or accident, and their short-term memory will also appear intact, but if you were to ask them routine questions, such as what they'd had for breakfast, or what they'd done yesterday, or who'd they'd met, they would probably have no idea whatsoever. In other words, their identity and most of their life story remains intact, but beyond this it's as if they are locked perpetually in the present. Amnesia is fairly rare, with stroke, closed-head injuries, and asphyxiation all possible causes of the kind of brain injury that can lead to memory loss. A condition called Korsakoff's syndrome, which is induced by poor diet linked with alcoholism, can also lead to amnesic-like symptoms.

Sometimes an amnesic patient may struggle to recall autobiographical memories from the period preceding the onset of their

Patient H.M.

It's not often that a car mechanic receives a prominent obituary in the New York Times, but in December 2008 that's exactly what happened when Henry Molaison died at the age of 82. Molaison, better known in the psychological literature as H.M., is the most studied individual in the history of neuropsychology, having been featured in literally hundreds of journal articles.

The interest began in the 1950s after Molaison, aged 27, awoke from brain surgery performed to help suppress his epileptic seizures. The surgeon, William Beecher Scoville, had removed slices from both temporal lobes of Molaison's brain in the region we know now is occupied by the hippocampi. Molaison's seizures were reduced, but so too was his memory ability. In one of the first documented cases of "pure" amnesia, Molaison had lost all ability to lay down new autobiographical memories. He cooperated with psychologists amicably for the rest of his life, working most often with Brenda Milner at McGill University and Suzanne Corkin at MIT. They documented how he lived each experience as if for the first time, and always greeted Milner and Corkin as if he'd never met them before. However, he was able to learn difficult lab tasks, such as mirror drawing, which depend on implicit, procedural memory.

Psychologists and brain scientists moved quickly to preserve Molaison's brain after he died, and in 2009 neuroanatomists were busy slicing and scanning it in order to turn it into a fully searchable digital atlas (see thebrainobservatory.ucsd.edu). Corkin is planning a memoir of Molaison's life based on the 45 years she spent studying him, and Columbia Pictures has already bought the film rights.

memory problems. This is a form of impairment known as retrograde amnesia, as opposed to anterograde amnesia, which is the more typical loss of ability to form new autobiographical memories. With retrograde amnesia, the memories from before the illness or accident will usually return, gradually getting closer to the onset of the amnesia, but falling short and leaving a permanent period of blankness.

As well as short-term memory, another form of memory that remains intact in amnesia is implicit memory. Psychologists have shown this by testing the ability of amnesics to learn tricky, lab-based tasks such as mirror drawing, which involves drawing using the mirror reflection of your hand as a guide rather than looking straight at it. Amnesics get better at this kind of task, just as a healthy person does, and they retain the ability when tested at later dates. However, unlike a healthy person, they won't remember having performed the task before.

Amnesia at the movies

Film-makers have been inspired by amnesia since the early days of cinema. According to neuropsychologist Sallie Baxendale, by 1926 ten silent movies had already featured the condition. Her entertaining article about portrayals of amnesia in film appeared in the *British Medical Journal* in 2004. But as Baxendale's analysis showed, Hollywood has generally provided an extremely inaccurate picture of what amnesia is really like.

One recurring misconception is the idea of memories being wiped out each night as an amnesic character goes to sleep, as befalls the private detective in *Clean Slate* (1994). It also happens to Lucy, played by Drew Barrymore, in *50 First Dates* (2004), which means that Henry, her would-be boyfriend (Adam Sandler), has to woo her afresh each day.

In a curious case of life imitating art, in 2010, a team led by Christine Smith at the University of California described a car-accident victim, FL, who actually did lose all her memories from one day to the next. However, brain scans revealed no brain damage, and research trickery, in which FL was tested on material from a previous day that she thought was from the same day, showed that she could actually recall earlier material. Smith's team concluded that FL wasn't feigning deliberately but that her symptoms were a form of psychogenic amnesia influenced by the film *50 First Dates*.

Another common distortion is the idea that a person's identity or morals are completely changed by their amnesia. In *Overboard* (1987), for example, Joanna (Goldie Hawn), a spoiled little rich girl, hits her head on a yacht. The resulting amnesia transforms her into a doting mother to the obnoxious children of her carpenter, played by Kurt Russell. In real life, however, amnesics generally retain their identities. Perhaps the most implausible idea about amnesia propagated by the movies is that a second bang to the head can cure amnesia. This happens to Tarzan in the film *Tarzan the Tiger* (1929), enabling him to overcome the baddie and rescue Jane.

Erasing unwanted memories

We tend to think of memory as a useful faculty, but sometimes people suffer traumatic experiences they'd really rather forget. In fact, traumatic or highly emotional memories can be incredibly long-lasting. We've all heard the cliché about people remembering exactly what they were doing when JFK, Princess Diana or Michael Jackson died, or where they were when the airplanes struck the Twin Towers in 2001. These kinds of memories are known as flash-bulb memories because

Baxendale also highlights two films that provide a refreshingly accurate portrayal of amnesia. The first is *Memento* (2000), starring Guy Pearce as Leonard, a man who develops amnesia after sustaining a head injury during an attack that leaves his wife dead. Leonard retains his identity and short-term memory, and spends the rest of the film hunting his wife's killer, all the while resorting to extreme measures, such as tattooing clues on his body, in an attempt to compensate for his memory problems. The other film is *Finding Nemo* (2003), an animation which features an amnesic tropical fish, Dory, who struggles to retain new information and pushes the patience of her friends to the limit – just as happens with real-life amnesics.

Struggling to remember. Guy Pearce and Carrie-Anne Moss in *Memento* (2000).

of their emotional salience and vividness. Similarly, when a person's life is in danger, there's a chance that they will later develop post-traumatic stress disorder, part of which involves involuntary vivid flashbacks to the traumatic experience.

Emotional or traumatic memories activate the amygdala housed in the temporal lobes (see p.39). It's believed that this triggers the release of the stress hormones adrenaline and noradrenaline, which subsequently influences the storage of memories in the hippocampus, somehow causing them to be particularly entrenched.

A woman carries her retrieved possessions through the streets of Leninakan (now called Gyumri), following the devastating Armenian earthquake of 1988.

The good news is that psychologists and psychiatrists appear to be getting closer to finding a way to erase unwanted, traumatic memories. The most widely tested approach has been to use the drug Propranolol (a common treatment for hypertension) to block the cell receptors that adrenaline and noradrenaline usually bind to. Back in 2003, psychiatrist Guillaume Vaiva and his colleagues recruited patients arriving at the emergency department of Douai and Lille Hospitals in France after they'd just been pulled from a car crash or suffered a physical assault. Eleven agreed to take propranolol three times a day for the next week, while eight others refused the drug but agreed to act as a comparison group. Crucially, Vaiva's team found that those given propranolol showed fewer signs of post-traumatic stress when they were assessed two months later.

Vaiva's study depended on treating people immediately, but it's possible there could be a way to help people with unwanted memories of a trauma that happened many years before. Research with animals has shown that when memories are recalled, there is a brief period during which they are particularly susceptible to disruption. Another psychiatrist, Roger Pitman, exploited this mechanism by asking nineteen trauma victims to recall an experience which had occurred an average of ten years earlier, and then giving half of them a dose of propranolol. A week later, the researchers played the participants a recording of their account of the trauma. Based on physiological measures like heart rate and sweating, it appeared that those previously given propranolol were far less traumatized by hearing their memories than those who'd just been given an inert placebo pill. The participants given propranolol could still remember their traumatic experience, but seemed less disturbed by it.

An obvious shortcoming of these studies is that they required participants to take drugs. However, late in 2009, psychologists showed that fearful memories could be wiped clean using a drug-free technique. At New York University, Elizabeth Phelps and her co-workers first trained participants to fear a coloured square by repeatedly pairing it with a mild but unpleasant electric shock. A standard therapeutic approach to removing this fear, known as "extinction", would involve exposing participants to the coloured square without the shock, in order to teach them that there is no longer any reason to fear the square. Phelps's team adopted this approach, but also applied the animal research that showed how memories are susceptible to modification just after they've been recalled. Phelps's team showed that the extinction therapy was significantly more effective when it was delivered just ten minutes after participants were given a reminder of the square, compared with six hours later or after no reminder at all. It's as if the reminder had temporarily rendered the "square-shock" memory particularly fragile, so that it was completely written over by the harmless experiences of the square without the shock.

All this sounds hopeful, but it's worth mentioning that some commentators have raised ethical concerns about the prospect of traumatic memory eradication. It's easy to understand their concerns. For example, what if the techniques were exploited to modify the memory of a witness to a crime? One defence is that the current approaches haven't actually been shown to eradicate memories, but rather to reduce their emotional salience. That still leaves some moral questions. For example, if drugs were developed that could strip a memory of its meaning, then what's to say people wouldn't start popping pills to clear their conscience? And without the guiding influence of guilt and regret, who knows how people might start behaving?

Déjà vu

Déjà vu is the term used for the unnerving sensation of experiencing a new situation as if it had happened before, the eerie feeling that you're retreading the path of an earlier existence. About two thirds of us experience it at one time or another, and it usually occurs in mundane circumstances, such as when sitting down for a meal at home or crossing a street on the way to work.

An early, popular explanation for déjà vu – which literally means "already seen" – suggested that it was caused by information from one eye, or one visual pathway, becoming desynchronized with the other, thus triggering a mistaken sense of familiarity with a scene when the later signal arrived milliseconds after the first. However, the psychologists Akira O'Connor and Chris Moulin at the University of Leeds challenged this account when they documented the case of M.T., a 25-year-old blind man who occasionally experiences déjà vu just as sighted people do.

Other clues have come from studying a rare complaint in some elderly patients in which it seems to them that life is constantly repeating itself. Moulin and his colleagues have identified several elderly people who no longer enjoy watching television, especially the news, because they feel as though they've seen it all before. The difference from classic déjà vu is that these individuals really believe that their experiences are repeated whereas healthy people know the situation is actually novel, even though it feels uncannily familiar.

Though it appears as if these older patients are delusional, antipsychotic drugs failed to alleviate the symptoms. Moulin suspects some kind of degeneration in the temporal lobes may be playing havoc with the patients' sense of familiarity and recollection, and that a temporary blip with the same system is at the root of classic déjà vu. The temporal lobes have been further implicated in déjà vu by reports that some people with temporal lobe epilepsy experience the sensation just before or during a seizure.

In research with healthy people, Moulin has shown that distraction during learning can lead to a later sense of "knowing" without a corresponding feeling of familiarity, and he's hopeful that his older patients could find respite from their symptoms by performing secondary tasks – for example, knitting while watching TV.

Research into déjà vu is hampered by the fact that it's well nigh impossible to catch people in the process of having the sensation. However, in an intriguing paper published in 2009, Alan Brown and Elizabeth Marsh claimed they may have found a way to simulate the sensation in the lab. Their method is based on Brown's idea that déjà vu could stem from implicit memories. Imagine glancing fleetingly at an unfamiliar street scene, being distracted by a poster in a window, and then returning your gaze to the street and experiencing a feeling of familiarity. It's possible that the déjà vu experienced in this scenario stems from that original, unnoticed glimpse of the scene, stored away as an implicit memory.

Brown and Marsh created a pared-down version of this situation in the lab. They presented participants with a range of symbols, some well-known, others completely new. The key finding was that flashing a novel symbol for just a few milliseconds (too quickly to be consciously seen) before presenting it again for a longer period led the participants to mistakenly claim to have seen the symbol before. Indeed, novel symbols not preceded by a subliminal flash were judged to be familiar just three percent of the time, compared with fifteen percent of the time when preceded by a subliminal flash. Moreover, after the experiment, half the participants said they'd experienced déjà vu during the study. The researchers concluded that their findings provided a possible mechanism for how false recognition – in other words, déjà vu – occurs in real life.

Nostalgia

An important mental activity made possible by memory is nostalgia – reminiscing sentimentally about "the good old days". The term was first coined in the seventeenth century by a Swiss doctor, Johannes Hofer, with reference to the homesickness experienced by Swiss mercenaries fighting in other countries. Possible causes cited at the time included the effect of changing atmospheric pressure on the brain and the noise of cow bells! For much of the twentieth century, nostalgia continued to be viewed as a negative emotion, synonymous with homesickness. Over the last decade or so, however, there has been something of a revolution in the way nostalgia is construed by psychologists. This is thanks largely to the research efforts of Constantine Sedikides, Tim Wildshut, Clay Routledge and their colleagues, who have shown that nostalgia actually plays a positive role in our mental lives.

One of nostalgia's key functions appears to be as a means of protecting against the effects of loneliness. In one study, Wildshut and his team triggered loneliness in university students by falsely telling them that they had achieved a high score on a loneliness questionnaire and were, indeed, lonely. Compared with the control group, the tricked students subsequently scored particularly highly on a measure of nostalgia that tapped how much they were missing things from their past (such as holidays they'd had or pets they'd owned). Of course, this only shows that feelings of loneliness trigger nostalgic thoughts, not that those nostalgic

Infantile amnesia and the reminiscence bump

Few people can remember anything from before they were about three and a half to four years of age, a phenomenon labelled "infantile amnesia". Experts still don't really know why this is. It's not that memory doesn't work before that age. Three-year-olds will happily and accurately talk about events that happened over a year ago. In a 2005 study, Carole Peterson at the Memorial University of Newfoundland in Canada investigated whether younger children have earlier first memories than older children. They found that children aged between six and nine years have slightly earlier memories – from about age three and up – but that the earliest memories of young people between ten and nineteen start at around the age of three and a half. The researchers couldn't explain what happened at age ten to prevent access to memories that were available at age nine. Another curious characteristic of memory across the lifespan is the "reminiscence bump". This is our tendency to have better recall for events that occurred during our late teens and early twenties compared with any other time of life. Some commentators have suggested that this is simply because events from those years are more salient – your first kiss, your first driving lesson and so on are bound to be more memorable than later examples. However a 2008 study by Steve Janssen showed that people of all ages were better at remembering impersonal news-related events that had occurred during their late teens and early twenties, thus suggesting memory for that period of our lives really is superior.

thoughts actually have any comforting effect. This evidence was provided by follow-up studies which showed that instructing participants to think about a nostalgic event from the past led them to feel in a better mood, and more loved and protected. Consistent with this, other research has shown that nostalgic thoughts tend to involve meaningful others, and often follow a so-called "redemptive sequence" where everything works out alright in the end.

Apart from boosting mood and guarding against loneliness, it seems that nostalgia could also ameliorate existential angst. In another study, participants were primed to think about their own mortality – for example, by asking them to imagine what will happen to their body when they die. Those participants who were more prone to nostalgia, or who were instructed to engage in some nostalgic reminiscence, subsequently had fewer death-related thoughts. "Regarded throughout centuries as a psychological ailment", Sedikides and his colleagues wrote in 2008, "nostalgia is now emerging as a fundamental human strength".

How to improve your memory

Psychologists say that anyone can train themselves to have an exceptional memory – it just takes practice. Most techniques used by people taking part in memory competitions involve translating boring material into graphic images, such as imagining the number 1 as a candle, or the number 8 as a snowman. And it seems that there's no intrinsic difference between memory champions and the rest of us, as psychologist Eleanor Maguire and her colleagues showed in a 2003 brain imaging study. But while they found no difference in the brain-structure of memory champions and normal controls, they did find differences in the way the brain was activated during memorizing. Specifically, the memory champions showed extra activation in regions associated with spatial navigation. This probably reflects their use of an ancient memorizing technique called the "the method of loci", which involves translating material to be learned into meaningful images and then imagining those images placed in various locations along a well-known route. When it comes to recall, it's just a case of walking the route in your mind and remembering where you put each item.

A good night's sleep is another useful memory aid, because when you're asleep your brain rehearses and consolidates what you've learned in the day. Scientists' first direct observation of this came through their study of maze learning in rats (see p.51). But it's not just the amount of sleep we get that's important, the quality matters too. An experiment conducted by Ysbrand Van Der Werf and his colleagues used beeping noises to disrupt people's deep, slow-wave sleep, while ensuring these participants had as much overall sleep as on a night when they were left undisturbed. Crucially, the participants remembered more images of doors and landscapes when they'd learned them before an undisturbed night compared with before a beep-disturbed night. Moreover, brain scans showed that disturbing deep slow-wave sleep seemed to have interfered with the usual functioning of the hippocampus.

Look back at the list of test words on p.76 and imagine being asked to make a note whenever a word contained the letter "a". If you were then given a memory test for the words, you probably wouldn't do very well. However, if you had been asked to look through the list and note whenever a word was related to tennis, you'd probably find that you performed much better. This is because we're more likely to remember things that we've processed more deeply. When it comes to real-life learning, long-term retention of information can be improved by summarizing the main points and reflecting on how they relate to prior knowledge and experiences. Explaining and summarizing what you've learned to other people can also help to integrate and consolidate your memories.

To improve knowledge retention, psychologists have shown that there's no point in continually studying material you've already mastered. According to Doug Rohrer and Harold Pashler, the optimum time to leave before revisiting mastered material depends on when you will be tested. Ideally, the period between initial study and revision should be ten to thirty percent of the time between the revision session and being tested. For example, in one experiment the researchers tested participants' memory six months after a revision session, and the most effective gap to leave between initial study and revision was one month. Related to this, Claudia Meltzer-Baddeley and Roland Baddeley have shown the efficacy of so-called adaptive learning, which is based on the idea of spending more time studying material you know less well. With computerized learning tools like Super-Memo that are based on this premise, items you recall correctly are left longer before being displayed again, whereas items you get wrong are presented again sooner.

Finally an exercise that sounds too simple to be true. In 2007 a study by Andrew Parker and Neil Dagnall found that wiggling the eyes from left to right for thirty seconds helped improve the memorizing of a list of words that had been presented just a few moments earlier. Parker and Neil Dagnall thought that the benefit could come from the eye move-ments improving communication between the two brain hemispheres. However, if you aren't strongly right-handed, you may want to give this technique a miss. In 2008, Keith Lyle and his colleagues showed that the eye-wiggle technique was actually detrimental to the memory perform-ance of left-handers and people who are only weakly right-handed. They think this is because left-handers already have ample crosstalk between their brain hemispheres, and in their case, the eye wiggling actually leads to activation of inappropriate information.

Decisions and emotions

Life is one decision after another. What shall I wear today? Which newspaper articles shall I bother reading? That's before the weightier decisions. Should my partner and I have children? Should I start a pension? Having a choice ought to be a good thing – it's a form of freedom after all. In the past a lot of decisions were made for us, whether it was working for the family business or who we should marry (choices which are still imposed in some cultures). But today's plethora of choices also brings disadvantages. In contemporary Western cultures we've experienced an explosion of choice so extreme that it can become overwhelming. A stroll down the aisles of the local supermarket reveals a dizzyingly diverse selection of products to choose from. Accompanying this abundance is an array of advice and information. No longer is it deemed prudent to book a hotel, for example, without reading the online views of former guests. And just when you think you've found the ideal place to stay, there's always that one disgruntled comment to put you off.

Spoilt for choice

One reason too much choice can be problematic is that it increases so-called **opportunity costs**. If you can holiday anywhere you like in the world, then once you've selected a single destination you've automatically and simultaneously forfeited the opportunities offered by all the other potential places. Plump for a city break and you've inevitably forfeited the chance to relax on the beach. This situation is particularly perplexing for people who are determined to make the best possible choice, dubbed "maximizers" by Swarthmore College psychologist Barry Schwartz, as opposed to those who are happy to make a good-enough choice, known as "satisficers".

In 2006, Schwartz and his colleagues showed that exhaustive searching might well lead maximizers to make better decisions, but tends to make them unhappy in the process. Schwartz's team categorized hundreds of students as either maximizers or satisficers, based on the answers they gave to various questions, for example: "when I am in the car listening to the radio, I often check other stations to see if something better is playing, even if I am relatively satisfied with what I'm listening to". By the following summer, the maximizers had landed jobs that paid twenty percent more on average than the satisficers' jobs, but they were less satisfied with their chosen job, more pessimistic, stressed, tired, anxious, worried, overwhelmed and depressed.

HEURISTICS AND BIASES

On its own, being swamped with choice wouldn't be such a dilemma if only we were rational decision makers. Unfortunately, evidence has mounted over the last few decades showing that much of our thinking is clouded by an array of **heuristics** – mental short cuts – and other **biases**. This new perspective on human thinking, much of it based on the work of **Daniel Kahneman** and **Amos Tversky**, has challenged the traditional view of economists that we make decisions largely in our own rational best interest. Controversies have arisen over how to judge the rationality or otherwise of these mental habits (after all, who is to say what is an acceptable level of risk, or a worthwhile reward?), so we should guard

Consumers in the developed world are presented with a bewildering array of choices.

against a crude description of all human thought as irrational. Nonetheless, these new insights into the apparent fallibility of our decision making have proven hugely influential and have led to the flourishing of a field known as **behavioural economics**, popularized by books like *Nudge* by Richard Thaler and Cass Sunstein. Because of the implications for policy making, the field has also attracted the attention of world leaders, including Barack Obama and David Cameron. Newspaper reports in the summer of 2010 claimed the latter has set up a "Nudge Unit" at 10 Downing Street charged with translating Thaler's ideas into policy.

To take one quick example from the field: a phenomenon known as the **status quo bias** describes the way most of us are swayed by the default option. It's been suggested that the shortage of organ donors in many countries could be remedied by making "donate" the **default option**, meaning that people would have to opt out if they didn't want to donate their organs. Some experts have argued that taking out a

Measuring wellbeing

How satisfied are you with your life? A surprisingly large amount of happiness research – for example, comparing happiness between nations – is based on people's answer to this single question, or one very similar to it. You don't need to be a psychologist to recognize that this approach, while straightforward, is extremely crude. Our emotions are regularly buffeted one way then the other, from one moment to the next, like a tree in the wind. To gauge these momentary fluctuations more accurately, psychologists use so-called "experience sampling" techniques. Participants are armed with hand-held computers or smartphones and asked to log their feelings and what they're up to – either at fixed time-intervals or whenever the computer buzzes at them. Researchers can then look at the effects of various activities on people's feelings, as well as seeing how a person's experience at one time-point affects their enjoyment of an activity at a later time-point. However, these diary-based methods can be intrusive and distracting. Just imagine the buzzer going off when you're settling down to eat or watch a good film. To avoid these disadvantages, Daniel Kahneman pioneered the "day reconstruction method". Participants recall the previous day, breaking it down into different periods of activity and recalling how they felt during each of these "chapters" of the day. This research has revealed that people report feeling happiest when with friends, as opposed to with their spouse or children. And rather than income being the most powerful factor affecting people's sense of wellbeing – as one might expect – it is having a good night's sleep that, apparently, makes the most difference.

pension plan and other socially desirable choices should similarly be made the default.

Kahneman and Tversky's most famous body of work was called **Prospect Theory** and has to do with our uneven emotional response to gains and losses. They showed that the size of the emotional effect of a loss is about twice as great as the positive effect of an equivalent gain – a discrepancy that affects our decision-making in predictable ways. For example, offered a gamble with the toss of a coin, most people will only agree to take part if they have the chance to win double (say £20) what they run the risk of losing (say £10). In the formal jargon, most of us are **loss-averse**.

Related to this is a phenomenon known as **framing**. Imagine two experimental vaccine programmes for treating a deadly virus contracted by six hundred people. Vaccine A will definitely save two hundred lives. With Vaccine B there is a one-third probability that six hundred people will be saved, but a two-thirds probability that nobody will be saved. Which do you choose? Phrased like this, Vaccine A appears to ensure the gains whereas Vaccine B carries the likely risk of losses. Because we're loss-averse, most of us choose A in this situation. Now imagine choosing between Vaccine C, using which means that four hundred people will definitely die, with two hundred saved, and Vaccine D which carries a one-third possibility that nobody will die and a two-thirds possibility that six hundred people will die. These outcomes potentially match those for A and B above, but phrased this way most people choose D over C. Definite losses are made salient by the phrasing of option C, which puts most people off.

Another tendency when making an important decision is to look for evidence that backs up our initial view. Psychologists call this the **confirmation bias** and it's easily demonstrated with a version of a task devised by Paul Wason in the 1970s. Imagine four two-sided cards, each with a letter on one side and a symbol on the other, placed on a table like this...

...and you are told that if a card has a vowel on one side of it, then that means it has a smiley face on the other side. Which card or cards would it be necessary for you to turn over to test the truth of the statement? Many people's response is to turn over the E and to turn over the card with the smiley face on top. But this is partly wrong. Imagine the E had a smiley face on the other side – that is consistent with the statement, but it doesn't mean it is always true. Imagine too that the smiley face-up card had a consonant on the other side – this wouldn't prove anything. The statement didn't say that smiley faces *only* appear on the reverse of cards with a vowel. The correct answer is to turn over the E card and the final card with a "no-entry" sign. If there were a vowel on the back of this card it would falsify the statement. Most get this task wrong because they look for ways to confirm the statement rather than to falsify it.

Here are a few more of the many other heuristics that influence our decision-making. The **endowment effect** describes the disproportionate value we place on things we own. The **sunk-cost fallacy** describes our anxiety to justify past investments. It explains why you're so reluctant to throw away that pair of shoes that you've only ever worn once because they don't fit well. **Hindsight bias** is our tendency to believe that things were more obvious at the time than they really were, given what we now know. We also tend to favour things that are more easily processed – a phenomenon known as the **fluency effect**. Research has shown, for example, that people rate hard-to-pronounce chemicals as more dangerous and that companies with simpler names tend to fare better on the stock market. We're also prone to an effect known as **anchoring**. If I asked you to pick a number between one hundred and one thousand and then estimate the year the Romans left Britain, the chances are your estimate would be biased by the random number that you chose. Shrewd credit-card companies appear to be aware of this effect. Research has shown that minimal payment levels (set by the company) reduce how much some people choose to pay off each month, thus increasing the amount of interest they end up paying to the bank.

CAN PEOPLE BE DEBIASED?

The wealth of research that's been conducted by psychologists into the flaws and biases in our thinking hasn't, unfortunately, been matched by an equivalent effort to find out how to alleviate these irrationalities. The situation isn't entirely without hope, however. Attempts to ameliorate the confirmation bias using "consider the opposite" or "consider the alternative strategies", for example, have met with some success, as have "delay and reflect" advice in the context of clinicians' diagnostic judgements. Other research has found some benefit in educating people about the heuristics and biases literature in general. Unfortunately, there have also been some setbacks. For example, attempts to redress the hindsight bias by asking people to list numerous alternative outcomes for a prior event have actually led them to feel more certain that the actual outcome was inevitable, perhaps because they found the hypothetical challenge so difficult.

But the greatest hurdle to successful debiasing is surely the fact that most of us think we are uniquely immune to the cognitive foibles which so afflict others. Emily Pronin at Stanford University provided an amusing demonstration of this when she asked 91 students to compare themselves with the average student on a range of positive and negative personality dimensions, including dependability and selfishness. Not only did 87 percent of the students give themselves better-than-average ratings, but the vast majority of them stuck by their ratings even after being told all about the "better-than-average effect" (also known as the Lake Wobegon Effect, see p.26) – the widespread tendency for most people to think they are better than other people.

CHOICE BLINDNESS

Perhaps more alarming than these biases and heuristics is other research suggesting how blind we are to the choices we're making. In 2005 Petter Johansson and his colleagues at Lund University in Sweden dramatically demonstrated this when they presented participants with pairs of photographs of women, and asked them to choose which face in each pair was the more attractive. Sometimes the participants were asked to justify their choice, in which case the photo they'd chosen was pushed across the table for them to consider further. Rather sneakily, Johansson's team occasionally used sleight of hand to pass a participant the opposite photo to the one they'd chosen. Bizarrely, on about a quarter of these sneaky photo-switches, the participants failed to notice the switch and then went about justifying the choice of a photo they had just rejected.

This **choice blindness**, as the researchers called it, is reminiscent of another decision-making anomaly represented by the infamous, oft-cited claim "I only read Playboy for the articles". This is our tendency to deny the real reasons for our choices, even to ourselves, if those reasons are not socially acceptable. Zoë Chance and Michael Norton, at Harvard Business

School, illustrated this in 2009 when they asked male students to pick between two sports magazines: one with broader coverage, the other with more features. Cleverly, the researchers manipulated the magazines so that one or the other also included a bikini special-feature. Predictably enough, the students picked the magazine with the swimsuits on three-quarters of occasions, whether this happened to be the broader-content magazine or the feature-filled option. Crucially, when asked to justify their choice, the students always pointed to either the breadth of coverage or abundance of features (depending on where the bikini special appeared), but never once admitted to the appeal of scantily-clad women.

In 2002 Daniel Kahneman became the only psychologist to win the Nobel Prize for Economics. It was awarded for his research on judgement and decision-making conducted with his long-time collaborator Amos Tversky.

TWO MODES OF THOUGHT

We're not equally prone to decision-making biases all of the time. In fact, psychologists say we have two modes of thought – an automatic, intuitive system and a deliberate, reflective system – and the extent to which our choices are swayed by mental short-cuts often depends on how much each of these systems is engaged. Take the phenomenon, mentioned above, known as anchoring: if we really concentrate and consider the question at hand we may find we can overcome an irrelevant anchor. It's our intuitive system that latches onto an anchor as a crude but often effective way to guide our guesswork. After all, we don't always have the time or inclination to consciously contemplate every choice and decision before us. That said, you shouldn't take away the impression that the intuitive system is always fallible, while the deliberate system is always superior. There are some circumstances where our **gut instinct** serves us well.

In 2009, with news of American and British troop casualities in Afghanistan a near-daily occurrence, a team of army psychologists was busy studying the ability of soldiers to spot the "improvised explosion devices" responsible for so much of the carnage. Using computer-based tests and mock ground-exercises, the psychologists found there were huge differences between individuals in their ability to spot the tell-tale signs of a hidden device. Usually it was the more experienced personnel who were more proficient at the tasks, but they often couldn't explain what had alerted them, beyond saying that they'd had a hunch. Recalling a real-life incident, one sergeant in the US army told the *New York Times*: "My body suddenly got cooler; you know, that danger feeling."

Indeed, this army research tallies with a classic study by neuroscientist **Antonio Damasio**, which showed that people's emotional reactions seem to guide their decision-making even before they realize it. Participants were presented with four piles of cards: those in piles A and B carried rewards of $100 each, but every tenth card had a penalty of $1250. Meanwhile, cards in piles C and D only brought rewards of $50, with every tenth card bringing a penalty of $250. The participants' challenge was to earn as much money as possible. Most people eventually caught onto the fact that it's better in the long run to take cards from piles C and D. However, Damasio's important finding was that before participants began consistently taking cards from these piles, they showed a heightened emotional reaction, as betrayed by their sweaty fingers, as they reached for piles A and B. It's as if their intuitive system – their gut instinct – already knew they were making a mistake before their conscious selves did.

Taken together, the army studies and the classic card-game research show that far from our emotions making us irrational, they sometimes improve our decision-making. So it's not surprising to learn that when patients with damage to the front of their brains, who had normal intelligence but impaired emotions, played the card game, they persisted with taking from piles A and B. In fact these patients weren't just poor at the card game, they were hopeless at making decisions in real life too.

The idea that emotions can make us *more* rational seems to fly in the face of common sense. Traditionally, emotions are seen as what makes us warm-blooded and fallible rather than mechanical and error-free. When rage or fear overwhelms the human veneer of cultured calm, we're reminded of our base, animal roots. But to view emotion as something that needs reining in, so that the intellect can assume total control, is to miss the point that emotions are an evolutionary adaptation with numerous benefits.

What are emotions?

Imagine a man receives a call to say that he has become a father. His face lights up in a smile, his pulse quickens and adrenaline rushes through his body. The man's interpretation of the news, his facial and bodily reaction, how he prepares to respond, and how he *feels* – all these are what makes an emotion, each element influencing the others. The words we use to describe emotions – happy, sad, afraid – generally capture only the feeling aspect of emotion. Contemporary psychologists recognize that the emotional process in fact begins as soon as we start appraising a situation. But imagine if the man's newborn child is the product of an illicit affair. The information reaching his brain is the same, but it may well have a different effect: on this occasion he bows his head in shame as his body braces for the awkwardness of telling the news to – or concealing it from – his wife. Neither spontaneous like a reflex, nor prolonged like a mood, emotion is the unfolding of these interconnected processes of interpretation, bodily reaction and expression.

Without emotions, our reactions would be spontaneous and robotic. Emotions imbue situations with meaning. There is a lull as new information is assessed and evaluated in relation to our past experiences, our ambitions and desires. Positive emotions motivate us toward

Let joy be unconfined. Happy and relieved Londoners celebrate the Allied victory that ended World War II in Europe.

Scared to death and the smell of fear

The idea that we can be "scared to death" is more than mere poetic hyperbole. Back in 1996 researchers at the University of Southern California, led by Jonathan Leor, accessed coroners' records from around the time of the huge earthquake that had struck Los Angeles at 4.31am on 17 January, 1994. The statistics were striking. On the day the earthquake struck, twenty-four people died from heart attacks, most of them within an hour of the first tremors. By contrast, the previous week's daily average was just five deaths a day – similar to other weekly averages from the same time of year from 1991–93. Further analysis confirmed that the extra deaths had nothing to do with exertion and instead seemed to have been triggered by the emotional stress of the quake. The demographics of the people who died from a heart attack that January day, combined with the sudden drop in heart-related deaths the following week, suggests that it was people who were already at risk of a heart-attack who had been scared to death by the quake. In her book *Emotional Rollercoaster*, Claudia Hammond summed up the implications of this research in a nutshell: "The fight or flight response, which usually works so well, giving us the focus and energy we need to deal with a situation, can backfire by stopping the heart completely."

It also seems that fear really does have a smell. According to a study conducted by psychologists in 2009, we can detect fear with our noses, but it doesn't have a perceptible odour. Alexander Prehn-Kristensen and his collaborators bottled fear by placing cotton pads under the arms of students waiting to give a stressful oral presentation. For comparison, they also collected sweat from cyclists. When the two sources of odour were delivered to participants' noses using an adapted oxygen mask, they couldn't consciously tell the difference between the two. Crucially, however, the smell of fear triggered extra activation in a swathe of brain regions associated with processing empathy and emotion. The finding suggests novelists could well be on to something when they write about the "stench" of fear in the air.

rewarding situations and resources, such as food, sex or shelter, negative emotions evolved to avert us from harm and distress. Emotions also ready our bodies for the action needed to obtain our goals and desires. When confronted by an attacker in a dark alley, fear sends blood rushing to our limbs, enhancing our ability to take flight. On stage before a gathered crowd, adrenaline courses through our veins, accelerating our thoughts.

Emotions also fulfil an important social function. Our facial expression, tone of voice and body language signal to others something of what we are thinking and feeling. The man's smiling face on hearing about his child's birth signals to others the pleasure and pride that he is experiencing. Watch the widening of eyes and sharing of smiles at airport arrivals, and you'll see how emotional communication begins long before words are uttered. When in danger, the survival value of these behaviours is clear. A look of terror warns companions, a shrill scream can startle the enemy.

AN EMOTIONAL DEBATE

Do the bodily changes associated with a given emotion provoke the feeling of that emotion, or instead, is it experiencing an emotion that triggers the bodily changes? Put another way, do we feel scared and then our heart races or does our heart race thus making us feel scared? Writing in the late nineteenth century, the pioneering American psychologist William James (see p.9) argued the latter. By his account, a situation, such as the sight of a bear, causes physiological changes, and it is the feeling of those physiological changes – the act of running and the racing heart – that gives rise to the emotion, in this case fear. Similarly, Charles Darwin's "facial-feedback hypothesis" proposed that physiological changes can give rise to emotions, rather than merely being a product of them.

As we've seen, contemporary psychologists see the different aspects of emotion – the feelings, the physiological changes, the appraisal of the situation – as affecting each other mutually in an unfolding process. And, in particular, so-called "appraisal theorists" highlight the role of our thoughts in emotional experience. According to their view, physiological changes alone can't dictate emotions, because the way the body reacts depends on how we construe a situation (as in the two scenarios in which the man heard the news of his newborn child). So whether a physical sensation, such as a racing heart, is felt as fear or excitement will depend on the context.

But this is not to say that James and Darwin were completely wrong. In fact, research conducted in the last decade has lent support to their theories, suggesting that emotions affect our bodies and our bodies affect our emotions. In a 2003 study, for example, Simone Schnall at Plymouth University and James Laird at Clark University showed that, for some people at least, thirty minutes spent pulling a smiling face led them to feel happier afterwards, while pulling a sad face led them to feel more sad (see box on p.102). More recent research has taken this even further, asking specifically whether it is the neural commands

THE ROUGH GUIDE TO PSYCHOLOGY

Why do we cry?

We do it a lot when we're babies, less when we're adult, but everybody cries sometimes. Quite why remains something of a mystery. When psychologists ask people about their real-life crying episodes, a substantial majority say that they felt better after a good session. This fits with the popular idea that crying serves a cathartic, cleansing function. By contrast, when crying is studied under laboratory conditions – for example, by showing participants a tear-jerker of a film – people usually show no benefits. If anything they feel worse. This mismatch between survey and lab research could arise from the role played by social context. In real life, a person who cries will often be comforted by those around them. In this context, we can see that crying serves an obvious social role, communicating to others that we are in distress. When crying has been studied in the laboratory, participants have usually been on their own, so perhaps it's no wonder they haven't experienced any benefit.

Researchers have also looked at whether some people benefit from crying more than others. Although women cry more than men, Jonathan Rottenberg's team at the University of Southern California found no evidence that they benefit more from crying. The most important characteristic in this regard was "alexithymia", which is a difficulty understanding the source and meaning of one's emotions. Rottenberg's team found that people fitting this description benefited the least from crying. Another approach of psychologists has been to

sent to the facial muscles that provoke emotional feelings, or if instead it is the feedback about the position of our facial muscles that affects the way we feel.

To find this out, Andreas Hennenlotter at the Max Planck Institute and his colleagues conducted an ingenious study in which they recruited women who had just had, or were due to have, cosmetic botox injections in their faces, thus rendering them unable to flex their frown muscles. Hennenlotter's team scanned the women's brains while they imitated angry facial expressions. All of them showed increased activity in the amygdala – a brain structure involved in emotional processing – when imitating an angry expression versus just looking at it. Crucially, however, this exaggerated amygdala activity was not as great in the women who'd had the botox. In other words, the influence of our facial expressions on emotional processing is not only about the neural commands sent to the muscles, feedback from the position of the facial muscles also seems to play an important role too.

characterize the different forms of crying. Judith Nelson, a psycho-therapist, has distinguished between at least three kinds: loud, protest crying; subdued, sad crying; and detached, tearless crying, of the sort provoked by hopelessness. Of course anyone who's been to a wedding will know that people also often cry when they're happy! The research on this kind of crying is even thinner on the ground.

ARE EMOTIONS UNIVERSAL?

Another question that engages researchers is whether or not emotional facial expressions are the same the world over. The seminal work in this area was conducted by Paul Ekman (now a consultant on the popular US series *Lie to Me*). He travelled the world, from Japan to the jungles of Papua New Guinea, carrying a set of photos of people pulling various emotional facial expressions, and he found that humans everywhere were able to interpret the emotions accurately. Other more recent research has shown that it's not just the facial expression of core emotions – happiness, sadness, fear and disgust – that are the same worldwide. Jessica Tracy at the University of British Columbia and David Matsumoto at San Francisco State University analysed photos taken of judo competitors at the 2004 Olympics and Paralympics, and found that all of them, wherever their country of origin and regardless of whether they were sighted or born blind, displayed shame and pride in the same way, with either slumped shoulders or raised arms, respectively. The blind competitors could never have seen another person display emotion in this way, which suggests that the display of shame and pride is innate rather than culturally learned.

But not everyone believes culture has no influence on the way that we express our emotions. Consider a controversial 2009 paper entitled "Cultural Confusions Show that Facial Expressions Are Not Universal" by Rachael Jack at the University of Glasgow. Jack's lab tested the ability of participants to categorize photos of emotional expressions and reported that people from East Asia had trouble distinguishing fear and disgust from, respectively, surprise and anger. The implication, the researchers

Six evidence-based ways to boost your happiness

1. **Smile** The Charlie Chaplin song *Smile* claims that you'll "find life is still worthwhile if you just smile". Research backs this up. Simone Schnall and James Laird instructed 46 participants to pull either a happy, sad or angry face intermittently for half an hour. Admittedly, no effect was observed for half the participants. However, for the others who were affected by their own facial expressions, those who'd been smiling subsequently felt in a happier mood than they had done earlier, and they were also particularly likely to recall happy events from their past when prompted by neutral words like "tree".

2. **Don't have kids** Some psychologists have argued, controversially, that our widespread belief that having children will make us happy is misplaced and is an example of a so-called "focusing illusion". We persist in thinking children will make us happy, these psychologists say, because we tend to focus on the good bits – such as our expected pride on hearing their first word – while neglecting to imagine the bad bits, such as changing nappies and the stress, worry and monumental effort involved in raising a child. In fact, several large-scale studies show that, on average, parents are less happy than non-parents.

3. **Be grateful** Remembering to count our blessings and show gratitude to others has been linked with increased happiness. What's going well in your life right now? What are you grateful for? Most of us can think of some small way that fortune has smiled on us. Martin Seligman, the founder of positive psychology (see p.349), showed that participants who wrote a letter of thanks and delivered it to someone who'd showed them kindness experienced increased happiness for up to a month afterwards.

4. **Become a political activist** The idea that active participation in society fulfils a basic human need, which can be traced back to Aristotle, is supported by recent research. In 2009 the positive

argued, is that these emotions are expressed slightly differently in East Asian cultures from how they are in Western cultures, thus causing the differences in recognition ability.

A neat compromise position on this debate was published by Matsumoto's group in 2009. Carefully re-examining the photos taken of the Olympic judo competitors, they discovered that for at least one to two seconds after losing a bout, competitors' emotional expressions were the same across all the different nationalities. However, after those initial revealing moments, cultural differences emerged, with judokas from collectivist cultures like China tending to mask their initial emotional expressions more than competitors from individualistic cultures like the UK.

psychologists Malte Klar and Tim Kasser surveyed hundreds of undergraduate students, and found that those who self-identified as activists were happier than those who didn't. It's not just that happier people are more likely to be activists. Klar and Kasser also encouraged a separate group of students to campaign for more ethical food-sourcing at their university cafeteria. These students subsequently reported feeling more energized compared with a control group who campaigned for tastier food and more choice.

5. **Seek out repeatedly enjoyable activities** Our tendency to adapt and adjust to those rare, profound changes, good and bad, that come our way – such as winning the lottery or becoming seriously ill – has led some experts to suggest that we're all stuck with a baseline level of happiness to which we will always return. However, Daniel Mochon and his co-workers challenged this in 2008 when they showed that repeated visits to religious services or to the gym left people feeling happier. They concluded that "the key for long lasting changes to wellbeing is to engage in activities that provide small and frequent boosts".

6. **Mix with happy people** A social networking study, involving over 12,000 people in Massachusetts, showed that happiness spreads through social groups like a smiley virus. A person's happiness isn't influenced merely by their friends' levels of happiness, the study found, but also by the friends of friends, and the friends of friends of friends. Using data collected over time, the researchers James Fowler and Nicholas Christakis were able to show that it isn't merely that happy people tend to congregate together. If a participant's friend was recorded as being happy at one time-point, the chance of that participant being happy when asked at a second, later time-point was increased, thus suggesting the friend's happiness really had played a causal role.

HOW MANY EMOTIONS ARE THERE?

Philosophers and psychologists have been grappling with this question for centuries. The grandfather of psychology, Wilhelm Wundt (see p.8), proposed that all emotions can be located along three dimensions – pleasantness vs. unpleasantness, excitement vs. depression, and tension vs. relaxation. This view was lent some credence by modern research showing that people find it easy to classify emotional words according to Wundt's first two dimensions. Other experts, including Paul Ekman, have followed Darwin's lead by arguing that there are a fixed number of "core" emotions, classifiable according to their distinctive and universally recognized facial expressions: happiness, disgust, surprise, sadness, anger and fear. But if Ekman and Darwin are right, how come we use hundreds of different words to describe our emotions?

The answer lies with another school of thought – championed by "appraisal theorists" like Klaus Scherer of the Centre for Affective Sciences in Geneva – which states there are probably as many emotions as there are meaningful situations to be encountered. By this account, while different types of facial expression are commonly associated with certain *kinds* of emotion, no two emotional experiences are ever identical. The numerous words we use to label emotions reflect the way, along with the use of metaphor and analogy, we struggle to convey something of what our emotions feel like.

Your development

That we feel any sense of a coherent self through our lives is little short of a miracle. Our bodies grow, blossom, mature, age and shrivel, so that externally we end up bearing little resemblance to our youthful origins. We change jobs, relationships, homes, sometimes even names and sexes. However, amidst all this confusion and drama there are discernible life-stages that we all live through: from our time in the womb, through to infancy and childhood, to adolescence, adulthood and ultimately retirement and old age. Historically, psychologists have focused mainly on the early stages, attempting to solve the enduring mystery of how a ball of cells becomes a fully-fledged person with hopes and regrets. Recently, however, that's begun to change, with the teenage and retirement years in particular attracting the interest of new research.

Embryonic psychology

It's dark and thunderously noisy and for approximately the first 38 weeks of your life, the womb is your home. Although it's the convention of many cultures to neglect the importance of this period, researchers are increasingly interested in foetal psychology. It's a time of astonishingly rapid change. At peak production, 250,000 new brain cells are created every minute and 1.8 million new neural connections formed every second. Double the number of brain cells are created that will ultimately be needed, with a later process of systematic pruning disposing of those cells that aren't required.

Pregnant mothers don't usually report feeling their baby's first movements until around sixteen to eighteen weeks, but thanks to ultrasound we know that foetal movements – which eventually include a repertoire of kicking, yawning, thumb-sucking and stretching – can actually begin from between seven to eight weeks. Remarkably, right- or left-handed-

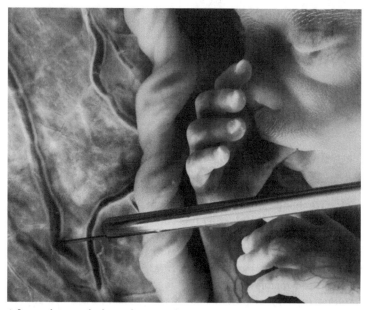

A foetus photographed at eighteen weeks.

ness is already evident from week ten, and the rapid eye-movements (REM), indicative of dream sleep in humans outside the womb, are seen in the last third of pregnancy.

Touch is the first of the **senses** to develop, at approximately eight weeks, with sensitivity initially apparent around the foetus's lips and cheeks. Taste and smell come next at about fifteen to sixteen weeks, with accounts of foetuses swallowing more if their mother's diet has sweetened the amniotic fluid. What you eat as a pregnant mother can even influence your baby's tastes once he or she is born – for example, children born to mothers who ate garlic during pregnancy show less aversion to this taste later in life. From 22 to 24 weeks, the foetus begins responding to sound, and by late pregnancy there's evidence for the recognition of different voices and speech sounds.

Foetuses show evidence of **basic learning** at 22 to 24 weeks. They will start to ignore or "habituate" to a sound or touch that is repeated. From 32 weeks, they show signs of associative conditioning, whereby the repeated pairing of one stimulus (such as a prod) with another subsequent stimulus (such as a specific kind of noise) leads the foetus to expect the second event to follow the first. A study published in July

Some parental dilemmas

❏ **To breastfeed or not?** Breastfeeding is associated with a range of physical and mental health-benefits for your baby and, if you can, the World Health Organization recommends sticking to breast-feeding for up to six months. However, claims that breast milk boosts a child's IQ are rather more controversial. A study by University of Edinburgh researchers, published in 2006, found the usual link between breastfeeding and children's IQ, but showed that this link mostly disappeared when family background was taken into account – that is, breastfed children tend to come from more advantaged backgrounds and to have mothers with higher IQs, which is probably why they too end up with a high IQ.

❏ **Is there any drawback to raising a child bilingually?** There are anecdotal reports that children raised to speak two languages show delays in their language acquisition relative to monolingual children. Such claims are largely unsupported by any scientific evidence, and what is certain is that any possible delays are only temporary. By contrast, there is ample evidence that a bilingual upbringing is advantageous. To take one example, a 2009 study by researchers at the International School for Advanced Studies in Italy found that babies raised in a bilingual home had superior cognitive control – they were better able to unlearn a puppet's prior location and then learn its new position.

❏ **What kind of pushchair should I buy?** Most pushchairs or baby buggies face away, so that your child is pointing away from you. However, the first psychological study of pushchairs, published in 2008, found that there could be advantages to having a buggy in which your child faces towards you. Developmental psychologist Suzanne Zeedyk of Dundee University found that parents talked to their infants twice as much when they were in a "toward" position – a good thing considering that parent-child interaction is known to be beneficial for language development. Moreover, the children in toward buggies were more likely to fall asleep and showed reduced stress-levels.

❏ **Imaginary friends** Experts and lay people alike used to think that for a child to have an imaginary friend was a bad sign, indicating social awkwardness. Today, psychologists recognize that not only are imaginary friends incredibly common – about half of all kids have one or more – but that children who have them are just as sociable and popular as those who don't. In fact, having an imaginary friend could come with advantages. A study by Gabriel Trionfi and Elaine Reese, for example, found that children with imaginary friends often have superior narrative skills, perhaps because of the practice they get describing them to curious family and friends.

2009 by Jan Nijhuis at Maastricht University involved placing a noisy, vibrating device on the tummies of women between the 30th and 38th week of their pregnancies. At first the foetuses squirmed and their heart rates increased. Crucially, however, they barely responded when the device was applied again ten minutes later – they'd evidently learned that there was nothing to be afraid of. The 34-week and older foetuses remembered the device was no threat even after a four-week gap.

Understandably, perhaps, a lot of foetal psychology research is focused on ascertaining whether or not foetuses can feel **pain**. It's a tricky area, because while there are indicators of pain processing from 23 weeks – in terms of the maturation of pain-nerve pathways and biochemical responses to needle punctures – there's no way we can know whether the foetus actually *feels* any pain. In 2010, however, the Royal College of Obstetricians and Gynaecologists in the UK published an authoritative report which concluded that foetuses of 24 weeks and younger *are* unable to feel pain, because they are in a sleep-like state of unconsciousness and their brains lack the necessary wiring between the periphery of their bodies and the cortex.

An area of embryonic psychology that's spilt over into the mainstream has to do with so-called "prenatal education". Given that by late pregnancy foetuses can hear and process sounds, it's perhaps no wonder that some companies have begun to make claims regarding the merits of

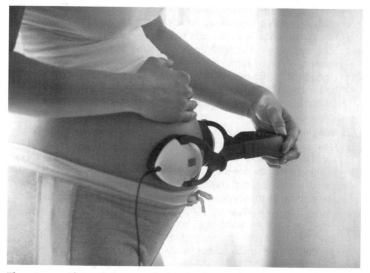

There is no evidence that pre-natal education has any benefits.

broadcasting various sounds into the womb. There's certainly evidence that newborns show a preference for the maternal voice and that they prefer music they were exposed to prenatally (although this usually disappears within three weeks). A study published in 2009 by Birgit Mampe at the University of Würzburg even showed that German and French newborn babies cry in a way that mirrors the intonation of their native languages. They seem to be mimicking the melody of the voices they've heard in the womb. But while these observations suggest that foetuses can process sounds in the womb and that this can affect their postnatal behaviour, there's very little, if any, evidence that this situation can be exploited for any kind of educational advantage. Some doctors have even warned that using commercial products to play loud sounds into the womb could be harmful.

What we do know for sure is that the pregnant mother's psychological state can affect her unborn child. More than a dozen prospective studies have shown that when a mother suffers from sustained **stress** during her pregnancy, this can have long-term consequences for her child, for example increasing his or her chances of having later attentional problems. This remains true even when researchers control for the effects of other relevant factors such as the mother's post-natal mood. One possible mechanism is via the stress-hormone cortisol, which can reach the foetus and affect brain development.

Infancy and childhood

Far from emerging into the world as a blank slate, as the philosopher John Locke argued in the seventeenth century, babies arrive with a suite of preferences and a host of predispositions, all of which serve to guide them in their new and strange circumstances. The baby's preference for the mother's voice, an infatuation with faces, a proclivity for mimicry, and a wide-eyed attention to what's going on – all these characteristics and many others ensure that the newborn bonds with the primary carer and learns about the world and the other people who inhabit it. These inbuilt capacities are perhaps most obvious when it comes to the numerous reflexes seen in newborns, including the **Moro reflex**, in which the infant flings out its arms in response to a loud noise or the feeling of falling, and the cute **stepping reflex**, in which the sensation of the ground on the soles of the feet causes the infant to step repeatedly as if trying to walk.

Of course it's frustratingly difficult to research what it's like to be a baby or young child, because they can't talk and we remember little

The truth about Little Albert

Little Albert is probably the most famous case study in child psychology. Aged eleven months, he was the subject of a series of experiments initially reported by the pioneering behaviourist John Watson (see p.14) and his wife Rosalie Rayner in 1920. The pair conditioned Albert to fear a white rat by repeatedly showing him the rat and simultaneously banging a steel bar and claw hammer together behind his head. Needless to say, this kind of experiment would never receive ethical approval today! Albert had previously been unafraid of the rat, but after Watson and Rayner's intervention, he cried whenever the rat was placed near to him. Watson and Rayner also tested Albert's reaction to other animals and objects to see how much his fear would generalize to things resembling a white rat. Their findings are often misreported – for example, some accounts have stated that Albert subsequently feared all furry animals. The historical record isn't helped by the fact that Watson and Rayner wrote several different versions of their experiments and never published the research in a peer-reviewed academic journal. What's clear from their writings is that the results were rather messy. For example, in a later stage of their experiments, the researchers used the metal bar to condition Albert to fear not only the rat, but also a rabbit and a dog. Yet later that same day Albert barely reacted when presented with these animals in another room. Another myth that often finds its way into reports of these experiments is the claim that Albert's mother took him away from Watson and Rayner before they could employ "desensitization" procedures to remove his recently acquired fears. In fact, the 1920 report of this work makes it clear that the psychologists were told well in advance when Albert would no longer be available.

There's a sad coda to this story. In 2009, the psychologist Hall Beck of Appalachian University reported the results of his efforts to find out what happened to poor Little Albert in the years after he was experimented on. Beck trawled Watson's personal and professional writings, as well as census data and other official archives, and even recruited the help of an FBI forensics expert. In the end Beck concluded that Little Albert was most likely a boy called Douglas Merritte, the son of Arvilla Merritte, a campus wet-nurse, who it is believed disposed of her maiden name, Irons, to hide the fact that her baby was illegitimate. According to Arvilla Iron's descendents, Douglas died aged just six, after developing fluid on the brain.

of our own infancy. Despite these obstacles, we do have some inkling. Because the lenses of babies' eyes are undimmed by age and their brains haven't yet learned to filter out unwanted sounds, the world will seem both blindingly bright and very noisy. There's also evidence that the senses start off cross-wired, so babies might well hear sights and see noises.

What about the infant's mind? One striking characteristic that differs from a mature mind is the baby's **attentional focus**. Whereas an adult surveys the world with the selective focus of a spotlight, the mind of a baby or young child is wider – in the words of developmental psychologist Alison Gopnik, it's more like a "lantern". Gopnik likens this state of mind to the experience of a first visit to a foreign city where every exotic sight and sound grabs your interest. By adult standards, the infant or child, like the tourist, might well appear woefully distractible and unfocused, but given the main goal of early life is to learn, the baby's mental openness is ideal.

You can demonstrate the advantage of lantern-style attention using a simple task in which you challenge children and adults to remember the left-hand card in a series of card pairs. As you might expect, compared with adults, children will usually perform less well at remembering the left-hand cards. However, given an unexpected test on one of the earlier right-hand cards, youngsters will typically outperform the adults. We're better at zooming in, but kids, it seems, are superior at processing the bigger picture.

Look this way

Psychologists who choose to conduct research with babies need to be extremely patient, as the little bundles of joy aren't always the most cooperative research participants. They can't be interviewed, fill out questionnaires or follow instructions. That's why psychologists often deploy a technique known as the "preferential-looking time" procedure. It draws on a reliable feature of infant behaviour, which is that they get bored when things don't change and look longer at things that surprise them. Show a baby a display with sixteen dots until they're bored, for example, then reduce the dots by half and they'll start looking again, thus suggesting they can tell the difference between quantities. The technique can also reveal preferences, for instance that babies prefer the sight of their mother's face to that of a stranger. And it can be used to test babies' expectations. They'll tend to look longer if you set up a mini-illusion in which a ball appears to roll through a solid object, thus suggesting they're born with an innate, (or rapidly acquired) sense of physics. A variation on the preferential-looking time procedure is the "high-amplitude sucking-preference procedure", which capitalizes on the fact that babies suck harder from a nipple when they're more interested in something.

The degree of **self-consciousness** evident in early childhood provides another insight into what it's like to "be" during this period. Rudimentary self-awareness itself emerges at around eighteen months. This can be tested with the red-dot challenge. If you surreptitiously splodge a one-year-old's forehead with red ink and place them in front of a mirror, they won't bat an eyelid. They don't recognize the person staring back at them. Repeat the stunt with a two-year-old, however, and they'll immediately reach for the red dot.

However, this initial self-recognition is far from fully developed self-consciousness. Before the age of about four, it's a sense of self that's rooted in the present. Show a two-year-old a home movie of his past self and he'll see a stranger. Even by three years, children don't seem to connect with their previous mental states. Ask a hungry three-year-old if they'd like a biscuit and most likely they'll say yes. But if, after they've scoffed a couple, you ask them if they'd wanted those biscuits a moment ago, they'll deny they ever did. It's not that young children can't remember the past – you'll find they're perfectly able to recall past events in a factual sense. It's that they somehow don't have a sense of ownership over their past selves. To use the terminology from Chapter 4 (on memory), they don't yet have a fully functional autobiographical memory that places them at the heart of an unfolding narrative. It's a similar story for the future, with the consequence that three-year-olds are hopeless at predicting their future needs. Whereas a four- or five-year-old will select sunglasses over a scarf for a trip to a sunny beach, a three-year-old will be as likely to choose the scarf.

Self-control is another key indicator of how an infant experiences the world. The human brain doesn't mature uniformly (unlike the brains of monkeys and other primates). In particular, the front of the brain responsible for self-control – the "prefrontal cortex" – is late to develop, and does not catch up with other regions, such as the auditory cortex, until about four years of age. According to a 2009 paper by Sharon Thompson-Schill and her colleagues at the University of Pennsylvania, while this feature of human development has obvious disadvantages for planning and controlling behaviour, these are outweighed by advantages for learning.

Imagine you are watching a tennis match (a game you know nothing about) and that at each point played, you are asked to estimate whether a player will come forward to the net. As an adult you observe the statistical probabilities during play and, based on this, on ten percent of occasions you predict the player will come forward, and on ninety percent that they'll stay on the baseline. This is known as **probability matching** and

Clever little scientists

Babies and young children are so adept at learning because they approach the world like clever little scientists weighing up probabilities and statistics. This can be demonstrated in the context of language learning, where infants face the daunting challenge of identifying word boundaries in speech. Sometimes fluent speakers pause between words, but a lot of the time they just let one word roll into another. One way to identify where a word ends and another begins is to pay attention to probabilities. Consider the phrase "hello Michael", in which "lo" comes after "hel" but before "mi". Baby Michael would hear "lo" come after "hel" much more often than he would hear either "lo" precede "mi" or other sounds precede "lo". This consistent pattern would reveal to him that "lo" somehow belongs to "hel", forming a word.

This is more than just a theory. A 1996 study by Jenny Saffran at the University of Wisconsin-Madison revealed that babies as young as eight months really do notice these statistical contingencies between syllables. When the researchers played the babies a repeating string of three nonsense-syllables, they grew bored just as you'd expect. But crucially, this boredom was broken when the babies were exposed to the same syllables paired together in a different order. It's as if, after just two minutes, the babies had already developed a sense of how likely one syllable was to follow another, and their interest was piqued when this probability changed.

it's the approach that most adults bring to these kinds of tasks. A toddler would also notice that players mostly stay at the back, but because of an infant's uninhibited thinking style, he or she will consistently predict the player will stay on the baseline. In this context, the toddler's crude approach will be right more often than a more nuanced strategy.

Thompson-Schill's team argued that this advantage translates to real-life infant challenges, such as language learning. Infants listening to adult speech will notice rules, only to hear them frequently broken. But thanks to their "maximization" approach, they tend to latch onto the rules and ignore the caveats, which is ideal when taking the first steps towards acquiring language. The psychologists Carla Hudson-Kam and Elissa Newport provided evidence for this in a study in which they exposed children and adults to a deliberately capricious artificial language. Children, but not adults, were found to zoom in on an unreliable rule and generalize from it.

In a series of classic experiments in the late 1980s, Walter Mischel of Columbia University tested the development of children's self-control.

He sat children in front of two large cookies or marshmallows and told them that they could have one now if they wanted, but if they waited five minutes for the researcher to return they could have both. Children younger than three couldn't resist the immediate temptation, but between the ages of three and five, reflecting the maturation of the prefrontal cortex, the children's ability to defer gratification improved. The older children even began using neat strategies to distract themselves from the temptation, such as covering their eyes or singing.

The role of the **imagination** provides a final insight into early childhood development. Babies are like little scientists (see box on p.113), but from about one year old, they're also like little novelists and film directors: personifying objects, role-playing, pretending and talking to imaginary friends. You could say these behaviours are laying the groundwork for what makes us distinctly human – the ability to consider other possible worlds, to think about what might be. The precociousness of the imagination is remarkable. One-year-olds already seem to grasp when someone is feigning surprise or rage. Two-year-olds know how to play along if an adult is pretending to be a bear and yet on another level they know that this isn't really the case. Three-year-olds understand that different fantasy worlds are separate – for example, that Batman can

Precocious talents

Infants and young kids aren't just great learners, they also come with a range of mental abilities that are either inbuilt or emerge extremely early on in life. An ability that parents can't fail to notice is that of mimicry. Classic studies in the 1970s showed that newborns are able to copy sticking out a tongue, lip-pursing, mouth opening, and even simple sequences of finger movements. Curiously, these abilities, like many others including face recognition, can briefly disappear or deteriorate before reappearing again – a sign that development isn't always linear, and that sometimes old tricks are later performed in new ways by a more mature mind.

Another great example of infant precociousness comes from research on the psychology of music. Ross Flom and his co-workers at Brigham Young University played a video and music to babies aged either three or nine months. The video showed a man or woman's face with a neutral expression and the babies soon grew bored of it. However, when the researchers switched the mood of the music, either from happy to sad or vice versa, the older babies became interested in the video again, suggesting that even at their tender age they could already hear the difference between happy jingles and mournful dirges.

touch his sidekick Robin, but can't touch the sea-sponge cartoon character SpongeBob.

Combine all these insights into aspects of infanthood – attentional focus, self-consciousness, self-control and imagination – and you start to get an idea of what it must be like to be a baby or young child. Every inch of the world is alive, dancing, screaming out for your attention. And meanwhile you're thoroughly immersed in each present moment, unrestrained, unhampered by any nagging connections with the past or worries about the future; uninhibited by the impossible, by what's real and what's not.

Developmental stages

Classic developmental psychologists like **Jean Piaget** used to think of children as passing through a series of discrete stages of mental maturity and that the errors they made on various tasks could reveal what stage they were at. It's certainly true that various developmental milestones emerge in a predictable order – crawling comes first, then walking; single-word utterances before sentences, and so on. Similarly, there are

Other early abilities have more obvious survival value. The classic "visual cliff" experiments conducted by Eleanor Gibson and Richard Walk in 1960 showed that most babies seem to be able to perceive depth as soon as they are old enough to crawl. The researchers placed babies aged between six and fourteen months on a glass table, part of which was patterned, giving the appearance of being solid, while the other part was see-through, appearing to be a sheer drop to the floor. With few exceptions, even the youngest babies refused to crawl onto the "drop" even if their mothers encouraged them to do so.

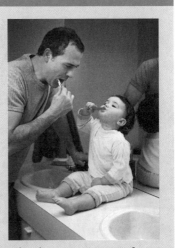

Babies have a great capacity for mimicry.

mental challenges that, say, a typical four-year old could pass but that any two-year-old would most certainly fail. A classic example is the **false-belief task**. Children are presented with a cartoon scenario in which a character empties a pencil tin of pencils and fills it with Smarties. A new character appears on the scene and the children are asked what she will think is in the tin. Children of four years of age and upwards understand that the new character has no reason to think the tin will contain anything other than pencils. By contrast, two- and three-year-olds tend to say the new character will think the tin is full of Smarties because they haven't yet grasped the notion that people can hold false beliefs.

However, psychologists are forever devising new ways to reveal infant and childhood abilities, with the result that Piaget's theory of errors and stages no longer holds up as well. It's not that these abilities are fully formed from birth, rather it's that the first signs of understanding – the building blocks – are being discovered at earlier and earlier ages. The findings reveal a picture of development that's more continuous than Piaget's abrupt stages implied.

For a good example, let's return to children's appreciation of other people's point of view – an ability psychologists call having a **theory of mind**. Piaget devised a test known as the "three-mountain task", inspired by the scenic landscape surrounding Geneva. The task involved sitting children in front of a model of the mountains and asking them to

Jean Piaget founded the International Centre for Genetic Epistemology in Geneva in 1955 and directed it until shortly before his death in 1980.

Jean Piaget (1896–1980)

Swiss-born Piaget is the second most highly cited psychologist of all time, behind Freud. He was an academic prodigy, publishing his first paper at the tender age of eleven, on the topic of the albino sparrow. Hundreds more research papers and more than 75 books would follow in a long and prolific career. His most influential works include *The Origins of Intelligence in Children*, *The Construction of Reality in the Child*, and *Play, Dreams, and Imitation in Childhood*. Early in his career, Piaget worked briefly with the famous psychoanalyst Carl Jung and later with the intelligence-test pioneer Alfred Binet (1857–1911). He married in 1923 and, like all self-respecting developmental psychologists, studied his own children Jaqueline, Lucienne and Laurent.

Influenced by evolutionary theory, Piaget founded a new area of academic enquiry known as genetic epistemology, which drew parallels between the developmental trajectory of a person's knowledge and the way that species adapt to their environmental circumstances. He is famous for arguing that thought develops through childhood in a series of a discrete, qualitatively distinct stages, which are always completed in fixed order. These are: the sensorimotor stage (from birth to about two years), the pre-operational stage (two to seven years), the concrete operational stage (seven to twelve years) and the formal operational stage (reached only by children in technologically advanced societies).

Piaget believed that a child at a given stage of cognitive development thinks differently from adults and from children in other stages, and that the stage a child is at can be revealed by the errors they make on certain tasks. Older children and adults understand that if nothing is added or taken away, then – despite appearances – the amount of something will not have changed. Piaget showed, however, that children in the pre-operational stage are still lacking in logical powers and overly reliant on appearances, and so can be tricked into thinking there is more of something if it takes up more space. Piaget called this "errors of conservation". You can test this with children under the age of five. Pour some water from a short, stubby glass into a tall, thin glass and they are quite likely to think there is more water in the second glass simply because the water level is higher.

imagine what the scene would look like from different perspectives – for example, they might be asked to select the photo that best showed the view from a position opposite to where they were sitting. What Piaget found was that children younger than four didn't understand the task, kids aged four to six understood it but were not very good at it, whereas seven-year-olds and upwards were far more successful. Piaget said this was because children younger than seven reason in an "egocentric" way, and that it's only when they reach what he called the "concrete-operational" stage of development (at around seven) that they are able to look at the world from other people's perspectives.

However, new research is challenging Piaget's conclusions, showing that a child's sense of other people's minds first emerges far earlier than his postulated concrete-operational stage. For example, experts now believe that babies as young as twelve months already have a rudimentary understanding of other people's intentions. Terje Falck-Ytter and his colleagues at Uppsala University's Baby Lab in Sweden recorded babies' eye movements as they watched videos of a person placing toys into a bucket. Babies of six months stayed fixated on the toys, but the gaze of those of twelve months, just like adults, leapt ahead to the bucket, as if anticipating the person's intentions. Further research has shown that a nineteen-month-old infant can tell the difference between a joke and a mistake, two-year-olds have a rudimentary understanding of ownership, and toddlers will routinely help you out if you drop some pens or can't quite reach an object that you're stretching for. A rather charming experiment by Betty Repacholi and Alison Gopnik even showed that eighteen-month-olds will feed broccoli to an adult, rather than their own favoured crackers, if that's what they've seen the adult enjoy earlier.

Another example of where Piaget's findings are being revised concerns "object permanence" – the understanding that objects continue to exist even when we can't see them. Piaget thought that this concept was beyond babies, and that their behaviour suggests that they think an object will come into existence as a consequence of their act of looking. For example, if you repeatedly hide a ball under a first cup and then, in full view, place it under a second cup, babies will still look for it under the first cup.

Contradicting Piaget, more modern explanations think this mistake and others like it have more to do with infant memory limitations or babies' inability to inhibit their temptation to look under the first cup when they've found it there so many times before. Perhaps the most recent and creative reinterpretation was offered in 2008 by Jozsef Topal and others at the Hungarian Academy of Sciences. They argued that when we communicate with babies using eye contact and chirpy chatter, they have an innate tendency to assume that what we're communicating to them is a general fact about the world. When the researchers repeated the ball-and-cup experiment without any patter or eye contact, the babies were far more likely to look under the second cup.

Moral development

The early signs of **altruism** speak to another area of child psychology – moral development – about which modern findings are also overturning traditional thought. Piaget, Freud, and the moral-development expert **Lawrence Kohlberg**, all believed that children don't fully understand morality until adolescence or even beyond. Indeed, influenced by Piaget, Kohlberg proposed a theory of moral development based on the levels: pre-conventional, conventional and post-conventional, each of which was further broken down into two stages. Kohlberg measured children's and young people's progress through the stages and levels according to their responses to moral dilemmas such as whether and why a man, Heinz, should break into a chemist's to obtain an overpriced treatment for his wife's cancer. Only when they reach the second and final stage of level three (the "universal ethical principals orientation"), which Kohlberg said happens from the mid-thirties onwards, do people rely on their own conscience with reference to universal moral principles, such as justice and the sanctity of human life.

The idea that morality takes time to develop is a view that's enshrined in many legal systems, and children are not expected to have a deep understanding of right and wrong. Piaget specifically argued that when judging the morality of an action, children younger than ten or eleven focus almost exclusively on outcomes and fail to take intentions into account, as adults do. According to Piaget, young children would consider a girl who breaks ten glasses attempting to reach a cookie for her mother as morally worse than a girl who broke one glass while in the process of attempting to steal a cookie.

In 2009, however, Gavin Nobes at the University of East Anglia and his colleagues appeared to show that young children do in fact take intentions into account – it's just that it can appear as though they don't because they haven't yet fully grasped the concept of negligence. Again, the argument isn't that moral reasoning is fully developed in childhood, it's just that the experts of the past hadn't fully uncovered the early building blocks of children's understanding.

Nobes's team presented dozens of children aged between three and eight years with illustrated stories involving bicycle crashes, dropped cups and games of catch, after which they asked the kids for their views on each protagonist's culpability and deserved punishment. A key difference from traditional research was that half the time the kids were told that a protagonist had taken care, whereas the rest of the time they were told that he or she had been reckless – for example, by trying to carry a tower of cups in one hand. Contrary to Piaget, the researchers found that overall, children, like adults, mostly based their moral judgements on whether a protagonist intended to cause harm. According to the researchers, the reason that the children's judgements sometimes diverged from the adults' is because, when bad outcomes occurred, they often failed to recognize as a mitigating factor the fact that a protagonist had taken care. To the children, a bad outcome meant the protagonist must have been negligent, even when they'd been told he or she had been careful. But as Nobes's team pointed out, this is an issue of delayed practical, not moral, understanding.

In another demonstration of children's advanced moral understanding, research published in the 1980s showed that young children can even tell the difference between the breaking of "arbitrary" social rules and actual harm. Judith Smetana, then at Rochester University, asked children aged between two and a half and nine years to judge the seriousness of a number of transgressions, including the breaking of school rules (such as wearing pyjamas to school) and morally bad acts (such as a hitting another child). Even the youngest children said that harmful acts were more serious than the breaking of rules, and they said that it would be wrong to hurt someone even if the rules said that you could. This contradicts Piaget's claim that young children are only able to see rules as fixed and absolute.

Although the Russian psychologist Lev Vygotsky (1896–1934) died young, and his major work *Thought and Language* wasn't translated into English until the early 1960s, his ideas about the importance of social interaction in children's development have been highly influential. Vygotsky emphasized that learning doesn't take place in a social vacuum. In particular, he argued that children's abilities are initially nurtured with the help of parents and teachers before becoming fully mastered – what he called the "zone of proximal development". His ideas have influenced educational practices, for example by highlighting the value of group work and peer learning.

Adolescence

Let's be honest, teenagers don't get the best press, at least not in Western cultures. The period between childhood and adulthood tends to conjure up thoughts of spots, sulks and strops, combined with a penchant for moody music, illicit drinking and other risky antics. These stereotypes are matched by the statistics. In the USA, for example, eighteen is the "peak age" of arrest for a range of crimes. For arson, it's even younger.

Oddly enough, adolescence is a uniquely human developmental stage. Even our closest relatives, the great apes, mature seamlessly from childhood into adulthood without an equivalent intermediary phase. The orthodox view of why we evolved with an adolescent phase was that it gave extra time for brain growth and for developing a body fit to walk long distances on two legs. However, this view has been challenged by recent controversial findings suggesting that our small-brained ancestor *homo erectus* may also have had an adolescent phase. Another explanation, proposed by anthropologist Barry Bogin of Loughborough University, is that adolescence improved the subsequent reproductive success of our immediate ancestors. By this account, humanoid girls look fertile before they really are fertile, allowing them time to practise the social and cultural complexities of adulthood without much risk of falling pregnant. By contrast, although teenage boys are fertile from a young age, their scrawny appearance reduces their appeal to women and their threat to adult men, thus giving them a safe time to practise being macho.

STROPPY TEENAGERS

When it comes to teenage angst, the default position among experts and lay people alike used to be to blame it all on the raging hormones. There's little doubt that the hormonal changes brought on by puberty do affect teenage behaviour, motivation and risk-taking. However, the picture we have today is more complete. An abundance of psychology and cognitive neuroscience research over the last decade suggests that the stereotypical teenager is coping not only with a hormonal surge, but also with a still-maturing brain.

Much of the evidence has come from brain imaging. While teenagers are beginning to look like adults on the outside, scans have shown that the brain continues to change in profound ways right through adolescence and into early adulthood. In particular, there's a major pruning back of excess grey matter during this time, combined with an increase in the "myelination" of brain cells, providing the fatty insulation that improves communication speed between neurons. Crucially, these patterns of maturation aren't uniform. Rather, regions involved in motor control and perception mature first, while regions at the front and side of the brain involved in weighing risks and rewards, self-control and thinking about other people's points of view tend to mature later on.

These brain differences between teenagers and adults have observable behavioural consequences. In 2004, for instance, Beatriz Luna and her colleagues in the Laboratory of Neurocognitive Development at the University of Pittsburgh tested nearly 250 people aged between eight and thirty years on a range of eye-movement tasks and found a series of performance differences between teens and adults. The tasks involved looking at an on-screen target as quickly as possible; ignoring the impulse to look at a target, looking instead in the other direction; and remembering target positions – these were tests of processing speed, inhibitory control and working memory (see Chapter 4), respectively. The researchers found that processing speed only reached mature adult performance at age fifteen, inhibitory control at age fourteen, while working memory didn't reach adult performance until age nineteen.

These performance measures may seem rather removed from real life. More recent research shows an important social skill – perspective-taking ability – also continues to develop right into late adolescence. Iroise Dumontheil at UCL and her colleagues tested children, adults, younger and older teens on a tricky computerized task that required them to move objects, such as balls and toys, housed on a set of shelves (see opposite). Crucially, the instructions came from a "director" who was located on the other side of the shelves and who could only see into those cubby holes that had no back to them. This meant that when he issued an instruction, such as "move the small rabbit up", and there was more than one rabbit on the shelves, the participants had to consider which cubby holes the director could and couldn't see, so as to disambiguate the command.

The teenager's viewpoint, from one side of the shelves, means that he can see three rabbits (two small and one large) and so has to disambiguate the director's command in order to identify the rabbit that is being referred to.

The director's viewpoint, from the other side of the shelves, means that he can only see two rabbits (one small and one large), because some of the objects have been blocked off from his sight.

As you'd expect, the teenagers outperformed the children, but the key finding is that the teens, even the seventeen-year-olds, made more errors on the task than adults. The researchers said their finding was consistent with the imaging research showing that the brain continues maturing right through to early adulthood.

ARE TODAY'S YOUTH REALLY MORE EGOTISTICAL?

With their swagger and sarcasm, the youngsters of today can seem full of themselves. But are they really? Or is it simply that we're stuck on an endless loop, such that each successive older generation eyes their juniors with suspicion, wondering why they're so pleased with themselves? According to a 2008 study, young people today really are more egotistical than in previous generations. A team led by Jean Twenge at San Diego State University trawled through published and unpublished data on self-reported undergraduate narcissism dating from the late 1970s to the present day, uncovering 85 samples involving 16,475 university students. These studies had asked young people to complete the "Narcissistic Personality Inventory", which features forty alternative statements to choose between, such as "I can live my life anyway I want to" or "People can't always live their lives in terms of what they want".

The results showed that levels of self-reported narcissism had risen year on year from the late 1970s to today, with the effect that two thirds of contemporary students scored above the narcissistic average for students tested in the years 1979–85. We should be careful before generalizing from these results – the study only looked at samples from the US, and only involved young people at university. Also, the researchers didn't look at contemporary adult egotism – perhaps we've all grown more full of ourselves.

Before we move onto adulthood and old age, it's important to mention that not everyone subscribes to the stereotype of stroppy teens and the role played by their maturing brains. In 2007, the psychologist Robert Epstein wrote an article for *Scientific American Mind* entitled "The myth of the teen brain". Epstein's main point was that many of the teenager brain-imaging findings were just as likely to be a consequence of cultural attitudes and the treatment of teenagers in western cultures, as to be a cause of what we think of as stereotypical teenage behaviour. He pointed to surveys he had conducted showing, for example, that teenagers in the USA have ten times as many legal restraints placed on their behaviour as adults. He suggests that it's little wonder teens

Do teenagers really need more sleep?

Staying up late and lying in the next morning are behavioural hallmarks of teenage life, but is it laziness or is the adolescent body-clock set to a different time? Recent research findings appear to support the latter view. A massive survey of 25,000 people aged between eight and ninety by Till Roenneberg at the Ludwig Maximilian University in Munich found that a person's time of optimum functioning becomes progressively later in the day through childhood and adolescence, reaching the latest time at about the age of twenty, after which it starts getting progressively earlier again. Meanwhile, Mary Carskadon at the E.P. Bradley Hospital Sleep and Chronobiology Research Laboratory looked at the brain waves of teenagers who'd been kept awake for 36 hours, and found that signs of "sleep pressure" appeared to build up more slowly compared to children. She told *New Scientist* magazine that this could account for why adolescents find it easier to stay up late. Some experts have even suggested that school lessons should be timetabled to start later so as to fit in better with the teenage body-clock. In 2009, Monkseaton High School in Tyneside, England decided to act on these recommendations, with lessons starting at ten in the morning for a five-month trial period. Preliminary results released in 2010 showed absenteeism at the school had plummeted during the trial period and grades in maths and English had improved significantly.

Dog tired. Teenagers may not need to have more sleep – just to get up later than the rest of us.

are so stroppy when their liberties are so compromised. Epstein also highlighted research conducted by the anthropologists Alice Schlegel and Herbert Barry III, examining teenage-hood in 186 pre-industrial societies. They found that that sixty percent didn't even have a word for "adolescence", and that antisocial behaviour in male teens was completely missing in around half. Historical analysis, Epstein further argued, shows that the very concept of what we think of as the teenage period is barely a century old, and he concluded that "we need to replace the myth of the immature teen brain with a frank look at capable and savvy teens in history, at teens in other cultures and at the truly extraordinary potential of our own young people today".

Adulthood, retirement and old age

For most people, the time between the end of adolescence and retirement is filled with a succession of monumental events – such as going to university, getting a job, finding a partner, having children, getting divorced, coping with bereavement, moving house, getting fired and so on. Some psychologists have posited that adulthood itself consists of several discrete sub-stages. The late **Daniel Levinson**, for example, proposed that men live through several "seasons": the first from 17 to 22 involving the acquisition of independence; the second, a period of establishment, finding a career and perhaps starting a family; then a few stressful years of reassessment and reality-checking, characterized by a fear that dreams might not be achieved; and finally, from about 33 onwards, a period of settling down in both work and family life.

As far as the brain is concerned, no sooner has it finished maturing than it begins to decline – at about the age of 27 or 28. Atrophy sets in and the brain starts to slow down, memory deteriorates and we gradually become less mentally agile. This decline is like the mirror opposite of our earlier development. The brain regions that were the last to fully mature, such as the frontal cortex, are the most vulnerable to the effects of ageing. Similarly, whereas through childhood and adolescence many functions became increasingly localized in one brain hemisphere or the other, ageing witnesses the reverse, as the hemispheres increasingly share the workload.

As people get older and more forgetful it's natural for them to start worrying that something could be seriously wrong. However, it's worth recognizing that everyone makes mistakes whatever their age. In 2007, Maria Jonsdottir and her Icelandic colleagues set out to establish just

Does brain training really work?

The evidence-base shows that the health of your brain can be enhanced by keeping physically active, avoiding smoking and excess alcohol, eating well, including plenty of vegetables and fish, and, of course, by keeping your mind active – reading, completing crossword puzzles and learning new skills, such as how to play a musical instrument. However, several commercial companies would also have you believe that you can help maintain your mental sharpness by purchasing and undertaking their "brain training" programmes. Market leaders include Dr Kawashima's Brain Training for Nintendo and CogniFit, which is endorsed by prominent neuroscientist Professor Susan Greenfield.

CogniFit has claimed that people aged over fifty who performed their computer-based brain-training exercises (including tests of task switching and dual tasking) for thirty minutes, three times a week for three months, subsequently showed superior mental performance compared with an age-matched control group who spent the same amount of time playing standard computer games. The trouble is, the science doesn't match these grand claims.

In 2009, *Which*, the respected, impartial UK-based consumer-rights group hired three leading scientists, including Chris Baird at UCL, none of whom had any vested interest, to assess the evidence for brain training. They concluded that proper scientific evidence for the benefits of brain training is almost entirely lacking. Many of the benefits claimed by these products can be achieved though everyday activities such as leading an active social life and surfing the web. Other improvements remain specific to the brain exercise without applying to real life in any useful way. Another expert, Cindy Lustig at the University of Michigan, thinks that past studies have also shown that older people, who have most to gain from brain training programmes, are actually the least likely to show any benefit. Her view is that "training programs aren't going to hurt you, and probably do have some benefits ... but they aren't going to turn an eighty-year-old brain into a twenty-year-old one."

how common such errors are. Nearly two hundred healthy participants aged between nineteen and sixty kept a diary of their lapses for a week, clocking up a total of 1217 mistakes. The average was for 6.4 lapses a week, with the most common kind being the sort that involves going upstairs only to forget what you've gone there for.

It's not all bad news. While the ability to think on our feet – what psychologists call "fluid intelligence" – declines with age, general knowledge and wisdom ("crystallized intelligence") usually continues

The last waltz. Keeping active and alert is the best way of staving off the negative effects of old age.

improving until the age of about seventy. There's also ample evidence that keeping the body and mind exercised can help stave off the effects of ageing. A study of over eight hundred nuns, priests and monks, by neuropsychologist Robert Wilson of the Rush Alzheimer's Disease Centre, found that those who kept their minds busy – for example by reading the newspaper – were less likely to have developed Alzheimer's disease when re-examined four years later.

As well as physical alterations to the brain, there's also evidence that growing older is associated with changes in thinking style. Margie Lachman at Brandeis University and her colleagues twice surveyed thousands of Americans over a two-year period and found that people aged over 65 were more realistic and accurate about their past and future happiness than younger and middle-aged participants. Whereas those under 65 tended to downplay past happiness and over-estimate future happiness, the older participants didn't. This more realistic outlook probably reflects older people's need to accept their life as they've lived it, and their greater awareness of people's ability to adjust to whatever the future holds.

What about the feeling that time goes faster as we get older? This is a tricky phenomenon to research. What we do know is that arousal and excitement seem to make time feel, in the moment, as though it is passing more quickly. Paradoxically, a day, week or month that was jammed full of activities can seem, in retrospect, to have trundled by. For older people then, perhaps time in the moment can feel as though it's passing slowly because they generally take part in fewer novel or exciting activities. Yet as they look back on the passing years, their less busy lives can make it feel as though time has whizzed by. Nevertheless, a study published in 2010 involving interviews with hundreds of people aged sixteen to eighty found no evidence that the last week, month or year felt like it had gone any faster for older people. It was only the last decade that seemed to have passed more quickly, and even here the difference between the ages was small. William Friedman and Steve Janssen, who conducted the research, suggested the maxim "time flies as you get older" was little more than a myth.

Retirement, when and if we get there, has particular psychological importance. For many people their career lends life meaning, as well as providing friends and status. It can be unsettling for this to suddenly end with the prospect of old age lying in wait on the horizon. When Marion Kloep and Leo Hendry at the University of Glamorgan in Wales interviewed 45 older people about the experience of retiring, they found that people generally fell into three groups. There was a "high distress"

Dementia

A consequence of rising life-expectancies around the world is that rates of dementia are also set to mushroom. There are currently 700,000 people in the UK with dementia, costing the economy £17 billion per annum. The number diagnosed is predicted to double in the next thirty years, with costs trebling. Dementia is common in old age (affecting six percent of those aged over 65; rising to thirty percent over age 95), but it is not a natural part of ageing. There are different types of dementia, with Alzheimer's being the most common and best known. Scientists still don't know the exact cause, although genetics is likely to play a key part, especially in early-onset varieties of the illness. In its advanced stages, Alzheimer's is characterized by a widespread loss of neurons, with the brain clogged up by clumps and tangles of diseased protein. Memory problems and confusion are the most obvious and immediate psychological effects. However, while Alzheimer's is devastating, there is room for hope. Books like *I'm Still Here* by John Ziesel describe the islands of intact functioning, such as the appreciation of art and music. Psychiatrist Sube Banerjee, the former joint leader of the UK's dementia strategy, has said that with the right psychological help and support, it really is possible to have severe dementia and still have a good quality of life.

group who'd experienced an accumulation of negative events, hadn't enjoyed work, but were nonetheless finding retirement challenging; a "work as lifestyle" group who'd been high achievers at work and were really suffering from the loss of status; and finally, a "life beyond work" group, which most participants fell into, made up of people living busy, active lives, meeting friends and getting stuck into hobbies.

According to a 2009 study, the key to a successful retirement could be to leave one foot in work while placing the other into retirement – taking on temporary, self-employed, or part-time duties in what the researchers called "bridge employment". Yujie Zhan's team at the University of Maryland looked at data from over twelve thousand participants collected between 1992 and 1998. Those who transferred to bridge employment enjoyed superior health compared with people who retired completely, even after taking baseline health into account. When bridge employment was in the same field as their main career, there were benefits for mental health too. Semi-retirement is probably beneficial because it avoids the shock of a sudden and complete role-transition; it keeps you active, but is less stressful than continuing with full-on duties.

Part II

You and me

7 Personal relationships

Relationships invest life with purpose and meaning; they define who we are, be it friend, father, daughter, tutor, rival or employer. Social bonds are also vital for our psychological wellbeing. Study after study has shown that people tend to be happier and healthier when they have sufficient meaningful relations with others. Orphaned babies who feel a human touch are more likely to survive than those who are deprived of such contact. Indeed, merely thinking about an intimate relationship can guard our self-esteem from the negative effects of hearing about our flaws and weaknesses.

Earliest attachments

Few emotional ties can be as intense and consequential as the one forged with the person (or persons) who looked after us when we were first born. Psychology, not surprisingly, has paid particular attention to these early bonds or **attachments**. Key twentieth-century pioneers in the field include the American psychologist and primate researcher **Harry Harlow** (1905–81) and the British psychoanalyst **John Bowlby** (1907–90). Their work challenged the Freudian belief that an infant bonds with its mother primarily because she satisfies its basic needs, or (in the psychoanalytic jargon) provides "drive reduction". Harlow and Bowlby emphasized instead the importance of touch and warmth, and the consequences if these are missing.

Harlow began his career by devising an intelligence test for monkeys, but then made a discovery that started him down the research path that would make him famous. He noticed how infant macaques grew attached to the ground blankets of their cages after being separated from their mothers and peers. If Harlow attempted to remove these blankets, the newly orphaned monkeys would go berserk. By contrast, they remained largely impassive when he took away their milk bottles after feeding.

An infant rhesus monkey clings to its surrogate mother.

In subsequent experiments in the 1950s, he built surrogate mothers for the infants, one out of wire that provided milk but no comfort; another out of wood and lined with soft cloth that provided warmth and comfort but no food. The monkeys would crawl to the wire mother for milk, but they spent the vast majority of their time cuddled up to the soft, warm mother. Contact, it seemed, was more important than food.

Meanwhile, John Bowlby and other child specialists had been making claims about the importance of maternal care for over two decades. Based on his studies of homeless and hospitalized children, Bowlby described a "human separation syndrome" that resulted in protest, despair and aggression. In 1951 he published an influential report for the World Health Organisation entitled "Maternal Care and Mental Health", in which he argued that infants have an instinctual need for motherly love. Bowlby's suggestion that infants deprived of this love will develop psychological problems later in life appeared to be supported by Harlow's research. The baby macaques raised by surrogate mothers, even cloth-covered ones, developed terrible behavioural problems later in life. They were incapable of successful mating and after artificial insemination they often killed their own offspring.

Harlow's work remains hugely controversial and is seen by many as unnecessarily cruel. Others made the obvious criticism that what's true of monkeys doesn't necessarily apply to humans. The impact of his research was undoubtedly magnified by its timing, as it was published during an era of great social flux. Before the orphaned macaques grew up and developed psychopathologies, the apparent success of the surrogate mothers was interpreted by some commentators as showing that human fathers could just as successfully rear young children, thus freeing women to pursue ambitions outside the home.

Bowlby's writings made a real impact – changing the rules in hospitals so that mothers could stay with their children – but they also attracted criticism. Scientifically-minded sceptics pointed out that the emotional problems of the children he studied could have been caused by a range of factors, not necessarily deprivation of maternal love and care. However, his central claim that the quality of an infant's relationship with its mother has life-long consequences for psychological adjustment has been confirmed by countless studies.

Textbooks often focus exclusively on Harlow's early research – the triumph of touch over food. Experts like Bowlby also tended to pay selective attention to these findings. But the reality is that Harlow's work took many unpredictable turns. Later studies showed that baby macaques deprived of maternal love grew up rather well-adjusted if they'd had the benefit of contact with peers, yet the opposite wasn't true. To have maternal contact but be deprived of the company of peers led to persistent social problems. Another curious finding was that the orphaned macaques who abused their first-borns tended to be loving mothers to their later offspring. We often want our scientific findings to be neat and easily interpretable, but Harlow's work illustrates how messy psychological outcomes can be.

> "Certainly, man cannot live by milk alone. Love is an emotion that does not need to be bottle- or spoon-fed, and we may be sure that there is nothing to be gained by giving lip service to love."
>
> Harry Harlow (1958)

MEASURING ATTACHMENT

In the late 1970s a colleague of Bowlby's, **Mary Ainsworth**, devised a test for identifying the attachment style of a child to her principal caregiver, versions of which are still in widespread use today. Known as the **strange-situation test**, the procedure involves observing what happens when a young child is separated from their parent and confronted by a stranger. A toddler who's distressed when their mother leaves but who is quickly comforted on her return is said to be "securely attached", while those who pay little attention and quickly move away from her when she returns are "insecurely attached". A study from the early 1990s by Gottfried Spangler and Klaus Grossmann used physiological measures, and found that even though these insecurely-attached children appeared unemotional on the outside, inside their hearts were beating away in

The cuteness response. In 2008 Morten Kringelbach at the University of Oxford showed that a region at the front of the brain – the medial orbitofrontal cortex – is activated within just over a tenth of a second when people look at baby faces, but not adult faces. This could be the neural correlate of our perception that babies are cute, a reaction that Charles Darwin and Konrad Lorenz saw as an evolutionary mechanism by which adults are prompted to care for infants. Kringelbach plans to test whether the reaction is also triggered by baby animals, and hopes the finding might one day offer a way to identify women at risk of developing post-natal depression.

distress. It seems they'd simply learned that to cause a fuss would make the situation worse.

Another reaction to the strange-situation task is for a toddler to become distressed when the parent leaves and remain inconsolable when she returns: this is known as "insecure-resistant" attachment. Finally, a more recent addition to the scoring of behaviour in the strange-situation task is so-called "disorganized attachment", in which the child reacts unpredictably, fluctuating from one attachment-style to another. Research using the strange-situation test has shown that attachment style tends to be passed from one generation to the next, and that parents who start thinking of their baby as a person before it's born tend to show more healthy attachment later on.

Siblings

To only children, the idea of having one or more siblings often conjures up idealistic images of life-long companionship and camaraderie. While some brothers and sisters do enjoy such rosy relations, many others endure bitter rivalry or a hurtful lack of interest. Unsurprisingly, parents are often keen to know just how to nurture their children so that they form amiable, supportive bonds. For instance, is it better to space children out over time or have them as close in age as possible? And do same-sex siblings get on better than siblings of the opposite sex? Despite the fact that the vast majority of people have siblings, there was little research on the psychology of sibling relationships before the 1990s. Today, however, psychology does have some preliminary answers.

We know, for example, that siblings can have a negative effect on each other. Children and adolescents who have a sibling who was hostile towards them in early childhood are more likely to suffer from anxiety, while teenagers who have one close in age who drinks too much alcohol are at increased risk from doing the same. Those whose parents argue are also more likely to experience friction between each other, although it's possible the causal effects here run in both directions (having children who don't get on may well lead to strife between parents). On a more positive note, there's evidence that having a sibling can lead to precocity when it comes to the ability to empathize and see another person's point of view. Research by Judy Dunn, now at the Institute of Psychiatry in London, showed that children who indulge in plenty of pretend play with a brother or sister, and who spend time talking about mental states with them, are likely to excel when tested on their understanding of emotions.

And then there are those pressing questions about gender differences and age gaps between brothers and sisters. According to a major ongoing study by Judy Dunn and her collaborators over the last ten years, these factors matter far less than parents think. Earlier sibling research had mostly relied on asking parents about the relations between their children. Dunn's team adopted the novel approach of using puppets to directly ask four- to eight-year-olds about their sibling relations. For example, one puppet called Iggy would say "My brother and I argue", then a second puppet, Ziggy, would respond "My brother and I don't argue. How about you and your brother?" The results showed that the warmest relationships were described by girls with a younger sister and the least warm by boys with a younger sister. A smaller age-gap between siblings was also associated with better relations, but these effects of gender and age were extremely modest. The household environment and the quality of the relationship between parents were more significant factors. Specifically, sibling relations were better when the household was more organized, with regular routines and little background noise, and when parents were happily married.

The love hormone oxytocin

A chemical called oxytocin, released by the hypothalamus in the brain, has been dubbed the "love" or "cuddle hormone" because of the important role it plays in social relationships. It's released in a rush during sex and to a lesser extent during other less intimate social activities. It seems to act as a kind of glue, making social bonds pleasurable. When scientists block oxytocin receptors in the brains of mother rats, the rats stop paying any attention to their pups. Similarly, blocking oxytocin receptors in the usually monogamous prairie vole causes it to play the field. In humans, sniffing oxytocin compared with a placebo increases trust and generosity, and improves emotion recognition. Markus Heinrichs at the University of Zurich, for example, asked participants to choose how much money to pass to a stranger in an investment game. The money would be tripled in the transaction, but there was no guarantee that the receiving investor would share any of the proceeds. Of the participants who inhaled oxytocin, 45 percent chose to invest the full amount, compared with just 21 percent of investors who inhaled a placebo. The same effect was not observed when investors gambled with a computer rather than another player, suggesting oxytocin specifically affects social trust, not risk perception in general. Trials are underway to test oxytocin's therapeutic potential for conditions such as social phobia and autism.

Friends

Whether we have one or a hundred, most of us probably like to think that we choose our friends judiciously. Psychological research, however, shows that friendship is influenced more by convenience, chance and vanity than by any form of taste or discernment. The influence of convenience on friendship was demonstrated by a classic study performed in the 1950s by social psychologist **Leon Festinger**. He looked at friendships among couples living in a student complex at MIT, which was composed of seventeen buildings, each with ten apartments over two floors. He found that students were ten times more likely to be friends with someone in their building than in another building; more likely to be friends with someone on their own floor; and more likely to be friends with another student on their floor the nearer that student's apartment was to their own.

Research on the role of chance in friendships was brought up to date in dramatic fashion by psychologists at the University of Leipzig in 2008. At the start of term, they had 54 new psychology students sit in randomly allocated chairs, arranged in rows. Amazingly, these seating arrangements on that first day were predictive of friendships a year later. Students who'd sat next to each other on day one tended to be better friends than people sat apart, with students who shared the same row tending to be better friends than students who'd been sat in different rows.

Another key influence on friendship choices is vanity: on average, we are more likely to be friends with people who are similar to ourselves – a phenomenon known as "homophily". Research by the social psychologist Robert Hays in the 1980s showed that, in general, friends tend to be more similar to each other across a raft of factors – including age, sex, ethnic background, marital status, personality and even IQ – than do people who know each other but aren't friends. Shared attitudes seem to be particularly important. Consider a 1970s study by William Griffitt and Russell Veitch which recorded the attitudes of thirteen male volunteers on 44 different issues, just before they spent ten days together in a simulated fall-out shelter. During and after the exercise, the men were asked to choose three others who'd they'd like to keep in the shelter. Predictably enough, they selected people with attitudes similar to their own.

> "I do not believe that friends are necessarily the people you like best, they are merely the people who got there first."
>
> Sir Peter Ustinov

There's an irony in the fact that we're drawn to people who share our attitudes, given that research consistently shows that most people tend to overestimate how much others (including their friends) agree with them – an error that's been called the "false consensus bias". In fact, we don't know our friends and lovers nearly as well as we think we do. William Swann Jr. and Michael Gill at the University of Texas demonstrated this in 1997 with a study that looked at how much students who were dating and college room-mates knew about each other, in terms of their sexual histories, hobbies and so on. The results showed that people's confidence in how well they knew each other increased the longer they'd been in a relationship or shared a room together, yet accuracy remained stubbornly resistant to improvement.

ABSENT FRIENDS AND RELATIONS

The meaningful others in your life can have a profound effect on you, even when they're absent. At Duke University, James Shah showed this by setting participants a task after first priming them subliminally

with the name of a significant relation, such as a parent, who wanted them to work hard and succeed. The effect was to cause the participants to work extra hard at the task. But in a twist to the experiment, a colleague of Shah, Tanya Chartrand, showed that the subconscious was able to resist this subliminal pressure when the significant other was perceived as overbearing. Chartrand primed participants in the same way as Shah, but this time the significant other was deemed to be not just ambitious for the participant, but also controlling. The result was that the participants tried less hard than usual at the task, an effect Chartrand called **nonconscious reactance**.

But thoughts of others don't have to be subconscious to have an effect. When Barry Schlenker at the University of Florida asked female participants to deliberately visualize a significant other, he tricked them into thinking the experiment was about the effect of visualization on heart rate. Appropriate medical equipment was in place, and part of the task required visualizing mundane items and experiences, as well as other people. After completing the task, the participants were asked to fill out personality questionnaires. Schlenker found that participants who'd visualized their parents subsequently rated themselves as less sensual, adventurous, dominant, extrovert and industrious than those asked to visualize a friend or romantic partner. Another version of the experiment showed that female students with low self-esteem who visualized a romantic partner rated themselves as less sensuous, relaxed and physically attractive than did students with high self-esteem.

A study from 2008 suggests these kind of absent influences could even be put to practical use. Simone Schnall at the University of Plymouth and her collaborators asked participants wearing backpacks to stand at the foot of a hill and estimate its steepness. Those who had a supportive friend standing nearby perceived the hill to be less steep than control participants. Crucially, so too did participants who merely thought about a supportive friend before making their estimate.

Loneliness

You can be surrounded by people, but if you feel no connection with any of them, loneliness will descend like a grey Sunday. A strangely paradoxical finding that emerged in 2009 was that loneliness is contagious. Paradoxical, because you'd think a loner would be the last person to start a trend. But according to psychologist John Cacioppo at the University of Chicago, loneliness, like happiness, spreads through social networks like a virus. The researchers took advantage of longitudinal data collected from thousands of people as part of an investigation into the risk factors for cardiovascular disease. Part of this research involved the participants answering questions about depression and loneliness, and it so happened that many of them knew each other. This enabled Cacioppo to make some curious observations, such as the fact that a participant was 52 percent more likely to say they were lonely if they had a friend who also described themselves as lonely. Having a friend with a friend who felt lonely increased the risk of loneliness by 25 percent. Even a lonely friend of a friend of a friend boosted one's own vulnerability to loneliness by fifteen percent! These effects were additive – the more lonely people a participant knew, the greater their own risk of feeling lonely.

Brain-imaging research shows that lonely people are more attuned to negative stimuli and show a suppressed neural response to positive scenes – almost as if they're actively on the lookout for potential snubs and slurs headed their way. Mixing with a friend like this is likely to make you feel lonely, which in turn will affect how you mix with other friends and so on. If all this talk of social isolation is leaving you feeling, well, rather lonely, you might benefit from switching on your favourite soap opera or sitcom. Another study published in 2009 by Jaye Derrick at the University of Buffalo showed that watching and thinking about the characters in our favourite TV shows really can help us combat feelings of loneliness and rejection – a benefit Derrick described as **social surrogacy**.

The Facebook generation

How has the Internet affected our personal relationships? Social networking sites like Facebook and Twitter have grown at a formidable rate, and the suddenness of their rise has led to plenty of

Mirror neurons

Successful relationships depend on us empathizing with one another, a skill that some scientists believe lies in the power of so-called "mirror neurons". These are cells identified in the forebrains of monkeys that are active both when a given action is performed and when that action is witnessed. The idea is that by simulating the emotions and actions of another, the cells can help us better understand what the other person was feeling and trying to achieve.

Mirror neurons were discovered, fortuitously, by Giacomo Rizzolatti and colleagues at the University of Palma in Italy in the 1990s. The researchers had implanted electrodes into monkeys' brains to find out how different brain cells were activated when they performed certain actions. According to science writer David Dobbs, team member Leonardo Fogassi entered the lab one day and happened to reach for the monkeys' raisins – it was then that the researchers realized that observing Fogassi perform this act led the same monkey neurons to fire as when the monkeys made the same rasin-reach movement themselves.

Brain-imaging experiments have since uncovered what seem to be mirror neurons in the brains of humans. The same patterns of activity are triggered in these cells both when we execute and witness a given action or facial expression. In fact, even hearing the description of a certain action appears to lead our postulated mirror-neurons to simulate the act in our own minds.

In 2010 Roy Mukamel and his colleagues at UCLA claimed to have found the first direct evidence for mirror neurons in humans, recorded from electrodes implanted into the brains of patients with epilepsy. The electrodes were being used principally for clinical reasons, but

doom-mongering. Even some scientists, who should know better, have predicted that the Facebook generation will be more atomized and lonely than earlier generations. In their eyes, digital interactions displace "genuine" face-to-face contact, to the detriment of relationships. The actual psychological evidence, however, is more nuanced and in most cases suggests Internet-based socializing can have its benefits.

Early seeds of concern about time spent on the Internet were sown in the late 1990s, when Robert Kraut and his colleagues at Carnegie Mellon University spent two years looking at the effect of Internet time on families living in Pittsburgh. Their study appeared to show that the more time the participants spent online (mostly for communication purposes), the less time they spent talking face-to-face with their families and the they allowed Mukamel's team to look for neurons with mirror-like characteristics, some of which were found in the front of the brain and in the temporal lobe.

This idea that the brain has its own simulation system in the form of suites of mirror neurons has led to an explosion of claims, some more grandiose than others. Writing in 2000, the neuroscientist Vilayanur Ramachandran even went so far as to say that "mirror neurons will do for psychology what DNA did for biology: they will provide a unifying framework and help explain a host of mental abilities that have hitherto remained mysterious and inaccessible to experiments". Indeed, some experts believe that conditions such as autism, characterized as it is by social problems, could be explained by abnormalities in the mirror-neuron system.

Other psychologists and neuroscientists are more sceptical. In 2009, Alfonso Caramazza and colleagues at the Universities of Harvard and Trento performed a brain-imaging experiment which they claimed disproved the existence of mirror neurons in humans. They concluded that executing a hand movement and then witnessing another person perform the same movement didn't lead to adaptation (reduced activity with repeated use) in relevant neurons, as ought to have happened if human mirror-neurons really existed. Caramazza felt that even the monkey research was open to interpretation. For him, just because certain cells are active both when performing and observing an act doesn't mean those cells play a causal role in understanding another person's (or monkey's) actions, as had been claimed. His view was that "so-called mirror neurons may be responding as a consequence of, and not as the basis for, action categorization."

smaller their social circles became, resulting in increased loneliness and depression. Kraut's team called this the **Internet paradox**, because the participants were supposedly using the Internet for communication, but were becoming more isolated. In 2001, however, the researchers returned to their original sample after another year had passed and found that the negative effects of Internet use had largely disappeared. What's more, a new investigation with a fresh sample appeared to suggest that time spent using the Internet was largely associated with positive outcomes, especially for extroverts.

This latter observation about the differential effect of the Internet on extroverts and introverts would prove to be prescient. Many subsequent studies suggest that social networking is beneficial for the majority of people who have healthy, happy social lives offline, but can be unhelpful for socially anxious people who find in-the-flesh interactions difficult. Research presented by Ben Ainley and his colleagues at the Association for Psychological Science annual conference in 2009, for example, showed that students who were lonely offline also tended to have fewer contacts online on sites like Facebook. Ainley concluded that "some of the obstacles to feeling connected in everyday life exist in virtual environments as well".

Although Facebook and similar sites are clearly no panacea for loneliness, numerous studies have hinted at their benefits. A 2006 study by Andrew Campbell and his team at the University of Sydney found no links between Internet use and anxiety, depression or social fearfulness, while those study participants who used the net for "online chat" told the researchers that they found their time online psychologically beneficial. The following year, a Michigan State University study led by Nicole Ellison reported that undergraduates who were regular users of Facebook tended to feel as if they were more a part of their university community than did less frequent users, and that Facebook use also helped students keep in touch with old friends from school.

Recognizing faces

Facial recognition is a vital skill in human relationships. Much like one pebble on a beach when compared to another, human faces are essentially pretty similar: all approximately spherical, with two eyes, a mouth and a nose. And yet most of us are expert at distinguishing one face from the next – and what's more, remembering which face belongs to which person. Even dim lighting and strange angles provide little challenge. But the science behind our face expertise is actually something of a battle zone between psychologists. There are fierce disagreements about whether this skill is innate or whether it is learned just like any other form of visual expertise, such as that displayed by a butterfly enthusiast distinguishing between obscure species.

The psychologists in the "face recognition is innate" camp point to the fact that looking at faces appears to activate a dedicated region of the brain in the temporal lobe, dubbed the **fusiform-face area**. People with brain damage to this region lose the ability to recognize faces, but their skill at distinguishing between other kinds of object remains unaffected. Supporters of the innate theory also highlight the so-called **face-inversion effect**, first described by Robert Yin in the 1960s, which suggests that turning faces upside down seems to have a detrimental effect on our ability to identify them, whereas upending, say, an aeroplane or a house seems to have little effect on whether we can recognize them. The face-inversion effect is thought to occur because we process faces in an unusually holistic fashion, paying careful attention to the distances between the different features – a procedure that's particularly hampered by inversion (as in the photograph on the right).

The Margaret Thatcher illusion. Apart from it being upside down, there doesn't seem much wrong with this picture of a smiling Margaret Thatcher. But turn the picture the right way up and it becomes freakishly apparent that the picture has been doctored in a way that makes her look extremely sinister. This illusion was first documented by Peter Thompson at the University of York, and it works in part because when the face is inverted we process the eyes and mouth separately from the rest of the face, whereas when the face is upright, we process the face and its distorted features simultaneously.

Psychologists who think face-recognition is a learned skill, on the other hand cite research by Isabel Gauthier from the 1990s. After training participants to distinguish between a set of weird putty-like figures called "greebles", Gauthier found that as they developed this skill, merely looking at greebles triggered activity in the fusiform-face area just as looking at faces did. Similarly, in the 1980s the MIT psychologists Rhea Diamond and Susan Carey claimed to have found a face-inversion effect among dog experts. This supported the idea that face processing represents a form of acquired visual expertise, distinguished from other examples simply because nearly all of us have developed it.

Those people who lack the ability to recognize faces are called **prosopagnosic** by psychologists, from the Greek *prosopo* meaning "face" and *agnosia* meaning "without knowledge". The condition was first described by the German neurologist Joachim Bodamer in the 1940s after he observed the defects exhibited by two patients who'd been brain damaged in World War II. For decades, the condition was thought to be extremely rare and nearly always a result of brain damage. However, recent research in Austria and the UK indicates that face-recognition difficulties are not that uncommon. Thomas and Martina Grueter at the University of Vienna and the Institute of Genetics surveyed 689 students and found that seventeen had serious face-recognition problems. Around the same time, Bradley Duchaine and his colleagues at University College London conducted a vast Internet survey of over 1500 participants and similarly found that about two percent had some degree of face blindness.

The people identified by these researchers appear either to have been born with their face-recognition difficulties or to have developed them early in life. There's evidence too that prosopagnosia can run in families. When Thomas and Martina Grueter carried out follow-up investigations on some of the seventeen students with face-recognition difficulties, they found that they all had family members with similar problems. So it's likely that "developmental prosopagnosia", as it's known, has been around for a long time. The fact that it remained undiscovered for so long was probably due to the embarrassment of those with the problem, combined with their ability to create alternative recognition strategies, such as focusing on people's clothes and voices.

Even more recently, psychologists have speculated that there may also be a minority of people who have a rare form of exceptional face-recognition ability – so-called **super-recognizers**. It seems that the research on developmental face-blindness was so widely reported in the media that this prompted several people to come forward claiming exceptional face-recognition powers. In a 2009 study, Richard Russell at Harvard University and his colleagues tested four such people and found that they outperformed 25 age-matched controls on a series of challenging tests. These included identifying the faces of celebrities before they were famous, and identifying previously presented faces from odd angles, or under poor viewing conditions. On these and other tests, the super-recognizers were superior to controls by an impressive amount, roughly equivalent to the degree by which developmental prosopagnosics are inferior to normal controls. Russell's team said that their discovery of super-recognizers had important implications for the real world – just think how useful it could be to have one of these people on your security team or in the witness stand.

Romantic interest

Should anyone be in any doubt about the importance of romantic relationships to our lives, they need only marvel for a moment at the international, multi-billion-dollar dating industry. Or consider all the thousands of dreamy poems, love songs and novels penned through the ages. That finding a romantic partner is such a priority for so many people should come as no surprise. The only reason most of us are here is because our biological parents successfully courted and then mated, and it's their genes, after all, that exert a powerful ongoing influence on our own amorous proclivities.

Evolutionary roots

Recognizing the importance of reproduction for our evolutionary ancestors, and the threats to it, can help illuminate many of our romantic tendencies today. When the evolutionary psychologist **David Buss** travelled the world observing the differing mate-preferences of 10,000 men and women across 37 cultures, from China to Sweden, he found a consistent pattern. Heterosexual women are attracted to men who appear to have status and resources, and who are a few years older than they are, while straight men tend to desire women who appear youthful, faithful and attractive. This pattern makes evolutionary sense – females want to know that a potential father is able to protect and fend for her offspring, while males want their kin to be as healthy as possible, and they want to be sure the child really is theirs (a younger female is less likely to have copulated with another male).

A study in 2010 seemed to back up this point about the differential appeal of status to the two sexes. Michael Dunn at the University of Wales Institute in Cardiff found that women rated a man as more attractive when he was seen sitting in a snazzy sports car rather than a bog-standard Ford Fiesta, but men's perception of the attractiveness of a woman was unaffected by whether she was sat in an old banger or something more swish.

Our evolutionary roots can even help explain some of our less savoury romantic habits. According to Steve Stewart-Williams at Swansea University, the reason some men insult their girlfriends or wives is out of fear that their partners might leave them. Stewart-Williams tested this idea by asking 245 men to admit how many times in the past month they'd insulted their partner. Those who admitted hurling more insults also tended to say that they indulged in other so-called **mate retention** behaviours, such as getting jealous when their partners went out without them.

The biological foundations of our love interests are also highlighted by the influence of the female menstrual cycle on the preferences of men

Homosexual relationships

Psychologists and sociologists have looked at ways that homosexual couples tend to differ from couples of the opposite sex. According to Victoria Clarke at the University of the West of England, research shows that lesbian and gay couples are more likely to achieve equality in their relationships in terms of household chores and wage earning.

Humans are far from being the only species in which same-sex individuals have sex. In fact, homosexual activity has been observed in as many as 1500 species, and our close relation, the Bonobo, has about half its sex with same-sex partners. However, whereas many human cultures tend to divide the majority of people into separate gay and straight categories, the norm among many animal species seems to be bisexuality – that is, there are few individuals who only mate with one sex or the other. Without the cultural and social pressure to pledge our allegiance one way or the other, it's possible the same would be true of more humans.

Homosexual behaviour can make evolutionary sense for many species – for example, it can help promote pro-social behaviour between individuals (bonobos are a far more peaceful species than the more heterosexual common chimpanzee), or sustain fertility in the absence of opposite-sex partners. This hasn't stopped several crank therapists from claiming the ability, and by implication the need, to alter people's sexual orientation. Such claims cast a dark shadow over the psychology of sexuality and prompted the American Psychological Association to make a formal declaration that such therapy does not work and could well be harmful. Their announcement in 2009 followed a task-force report that scrutinized 83 relevant studies, published between 1960 and 2007.

It seems that indicators of high male status, such as a flashy car, really do have an impact on women.

and women. For example, it's been shown that men prefer the smell of a woman when she's near ovulation, compared with the low-fertility stage of her cycle. Similarly, women show a heightened preference for masculine traits when they are at the fertile stage of their cycle, and they also take greater care over their appearance at this time.

Falling in love

According to the anthropologist Helen Fisher at Rutgers University, humans have evolved three brain-systems for close relationships: one is lustful and supports our sexual drive, another is activated when we fall in love, and the third allows us to develop long-lasting, deep-seated attachments – sometimes referred to as **companionate love**. Fisher and her colleagues have scanned the brains of people who are in love and found that the state appears more akin to an obsessive drive than an emotion. When these lovers viewed a photograph of their partner, their brains responded as if they'd just enjoyed a drug-fuelled high. Dopamine-rich reward areas such as the ventral tegmental area in the limbic system (see p.39) lit up like a Christmas tree.

The evolutionary purpose of our sexual drive is obvious – it motivates us to mate and therefore reproduce. Fisher believes that the act of falling in love allows us to zoom in on one partner, rather than endlessly chasing every potential mate who passes by. When we're in love, the rest of the world fades to grey and all that matters is the object of our passion. We're enchanted by their every move, their every word, that smile, those lips. Indeed, the experience can be so intense that psychologists have even noted how the symptoms overlap with psychiatric conditions such as mania and obsessive-compulsive disorder. Some people really are madly in love.

As well as the rush of rewarding chemicals in the brain, falling in love is also aided by a series of psychological illusions. Research shows, for example, that heterosexual men are prone to interpret a woman's smile or laugh as a favourable response to them personally. A study in 2010 reported that men more prone to this bias tend to fall in love more often. Yet further research shows that men claim to believe in love at first sight more often than women. Again, this all makes evolutionary sense. For male reproductive success, it's less costly to suffer the temporary embarrassment of reading too much into a woman's glance than it is to regularly miss out on mating opportunities. By contrast, women have to make a far greater personal investment in reproduction, so it's sensible for them to be more picky to ensure the potential father of their offspring is really committed.

In search of human pheromones

In 1959 the biochemist Peter Karlson and entomologist Martin Luscher coined the term "pheromone" to describe a chemical message passed from one member of a species to another. Since then, the search has been on for a human equivalent. The discovery of a substance, released by one person and causing an involuntary reaction in another, would be a revelation – especially if that reaction was one of enhanced sexual interest. However, despite the dubious claims made by various peddlers of love potions and the like, no human pheromone has yet been definitively identified. That's not to say there are no plausible contenders. Two candidates are the testosterone derivative 4,16-androstadien-3-one (AND), found in men's sweat, and the oestrogen-like steroid estra-1,3,5(10),16-16-tetraen-3-ol (EST), found in female urine. In a 2005 brain-imaging study, Ivanka Savic at the Karolinska Institute found that the smell of AND triggered increased activation in the anterior hypothalamus (known to be involved in sexual behaviour) of heterosexual women and homosexual men, but not heterosexual men. By contrast, it was the chemical EST that excited this region in straight men.

Once we're in love, other sleights of mind help to ensure that we stay together. We tend to denigrate past partners and see our current lover in a flattering light. According to tradition, love is blind, and the evidence backs this up. Research by Viren Swami, for example, has shown that people nearly always rate their partner as more attractive than themselves. Faby Gagne at Wellesley College similarly found that 95 percent of people believed their partner was better-looking than average, more intelligent, loving and witty.

These kinds of biases may seem a little delusional but there's evidence that they help keep us together once the buzz of early attraction has faded. Research by Paul Miller at the Ontario HIV Treatment Network followed 168 newly-wed couples for 13 years and found that those with a more idealized perception of each other early on were more likely to still be in love years later. Similarly, Sandra Murray at the University of Waterloo found that those people who idealized their partners tended to be more happy and satisfied with their relationships. Other research has shown the power of enduring love. A brain-imaging study presented at the Society for Neuroscience conference in 2008 found that couples who claimed to still be in love after decades of marriage still experienced – in terms of brain activity – the drug-like rush and craving of an early romance when they viewed a picture of their partner. The research, by Bianca Acevedo at the State University of New York, also showed that the sight of their partners prompted long-term lovers, but not new partners, to experience increased brain activation in regions associated with calmness and pain suppression.

From kissing to orgasm

Conjecture is thicker on the ground than evidence when it comes to explaining why humans like to lock lips and swap mouth fluids. An account that's popular with anthropologists is that the habit evolved from a tendency among our ancestors for mothers to feed their young mouth-to-mouth – a behaviour still indulged in by our chimpanzee cousins. An alternative theory, suggested by neuroscientist Vilayanur Ramachandran, is that the lure of red lips can be traced back to our penchant for ripe fruit.

Other experts have proposed that kissing acts as a kind of early relationship trial. Testing this claim, psychologist Gordon Gallup at the University of Albany surveyed nearly two hundred men and women and found that 63 percent said they'd ended a potential relationship after the

Women, more than men, see kissing as a good way of establishing the quality of a potential mate.

first kiss went badly. Another survey of over a thousand college students suggested that more than men, women use kissing as a way to assess a potential mate – female students were more likely to report making judgements based on their partners' breath, taste and teeth, and were less likely to engage in sex without kissing first.

Whatever the evolutionary reasons for our lip-touching habits, a study in 2009 suggested that kissing is an ideal stress-reliever. Kory Floyd and his colleagues at Arizona State University recruited 52 participants who were either married or living with a partner. Half of them were instructed to up their kissing time. Six weeks later the kissing group felt less stressed, happier with their relationship and measures of their blood lipids suggested they really were more relaxed.

Moving swiftly on from first to last base, scientific insights into orgasm have increased over recent decades, in part because of the growing use of drugs for treating depression and psychosis. Certain anti-depressants that increase the availability of the neurotransmitter serotonin, have been shown to suppress orgasm – a side-effect called anorgasmia. This has led to suggestions that serotonin acts as a kind of orgasm brake, and there are even anecdotal reports of men using anti-depressants as an unlicensed treatment for premature ejaculation.

Believe it or not, researchers have even managed to scan the brains of participants in the throes of an orgasm. For a 2003 paper, neuroscientist Gert Holstege at the University of Groningen scanned eight men's brains whilst their female partners masturbated them to ejaculation. The results showed that male orgasm was associated with a rush of act. reward-related regions – no surprise there. Less expected was a dro̞ activity in the amygdala, perhaps reflecting a lowering of vigilance, and an increase in activity in the cerebellum, the cauliflower-like structure at the back of the brain that's traditionally associated with motor coordination. Holstege's team thought that the latter finding suggested that the cerebellum also plays a role in emotions. In research published in 2006 the roles were reversed, and twelve men stimulated their brain-scanned female partners to orgasm. The most striking finding here was that the women's climax was associated with a sudden drop of activity across a

Evidence-based seduction

If reading this chapter has got you in the mood for some lurve, here are some evidence-based tips to help you out.

If you're a man seeking a woman, use chat-up lines that reveal your helpfulness, generosity, athleticism and culture. Psychologist Christopher Bale asked over 200 students, including 142 females, to read chat-up scenarios, and these were the kind of lines rated as most likely to succeed, whereas jokes, empty compliments and sexual references were given the thumbs down. For women seeking a man, research by psychologist Joel Wade suggests you should be as direct as possible. Eighty undergraduates said that lines such as "Want to meet up later tonight?" were more likely to succeed than subtler attempts such as "Hello, how is it going?" or the humorously suggestive approach, as in "Your shirt matches my bedspread, basically you belong in my bed".

Apart from deploying the right verbal weaponry, other research suggests that wooing skills could be helped by lightly touching your preferred date on the arm. Psychologist Nicolas Guegen recruited a good-looking man to approach 120 women in a nightclub over a period of three weeks, and ask them to dance. Of the 60 women he touched lightly on the arm, 65 percent agreed to a dance, compared with just 43 percent of the 60 women whom he asked without making any physical contact.

If the silky chat-up lines and the sneaky arm-touch don't work, you could try recruiting some friends of the opposite sex to help you out. Benedict Jones and his colleagues at Aberdeen University's Face Research Laboratory showed that women rate a man as more attractive after they've seen another woman smiling at him. Jones said this suggests our preference for a man's face is affected by social cues we pick up from how other people look at him. Apparently, a similar phenomenon occurs in the animal kingdom – for example female zebra finches prefer a male who they've previously seen paired with another female.

n regions, perhaps reflecting an abrupt loss of inhibition. on the female orgasm has found that it blocks pain whilst y increasing sensitivity to touch.

ologists have investigated what turns people on in the first -reported study by Meredith Chivers, now at Queens University in ..., found that straight women are more aroused by what they see people (or animals) doing, whereas men, gay and straight, are more concerned by gender. Participants watched videos featuring gay male sex, gay female sex, straight sex, solitary masturbation, people performing exercises in the nude and sex between bonobos. Subjective and physiological measures of arousal showed that, overall, all the participants were most turned on by sex and least turned on by watching nude people exercise.

However, clear gender-differences also emerged, such as that the straight women didn't care much about the gender of who they were watching: it was what they were doing that mattered (although gay women were more selective and were unaroused by men). The female participants even showed some arousal in response to the mating bonobos. In contrast, men were particularly excited when the video matched their sexual orientation – gay men being most titillated by the sight of other men, straight men by the sight of straight women.

Another study by Chivers looked at the results from dozens of previous experiments to see how much correspondence there was between people's subjective reports of their sexual arousal and physiological measures of their genitals. This showed that men have a consistently greater correspondence than do women between how they feel and what their body is doing. The research was inconclusive, but one reason could simply be that getting an erection makes it easy for men to know when they are sexually aroused.

Ways to stay together

If all these facts about kissing and orgasms aren't enough to motivate you to stay with your husband or wife (perhaps they've tempted you to find a new lover), you would do well to heed the findings of a 2006 epidemiological study which showed that having a spouse can prolong your life. A follow-up survey of nearly 67,000 people interviewed in 1989 revealed that 5,876 (8.8 percent) had died before 1997. Analysing the data, and controlling for age, health and socioeconomic factors, Robert Kaplan and Richard Kronick of the University of California discovered that the death rate among those people who had never married was 58 percent higher than among their married peers. The unmarried participants were at greater risk of death from infectious disease and cardiovascular disease, as well as accidents, murder and suicide.

There's no shortage of agony aunts, relationship therapists and self-help books available and willing to offer sure-fire advice on how to make a relationship last. The reality is that psychological science doesn't have any definite answers – no two relationships are the same, and sometimes there's no avoiding the fact that a partnership has simply run its course.

However, examining the characteristics of couples who have stayed together compared with those who split up can be revealing. The marriage expert **John Gottman**, director and co-founder of the Gottman Relationship Institute in Seattle, videoed couples talking to each other about their past or about an issue they disagreed on, and followed them up three years later. Looking back at the tapes showed that those who remained together had used a 5:1 ratio of positive to negative statements when conversing with

> "Beauty is all very well at first sight; but who ever looks at it when it has been in the house three days?"
>
> George Bernard Shaw, *Man and Superman* (1903)

each other. By contrast, the couples who ended up splitting had uttered as many negative as positive comments when interacting. The lesson, it seems, is that if you haven't got anything nice to say, don't say it – at least not if you want your relationship to last.

Other findings worth noting involve what psychologist Brooke Feeney calls the **dependency paradox**. Feeney, a professor at Carnegie Mellon University, followed 165 married couples and focused on cases where one partner had given the other plentiful, unconditional support. Rather than the support fostering a neediness, supported partners six months later tended to have achieved more goals and were more self-sufficient and secure than they were before. That's not to say that we shouldn't strive for balance in our relationships. After monitoring 101 student couples for nearly five years, Susan Sprecher at Illinois State University found that individuals who felt they were investing more in a relationship than they were getting out of it tended to be less satisfied with – and less committed to – that relationship, making it more likely to end. Other research suggests that making each other laugh, performing new activities together, sharing secrets and treating each other with respect can all help prolong a relationship's longevity.

9 Talking to each other

Words enable me to share with you my innermost thoughts. I can describe my own sensations, such that you're able to recreate in your mind an experience I had a thousand miles away, or a hundred days ago. My words are literally altering your mind. We can talk about things that haven't happened yet, or even about things that never will. I can utter a sentence that's most likely never been said or written before: "*The Rough Guide to Psychology* is my favourite book", and still you and every other English speaker can decipher the meaning. This is possible through a mixture of acquired vocabulary and syntactical awareness – the ability to interpret the rules about the way words are ordered and the relationships between them.

Language and its development

Linguistics is a vast, cavernous discipline in its own right and there's only the space here to touch on a few key principles and debates. Psychologists are particularly interested in how we acquire language in the first place, and also how language is represented and processed by the brain. But most of all, they're curious about the links between thought and language, with some experts even going so far as to suggest that we are unable to think about things for which we lack the words.

The scholarly tussles in the field of language development have largely revolved around whether or not the capacity for language is innate. Of course, we know that the family environment that a child is brought up in plays at least some role, because English children raised by English-speaking parents don't suddenly start babbling in Mandarin but invariably end up speaking English, just like their parents. In fact, babies start out with the ability to hear foreign speech sounds, but lose this over time as they adapt to their particular linguistic environment. A study in the 1980s showed this in relation to Japanese babies and the sounds denoting "R" and "L", which don't exist in Japanese. Babies who were younger than nine months could hear the difference, but their infant compatriots older than this could not.

We also know that when speaking to an infant, adults – in fact, even children as young as four – adopt a slower, simpler, and more repetitive style of speech, known as "motherese", that ought to make it easier for infants to learn from. It's clear too that when interacting with their children, parents tend to talk about whatever it is that their child is

Is language unique to humans?

We used to think that tool use was uniquely human, but then chimps were seen using branches fashioned into rods to fish for termites. Crows have also been spied using sticks to extract larvae from holes in dead wood. That left language as the final preserve of human distinctiveness. True, monkeys were known to have their alarm calls – one each for eagle, snake, leopard and other threats – but crucially it was thought that these were never combined to make sentences. Grammar remained uniquely ours. But now some animals appear to have taken the gloss off that achievement too. Late in 2009, Alban Lemasson, a primatologist at the University of Rennes, reported instances of male Campbell's monkeys in the Ivory Coast combining their limited repertoire of six calls, "Boom, Krak, Hok, Hok-oo, Krak-oo, and Wak-oo", to create new meanings. To take just one example, a series of Boom calls

on their own was a message for the rest of the group to gather closer, whereas Boom calls followed by a Krakoo was a warning about falling branches. Adding a Hok-oo to that series created a new message about a territorial threat from a neighbouring monkey-group. This isn't evidence for complex grammar of the kind seen in human language, but it is a kind of proto-syntax more complex than anything seen in animals before. Lemasson's team concluded that the evolution of complex morphology had "begun early in primate evolution, long before the emergence of hominids".

Male Campbell's Monkeys have developed a language with its own rudimentary syntax.

focused on. So if the child glances at Ruby the dog, the parents tend to go "Ooh, there's Ruby the dog, say 'hello Ruby'", and so on. Then the child reaches for a ball: "There's your ball, darling. Do you want your ball?" Taken together it can seem as though these conditions provide an ideal learning environment for children to acquire their native language.

ACQUIRING THE RULES

And yet, while this might well be true for vocabulary, psycholinguists have known for some time that the spoken language children are exposed to is not sufficient for them to learn all the rules of grammar. In the formal jargon, this is known as the "poverty" of the linguistic input. Psychologists have pored over transcripts of children and parents talking to each other, and while the latter do occasionally correct their children's grammatical errors, they don't do it nearly often or systematically enough to explain how children are able to perfect their language as effectively as they do. What's more, the children's errors – for example over-generalizing the rule of applying an "s" to make a plural – have been found to continue beyond the period when the adults were vigilant in providing corrections. These observations about the poverty of the feedback have been combined with other observations about the constraints of the world's languages – what the pioneering linguist and intellectual **Noam Chomsky** called a "universal grammar". It's not the case that just anything goes. Instead, all languages seem to share key grammatical commonalities, even if these are tweaked slightly from one language to another. For example, most experts agree that all human languages contain nouns (dissenters from this view highlight a handful of exceptions, including Straits Salish, a North American indigenous language). Taken together, this evidence is used to argue that human infants come with a language-faculty built in – what Chomsky called a **language acquisition device** (LAD).

Chomsky's idea is that on hearing language spoken, various grammatical switches or "parameters" are pushed one way or the other as the child adjusts to its native tongue. Consider word-order. In English, the rule is subject-verb-object, whereas in Japanese it is subject-object-verb. The child's "language instinct", to borrow the title of Steven Pinker's best-selling book, means that their brain recognizes the importance of word order and other rules in language. Repeated exposure to the subject-verb-object or other convention then tunes this particular grammatical parameter in the child's brain.

The linguist Noam Chomsky has argued that all human infants have a built-in language faculty and that all languages are underpinned by a universal grammar.

Language and the brain

The most widely known fact about language processing is that, for most people (over 95 percent of right-handers and 60 percent of left-handers), it is predominantly performed by the left hemisphere. More detailed clues as to how the brain processes speech come from two sources – the study of patients with brain damage, and from recording people's brain activity while they're engaged in language tasks.

Speech problems that arise as a result of brain damage are known as **aphasia**, and there are two main types – fluent and non-fluent. Fluent or "semantic" aphasia – characterized by garbled, flowing speech conveying little concrete information – tends to follow damage to the temporal lobe, near its junction with the parietal lobe (Wernicke's area). By contrast, non-fluent aphasia – characterized by staccato speech with few verbs or little use of grammar – tends to occur after damage to the Broca's area in the frontal lobe (see p.41). Stated crudely, these impairments suggest that language functioning is divided into two specialisms: Broca's area for processing **syntax**, and Wernicke's area for decoding **meaning**.

Other clues about language-processing come from patterns of dyslexia acquired through brain damage. Some patients develop **phonological dyslexia**, which means they have difficulty translating letters into sounds. This affects their ability to read new words that they've never seen before.

A language switch?

Why don't people who are bilingual or multilingual get confused more often, flitting back and forth between their different languages? A popular view is that they have a neural switch at the front of the brain that shuts down languages that aren't currently in use. This idea found support in a 2007 study, led by Khuan Ko and his team at the University Medical Centre in Utrecht, which involved probing the brains of people undergoing surgery for epilepsy. The principal purpose of such probing is to ensure that the surgeons don't cut the wrong bits of the brain, but it also provides a rare opportunity for experimentation. In one case a French-Chinese bilingual was asked to count as the researchers prodded his brain looking for language regions. The man began counting in French, then when he reached seven (...*quatre, cinq, six, sept*), the stimulation was applied to the lower, left-hand side of the front of his brain, at which point he involuntarily switched to Chinese (...*ba, jiu, shi*). When the stimulation ended, he reverted to French. It's as though the researchers had accidentally flipped the switch that inhibits whichever language isn't in use.

On the other hand, they can read most words that they know "whole", without having to decode them letter by letter. By contrast, other patients have **surface dyslexia** and show the opposite pattern of impairment: they can read words letter by letter, but they can't read words "whole". This means they come unstuck with irregular words, such as "yacht", that don't obey the normal letter-to-sound correspondence rules. Taken together, these and other findings suggest we have at least two routes for processing words – one is by whole word or lexicon, while the other is piecemeal, letter by letter.

Another condition caused by brain damage is the inability to dig up the right word for objects, places or concepts, known as "**anomia**". Curiously, anomia can affect some categories of words but not others. A patient might be able to name objects, for example, but not living things.

Finding the right words for things obviously depends in part on our semantic memory – our knowledge about the world. A 2009 study by Faye Corbett, at the University of Manchester, took this idea further by suggesting that the brain's semantic system is comprised of two parts: a core store of knowledge in the temporal lobes, and a search-and-control system, embodied in the frontal cortex and temporo-parietal junction, which navigates through the corridors of the mind finding and comparing word meanings.

Corbett provided evidence for this by comparing the anomia displayed by eight patients who had a form of dementia affecting their temporal lobes with the difficulties shown by seven stroke-patients who had damage either to the left, frontal part of their brains, or the temporo-parietal junction. Superficially, the two groups of patients had remarkably similar impairments. They all struggled to find the correct words for things, and their factual knowledge and comprehension also seemed affected. However, there were some important differences between the two groups.

The dementia patients appeared to have entirely lost their core knowledge for certain word-meanings – if they struggled with a word in one kind of task, such as matching words to pictures, then they would also struggle with that word in other tasks, such as miming the meaning of a word. Moreover, the more unusual a word, the more likely these patients were to have a problem. By contrast, the stroke patients performed well on simple tasks, such as pointing to a picture of a hammer when prompted with the word, but struggled as soon as a task was made more complicated – for example, pairing objects that are related by their function, such as matching a hammer and chisel. Also, whereas the dementia patients could either mime an object's use or not, the stroke patients would frequently get some of the mime correct, but would then perform an inappropriate action, as if they were suddenly using a different type of object. For the stroke patients, then, it was as if their core knowledge was intact but their search-and-control system had gone awry.

Other research has used **electroencephalography** to record the surface electrical activity of the brain during

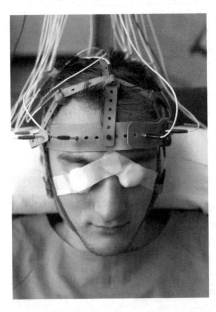

Electroencephalography (EEG): when brain cells fire, they generate electrical activity which can be recorded by electrodes placed on the scalp. Unlike functional magnetic brain-imaging, the spatial resolution of EEG is poor. However, its "temporal resolution" is excellent, meaning that it can be used to chart activity changes over sub-second time-intervals.

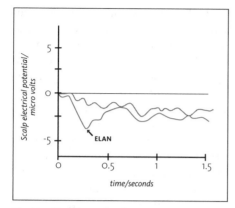

The blue line shows the characteristic spike in negative electrical activity triggered by an ungrammatical sentence.

language tasks. This line of work has complemented the patient findings, suggesting that syntax is processed first, separately from meaning, followed by a secondary process of integrating syntax with meaning.

How do we know this? A consistent observation is a short, sharp burst of negative electrical activity (or spike) over the frontal lobe, known as the **early left anterior negativity** or ELAN, which occurs within two hundred milliseconds of encountering a syntactic anomaly, as in the sentence "The Rough Guide enjoyed I was". In contrast, a semantic anomaly, as in "he spread his warm bread with socks" usually elicits a negative wave of activity over central/parietal regions after 400ms, and is known as the **N400**. Finally, there's a positive, more posterior spike after 600ms, known as the **P600**, that tends to follow not only syntactic anomalies but also perfectly grammatical sentences that surprise us, triggering a reassessment of our initial interpretation, as in: "After a long battle, the king was surrounded by attackers on all sides, but still the chess grandmaster was confident of a win." The P600 reflects the cognitive effort that's required to mentally adjust to the surprising context. It seems that these processes occur in series. If a sentence contains both syntactic and semantic anomalies, only the ELAN is provoked, suggesting that a breach of grammar puts the brakes on subsequent decoding of meaning.

The language of thought

Can we think about concepts for which we lack the words? Can we have words for things that we can't think about? The formal term for the idea that language dictates what we can and can't think about is "linguistic determinism", and it's perhaps most famously expressed in the **Sapir-Whorf hypothesis**, named after the linguist Edward Sapir and his student Benjamin Whorf. The idea can be illustrated by the urban myth about Eskimos having more words for snow than the rest of us, thus enabling them to identify differences in snow types that others are blind to. In Ludwig Wittgenstein's words, "The limits of my language mean the limits of my world."

Supporting this idea is a series of studies conducted by the psychologist Peter Gordon with members of the remote **Pirahã tribe** of Brazil. The Pirahã, like many other hunter-gatherer societies, only have words for the numbers one, two and many. They have no currency but instead barter goods. Gordon tested tribe members on a series of numerical matching tasks – for example, he would place a number of batteries in a row, and their task was to lay out the same number underneath. Crucially, their performance suggested they were unable to think about numbers for which they lacked the words. They did fine when there were

That tip-of-the-tongue feeling

There are few things more frustrating than knowing you know a word but not being able to dig it out of your mental filing-cabinet. What's particularly irritating is that we often experience this retrieval failure for the same words. According to the psychologists Amy Warriner and Karin Humphreys, it's not that some words are particularly tricky, it's that when we're in a tip-of-the-tongue state, we're actually learning the wrong way of finding a word. It's as if we're repeatedly looking in the wrong drawer for our keys, to such an extent that it becomes habitual.

Warriner and Humphreys tested this idea by giving definitions of obscure words to thirty students. Whenever the students experienced a tip-of-the-tongue state, the researchers waited either ten or thirty seconds before giving them the answer. Two days later, the students were more likely to have a repeat tip-of-the-tongue state for a given word if they'd previously experienced thirty seconds of having the word on the tip of their tongue – rather than just ten seconds. This is consistent with the idea that when the students were made to wait thirty seconds, they were spending more time reinforcing the incorrect pattern of activation that was causing their tip-of-the-tongue sensation in the first place. "Metaphorically speaking," the researchers explained, "this is akin to spinning one's tyres in the snow, resulting in nothing more than the creation of a deeper rut." So, to avoid repeat tip-of-the-tongue experiences, the secret is to find out what the elusive word is as soon as possible, either by looking it up, or asking someone. Once you have the correct word, say it to yourself, out loud or mentally, so as to consolidate the correct memory. On the other hand, if you can't get any help locating a word, stop trying, because all you're doing is reinforcing the habit of looking in the wrong place.

one, two or three batteries, but for any numbers greater than this their performance grew progressively more inaccurate. Gordon concluded with some gusto that this was a "rare and perhaps unique case for strong linguistic determinism".

However, in his book *The Stuff of Thought: Language as a Window into Human Nature*, Steven Pinker pours cold water on this interpretation of the Pirahã findings, arguing that Gordon has cause and effect the wrong way around. In Pinker's view, the tribespeople's lack of numerical words and poor numerical performance are both consequences of the fact that their way of life doesn't require them to think about or communicate in precise numerical terms larger than three. The same logic can be applied to the Eskimo myth. Eskimos spend more time thinking about snow than the rest of us because they're surrounded by the stuff. And thinking about snow so much means they've had more cause to invent new ways of talking about it.

Besides these logical objections there's also ample empirical evidence that refutes linguistic determinism. For example, the French neuroscientist Stanislas Dehaene studied another Amazonian tribe called the **Mundurukú** who have no words for spatial relations. Despite this, Dehaene demonstrated that members of the tribe were able to solve geometric problems and learn how to use a map. Also, in an inversion of the Pirahã research, Dehaene showed that the Mundurukú were poor at numerical tasks involving quantities of three and greater, even though they have words for numbers up to five. As Pinker puts it: "The prerequisite for exact number concepts beyond 'two' is a counting algorithm, not a language with number words."

Although language doesn't *determine* what we can and can't think about, it's worth pointing out that there is ample evidence that the conventions of different languages can affect our *habits* of thought. For example, speakers of languages which require them to attribute genders to objects have been shown to think about those objects as if they really do have the qualities of the gender attributed to them. Native Spanish speakers, for example, think of bridges (male in their language) as having more masculine qualities, whereas the Germans (for whom bridges are female) think of bridges as being more feminine. Perhaps the most striking example of language conventions influencing mental habits comes from the Australian aboriginal language Guugu Yimithirr. Speakers of this tongue refer to all spatial relations in terms of the cardinal directions (East, West and so on) and never egocentrically, as in left, right, behind, in front. This convention obliges them to pay constant attention to environmental cues so that they know the geographical coordinates in any given situation. As you might expect, native speakers of this language have been shown to have extraordinary spatial skills and memories.

Arguably a rather more convincing account of the relation between thought and language than the Sapir-Whorf hypothesis is provided by **conceptual semantics**. This is the idea that there is a wordless "language of thought" underlying the way we use and categorize our words. This pre-verbal language reflects the way we construe the world. It's based on issues relating to giving, changing, moving and whether an action is continuous or discrete. Consistent with this, the way we organize our words, for example into transitive (involving acting on another object or person) and intransitive verbs (something you do by yourself, such as sleep), is grounded in questions of change, permanence and physics.

METAPHOR AND ITS USES

The physical foundations of language are also revealed through our ubiquitous use of **metaphor**. When we think about concepts like power,

Bl**dy h*ll!

Just what the fuck is it about swear words that makes them so special? Excuse my language, but by shocking you I was attempting to demonstrate that a key characteristic of taboo words is their raw emotional power. This has been confirmed with brain-imaging and brain-wave recordings. Just like loud noises and the sight of angry faces, taboo words cause our amygdala – the almond-like brain-region involved in processing emotional memories – to fire up. The trouble is that this really just provides physiological proof for what we already know from first-hand experience. Quite why these words wield such power probably has to do with the things they refer to. In most, if not all, languages, swear words tend to refer to sex, sexual organs, excreta, death, decay, God and outcast social groups. And whereas technical or scientific terms for these things are used in a way that's intended to be as insipid and precise as possible, swear words have the opposite function – designed to highlight the disgustingness or earthy lustiness of the substance or act. Research shows that men swear more than women, teenagers more than the rest of us, and that we all swear more when in the company of our own sex. Depending on the social context, we can invoke taboo words strategically. The orator can build up to a crescendo, insert a "fucking" in her concluding line, and ensure her passion leaves a lasting impression on the audience. Footballers sharing a drink post-match can exchange carefree "shits" and "fucks", thus putting on display their unshockable machismo.

for example, we invoke the metaphor of height – we talk about someone being on the bottom rung of the ladder, or a person being "high up" in the office hierarchy. For time, we invoke the metaphor of movement through space. You can test this out yourself by considering which day of the week a meeting has changed to, if it was originally planned for Wednesday but has been moved forward two days. If you think it's now changed to Friday, so the argument goes, then you're someone who thinks of themselves as moving through time, while if you think the meeting is now on Monday, then you're more passive, and you think about time passing you by. A study by David Hauser and colleagues in 2009 even suggested that angrier people are more likely to think the meeting has moved to Friday, reflecting the fact that they have a more assertive, forward-moving attitude.

This idea that our thoughts are not only grounded in but also affected by physical metaphors is known as **embodied cognition**. Other examples include the finding that people in a warm room are more likely to say they feel socially close to an experimenter than research participants in a cool room, and that people tend to assume a serious book will be heavier than a flippant one. These kinds of examples have led some linguists – most famously George Lakoff – to go so far as to suggest that the language of thought that underlies our use of words is fully rooted in the physical. According to this extreme account, we can only understand abstract concepts like importance and time by referring to physical concepts like weight and distance. Most experts believe this is taking the role of metaphor in our mental lives too far. Pinker, for one, points out that while metaphors clearly play an important role in language and thought, they are ultimately based on a separate conceptual foundation. He says this is revealed graphically by our ability to "see through" metaphors (as in US comedian Steven Wright's question: "If all the world's a stage, where is the audience sitting?") and, in the case of the "time-as-space" metaphor, by the existence of brain-damaged patients who no longer understand prepositions for space (as in "she's at her desk"), but do still understand prepositions for time (as in "he daydreamed through the meeting").

A helping hand

We've focused on words so far, but watch any person speak for a few minutes and you'll doubtless see them waving their hands about as if conducting an invisible orchestra. In fact, some experts believe that

Politicians will often use exaggerated gestures to reinforce a point or to fire up an audience. This is Edward Kennedy in 1962 trying to win the Democratic nomination to run for Congress.

language may have evolved through gestures first, with spoken language only emerging later on. Consistent with this idea is the fact that Broca's area in the brain is involved in controlling hand-gestures as well as its role in language.

Recent studies have confirmed that **gesticulations** aren't just a silly habit, they actually play an important role in helping us communicate. Consider a 2004 study by Susan Wagner at the University of Chicago, which involved videoing 72 students while they explained maths problems they'd solved earlier. Crucially, during each explanation, the students had the additional task of remembering letters or arrangements of dots presented to them before they began their explanation. Students who were allowed to use gestures during their explanations subsequently recalled more of these items to be remembered than students who were prevented from gesturing. The finding suggests that using their hands made the explanation part of the task easier, thus freeing up more mental resources for the memory part of the task.

As well as aiding the thought processes underlying speech, gesturing can be beneficial to the listener. Research by Pierre Feyereisen at the University of Louvain suggests that people find it easier to remember statements that are accompanied by gestures, as long as the gestures are appropriate to what is being said. Feyereisen showed 59 students a video of an actor uttering different sentences while making either a meaningful or a meaningless gesture. Those accompanied by a meaningful gesture – for example, the actor pointing his index finger downwards and drawing a circle, while stating "the buyer went round the property" – were remembered more than sentences accompanied by a meaningless gesture (for example, the actor holding his right hand open, palm upwards and saying "He runs to the nearest house").

Of course, hand movements can even be choreographed to create entire languages – as demonstrated by the **sign languages** used by deaf people, including British Sign Language and American Sign Language. These are fully formed language-systems with their own syntax and vocabulary based on hand-shape, location, orientation and movement. Amazingly, in the absence of formal tuition, deaf children invent their own signs. Indeed, it's thought that this spontaneous process led to the formation of Nicaraguan Sign Language in the 1970s, after children in one of the country's main schools for the deaf were encouraged to read lips and speak rather than use signs.

Part III

Same difference

10 Nature – Nurture

In the making of a human, how much is nature, how much is nurture? That is to say, what is the relative influence of genetic inheritance versus the effect of parenting and experience? These are questions with political as well as scientific import. It's an unpalatable fact to some, but we're certainly not born equal. Some people are predisposed to be more intelligent than others, some faster, bigger, nastier, lustier. However, there is no optimum human form – different people are better suited to different situations. We're each equipped with the characteristics and inclinations that allowed our ancestors to thrive in the social and physical worlds in which they lived.

Why we differ

Broadly speaking, there are three main influences that make each of us unique. There is our genetic inheritance; there's the family environment, which we share with any siblings we may have; and, finally, there are unique environmental effects, which are those experiences that we alone encounter. Untangling these three influences is no mean feat, but great progress has been made in recent decades, particularly through the use of twin- and adoption-studies in an emerging field known as **behavioural genetics**.

Monozygotic (identical) twins develop from the same ovum and sperm and therefore share all their genes. Whether raised together or not, such twins tend to be far more similar in numerous traits, including personality and intelligence, than raised-together dizygotic, non-identical twins who are formed from separate eggs and sperm (and so share only half their genes). This provides compelling evidence that genes play an important role in shaping our psychological make-up.

Consider the gene that codes for brain-derived neurotrophic factor (BDNF) – a protein that encourages neuron growth. There are two possible versions of this gene, one containing the amino-acid methionine, the other containing the amino-acid valine. Each person carries either one of each, or two copies of just one of the versions (known as val-mets, val-vals, or met-mets, respectively). Crucially, the permutation you have is strongly linked to the personality dimension of neuroticism (see p.178). Met-mets tend to be the most neurotic of all, suffering from more depression and anxiety. Val-mets, in turn, tend to be more neurotic than val-vals.

On its own, variation in the gene for BDNF only accounts for about four percent of the variation in people's neuroticism, so other genes and the environment must also be involved. The overall influence of genes on any given characteristic is known as that characteristic's **heritability index**. Genes explain about sixty to eighty percent of variation in height, for example, and about fifty percent of the variation in personality. However, it's important to treat these kinds of estimates with caution. Whenever a study cites the relative contributions of genes and the environment, this pertains to the particular sample under investigation at that particular time in those particular circumstances. The larger, more varied and widely distributed the sample, the more trustworthy the heritability estimate.

Danish identical twins taking part in a study of the genetic and environmental factors that affect ageing. The Danish Twin Registry started recruiting in 1954 and by 2005 contained more than 75,000 twin pairs born between 1870 and 2004.

The fact that identical twins aren't identical in every respect tells us that genes aren't the whole story. By comparing identical twins raised together and identical twins raised apart, via adoption, psychologists can further disentangle the influence of shared and unique environmental effects. The shock result to come out of this kind of research is that identical twins raised together are no more similar to each other than identical twins raised apart. Similarly, a child adopted into a family ends up no more similar to her adopted siblings than if he or she had been raised in another family. Stated starkly, this research suggests that the family environment plays little if any role in the shaping of a child's personality. Unique environmental effects, such as a child's circle of friends and their experiences at school, are far more influential.

This revelation was popularized in a controversial 1998 book by the psychologist Judith Rich Harris called *The Nurture Assumption: Why Children Turn Out The Way They Do*. For years, psychologists from Freud onwards had assumed that parents play a powerful role in the shaping of their children's personalities, but here was compelling evidence that

Fear of snakes – it's human nature

While mainstream psychology has tended to concentrate on ways that people differ from one another – known as **individual differences** – anthropologists and evolutionary psychologists have documented the characteristics that we have in common. Indeed, in his book *Human Universals* (1991), the anthropologist Donald Brown lists over one hundred physical and behavioural traits that are common to all cultures, such as language, music and humour. Rather than being learned, these behaviours are considered to be part of human nature. Take the example of the fear or wariness of snakes. Of course, it is possible to learn to fear virtually anything. But our evolved human nature means that most of us are quicker to learn to fear snakes (and spiders, heights, the dark, confined spaces and so on) than modern threats, such as guns – a phenomenon known as **prepared learning**. Back in the 1980s Edwin Cook and his colleagues conditioned participants to fear snakes and guns by repeatedly pairing them with a loud, unpleasant noise. Despite the fact that a loud noise is more consistent with the threat of a gun, the procedure led to a far deeper and longer-lasting fear of snakes than guns. This is an example of human nature in action. Snakes were obviously more of a threat to our ancestors than yet-to-be-invented guns, and individuals quick to learn the threat of snakes were more likely to pass on their genes, including an inclination for snake wariness, to later generations.

their influence is far more modest. So whereas research had shown that, say, conscientious parents tend to raise conscientious children, the new field of behavioural genetics demonstrated that this was probably because of genetic factors, not parenting style. For a post-war culture obsessed with the importance of parenting, these claims were explosive. It's important to add a caveat here. The findings showing the modest role played by the family environment pertain to unexceptional circumstances. There's no question that neglect or abuse can have a devastating effect on a child's development.

It's also important to recognize that genetic and environmental effects are not separate. A person's genetically influenced traits and endowments affect the kind of environments they place themselves in. A more intelligent child is more likely to end up at a superior school; a lanky teenager more likely to wind up on the basketball court and thereby receive more coaching. Similarly, many genes are like switches, turned on by particular environments. In fact there's a whole field, known as **epigenetics**, which seeks to discover the processes that control whether or not a particular gene is expressed. This means that for many traits and illnesses, it is impossible to say whether the cause is either genetic or environmental. A good example of this is phenylketonuria, a genetic condition which prevents the digestion of phenylalanine, an amino acid found in fish, meat and other foods. With the right diet, phenylketonuria causes almost no problems. However, if a person with phenylketonuria eats foods containing phenylalanine they develop severe cognitive deficits. Are these problems caused by genes or the environment? The answer, as with so many other outcomes, is surely both.

BIRTH ORDER

One of the most popular folk-psychology explanations for why we differ is birth order – first-borns are traditionally considered to be high-achieving go-getters, while younger siblings are often seen as more rebellious and creative. There's certainly plenty of anecdotal evidence to back this up. First-borns are hugely over-represented among past leaders from all over the world, including British and Australian Prime Ministers and American Presidents. Similarly, a recent survey of international corporations reported by *Time* magazine found that 43 percent of chief executive officers were first-borns whereas just 23 percent were last-borns.

In some ways, the apparent success of firstborns makes sense. After all, they have all the attention and resources of their parents to themselves, whereas later siblings have to share or perhaps even go without. But it's not all bad news for younger siblings. Research shows that they are more skilled at understanding other people's emotions and considering alternative points of view, perhaps because they've needed these social and political skills to cope with their junior rank in the family.

Regarding personality traits, first-borns are often found to be more hard-working and diligent, while younger siblings are more sociable and creative. However, some psychologists are sceptical about these personality findings. The results are usually inconsistent and mostly come from studies that relied on siblings rating each other's personalities. That young siblings should rate their older brothers and sisters as highly conscientious, while first-borns rate their younger siblings as rebellious is little wonder if you consider that they're probably drawing on childhood memories of the family home.

11 **Personality**

This chapter will focus on psychology's attempts to categorize and understand people according to pervasive differences in their behavioural tendencies – their "personalities". The idea that each of us has a distinct, consistent personality is essential to our folk psychology. We deal with each other on the basis that a person who's been amiable and garrulous in the past is likely to be so in the future – and the same goes for any other personality traits. Were it any other way, our social relations would doubtless descend into chaos.

Critics of personality theory argue that more weight should be given to the power of a situation to explain our behaviour. Forget personality they say, a person is more likely to be brave if surrounded by friends; to be outgoing at a party full of people they know; more likely to work hard in an office shared with conscientious colleagues. In fact, there's a phenomenon in social psychology known as the **fundamental attribution error**, which describes our tendency to downplay the influence of situational factors when interpreting other people's – but not our own – behaviour.

These criticisms aside, science generally backs up the idea of consistent personalities. One study compared people's scores on the same personality test carried out twelve years apart and found little change. Measures of personality also effectively predict later outcomes, such as marriage and occupational success, thus suggesting that personality exerts a consistent effect throughout a lifetime. In a 1987 study, for example, Lowell Kelly and James Kolney followed three hundred couples from their engagement in the 1930s until 1980. Personality scores obtained in the 1930s were strongly predictive of marital outcomes. For instance, divorce was more likely if either the man or woman had scored highly in neuroticism (see p.178).

Personality categories

Somewhat trickier than establishing the consistency and predictive power of personality has been the age-old conundrum of how exactly to categorize the different personality traits. The idea that each of us has one of four temperaments or humours – phlegmatic, choleric, sanguine or melancholic, depending on the predominance in the body of either phlegm, yellow bile, blood or black bile – dates back at least as far as the Ancient Greeks and formed the basis of Hippocratic medicine. Over the last hundred years, psychologists started to develop theories with a more scientific basis. The model devised by **Hans Eysenck** (1916–97), for example, had an extrovert/introvert dimension, a neurotic/stable dimension, and later on, a psychotic/socialization dimension. **Raymond Cattell** (1905–88) proposed sixteen personality factors, including warmth, vigilance and dominance. By the end of the last century, a gratifying consensus emerged, based on the idea of stripping out any redundancy in different personality traits – a process known more formally as **factor analysis**.

For example, given that being sociable and being enthusiastic nearly always go together, it makes sense to collapse these into a single trait. Applying this idea to a multitude of different personality characteristics, psychologists today largely agree that there are five main personality traits – known as the **Big Five** – that can't be reduced down or lumped together any further. These are Extroversion, Neuroticism, Conscientiousness, Agreeableness, and Openness (to identify your own scores on these factors see p.184). All are continuous dimensions, rather like height or weight. The fact that so much variation in these traits has persisted in the human genome suggests that, in the past, a mix of environmental circumstances allowed different personality types to thrive. Underlying variation in each of the Big Five traits is the functioning of a particular brain system or systems.

Extroversion describes how motivated a person is in the pursuit of reward. High scorers on this dimension tend to be doers and seekers. They go to more parties, have more sexual partners, and are more thrill-seeking than low scorers. Put an extrovert in a brain scanner, show them positive images, such as of an erotic couple or a delicious meal, and their brain will fire up far more explosively than a low scorer on this dimension. The implication is that the reward pathways of their brains are more sensitive. It's worth noting that a low scorer on the extroversion trait is not necessarily sad and withdrawn. Rather it's that they're less affected by and driven towards positive reward.

Shakespeare's Hamlet, who embodies the Renaissance melancholic type, would nowadays be considered highly neurotic.

Neuroticism is the flip side of extraversion and describes a person's sensitivity to negative emotion. High scorers are hesitant, vigilant and nervous. Place them in a scanner, show them negative images and their brain will flare up far more than the brain of a low scorer. Unsurprisingly perhaps, high scorers on neuroticism tend to suffer from higher rates of depression and anxiety. It's the deep brain structures of the limbic system that underlie neuroticism, including the reactivity of the amygdala (see p.39). The reason evolution hasn't eradicated neuroticism from the genome is because in dangerous circumstances, caution pays.

Conscientiousness is akin to will-power. It describes our ability to resist immediate temptation for the benefit of later gain. A high scorer on this dimension will be disciplined and well-organized. Research shows that highly conscientious personalities live longer and excel at work. The relevant brain system here is the inhibitory mechanisms of the frontal lobes. The price of too much control is a loss of flexibility and spontaneity, which can manifest as obsessive compulsive personality disorder. People who match this description tend to live by exceedingly strict routines and find it difficult to cope with any unpredictability.

Agreeableness describes a person's friendliness and ability to engage with others. The extrovert may seek out human company, but isn't necessarily a pleasant person to be around. A high scorer in agreeableness, by contrast, is defined by their ability to understand and relate to other people's emotions. They are likely to work in a caring profession, be family-oriented and a good listener. The brain systems underlying this trait have to do with the ability to empathize and think of things from other people's perspectives. We haven't all evolved to be high scorers on this dimension, because caring too much for other people's needs is never going to be a winning strategy, especially when there are others in the world ready to exploit your selflessness.

Openness is probably the least well-defined and understood of the Big Five traits. High scorers on this dimension tend to appreciate high culture and new experiences. They see connections in meaning between superficially unrelated concepts – a skill that can manifest itself in poetry, storytelling and other forms of creative expression. A weakness of this trait, from a theoretical point of view, is that it tends to get tangled up with intelligence. High scorers on openness also tend to score high on intelligence tests, but the two factors are not the same thing. Intelligence describes the overall fitness and efficiency of a person's nervous system (see Chapter 12), whereas openness is more specifically about appreciating and having original insights. Openness also tends to correlate with having unusual perceptual experiences and believing in spirituality and the paranormal. At its most extreme, openness can manifest itself as psychosis or a schizophrenic-like personality, which is when a person has a tendency to see meaning where there is none.

It's important to remember that these factors are intended to be dimensions, not black-and-white categories. One way to think about people's scores on the different factors is as varying thresholds which must be passed before they are prompted to behave or react a certain way. Everyone is capable of feeling nervous or fearful: it's just that to a high-scorer on neuroticism, these reactions are more easily triggered. We're all susceptible to temptation – it's just that to the high scorer on conscientiousness, the lure required is so much greater. Another thing to bear in mind is that while it helps for descriptive purposes

George Kelly (1905–67) and the idiographic approach to personality

While many psychologists have attempted to identify the principal dimensions of personality that we all share (the "nomothetic" approach that led to agreement on the Big Five factors), George Kelly's **Personal Construct Theory** attempted to understand how each of us is unique (the "idiographic" approach). Personal constructs, which vary from person to person, are those "bipolar" aspects of reality through which we each comprehend the world – such as whether people are punctual or tardy, whether products are cheap or expensive and so on. Each individual's personal constructs are not fixed, but can be updated through their lives. Kelly believed that by uncovering the principal constructs through which a person construes the world, we can come to understand the kind of person they are – their unique personality.

to explore the extremes of personality, many people will of course score moderately on one or more factors reflecting subtle differences in character.

Measuring personality

Personality is usually measured with the use of self-report questionnaires, in which a respondent rates their agreement with a series of descriptive statements, known as test items (see box on p.184). When psychologists devise these tests, they make sure that the different items really do measure what they're supposed to be measuring – a quality known as **validity**. To do this, they will check that an affirmative answer to one item that's supposed to measure, say, extroversion, tends to go hand in hand with affirmative answers to the other items intended to measure that same factor. The psychologist might also check that scores on the new test agree with scores on an already established measure. Finally, they might consider ensuring that the test correlates with other corroborating evidence, such as the respondent's diary records or the verdicts of their friends and family.

Another quality expected of an established personality test is that it should have **reliability**. That is, the same or similar score should be achieved when the same person is tested repeatedly, or when the test is completed by different people who ought to achieve the same score because they have the same or similar personality-type. It's also important to establish "norms" for a new personality test, which requires getting as many people as possible to complete the measure, so that some sense can be built up as to what constitutes a "normal" or common score and what constitutes a more extreme or unusual score.

A major drawback of self-report questionnaires of the kind used to measure personality is many people's concern to make a good impression – a phenomenon known as **social desirability**. After all, who wants to reveal to an unfamiliar researcher that they are lazy, obnoxious or neurotic? Of course, where possible, making a test anonymous helps. Also, some personality tests include "too good to be true" items designed to detect when social desirability is likely to be distorting the results (see p.264).

More old-fashioned approaches to measuring personality are today considered to be lacking in reliability and validity. This includes the **Thematic Apperception Test** devised by Harvard psychologist Henry Murray in the 1930s. The TAT requires participants to generate stories in response to ambiguous picture cards, for example of a woman lying

A doctor at New York's Montefiore Medical Center using the Rorschach personality test to establish whether a patient's headaches have a psychological origin.

in bed, eyes closed, with a man standing nearby, hand over his face. A male respondent who told a story in which the man had murdered the woman would be perceived by a psychologist as harbouring hostility towards women.

Another traditional measure that still generates a great deal of controversy to this day is the **Rorschach inkblot test**. Users of this test are instructed to look at a series of inkblots and to describe what they see. Their answers are scored according to the parts of the blot that they focus on; the shape, movement and colour that they perceive; and the content they recognize in the blot, such as an anatomical feature or animal. Many psychologists, especially in the US, remain convinced of the value of the Rorschach. However, the test is rarely used in other countries (such as the UK) and many scientifically-oriented psychologists are extremely critical of its continued use. The controversy reached boiling point in 2009 when a Canadian physician published all ten of the official inkblots on Wikipedia. Defenders of the test were outraged and complained that the Internet leak would render the tool useless.

READING PERSONALITY IN THE EYES, FACE AND FINGERS

A popular method for discerning personality in Ancient Greece was to look for clues in the face. The idea that a person can look evil or friendly strikes an intuitive chord, and **physiognomy** (as it's known) has had a long but chequered history. Dismissed by Leonardo Da Vinci as unscientific, and outlawed by King George II of England, it nevertheless remained an influential idea, and in the nineteenth century was commonly used as a way of identifying criminals and assessing types of lunacy. Although by the twentieth century it was widely regarded as a pseudoscience, new findings suggest that aspects of personality really do have correlates in the face, the eyes and even the relative lengths of the fingers.

In a 2009 study, carried out by Justin Carré at Brock University, participants were shown photographs of men whose levels of aggression had been assessed earlier and asked to judge how aggressive they thought they were. Remarkably, the participants were largely accurate in identifying the more aggressive types, with further analysis suggesting that they were using the facial width-to-height ratio to make their judgements (in other words the wider a face was relative to its length, the more aggressive it was judged to be). The reason that this is seen as an indicator of aggression may well be because a face with this shape more closely resembles an angry facial expression. Separate studies have confirmed that face-width is a valid marker – men with such faces have higher testosterone levels, and an investigation involving ice hockey players found that those with wide, short faces had been penalized more often for violent acts during games.

Other related research has shown that it's possible to discern the sexual orientation of a person from the briefest of glimpses of their face; that a glance at the face of a chief executive can provide a rough idea of the profitability of a company; and that baby-faced men are more likely to be judged innocent in court.

Focusing on the eyes, Mats Larsson at Örebro University found in 2007 that participants who had more features called Fuchs' crypts on the surface layers of their iris (reflecting thicker tissue) tended to form warmer and more trustful attachments to other people, and experienced more positive emotions. Participants with more "contraction furrows", another indicator of tissue density, tended to have more impulsive personalities. Unfortunately, eye colour wasn't linked to personality, although a separate study published in 2010 found that white men with brown eyes are perceived as more dominant than their blue-eyed counterparts. Larsson thinks the basis of the association between the iris and personality lies with the Pax6 gene, which is linked with tissue growth both in the iris and the brain.

When it comes to the fingers, a common test is to compare your index fingers (second digit; 2D) and ring fingers (fourth digits; 4D). Are they roughly the same length or is the index finger shorter? Much research over the last couple of decades has suggested that having a shorter index finger relative to the ring finger is a sign of having been exposed to more testosterone in the womb. Not surprisingly, women tend to have a higher 2D:4D ratio than men. Among both sexes, the 2D:4D ratio has been associated with personality and behaviour. In women, for example, a lower 2D:4D ratio is associated with more exhibitionism and in men with lower agreeableness. Other research in this field is quite bizarre. In a study published in 2006 by Bernhard Fink, dancing men with lower 2D:4D ratios were rated as more attractive by women than dancing men with higher 2D:4D ratios!

Multiple personalities

If the notion of different personality dimensions is now widely accepted by psychologists, what of the unsettling idea that some people have multiple personalities? There is a psychiatric diagnosis that describes this very situation. It used to be called **multiple personality disorder** but is known today as **dissociative identity disorder**.

Among the most famous cases is Chris Costner Sizemore, whose alter egos included Eve White, Eve

A publicity still for the 1957 movie *The Three Faces of Eve*. Joanne Woodward won the best actress Oscar for her performance in the title role(s).

Black, Jane and many others. According to her psychiatrists, these other personalities emerged as a coping mechanism in response to early trauma. Before the age of three, Sizemore witnessed her mother badly injured, saw a drowned man pulled from a ditch and another man sawn in half at a lumber mill. Her story was made into an Oscar-winning film in 1957 called *The Three Faces of Eve*, starring Joanne Woodward. In 2009 Sizemore appeared on the BBC's *Hardtalk* interview programme

Measure your personality

Read the following statements, and for each give yourself a score from 1 (that's not me at all) to 5 (that's me exactly).

1. If I see someone upset, it often moves me too
2. I enjoy novels
3. I like throwing parties
4. I sometimes feel very low
5. I rarely get anxious
6. I'm punctual
7. I'm not afraid to insult people
8. I like to eat at the same times each day
9. I often strike up a conversation with strangers
10. I like to plan ahead
11. I avoid horror films
12. I'd like to do more for charity
13. I often wonder about the meaning of life
14. I rarely get over-excited about things
15. Music is unimportant to me

Scoring
Now tally up your results as follows (to reverse score an item, 1 becomes 5, 2 becomes 4 and so on).
Extroversion: Add your scores for 3, 9 and 14 (reverse scored).
Neuroticism: Add your scores for 4, 5 (reverse scored) and 11.
Conscientiousness: Add your scores for 6, 8, and 10.
Agreeableness: Add your scores for 1, 7 (reverse scored) and 12.
Openness: Add your scores for 2, 13, 15 (reverse scored).

A score of 11 to 15 for any trait is high, 6 to 10 is medium, and 1 to 5 is low. By comparing your scores for the different traits, you'll get some sense of how dominant each trait is in your own personality. However, to get a big-picture feel for what your score means, you'll need to ask friends and family to have a go too, so that you can compare each other's personalities. Note that this test is just to give you an idea – it hasn't been checked for validity or reliability (see p.180).

and claimed that "one minute I'd be one person and the next minute I'd be somebody else." She believed that her first husband had married Eve White, not her, and that her first daughter was Eve White's daughter, not her own. Sizemore today claims to have lived as one personality for the last thirty years, with all her alter egos combining to form her newfound singular identity.

What is happening in a case like this? Can it really be possible for a single brain to give rise to multiple personalities? A diagnosis of dissociative identity disorder is highly controversial, and it's rather suspicious that the number of reported cases has waxed and waned according to the publicity given to the condition. In particular, there was an "epidemic" in the 1980s and 90s when awareness of the diagnosis was at its zenith.

Today, dissociative identity disorder is considered one of a family of conditions alongside depersonalization disorder (feeling that nothing is real), fugue state (forgetting who you are) and dissociative amnesia (forgetting key episodes of your life). These diagnoses are only made in the absence of a possible organic cause of the symptoms. Psychiatrists and psychologists have tried to shift the focus away from the sensational notion of multiple personalities, to concentrate instead on the memory loss and breakdown in continuity of consciousness that's common to all these conditions. As with the case of Chris Sizemore, the most popular theory is that dissociative identity disorder emerges as a coping mechanism after trauma. In line with this theory, people exhibiting a purported case of split personality will often claim that one or more of their identities has no recollection of a particularly traumatic memory.

One of the leading authorities on dissociative disorders is John Kihlstrom of the University of California. His authoritative overview, published in 2005, called on people to keep an open mind. "As complex as [dissociative disorders] are," he said, 'they deserve to be studied in a spirit of open inquiry that avoids both the excessive credulity of the enthusiast and the dismissal of the determined skeptic." Today, most of what we know about dissociative identity disorder remains anecdotal and based on single case-reports. There's been little systematic study to find out how a single person's multiple identities score on a personality test.

12 Intelligence

The subject of human intelligence and how to measure it has a dark history and remains one of the most controversial areas in psychology. Despite this, intelligence tests are still used in many countries to inform sensitive decisions – from whether a child is provided with extra help at school to whether a job candidate should be hired or not.

What is intelligence?

In everyday life, intelligence is a familiar but incredibly vague concept. We might all agree that a professor of astrophysics is in some sense highly intelligent. But imagine if the same professor made a habit of getting lost, offending colleagues or losing money on risky investments. In these cases we might just as readily say that they were rather stupid, socially inept or unwise. Conversely, a gangster with no qualifications to their name might not be considered intelligent in an academic sense, but we might refer to their street smarts – their understanding of who to trust and how to avoid trouble. Common sense, creativity, tactical nous, mathematical genius, people skills, literary talent – in common parlance, all these abilities are at times seen as forms of intelligence.

The mainstream scientific view of intelligence is that it reflects the "fitness" or efficiency of the brain and nervous system. The idea that intelligence is more than just an abstract or subjective concept has been supported by findings showing that someone who displays evidence of cleverness in one domain, say maths, also tends to excel in other domains too, such as language and spatial processing – an observation that has come to be known as **g** or **general intelligence**. Moreover, people's performance on written or computerized tests of their mental skills and knowledge also correlate with extremely basic tests of their reaction time (their **speed of mental processing**), providing further support for the idea that intelligence is the manifestation of an efficient nervous system.

Still more evidence that there really is such a thing as intelligence comes from the fact that people's performance on tests of their mental skill and reaction times remains consistent over time, is partly inherited from their parents, and successfully predicts outcomes such as school achievements, career success and even longevity.

Recent research has started to explore the neural correlates of intelligence. A 2009 study used a brain-scanning technique, known as **diffusion tensor imaging**, to illuminate the efficiency of neural pathways in the brains of 92 identical and non-identical twins. Participants who scored higher on an intelligence test also tended to have quicker, more efficient neural

As if formulating the Theory of Relativity wasn't enough, Albert Einstein was also a gifted amateur violinist.

pathways. At the time the results were released, the project leader Paul Thompson at the University of California put it this way: "When you say someone is quick-thinking, it's generally true – the impulses are going faster and they're just much more efficient at processing information and then making a decision based on it."

Thompson's study focused on white-matter tracts in the brain, which are insulated with fatty material to speed nerve conductance. Other research shows that intelligence is also linked to quantities of grey matter (the cell bodies) in different brain regions. In 2007 Rex Jung and Richard Haier analysed the results from 37 brain-imaging studies and came to the conclusion that intelligence is associated with grey-matter volume in fourteen key areas spread throughout the frontal and parietal cortices. Jung and Haier called this the P-FIT network (as in "parieto-frontal integration theory") and they speculated that one day, by focusing on these areas, brain scans will be able to identify a person's intelligence profile.

It's all in the reflexes

Speed of mental processing is measured using: 1) **simple reaction-time** tests, in which the participant must press a button as quickly as possible in response to the appearance of a certain stimulus (for example, a light); (2) **choice reaction-time** tests, in which there are two or more response buttons and the participant must press the correct one depending on which stimulus has appeared and; (3) **inspection-time**, tests in which the participant must compare two stimuli as quickly as possible (for example, identify which of two parallel lines is the longer).

This picture, taken in 1925, shows Phil Scott, the British heavyweight boxing champion, completing what appears to be a simple reaction-time test at London's Middlesex Hospital.

HOW MANY KINDS OF INTELLIGENCE ARE THERE?

There's general agreement that intelligence can be broken down into **crystallized intelligence**, which reflects things like general knowledge and vocabulary, and **fluid intelligence**, which is about abstract reasoning and the ability to think on your feet. The US psychologist **Howard Gardner** has put forward an account, popular but largely unaccepted in mainstream circles, claiming there are seven further sub-types of intelligence: verbal, logical, spatial, musical, body-kinetic, interpersonal and intrapersonal. Gardner's compatriot **Joy Guilford** (1897–1987) has proposed a staggering 180 different factors in intelligence, from kinesthetics to memory prowess. The trouble with these wide-ranging accounts is that they risk becoming so broad as to be meaningless.

Gardner's final two intelligence-types (the interpersonal and intrapersonal) resemble the idea of **emotional intelligence**, made famous by **Daniel Goleman** in his 1995 best-selling book *Emotional Intelligence: Why It Can Matter More Than IQ.* Emotional intelligence (EI) refers to the ability to understand, recognize and manage your own and other people's emotions. The idea of emotional intelligence has proved popular with the mainstream media and public, but remains controversial in academic psychology. Critics point out, for example, that if someone performs well on one of the EI sub-tests (for example, measuring their understanding of their own emotions), they don't necessarily perform well on the others (such as a test of their ability to understand other people's emotions). In other words, EI probably isn't a coherent, unitary concept at all. Another criticism is that unlike traditional intelligence, EI doesn't successfully predict real-life outcomes, such as people's success at work. When the American Psychological Association published its working-party report "Intelligence: Knowns and Unknowns" in 1996, the term emotional intelligence wasn't even mentioned.

Robert Sternberg, a former president of the American Psychological Association, is another influential voice in the field who believes that the traditional scientific conception of intelligence is too narrow, and that too much emphasis is placed on **g**. His theory of **successful intelligence** includes three aspects: a memory-analytic component (similar to the traditional conception of intelligence), a creative component and a practical component.

Measuring intelligence

Intelligence is measured using written or computerized tests, often with a multiple-choice format. Crystallized intelligence is probed by a series of items (i.e. a "subscale") that focuses on vocabulary and general knowledge, whereas tests of fluid intelligence are presented in the form of abstract visual problems, the most famous being **Raven's Progressive Matrices**, developed in the 1930s by psychologist John C. Raven. In an attempt to prevent cheating, official standardized intelligence tests and their answers are only released by publishers to licensed psychologists.

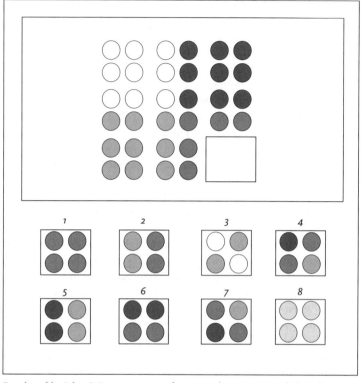

Developed by John C. Raven as a way of gauging abstract, non-verbal intelligence, Raven's Progressive Matrices are still considered to be one of the most effective ways of assessing general intelligence. (The correct answer is No.1.)

Modern intelligence tests give the test-taker a standardized score, known as their **intelligence quotient** (IQ), that shows how well they have done relative to a large comparison-sample of healthy adults or, in the case of a child, in comparison with other children of their age. When someone achieves a raw score that equates to the average performance of the comparison sample, this is converted to 100. Approximately half the general population has an IQ lower than 100, while has have a higher intelligence. A difference of one standard deviation from the average intelligence – standard deviation is the square root of the average amount of deviation from the average score – equates to about 15 IQ points. This means that a person with an IQ of 115 is considered to have scored higher than 84 percent of the population. Traditionally, an IQ score of 70 or less is considered

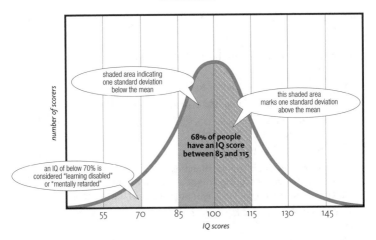

shaded area indicating one standard deviation below the mean

this shaded area marks one standard deviation above the mean

68% of people have an IQ score between 85 and 115

an IQ of below 70% is considered "learning disabled" or "mentally retarded"

number of scorers

55   70   85   100   115   130   145

IQ scores

extremely low or "mentally retarded" (although this term is quickly falling out of favour).

Intelligence testing remains highly controversial. Critics, such as Stephen Jay Gould, have argued that the tests are culturally biased; that people can improve their performance through practice; that results are contaminated by factors like motivation and educational background; and that not enough weight is given by the tests to soft skills such as empathy and creativity. (Recognizing some of these concerns, tests designed to measure Sternberg's "successful intelligence" are more varied and include practical and creative tasks alongside more traditional items.)

There are also objections to the uses intelligence-tests are put to, for instance determining whether a person gains access to certain psychological or social services; filtering schools admissions; appraising job candidates; and assessing a person's legal capacity (i.e. their ability to look after their own affairs). Often these life-changing decisions are based on what many regard as arbitrary cut-offs, such as whether a person has an IQ of 70 or less, or above 130, the latter considered by some test administrators as a sign of "giftedness". If the tests are flawed and biased, so the argument goes, then it is scandalous that the tests can have such influence on people's lives. Negative feedback from a test can also be self-fulfilling, damaging a person's confidence and affecting their life choices. To fully appreciate the controversies that cloud intelligence-testing, it's worth taking a step back in time to see how intelligence-testing evolved and how it has been abused.

Test your intelligence

Here are a few examples of the kind of items you might expect to find in a typical intelligence test.

1) Pebble is to beach as book is to ... which of the following:

a) page b) library c) magazine d) sea e) onion f) print.

2) Study the series of numbers 20, 21, 18, 19, x, 17 and select the correct missing number for x from:

a) 100   b) 20   c) 16   d) 14

3) Jon scores 20 goals in four matches. He scores a tenth of these in the first match while scoring an equal number in the remaining three matches. How many goals did he score in each of the last three games?

4) Who is the founder of Microsoft?

5)

//	|||	\
		\\	///
\\\	/	?

Select the icon that's missing from the final cell in the table:

a) ||| b) 0   c) \   d) || e) \\

6) Tennis Hockey

Which one of the following has something in common with the above words, which it does not share with the others: a) darts b) skiing c) toast d) cricket e) wrestling f) monkey

Answers: 1) b; 2) c – the rule from left to right is add one, minus three, add one, minus three; 3) 6; 4) Bill Gates; 5) d; 6) d (all are ball games).

A brief history of intelligence testing

It all started with the Victorian adventurer and polymath **Francis Galton** (see p.11). Obsessed with measuring anything and everything, Galton eventually set his sights on human ability, establishing an **Anthropometric Laboratory** at the London International Health Exhibition in 1884. Although many of Galton's instruments were physiological – among other things, he recorded people's height, weight, hearing, vision and punching power – his ultimate purpose was to identify people's innate mental ability. In line with his belief that geniuses are born, not made, Galton thought his tests could encourage breeding between clever folk and discourage it among the "feeble-minded" – a disturbing but influential idea that developed into the **eugenics** movement.

Across the channel in turn-of-the-century France, universal education was being introduced, and for the first time it was deemed necessary to identify children with abnormally low intelligence. The psychologist **Alfred Binet,** who'd read about and improved upon Galton's techniques, was given the responsibility by the French government for devising a test that would identify children who were "retarded". Together with his colleague **Théodore Simon**, Binet devised a series of systematic mental tasks that tapped language, abstract reasoning and other faculties, and they pioneered the idea of comparing a child's actual performance with what he ought to be able to do given his age. In 1905, the **Binet-Simon test** was born – the world's first modern intelligence-test.

Around the same time as Binet and Simon were developing their test, the English army officer and psychologist Charles Spearman discovered that if a person is a skilful performer on one kind of mental task, the chances are that he or she will also excel on other mental tasks – leading him to propose and name the idea of g (general intelligence), which has since become a foundation stone of intelligence testing.

Meanwhile, in the US, the psychologist **Henry Goddard** had started using a translation of the Binet-Simon test to filter immigrants arriving at Ellis Island, and to classify "mentally-retarded children". But it was the demands of World War I that would give the intelligence test an unstoppable momentum. At a time when psychology was still a nascent discipline, the American Psychological Association's President, **Robert Yerkes**, together with **Lewis Terman**, Goddard

Alfred Binet – the father of intelligence testing.

and a few others, managed to convince the US military of the value of their new-fangled intelligence tests. In the end, the psychologists tested 1.7 million men, ostensibly to help identify those too feeble-minded to be of any use to the war effort. The war "put psychology on the map" was how **James Cattell**, another pioneer in the field, put it. After the war, Terman oversaw the rise of routine intelligence testing in schools. By the mid-1920s, nearly four million American children took an intelligence test every year.

In the UK, the educational psychologist **Sir Cyril Burt** adapted the Binet-Simon test and became a vocal proponent of the idea of g and inherited intelligence. Burt believed that people often ended up in jobs and social roles not befitting their intellectual capabilities, including less intelligent people in senior positions and those in lowly roles who weren't fulfilling their potential. He saw intelligence tests as a way of sorting people more effectively. The main outcome of campaigning by Burt and other like-minded psychologists was the eleven-plus (11+) – an examination taken by every child in England and Wales, the results of which determined whether they were granted access to a superior grammar school or a less desirable secondary modern school.

The Cyril Burt affair

Regarded as one of the world's leading educational psychologists in his lifetime, Cyril Burt (1883–1971) was accused of serious scientific misconduct in the years that immediately followed his death. The accusations concerned his research into the heritability of intelligence, which had involved studies of identical twins reared apart. Doubts were raised about the number of identical twins he claimed to have studied, and detractors observed that his results were too uniform to be true. Further suspicion was aroused by the elusiveness of two of Burt's research assistants. Many psychologists leapt to Burt's defence. It was pointed out that his assistants may have worked under pseudonyms, and that much of Burt's identical-twin data cited in the 1950s and 60s actually originated from research conducted before the war, having been lost for many years. Despite these explanations, in 1980 the British Psychological Society formally condemned Burt's work on the genetic inheritance of intelligence. However, the controversy rumbled on, and in 1992 the BPS declared that it no longer had a "corporate view" on the truth of the allegations. Subsequent research has confirmed that a large amount of variation in intelligence is accounted for by genetic factors, with the upper estimate being about 85 percent.

A US Army recruiting officer testing the mental ability of an applicant by means of cutout blocks.

Most of the standardized intelligence tests in use today were developed by **David Wechsler**, a test administrator for the US army during World War I. Before and after the war, Wechsler worked with most of the leading proponents in the field, and in the 1930s he put together what he considered all the best bits from the various tests then in use, including verbal and non-verbal questions, to create a new comprehensive exam that became the gold standard of intelligence tests. Today, different versions of his test are used for different age-groups, including the Wechsler Preschool and Primary Scale of Intelligence (WPPSI; pronounced Whipsee), the Wechsler Intelligence Scale for Children (WISC) and the Wechsler Adult Intelligence Scale (WAIS).

THE DARK SIDE OF INTELLIGENCE TESTING

The idea of using intelligence-test results as the basis for rejecting immigrants or selecting school pupils raises ethical questions all of its own. But the dark side of this field really emerged when Terman and his colleagues began analysing all the data they'd accumulated during their military work. As well as providing the alarming finding that half of all tested Americans were officially "morons", the data also revealed differences between social groups, including between black people and white people (little wonder, given that black people were generally less educated and poorer). When these results were combined with a highly dubious 1912 analysis by Goddard entitled "The Kallikak Family: A Study in the Heredity of Feeble-Mindedness", the eugenics movement had all the ammunition it needed. By 1932, twenty-seven states in America had passed laws permitting the sterilization of people regarded as feeble-minded. Stephen Murdoch, the author of *IQ: How Psychology Hijacked Intelligence* (2009), estimates that over sixty thousand people in America were sterilized in the twentieth century – the specious aim being to stop the spread of unintelligent genes. In Nazi Germany, the figure reached over four hundred thousand.

Claims and counter-claims about racial differences in intelligence continued to be bandied around for most of the twentieth century, culminating most famously in *The Bell Curve*, a controversial 1994 best-seller by the late Richard Herrnstein and Charles Murray. In a recent review of the field, the psychologists Stephen Ceci and Wendy Williams at Cornell University defended the continued study of race differences in IQ, arguing that unsavoury claims are best countered through empirical research. They say their own findings suggest racial differences in IQ are due to environmental, not genetic, factors.

Another highly sensitive social issue thrown up by intelligence testing concerns death sentencing in US courts. Following the case of *Atkins vs. Virginia*, in 2002 the US Supreme Court ruled that a criminal deemed to be mentally retarded cannot be sentenced to death. This has led to trials in which expert witnesses (usually psychologists) for both the defence and prosecution clash over how highly a defendant has scored on intelligence tests.

Are we getting cleverer?

When the test scores of today are compared with those in previous decades, going back to around 1900, a consistent pattern emerges – scores seem to be progressively higher. In statistical terms, the size of this increase is one standard deviation or 15 IQ points in the last fifty years (in Britain this would mean that, measured against today's standards, seventy percent of Victorians would have an IQ of less than 75 – close to official "mental retardation" levels). This phenomenon has come to be known as the **Flynn effect**, after the New Zealand political scientist **James Flynn** who first documented it. By his account, the trend has been found in every country for which we have the necessary data, which in 2007 stood at over thirty countries. Rather than our brains having undergone some kind of collective upgrade, however, Flynn thinks the explanation lies in the rise of science education and technology.

If you look closely at the intelligence-test subscales, our collective improvement hasn't been uniform. On general knowledge, maths and vocabulary we've barely budged, whereas our skill at typical questions about similarity (such as "in what ways are dogs and rabbits alike?") have rocketed. This fits Flynn's explanation, because he says that a youth of today would be taught that dogs and rabbits are both mammals (the kind of answer that a typical intelligence-test would be after), whereas the youth of yesteryear would be taught to focus on what things are for, in this case that a dog is for hunting rabbits. We've also shown significant average improvement on Raven's Progressive Matrices and other abstract tests. Again, Flynn says that this probably reflects the ubiquity of visual and abstract stimulation in the modern world, in the form of video games and TVs.

After years of IQ increases, a surprising study published in 2008 suggested that a recent change of direction might have occurred, with average intelligence-test performance beginning to decline. Thomas Teasdale at the University of Copenhagen and David Owen of the City University of New York took advantage of the Danish tradition of testing the intelligence of all eighteen-year-old men prior to conscription into military service. Consistent with the Flynn effect, the 25,000 young men assessed for military service in Denmark in 1999 performed significantly better, by about two IQ points, than the 33,000 tested in 1988. However, the 23,000 men tested in 2003–2004 performed significantly worse than the 1998 group, at a level almost equivalent to the 1988 group. A similar observation has been made among Norwegian conscripts.

What could be causing this reversal in braininess? Teasdale and Owen ruled out diet change as the cause – after all, there had been no shift in average height, which you'd expect if diet had altered. They also rejected the suggestion that the decline could be due to malingering, since test performance was actually higher among men with a more negative attitude to the military. Instead, the researchers surmised that there has been some kind of reduced emphasis on abstract reasoning and problem-solving in the Danish educational system, or a decreased emphasis on speed. Whatever the cause, Teasdale and Owen predicted that this new trend could meet with the emerging Flynn effect in Third World countries, thus leading to a levelling of IQ scores around the world.

Creativity

A key aspect of mental prowess and career success that most psychologists agree isn't tapped into by traditional intelligence-tests is creativity. Indeed, in some ways, creativity is the antithesis of intelligence as traditionally measured, and extremely high scorers on IQ tests tend to do poorly on creative tasks. Whereas many psychometric tests and school exams require you to zoom in on the correct answer, drawing on a "convergent" thinking style, creative tasks ask you to think originally, in a "divergent" style.

Standard measures of a person's creativity include the "novel uses" test. To try this out, spend two minutes thinking of as many non-conventional uses for a paper clip as possible. Then do the same for a brick. A psychologist would give you a total score for the number of uses you came up with, as well as scores for the originality and usefulness of your ideas. There's also the "Remote Associates Test". For example, which one word can form a compound word or two-word phrase with: a) widow; b) bite; c) monkey? Or another one – which word goes with: a) blood; b) music; c) cheese?

Five tips for boosting your creativity

Do the groundwork There's an unfortunate cultural myth that says only a select few people are capable of creativity; that new and brilliant ideas simply flow from their minds. The truth is that creativity takes hard work and exhaustive preparation. If you want to innovate in a given field, you must first master all that has gone before. But don't become too narrowly focused: keep an open mind and stay curious. Most important of all, don't forget to capture your ideas. Many wonderful insights are lost because people mistakenly assume they'll remember an idea.

Spend time living abroad Anecdotal evidence abounds, but it was only in 2009 that William Maddux and Adam Galinsky provided scientific evidence that a lengthy foreign sojourn really can set the creative juices flowing. They found that students who'd spent more time abroad were more likely to solve Duncker's candle problem (see p.199) and more likely to succeed in an awkward negotiation task that required a creative solution. They also found that students primed to think about a time they'd lived abroad tended to be better at the Remote Associates Test (see above).

Paint your walls blue People sat in front of a blue, rather than a red, computer screen have been shown to generate better quality and more creative ideas for things to do with a brick. In the same 2009 study, Ravi Mehta and Rui (Juliet) Zhu at the University of British

(Answers at the bottom of p.201.) Another popular measure of creativity is Karl Dunker's Candle Problem. Imagine you have a box of tacks, a candle and some matches. Your task is to fix the candle to the wall in such a way that it doesn't drip wax on the floor. The solution is to use the tacks to pin the tack box to the wall and then use it as a candleholder.

Psychologists usually break creativity down into three component parts. First there's the research stage: even the most creative geniuses need to do the groundwork. In fact, people often underestimate the importance of getting to know a problem inside out from every conceivable angle. Creativity often depends on bringing established ideas together in novel ways, so the more raw material you have to work with, the more likely you are to come up with a novel and useful idea. Second is the incubation period, which has been the subject of some intriguing psychological research suggesting that there really is some truth to the old adage about sleeping on a problem. Finally, there's the Aha! or eureka moment, as when Archimedes allegedly leapt out of the bath as he realized that the height of the water provided an index of volume.

Columbia also found that participants created more novel and original toys when given blue (rather than red) parts to make them with.

Wiggle your eyes back and forth Psychologists at Stockton College asked participants to invent new uses for everyday objects, including bricks and newspapers, before and after performing horizontal eye-exercises for thirty seconds. After wiggling their eyes, the strongly right-handed and left-handed – but not the ambidextrous – participants came up with more original ideas and more categories of use than a control group who didn't perform the eye exercise. It's thought that the wiggling helps to improve communication between the hemispheres. The same exercise also boosts memory (see p.88).

Stop thinking so hard Distract yourself and you'll give your non-conscious mind the chance to grapple with the problem at hand. Ap Dijksterhuis and Teun Meurs showed this in a 2006 study in which they asked 87 students to think of as many new names for pasta as they could, after giving them a head start with five examples of existing names that all began with the letter *i*. Those students who first engaged in a distracter task for three minutes before giving their suggestions thought of far more varied names than students who spent the same time simply thinking of new names (the latter group mostly thought of new names beginning with *i*).

It's the final eureka stage that leads us to forget all the hard work and thought that's gone before it, and it's the stage that usually enters popular folklore. Kary Mullis, who won the Nobel Prize for his discovery of the polymerase chain-reaction, a technique that led to DNA fingerprinting and other biomedical breakthroughs, said the idea came to him in a flash when driving home one day. Similarly, Michael Jackson, one of the hardest workers in the entertainment industry, described how his hit song "Billie Jean", and others like it, landed in his lap as if a gift from God. He even joked that if he hadn't acted as the receptacle for the ideas, God would have give them to someone else like Prince.

Several studies suggest that insight is achieved largely via the brain's right hemisphere, which is characterized by more diffuse, but weaker, activation than the left hemisphere. For example, research shows that if you present a person with the solution to a problem that they couldn't solve, they're quicker at reading it with their right hemisphere. This can be tested by presenting the solution to just one side of the person's brain at a time, by making it visible on just one side of space (the left side of space is processed by the right hemisphere and vice versa). The quicker reading by the right hemisphere suggests that it was nearer to finding the solution. Brain-imaging results back this up. Scans of brains that have solved a problem via insight, rather than piecemeal, show more activity in the front part of the right upper-temporal lobe (the superior temporal sulcus).

Expertise and giftedness

Related to creativity is the notion of genius or remarkable talent. Whether we're talking about the musical wonder of Mozart and Beethoven or the sporting prowess of David Beckham and Michael Jordan, there's a deep-rooted belief that genius is founded on innate talent. However, years of research, much of it by the Florida-based psychologist Anders Ericsson, has exploded this myth. Having the appropriate genetic endowments helps up to a point, but when it comes to truly exceptional talent, the secret lies in practice – lots of it and of the right type.

In a 1993 paper, Ericsson investigated the practice habits and history of violinists, including several from the Berlin Philharmonic Orchestra and the Radio Symphony Orchestra, and pianists from the Music Academy of Berlin. His key finding was that the most accomplished musicians had totalled around ten thousand hours of practice by the age of twenty, whereas the lesser accomplished had totalled only five

The "King of Pop", Michael Jackson was just five years old when he became lead singer of the Jackson Five. A renowned vocalist, dancer, song-writer and producer, he became the best-selling male pop artist of all time. At the time of his death in 2009, Jackson was preparing for an unprecedented run of fifty London shows, tickets for which sold faster than for any concert in history.

thousand. Serious amateurs, by contrast, clocked in at just two thousand hours. More recently, in 2008, Joanne Ruthsatz at Oberlin College assessed the IQ, musical ability and practice habits of 178 high-school band members and 83 elite conservatory students. Among the high-school band members, musical achievement was associated with a mixture of past practice, IQ and musical aptitude (in terms of tone and rhythm perception skills). All three of these factors were higher among the conservatory students, as you'd expert, but crucially, differences in musical achievement among these elite musicians was associated only with past practice-habits. Among elite performers, in other words it is more practice that makes all the difference to success.

It's important to note that not just any practice will do. Rather, Ericsson refers to "deliberate practice" being key. According to David Shenk, author of *The Genius in All of Us*, this "requires the mindset of never being satisfied with your current ability ... a constant self-critique, a pathological restlessness, a passion to aim just beyond your capability so that you actually long for daily disappointment and failure. Most importantly, it demands a never-ending resolve to dust yourself off and try again."

Answers to the questions on p.198: 1) Spider; 2) Blue.

13 Gender and species differences

If you're at a dull dinner party and you want to spice things up, the topic of gender usually works a treat. Which sex is more intelligent? Do women really talk more than men? Thanks to the popularity of books like John Gray's *Men Are from Mars, Women Are from Venus* it's easy to forget that we're even members of the same species. Yet human we all are. Women and men alike feel emotion, need sleep, enjoy sex, form friendships and appreciate art. On the other hand, there are also real differences between the sexes, rooted in biology and manifested psychologically. Another topic that seems to endlessly fascinate is animal intelligence and the question of what, if anything, makes humans unique. Chimps aren't likely to win a Nobel prize anytime soon, but the dividing lines between animal and human cognition are not as pronounced as they once seemed.

Where gender difference begins

It's the all-important Y-chromosome that sets the foetus on the path to masculinity. Testes develop, testosterone is released, and as a consequence, men tend to be more aggressive and to take more risks. They have a greater fondness for casual sex and pornography. Despite the "man flu" jibes, they're also more tolerant of pain and more willing to fight physically for their status and reputation. Women, by contrast, tend to have more empathy and to have more intimate friendships. They're also about twice as prone to depression.

In terms of the brain, the differences are subtle, but they do exist. Men generally have bigger brains (by eight to ten percent) and more white matter, which is the insulated, connective type of neural tissue. Women's brains tend to be less lopsided, in the sense that functions are shared more equally between the hemispheres. They also have more grey matter – those areas made up of densely packed cell bodies – and more connectivity between the hemispheres. One

brain structure that shows particularly striking differences between the sexes is the hippocampus, which is larger, relative to overall brain size, in females.

It's imortant to note that not all studies uncover these results, and random variation between individuals will often overshadow any averaged gender differences. Also, as Cordelia Fine warns in her 2010 book *Delusions of Gender*, we should be cautious when making inferences about sex differences in behaviour and cognition based on observed sex differences in brain structure and function. The links between brain activity and mental processes are far from straightforward and different brains can use different neural means to reach the same mental ends.

That said, the genders do seem to differ in specific abilities. Although men and women don't differ in overall intelligence, women are generally better at reading facial expressions and superior at certain language tasks such as spelling and verbal memory. On the other hand, men consistently outperform women on tests of spatial prowess, such as mental rotation and map work. Bear in mind, though, that as Fine argues in her book these differences may well be exaggerated by men's and women's culturally learned expectations of how they ought to perform, given their sex. Indeed, a 2006 study by Angelica Moè and Francesca Pazzaglia at the University of Padua found that gender differences in mental rotation ability disappeared when male and female high-school students were fed the lie that women are generally considered superior at spatial tasks (see also p.218).

Another consistent finding in gender research is that the range of male ability tends to be more spread-out and extreme. That is, many more men than women tend to display either extremely poor or extremely strong ability in a subject. Female performance, by contrast, tends to clump much more around the average. Consistent with this, conditions like autism and ADHD are far more common in boys and men (in fact, a popular theory is that autism is the manifestation of a having an extreme male brain; see p.318).

Innate or culturally determined?

Gender feminists have argued that, rather than being innate, the behavioural differences we see between boys and girls are the result of socialization. By this account, boys like fighting and guns, and girls like chatting and dolls, because they were brought up in a culture that impressed those choices and dispositions upon them. This view, while popular, doesn't stand up to much objective scrutiny.

Consider a 2008 study by Kim Wallen and co-workers at Emory University in Atlanta. Because it's tricky to separate out biological and cultural effects with human children, these researchers looked at gender-related toy preferences in our close relative, the macaque monkey, in whom cultural influences on play are absent. Like human boys, male macaques were fussier than their female counterparts, tending to play much more with wheeled toys (taken to be masculine) than cuddly toys (feminine), given the choice of both. The female macaques, by contrast, didn't show a preference between the two, with the consequence that they played with the cuddly toys more and the wheeled toys less than the males did. The findings don't rule out the role of societal influences on children's toy preferences, but they provide strong evidence for the part played by biology.

Perhaps the most powerful evidence against the idea that gender identity is purely learned is a 2004 paper by William Reiner and John Gearhart at John Hopkins University, in which they assessed sixteen boys from the age of five to sixteen years who had been born with their penis missing – a rare condition known as cloacal exstrophy. Fourteen of these boys were raised from birth as if they were girls, even to the extent of having further sex-change surgery. Despite this, eight of these fourteen declared themselves male during the course of the study, and all sixteen participants were judged to have moderate to strong interests typical of males.

Related to this is the story of David Reimer, a Canadian man whose penis was destroyed in a botched circumcision operation when he was eight months old. Reimer was brought up as a girl and renamed Brenda,

Do women talk more than men?

What about the popular belief that women talk much more than men? Triumphant headlines in 2006 declared this to be scientific fact. "Women talk three times as much as men, says study" was how the British *Daily Mail* put it. The source of this claim turned out to be the just-released book *The Female Brain* by neuropsychiatrist Louann Brizendine. Women average twenty thousand words per day, the book claimed, whereas men manage an average of only seven thousand. Thanks to the investigations of *Boston Globe* journalist Mark Liberman, it's since been revealed that Brizendine borrowed these figures from a self-help book, not from a proper scientific study. Such a study was, however, published in the prestigious journal *Science* in 2007. Matthias Mehl at the University of Arizona asked hundreds of participants to wear a recording device that captured thirty-second snippets of their daily speech every twelve and a half minutes. Extrapolating from several days' worth of these snippets, Mehl's team estimated that men and women alike averaged around 1600 words per day. In North America at least, it seems the idea that women are more verbose than men is little more than a myth.

after his parents took the advice of a psychologist, John Money, who believed that gender identity results from the way a child is raised. To help with the reassignment, Reimer's testicles were removed and he was given female hormones. Money originally claimed the outcome was a success, but the truth, as revealed by Reimer in a book by John Colapinto

As Nature Made Him: The Boy Who Was Raised as a Girl, was that he never took to being a girl. Reimer resumed his male identity at age fourteen and later underwent surgery to restore his maleness, as far as this was possible. He married and became a stepfather to three children. Sadly, Reimer committed suicide in 2004 – his wife had recently left him and his brother had died from a drugs overdose in 2002.

GENDER BIAS

Another area that's seen a great deal of controversy in recent years is the under-representation of women in science and maths. A media storm kicked off in 2005 when the then Harvard President Lawrence Summers suggested that one reason why women are a rare sight in science and engineering is because of innate biological differences between the sexes. As we've seen, it is certainly true that outstanding ability in maths is more common among males than females. However, the size of this difference is not enough to explain the massive gender disparity in science and engineering.

An alternative explanation was provided in 2009 by the psychologist Stephen Ceci and his colleagues at Cornell University, after they reviewed more than four hundred journal articles and book chapters on the topic. They found that it was women's decisions to have children and their related career-choices that was the strongest factor. For example, the researchers found that women with strong maths skills were less likely than their male peers to choose to go into science, perhaps because, unlike most men, they also tended to have superior verbal skills. This inclined many of them towards careers in law and medicine, which are often more accommodating with regard to starting a family.

A related study, also published in 2009, used an Internet quiz to test the implicit gender beliefs of more than half a million people across 34 countries. Brian Nosek and his team compared these results with actual science performance scores achieved by twelve-year-olds in these same countries. The researchers' finding was that the two correlated: those countries with old-fashioned gender stereotypes tended to be the same countries where girls underperformed in science. The study can't show which way the causal direction flows, but given that other research has shown that stereotypes can harm people's performance, it looks as though traditional ideas about gender roles could be holding back female success in science.

Another gender bias that affects women's careers is known as the **glass cliff**. This is the tendency for women to be chosen to lead organizations that are in a crisis. Recent examples include Lynn Elsenhans's appointment as CEO of the oil company Sunoco in 2008, after their shares had plummeted in value; and Jóhanna Sigurðardóttir's election as prime minister of Iceland, soon after her country's economy had been devastated by the global financial crisis. These real-life examples are backed up by laboratory studies in which participants have been shown to favour female candidates when choosing a leader for fictional organizations described as being in a crisis. The glass cliff is bad news for women because, in general, leaders of organizations that are struggling are less likely to enjoy career success in the future.

A 2010 study by Susanne Bruckmüller and Nyla Branscombe at the Universities of Erlangen-Nuremberg and Kansas, suggested that the glass cliff is related to gender stereotypes and stereotypical beliefs about what kind of leader is needed in a crisis. Using fictional company scenarios and fictional leadership candidates, the pair showed that in a crisis situation, male candidates were less likely to be perceived as having female attributes, such as strong communication skills and empathy, and were consequently judged as less well-equipped to lead. Almost by default, therefore, female candidates ended up being preferred in a crisis. The researchers highlighted the double irony of their finding, writing: "When women get to enjoy the spoils of leadership, (a) it is not because they are seen to deserve them, but because men no longer do, and (b) this only occurs when, and because, there are fewer spoils to enjoy."

A man walked into a bar...

Men and women have their differences, but apparently their sense of humour isn't one of them. Both sexes laugh as much as each other and they laugh at the same things. In a 1999 paper, Rod Martin and Nicholas Kuiper asked eighty men and women to keep a diary record of their laughter for three days. There was huge individual variation – one person reported laughing 89 times in one day! – but men and women didn't differ in how much they laughed. More recently, Eiman Azim at Stanford University scanned the brains of ten men and ten women as they rated the funniness of seventy cartoons. Intriguingly, although there were no sex differences in the type of cartoons deemed to be funny, or in the amount of amusement they caused, there were differences in underlying brain activity. Women seemed to take longer to decide whether a joke was funny, and they showed greater activity in reward-related brain areas, suggesting that, compared with men, they were more surprised when a cartoon made them chuckle.

Comparing Species

Whether it's "Dog dials 999 to rescue owner" or "Monkey solves crossword!", barely a week goes by without the papers reporting on some feat of animal intelligence. Comparisons with human intellect usually ensue, a traditional pastime that dates back to Aristotle and probably beyond. For centuries, those seeking to highlight the ways that humans differ from animals used to be spoilt for choice. Language, culture, emotions, tool use … the list went on. Over the last few decades, however, each of these prized bastions of human uniqueness has been washed away like so many sand castles lost to the tide. Crows use tools, monkeys scream alarm calls, and elephants mourn their dead.

Time and again, experts have attempted to draw new dividing-lines. So when apes were taught to communicate with signs, or macaques were heard issuing alarm calls, the boundary was moved. Okay, animals can communicate with sounds and gestures, so the argument went, but it still remains beyond any animal to put different calls together to form new meanings – only humans can do that. But then, late in 2009, scientists observed monkeys in the Ivory Coast stringing different calls together in rule-based fashion, creating new meanings (see p.157). This pattern of shifting the boundaries and then new discoveries being made is one that keeps being repeated across different forms of behaviour and mental functioning.

Take another key skill once considered the preserve of humans – **deception**. There have now been many examples of chimps and other animals taking another individual's perspective into account and using that information so as to further their own aims. Brian Hare and his colleagues showed this in 2006 when they set up a situation in which chimps competed with a human researcher for food. The chimps soon learned to sneak up to the food using a route that was hidden from the human's view.

What about a sense of justice and morality? In fact, animals seem to have these too. There's a classic study from the 1960s by Stanley Wechlin at the Northwestern University Medical School in Illinois, in which he and his team observed hungry macaque monkeys refusing to take food if taking it meant another monkey would get an electric shock. Even your pet dog has a sense of **justice**, albeit a selfish one. Late in 2008, Friederike Range at the University of Vienna tested dogs on a task in which they had to offer their paw as if shaking hands. Crucially, when the dogs were tested in pairs and only one dog was rewarded with treats, the unrewarded dog stopped playing along. In fact, the dog that was treated unfairly shook paws fewer times than when both dogs had performed the task together without any treats. In other words, dogs are happier to perform for no reward than to perform when another dog is getting a reward, but they aren't.

When it comes to animals behaving in what we consider to be a human-like fashion, surely the example to trump them all is a study from Georgia State University in Atlanta. Here in 2007 Michael Beran and his colleagues set up some apparatus in which a jar continued filling with sweets until a chimp grabbed and took it. You'd think the chimps would lack the restraint to wait very long before making a greedy lunge. This was certainly the case when there was no distraction. Amazingly, however, when the researchers provided some toys, the chimps played with these and were able to wait for much longer before grabbing the jar, thereby gaining more sweets. It's not that the toys themselves were an irresistible lure. If the jar was put out of reach, the chimps didn't bother playing with the toys nearly as much. It seems they really were using them as a form of **self-distraction.**

Not content with showing that animals are often able to match human mental ability, a recent study went further and provided an example of human intelligence being surpassed. Sana Inoue and Tetsuro Matsuzawa

Boy and chimpanzee studying a leaf together.

The human and animal brain compared

From the outside, it's not immediately obvious what it is about the human brain that marks us out from the rest of the animal kingdom. It certainly isn't sheer size. Whereas a human brain weighs in at about 1.4kg, an elephant brain is over 4kg, whilst the typical sperm whale boasts a brain of 8 to 9 kilos! What about brain size relative to body size? This measure paints humans in a more favourable light – we have one of the biggest brains in the animal kingdom for our body weight. But still, using this measure, we're beaten by little animals like squirrels. Another index is known as the encephalisation quotient, which looks at expected brain-weight for a species given the taxonomic class it is in, such as mammal, bird or reptile. By this measure, humans do really well, having a brain about eight times heavier than you'd expect for a mammal of our size.

Another distinguishing feature of the human brain that's often mentioned is the size of the cerebral cortex. While it's true that this structure is particularly large in humans, it's the organization of the brain and the way it's wired up that's more important. Humans have more tissue devoted to so-called association cortices than any other species. These are regions that aren't dedicated to any one particular function, but rather to higher-order integration. The human brain is also more densely packed with brain cells than any other species, with the result that we have even more neurons than the enormous whale brain. Finally, the myelin insulation that surrounds some neurons is thicker in human nervous systems than in other animals, improving the efficiency of inter-neural communication.

created a test of **eidetic** or "photographic" memory. Human participants and two chimps watched a computer screen on which numerals were quickly replaced by blank squares, with their task being to touch the squares in the correct numerical order. The humans beat the older of the chimps for accuracy, and both they and she showed a tendency to become less accurate as the presentation time of the numerals was decreased. However, the younger chimp, Ayumu, was more accurate than the humans, and his performance didn't deteriorate with reduced presentation-time.

All these demonstrations of surprising feats by animals is all well and good, but it remains the case that capuchin monkeys don't author books, and building cities and cathedrals is beyond even the brainiest bottle-nosed dolphins. The dividing lines may be fuzzier than they once were, but the human ability to produce sophisticated inventions – from written language to the Internet – still puts mankind in a league of its own. What is it, then, that's allowed the human mind to scale new heights of achievement and culture? The Harvard University psychologist Marc Hauser believes he has pinned down the four key ingredients.

According to Hauser, only humans are capable of **generative computation**, which is the ability to combine elements, be they words, musical notes or math symbols, to form new meanings (although perhaps the Ivory Coast monkeys have demonstrated this ability). Related to this is recursion – the repeated application of a rule that allows us to embed meanings in other meanings, potentially ad infinitum. Also said to be uniquely human is what Hauser calls the **promiscuous combination of ideas**. This is our ability to see and make links between ideas from disparate realms such as law, music and morality. The third key factor

Hauser investigated

The field of animal cognition was rocked in 2010 when Harvard University announced that Marc Hauser had been found guilty of scientific misconduct and would be on leave until the autumn of 2011. Hauser had established an impressive reputation for demonstrating cognitive feats in monkeys that other experts had previously thought unique to humans and great apes. With the retraction of two scientific papers and concerns about three others, the research community were left wondering which findings from the Hauser lab could be trusted and which couldn't. Frans de Waal, a renowned primatologist at Emory University, Atlanta, told *Scientific American*: "It is disastrous. This is a very small field – if one prominent person is under suspicion, then everyone comes a little bit under suspicion." The *Chronicle of Higher Education* managed to obtain the letter, written by a lab assistant, which had triggered the investigation of Hauser's research. This revealed that suspicions were first aroused during the coding of videos of Cottontop Tamarin monkeys. Hauser's coding suggested that the monkeys spent more time looking at a speaker when the pattern of sounds it was playing changed (this pattern recognition could be an important precursor to language). But when the research assistant and another colleague played back the video, they saw something completely different – the monkeys were actually looking the other way. Commentators were divided on whether Hauser was guilty of deliberate fabrication, or if instead he had simply seen what he hoped to see (investigations by Federal funding bodies were still underway in September 2010). Either way, the affair exposed how tricky research on animal behaviour can be, and how important it is that strict measures and crosschecking are in place to ensure that scientists' expectations don't contaminate results.

is **mental symbols**, allowing us to represent events, real or imagined, through art and language. Finally, Hauser points to our unique capacity for **abstract thought**, granting us the ability to ponder the existence of an afterlife, gods and concepts like justice. Whether these four distinguishing features of human thought will remain in place after another decade of animal research remains to be seen.

Reports of animal feats never cease to fascinate people, especially newspaper editors. However, there is a more serious side to showing what animals are capable of and understanding what makes humans unique. Comparative psychologists believe that identifying areas where our abilities overlap with those of other animals, and those where our abilities have diverged, can help us to understand the evolution of mental mechanisms. Consider the demonstration by Daniel Weiss at Pennsylvania State University, which showed that, like humans but unlike some other primates, Tamarin monkeys form an anticipatory thumb-down grip shape when reaching for an upside-down glass. Because Tamarins don't use tools in the wild, this finding contributes to the hypothesis that anticipatory motor planning is a necessary but not a sufficient skill for the development of primate tool-use. Studies like this help to reveal the evolutionary roots of our mental abilities, and from there we can begin to uncover how genes came to build the brains that made us human.

Part IV

All of us

14 Prejudice and racism

Humans have a powerful instinct for forming into tight-knit groups, be they tribes, sports clubs, countries or political parties. This makes sense – we can achieve more together than alone, and no doubt those of our ancestors who were motivated to form such groups were more successful and more likely to procreate than those who operated individually. Moreover, an inbuilt inclination to in-group loyalty and bias can help foster cooperation and improve group effectiveness. But there is a serious downside to this behaviour. The demon twin of in-group loyalty is out-group prejudice. With such powerful impulses, it's no wonder that human history is pockmarked by deadly wars and skirmishes, with one gang, tribe or country facing off against another.

A classic study from the 1970s by the British psychologist **Henri Tajfel** showed just how arbitrary in-group loyalty can be. Tajfel and his colleagues divided schoolboys from Bristol into two arbitrary groups based on their stated preference for the abstract art of either Klee or Kandinsky. Next, the boys were asked to make a series of decisions with regards to allocating money between pairs of their peers. Crucially, the identity of these peers was hidden except for their group membership. The boys showed some effort at distributing the money fairly, but they couldn't help themselves from consistently allocating more money to other boys who were in their recently created group.

Racial prejudice

One of the banes of modern life and one of the most divisive expressions of **in-group bias** is racism – people making assumptions about another person on the basis of his or her apparent racial background. Plenty of research shows that this tendency to categorize and judge people by outward racial appearance begins from an early age. Four-year-olds recognize other people this way and begin to show increasing bias towards others who look like they do – for example, choosing to play with another child of the same, rather than a different, skin colour to themselves (they also show a preference for other kids of the same sex, similar age and who have a similar accent).

By the age of nine children are already attempting to appear racially colour-blind – a sign, perhaps, that they're aware of the inappropriateness of their underlying biases. Evan Apfelbaum showed this by using a game reminiscent of Guess-Who? Children were presented with photos of forty people who varied according to four key dimensions, and their task was to find out with as few yes/no questions as possible which one of the photos the researcher had in their hand. The nine- to ten-year-olds actually performed worse at the task than the eight- to nine-year-olds, because they avoided asking questions about race.

THE EVOLUTIONARY ORIGINS OF RACISM

It would have been highly unusual for our distant ancestors to encounter a person of a markedly different skin-colour. However, it would probably have been useful for them to use visual cues – clothing perhaps, or symbols – to identify quickly whether another person was from the same or a different group. No doubt the salience we give to racial appearance today is an unfortunate extension of this once-useful habit. However, as well as being morally dubious, it is clearly a mistake for us to continue to do this. Modern research shows that a person's racial background is an unreliable indicator of their underlying traits – there's far more genetic variation between members of the same racial group than there is between members of different racial groups.

Underlying our unfortunate tendency for out-group prejudice is the emotion of disgust, which probably first evolved as a way to protect us from contact with potentially toxic substances such as faeces and rotten meat. The biologist Marc Hauser thinks that evolution may have co-opted this emotion and applied it to social behaviour. In the same way that disgust helps keep outside of us those things that are best not ingested, it may similarly motivate us to avoid contact with outsiders – people who are not members of our tribe.

Why should we have evolved a tendency to reject outsiders in this way? One theory gaining popularity is that we have a **behavioural immune-system.** This refers to behaviours that have evolved as a way of avoiding contact with parasites. It's likely that our ancestors used an outsider's

Was the election of Barack Obama bad for racial equality?

The US may have inaugurated its first black president in 2009, but the country's racial inequalities – in terms of education, health, incarceration and wealth – remain rife. What's more, findings published in 2009 suggested that the mere fact that a black man was a candidate, and subsequently got elected, may ironically have been a bad thing for racial equality, at least in the short term.

In 2008, Daniel Effron of Stanford University asked a group of predominantly white students which candidate they planned to vote for in what was then the upcoming presidential election. He also presented them with a range of hypothetical scenarios, such as making decisions about hiring, that would reveal their racial bias. Some students stated their voting intentions first and dealt with the hypothetical scenarios second; other students did things the other way around. The awkward finding was that students who declared their intention to vote for Obama and then answered the fictional scenarios subsequently showed more favouritism towards white people than the students who made the hypothetical decisions first. Effron thought there was a possibility that having the opportunity to vote for Obama had led some people to feel it gave them licence to be prejudiced in other decisions.

Another study at the University of Washington raised similar concerns. Cheryl Kaiser compared the support of a group of predominantly white students for anti-racist social policies ten days prior to, and one week after, Obama's election. She found that support for anti-racist social policies – for example, encouraging diversity in business – was lower after Obama's election compared with before. The fear, she said, is that Obama's success led people to believe that combating racial prejudice was no longer as important an issue.

unusual appearance as a crude cue for the risk that that person was carrying a parasitic infection. Somewhat alarmingly, there's evidence that these instincts still influence us today. Jason Faulkner at the University of British Columbia found that participants expressed more xenophobic attitudes after they were reminded of the ease with which bacteria and

Stereotype threat

The mere knowledge that other people expect certain things of you because of your age, race, gender or other categorization is enough to have a detrimental effect on your behaviour, especially if you fear that your underperformance will be used to bolster a stereotype. Psychologists call this effect "stereotype threat" and it can occur even in the absence of any overt prejudice or mistreatment. Women, for example, have been shown to struggle with a maths task in the company of men, but not a verbal task, presumably because the pressure not to conform to negative stereotypes about female mathematical ability has a detrimental effect on their performance. Similarly, black students have been found to perform better at school tests administered by a black examiner than

by a white examiner. In 2007, Armand Chatard, now at the University of Geneva, showed that stereotypes can even affect our memories. Female high-school students primed with a highly salient reminder of gender stereotypes, including statements like "men are gifted in mathematics" and "women are gifted in the arts", subsequently underestimated maths grades they'd achieved when they were younger. Armand said this could have real-life consequences. For example, women might be reluctant to pursue science careers if gender stereotypes have led them to downplay their past achievements.

King Carl Gustaf XVI presents the 2009 Nobel prize for Economics to US economist Elinor Ostrom – the first woman to win the award, and one of five female prizewinners that year. In the 108-year history of Nobel prizes, however, only 41 have been awarded to women, compared with 778 awarded to men.

germs are transmitted. Similarly, Carlos Navarrete at Harvard University surveyed pregnant women and found that those in the first trimester of pregnancy, when risk of infection is highest, expressed more in-group bias and out-group prejudice than women in the second and third trimesters.

Fear of contamination may explain our motivation for out-group prejudice, but the ease with which we are willing to act on this prejudice appears to be related to our ability to dehumanize outsiders. This was demonstrated graphically in 2006 when the Princeton University researchers Lasana Harris and Susan Fiske scanned the brains of students as they looked at pictures of people from different social groups. When the students looked at sporting heroes, the elderly and businessmen, activity was triggered in the medial prefrontal cortex, a region of the brain known to be associated with thinking about people. By contrast, when the students looked at pictures of the homeless or drug addicts, activity in the prefrontal cortex was missing (just as it was when the students looked at pictures of objects). Rather disturbingly, activity was instead observed in brain regions related to disgust.

Beating racism and prejudice

The most powerful antidote to out-group prejudice, according to several decades of research in social psychology, is meaningful, positive contact with out-group members – an idea that psychologists call **contact theory**. Research in Bradford in the UK, for example, has shown that young white adults with more Asian friends tend to have more positive attitudes towards Asians in general, see them more as individuals, and are more trusting of them as a group. Similar findings have been reported around the world, from Northern Ireland to India. According to the Oxford University social psychologist Miles Hewstone, the benefits of such contacts are that they reduce the "discomfort of strangers" and diminish anxiety. When a person has a friend from an out-group, they share intimacies. This "self-disclosure" helps them identify with each other as real people experiencing the vicissitudes of human life. If prejudice is facilitated by people seeing outsiders as somehow less than human, then contact, it seems, has the opposite effect – humanizing members of other social groups.

One obvious criticism that's been levelled at contact theory is that the causal direction could quite plausibly run in the other direction. People with more positive and tolerant attitudes towards members of other social groups are surely more likely to have friends from those groups. While this is true, longitudinal research has been conducted showing that inter-group contact really does have a beneficial effect on people's attitudes. To take one example, Jens Binder at the University of Manchester surveyed hundreds of school students in England, Germany and Belgium, and found that kids who were members of the majority ethnic group, and who had more contact with ethnic-minority students, exhibited reduced prejudice towards that group when re-tested six months later.

What's particularly promising about research in this area is that so-called "extended" social contact also appears to help reduce prejudice. That is, having a friend who has a friend from another social group can dissolve prejudice. In fact, a 2009 study by Rhiannon Turner and Richard Crisp showed that merely imagining having positive contact with out-group members could have a beneficial effect. Turner and Crisp asked one group of students to think about Muslims for two minutes while another group spent the same amount of time imagining a positive encounter with a Muslim person. Afterwards, the latter group exhibited reduced prejudice towards Muslims as measured using both explicit tests and implicit tests (see box below).

The Implicit Association Test

When psychologists conduct research into prejudice they soon encounter an awkward problem. Participants will often conceal their true feelings so as to give the appearance of being more tolerant than they really are. They may even hide their true feelings from themselves. One way researchers overcome this problem is using so-called "implicit measures". Perhaps the best-known is the Implicit Association Test. This is a computer-based task based on the premise that a person will find it easier to use the same computer key to respond to two categories which they subconsciously associate. So, for example, the logic of the test predicts that an Islamophobe will be quicker when the same key is used to respond to Muslim names and negative words than when the same key is used to respond to Muslim names and positive words. The standard format for these tests is to have four categories, two allocated to one key and two allocated to another, for example: one key for Muslim names/ negative words; another key for Western names/positive words, and then the reverse, Muslim with positive, Western with negative. There are plenty of examples online for you to try out yourself, for example at implicit.harvard.edu/implicit.

PERCEPTUAL BIAS

Besides contact theory, psychologists have also been pursuing less obvious anti-prejudice interventions. One such approach has targeted the well-established finding that people are better at distinguishing between faces belonging to people of their own racial background. This is the polite way of describing the "they all look the same" experience, whereby members of other racial groups seem to look more similar to each other than to members of our own racial group. Sophie Lebrecht at Brown University reasoned that this perceptual bias could fuel prejudice. She and her colleagues trained a group of white students to better distinguish between African-American faces while a control group spent the same amount of time just looking at African-American faces. Afterwards the trained group showed reduced prejudice towards African Americans relative to the control group. This makes intuitive sense – presumably learning to see the visible differences between people of another race makes it harder to lump them altogether from a social and cultural perspective.

For people trying too hard to conceal their racist tendencies, be they real or imagined, it's worth bearing in mind that attempting to appear

The Implicit Association Test is a favourite toy of researchers and lots of studies show that it predicts people's actual behaviour and their explicit attitudes. But the test is not without its critics. For example, it's possible that people might associate two categories more easily, not because of their implicit attitudes, but simply because those two categories are frequently paired together in the media. To return to our earlier example, just think of all the news coverage given to Islamic fundamentalism. Supporting this concern, in 2006 Anna Han at Ohio State University showed that participants' implicit attitudes towards two Japanese Pokémon toys was easily influenced by a brief video featuring a child saying that she preferred the toy which, based on information presented earlier, was clearly inferior. Another criticism is that participants' responses in the test are not entirely the product of their subconscious attitudes, and that they are exercising some sort of control over them. For example, another 2006 study, this time by researchers at Iowa State University, found that heterosexual students showed less homophobia on the Implicit Association Test when they thought the results would be made public than when they thought the results would be kept private.

"colour-blind" can backfire. This was demonstrated by Michael Norton at Harvard Business School by having white participants play an identification game (similar to the one used by Evan Apfelbaum with children) with black participants. The participants had before them 32 photos of people: half were male, half were female; half were old, half were young; half were black, half were white and so on. On each turn, the participants had to identify which one of these 32 people their playing partner was currently looking at, by asking as few "yes/no" questions as possible. Crucially, those white participants who avoided using race as an identifying factor not only performed less well at the task, they also made less eye-contact with their partner and were perceived to be less friendly by a pair of judges who watched a recording of their behaviour.

COMBATING HOMOPHOBIA

Most psychology research into prejudice has been focused on racism, but of course, members of any social grouping can be victimized in this way, and one of the most inventive anti-prejudice interventions by a psychologist relates to homophobia. At Brock University in Canada, Gordon Hodson asked heterosexual students to imagine landing on a planet that's populated by aliens who look exactly like humans, but who don't allow any public displays of affection, live in same-sex housing and reproduce by artificial insemination. The idea was that this would provoke heterosexual students into imagining what it's like to be homosexual, without realizing that's what they were doing – thereby overcoming any resistance they might have had to this prospect.

The participants also answered questions about how they would cope with life on the planet and maintain their lifestyles. They also shared plans for how to behave romantically in secret and how to identify other humans. Afterwards, this alien intervention group were more able to take the perspective of homosexuals than were control participants who had attended standard anti-homophobia lectures, and this in turn was associated with more empathy towards people who are homosexual, a greater tendency to think of homosexuals and heterosexuals as all belonging to the same category (that of being human), and ultimately to more positive attitudes towards people who are gay. Promisingly, these advantages – compared with the control group – were still evident a week later.

15 Beliefs and morals

Throughout history, people have been united and divided by their beliefs and moral codes. To those of religious faith, God or gods dictate what is right and wrong, provide guidance on how to live and bring comfort in the face of the inevitability of death. Psychological research, in contrast, is showing the biological basis and evolutionary roots underlying morality, existential stoicism, altruism and even the emergence of religion itself. Traditionalists fear that these avenues of research implicitly endorse a moral relativism which risks undermining our very humanity. But as Steven Pinker has argued, "far from debunking morality ... [this research] ... can advance it, by allowing us to see through the illusions that evolution and culture have saddled us with and to focus on goals we can share and defend".

Religion

Across the world and through the ages, human cultures everywhere have developed religions. This gives the impression that religious belief and ceremony, like language and music, is an essential part of human nature. The explanations for why this should be fall largely into two camps. There are those who believe that religion evolved as an adaptation that encouraged group cohesion and cooperation. According to this view, the loyalty and organization of religious cultures would have given them the edge over godless rivals. The other explanation sees religion not as an evolutionary adaptation per se, but rather as a side-effect of the way the human mind has evolved for other, especially social, purposes. By this reckoning, cognitive adaptations – such as being able to think about the beliefs and intentions of a person who isn't physically present – predisposed the human mind to religiosity.

Supporting the first view of religion (as an adaptation that fostered group loyalty) are studies such as the one conducted by Joseph Bulbulia

The religious process. Russian Orthodox monks lead a crowd of pilgrims at Solovetsky Monastery.

and Andrew Mahoney at the Victoria University of Wellington in 2008. The researchers invited Christians in New Zealand to play a financial game with anonymous Christians in Canada (unbeknown to them, a computer actually controlled the Canadian responses). The performance of these New Zealand Christians was compared against the performance of New Zealand citizens in Wellington, who thought they were playing with anonymous New Zealand citizens in Auckland (again, these players were fictional and a computer controlled their actions). Bulbulia and Mahoney's key finding was that the New Zealand Christians were far more generous toward their anonymous fellow Christians in Canada than were the Wellington citizens towards their Auckland counterparts. This finding and several others like it suggest religious identity can bond people across the world far more powerfully than secular connections do.

Consistent with this account of religion as a social glue are findings showing how belief in an omnipotent deity or deities can foster a sense of always being watched, the hope that one might be rewarded for good behaviour and a fear of punishment for disloyalty. It's easy to see how such an arrangement could benefit discipline and help unite large groups in a common cause.

Advocating the "religion as a side-effect" explanation are psychologists, such as Pascal Boyer at Washington University in St Louis, who have noticed that many of the elements of religion appear to have piggybacked on cognitive abilities that we've developed for other purposes. Consider our ability to make sense of the world by grouping things into distinct categories. We learn early on, for example, that something furry, with four legs and that barks is a dog. Boyer points out that many religious entities tend to exhibit all the key characteristics of the group to which they belong, but with one or more salient violations that render them eminently memorable. The idea of a man with two legs, two arms, who laughs, talks and so on, but who can also walk on water and return to life after death, is difficult to forget.

It's a similar story with regards to our ability to rehearse and plan dialogue with people who aren't physically with us. From this it's but a small step to prayer. Or consider religious ritual. In this case, the same mental machinery that supports our understanding of social cause and effect allows us to appreciate the idea that *who* is carrying out an action (such as a priest) is important for a certain effect (for example a baptism) to be achieved, because only certain people are endowed with religious authority by God. It's these same cognitive processes that enable us to appreciate the rules underlying other more mundane social exchanges – for instance, my pay rise only counts if it is my boss who gives it to me.

Of course, these two ideas – of religion as evolutionary adaptation or as piggy-backing on other cognitive abilities – are not mutually incompatible. The evolution of key social cognitive abilities could have provided a fertile breeding-ground for religious thought and behaviour to emerge, and from there religion could have bestowed survival advantages on certain groups and eventually come to be favoured by natural selection in its own right.

Consistent with both evolutionary accounts are studies showing just how early in life religious-like thought emerges. Jesse Bering at Queens University Belfast, for example, has used puppet shows to test kindergarten children's understanding of death. He's found that while they recognize that biological needs, such as the requirement for food, will cease when a fictional character dies, they also tend to claim that psychological states, such as feeling hunger, will continue. Bering has further found that these beliefs in the persistence of function beyond death actually diminish with age, which appears to run counter to the idea of religious beliefs arising principally through cultural indoctrination, showing instead the natural inclination we have for spirituality. In other research, Deborah Kelemen at the University of Arizona in Tucson, has shown that children aged between six and ten have a natural inclination to see intention behind the way things are made. Mountains are described by children as existing so that people can go climbing; rivers so that boats can come and go on the water. It's easy to see how religious belief could flourish in minds predisposed to see the world in this way.

All this focus on explaining the ubiquity of religion ignores an elephant in the room – atheism. If the human mind is so predisposed toward religion, how come so many people are atheists? A recent British survey, for example, found that 43 percent of respondents reported having no religion. This is actually a little-researched field and psychology doesn't as yet have many answers. Watch this space, however, because academics are hoping to rectify the situation soon. Late in 2008 Lois Lee at the University of Cambridge and Stephen Bullivant at the University of Oxford together set up the Non-religion and Secularity Research Network – an interdisciplinary and international organization – for just this purpose.

Is there a God spot?

Calling it a God spot may be crude, but there's certainly ample evidence that the temporal lobes, located near the ears, are especially implicated in various religious and spiritual states, such as feeling at one with the world. For over a century there have been documented associations between temporal-lobe epilepsy, where the seizure epicentre is located within the temporal-lobes, and powerful feelings of religiosity. There's also the work of Michael Persinger at Laurentian University in Ontario – he claims that his "God helmet", which applies weak electrical stimulation to the temporal lobes, reliably provokes feelings of oneness and a sensed presence in volunteers.

Other researchers, however, say that it's more accurate to think of a "God network" rather than a God spot. Andrew Newberg at the University of Pennsylvania scanned the brains of Tibetan Buddhists and Franciscan nuns, meditating and praying, respectively, and found that feelings of oneness with the world tended to co-occur with attenuated neural activity in the left-orientation area of the parietal lobe – an area that under usual circumstances represents where our body ends and the world begins. Mario Beauregard at the University of Montreal, meanwhile, has scanned the brains of fifteen nuns recalling a time when they had a powerful connection with God. Compared with recollection of an intense social experience, memories of this religious connection were associated with extra activity in a whole swathe of brain regions. These included the insula, involved in representing internal bodily states, as well as the medial orbitofrontal cortex, involved in emotion and reward.

EXISTENTIAL ANGST

One aspect of being human that marks us out from the rest of the animal kingdom is our knowledge that one day our existence will come to an abrupt end. People often assume that religion emerged as a way of coping with this existential awareness, but this is unlikely to be true. While the idea of salvation is associated with some religions, including Christianity and Islam, it is unheard of in many others, including heathen traditions. Also, the idea that religions evolved as a way of providing relief from existential angst is undermined somewhat by their common focus on hell and vengeful spirits.

Psychologists seeking to understand how we cope with the reality of our finite existence have instead focused on the idea that we have an inbuilt psychological immune-system, one that works tirelessly beneath our conscious awareness, tuning our mind to a more positive channel whenever we think about death. This involves finding ways to boost our self-esteem and connect with a cultural worldview that imbues life with meaning. This **Terror-management theory**, as its known, is itself part of an emerging field known as experimental existential psychology. Supporting the terror-management approach, there's research showing that self-esteem helps to relieve existential angst, and also that thoughts of mortality cause us to seek out self-esteem boosting opportunities.

Jeff Greenberg at the University of Arizona, for example, played participants gory film-clips and measured the effect this had on their physiological arousal. He found that participants were less affected by the clips if they'd just had their self-esteem massaged by falsely-inflated positive feedback on an IQ test. Other research has shown that reminding people of their mortality – by having them

Bruce Campbell gets his comeuppance in *Evil Dead II*.

describe what they think will happen to their body when they die – leads them to want to make themselves more attractive (a form of self-esteem boost), for example through planning to get a sun tan. Mortality reminders also cause us to cling more strongly to our own worldview. A study in which US participants were prompted to think about their own deaths found they subsequently showed increased bias in favour of a job candidate who expressed pro-American views in an interview.

Also supporting the terror-management theory was a clever 2007 study by Nathan DeWall and Roy Baumeister in which they asked students to complete word-stems such as "jo_". DeWall and Baumeister found that those students who'd just been asked to think about their own mortality were far more likely to complete the stems to form positive words (such as "joy") than neutral words (like "jog") than were students who'd spent time thinking about a painful visit to the dentist. The researchers said this was another example of how reminders of death trigger an automatic buffer-system that searches for happy thoughts.

The findings from terror-management theory have some curious implications for real life. Think about the actions of terrorists who seek to subdue and coerce civilian populations by spreading fear of death. Ironically, they may end up doing just the opposite. In 2009, Inbal Gurari, who was then based at Washington University in St Louis, told 52 Jewish Israelis about recent terrorist attacks that had taken place in their country, and asked them to indicate how many times over the last six months they'd been near to where those attacks occurred. The idea was to make them think about how close to danger they'd been. Crucially, participants who did this before their self-esteem was measured subsequently showed enhanced self-esteem compared with participants who had their self-esteem measured first, before thinking about the attacks. The findings also match the way populations have been seen to respond in real life after terrorist attacks. Just think back to the days and weeks after 9/11 – the American flag was flown, religious attendance rocketed and government approval-ratings soared.

Morality

Another argument proposed for religion's purpose is that it provides us with morality, a collective understanding of what is right and wrong. As with the idea that religion relieves existential angst, this argument has intuitive appeal, but is likely to be wrong. A growing body of evidence suggests that human morality is to some extent hard-wired. According to

Marc Hauser's increasingly influential account, we humans have a kind of **universal moral grammar**, akin to the universal grammar that underlies our linguistic capabilities (see p.158). Like its language equivalent, the universal moral grammar provides a series of default principles set in stone, with various parameters that can be tweaked one way or the other according to local cultural variation.

Hauser has provided some preliminary evidence for the idea of a universal moral grammar by using a website (moral.wjh. harvard.edu/) to collect the moral judgements of thousands of people across the world. In a 2009 paper, Hauser and his colleague Ilkka Pyysiäinen at the Helsinki Collegium for Advanced Studies, observed that "in dozens of dilemmas, and with thousands of subjects, the pattern of moral judgements delivered by subjects with a religious background do not differ from those who are atheists".

> **"Two things fill the mind with ever new and increasing admiration and awe, the oftener and more steadily we reflect upon them: the starry heavens above me and the moral law within me."**
>
> Immanuel Kant, *Critique of Practical Reason* (1788)

What emerges from these thought experiments conducted on the Internet is that three moral codes appear to be near-universal across cultures: the action principle; the intention principle; and the contact principle (see box on p.231). The **action principle** refers to the idea that harm caused by deliberate action is morally worse than harm caused by inaction. The **intention principle** refers to whether a person is deliberately harmed for the greater good, or if instead a person is harmed as an unfortunate side-effect of an action that leads to the greater good. Although outcomes are the same in each case, the former, deliberate-harm condition is usually judged as morally worse. Finally, the **contact principle** refers to whether or not physical contact is involved in an action that leads to harm. Harmful actions involving physical contact are usually judged more harshly than actions that don't involve such contact.

A shortcoming of much of the existing research in this area is that the participants have nearly always been from urban, technologically advanced cultures. However, in 2010, Hauser took translations of the usual hypothetical scenarios to the highlands of Chiapas in Mexico to study a rural Mayan community. Like most other surveyed participants, the Mayans regarded deliberate harm caused for the greater good as worse than harm caused as a side-effect for the greater good. However, they didn't think harm caused through inaction less bad than harm caused through action, as most previous participants had done. Hauser and his colleague Linda Abarbanell concluded that the action principle could be an aspect of morality that is culturally determined, and that perhaps other close-knit communities with extensive social obligations between members also see harmful inaction as being just as immoral as harmful action.

These ideas about a moral grammar also chime with the work of the psychologist Jonathan Haidt at the University of Virginia. He conducted studies in which he presented participants with odd stories in which nobody gets hurt, but which nonetheless provoke in participants the sense that something is morally wrong. In one example, a brother and sister decide to try having sex together, taking all the necessary contraception precautions. In another, a family decide to cook and eat their dog after it is killed in a traffic accident. People react with moral disgust to these scenarios and yet they struggle to explain why – a phenomenon that Haidt calls **moral dumbfounding** – thus bolstering the idea that we have an inbuilt moral intuition divorced from reason. This modern view of morality as an intuition or a universal grammar flies in the face of more traditional theories, such as those of the Harvard psychologist Lawrence Kohlberg, in which moral judgement was seen as emerging from rational thought and consideration.

In a further development of his ideas, Haidt proposed that our moral intuitions are grounded on **five foundations**, each of which is calibrated according to our cultural background. These are Harm/care (relating to kindness and nurture); Fairness/reciprocity (issues of equality and treating others as you would wish to be treated); Ingroup/loyalty (patriotism and self-sacrifice), Authority/respect (leadership and tradition); Purity/sanctity (taboos around the body and diet). According to Haidt, the first two are universal, tend to correlate with each other, and are especially valued by liberals. The remaining three also tend to correlate with each other, but are less universal, and tend to be valued more by conservatives. See which dimensions you value most highly at www.yourmorals.org.

Haidt argues that for a successful society there needs to be a balance between the five moral foundations – a blend of the liberal and conservative positions. He recognizes that the danger with his own self-declared liberal position is that it downgrades the Authority, Ingroup and Purity moral dimensions, associating these values with racism and segregation. And yet, it is the order, tradition, and sense of community and belonging (associated with the loyalty, authority, and purity dimensions) which Haidt believes makes people happy. Without these, he says, you risk ending up with a "nation of shoppers who feel empty inside".

Haidt's theory of morality has the potential to help inter-group relations, including America's Culture Wars, by fostering in people greater understanding of other viewpoints. Indeed, different groups will often judge the same issues in the context of a different moral dimension. For example, liberals typically consider immigration issues in terms of fairness/reciprocity, perceiving the conservative position to be racist and immoral. Haidt's theory suggests that it is not necessarily that conservatives are racist but rather that they interpret this issue in terms of the in-group/loyalty moral dimension, which is prioritized in their cultural

Trolleyology

To investigate people's moral judgements, psychologists use fictional scenarios, often involving a runaway trolley, a convention which they've borrowed from the philosophers Philippa Foot and Judith Jarvis Thomson. Take the three principles identified by Marc Hauser as possible moral universals, described on p.229. These can be fleshed out using versions of the trolley problem. Imagine a heavy runaway trolley is running down a track towards a crowd of five people, imperilling their lives. Now imagine pulling a lever to divert the trolley down a different path such that you save the five people, but a single man on the new path will be killed. This is an example of a harm happening as a side-effect in the pursuit of a greater good. Now imagine that instead of pulling a lever, you push a man into the path of the trolley, saving the crowd of five but killing the man. This is an example of deliberately causing a harm in the pursuit of the same greater good.

This last example also involved direct physical contact, which most people judge to be morally worse than harmful actions instigated at a distance. If you pulled a lever which opened a trap door which dropped the man into the path of the trolley, thus saving the crowd, this would be an example of causing a deliberate harm without direct physical contact, with the aim of achieving a greater good. Most people judge this to be less morally bad than pushing the man with your bare hands. Finally, imagine you see the trolley hurtling towards the crowd of five and you choose to do nothing. Most people judge this as morally bad, but not as bad as if the trolley was hurtling down an empty track and you then switched a lever deliberately so as to divert the trolley towards a crowd of five people. A rural community of Mayans, however, consider harm caused through inaction to be just as morally bad as active harm (see pp.229–30).

view. In the same vein, the beliefs and practices of traditional cultures and orthodox religions, such as the Jewish taboo of eating pork, or the ban on blood transfusions among Jehovah's Witnesses, can be seen in terms of their placing high moral value on the Purity/sanctity dimension.

Altruism

The idea of cooperation between people makes sense in obvious, hands-on ways. Working together enables us to achieve physical objectives that simply wouldn't be possible alone. Just think how our ancestors cooperated as an efficient hunting unit, or consider the way we exchange skills. Few us can be doctors, builders, cooks and artisans, all in one package. Instead we specialize, offering our skills to society in exchange for those offered by other people.

Cooperation also makes sense in small family groups because of the sharing of genes between close family members. Your parents, siblings and children share fifty percent of your genes, so by helping them you're helping your own genetic legacy. From this perspective, it makes sense that the genes that influence people to help their close family have an advantage when it comes to being passed on from one generation to the next.

More problematic for psychology is how to explain the human tendency to altruism – the provision of help to others with no obvious

All-round benefit? A man gives money to a young homeless family on the streets of New York.

selfish gain. What motivates a person to donate large sums of money each year to charity to help people on the other side of the world? Or what about the mundane kind of altruism that leads someone to help a stranger carry a pushchair up an escalator? One compelling answer is that visible demonstrations of altruism, especially by men, are appealing to the opposite sex. By this account, men who are more altruistic are more attractive to women and therefore the genes that influence altruistic behaviour are more likely to be passed down the generations.

In support of this idea, research has shown that men in the early, wooing stages of a romantic relationship are more inclined to give money to street beggars than men in a more established, long-term relationship. For instance, a study by Wendy Iredale at the University of Kent involved men and women playing a financial game and then being asked at the end how much of their winnings they'd like to donate to charity. If an attractive woman was watching when they made their donating decision, the male participants donated more money than if a man was watching or no one at all. In contrast, the female participants' donating decisions weren't affected in this way.

So it seems there's evidence that men are motivated to impress women with their altruism. What about the female perspective – do they find altruistic men more attractive? Iredale had female participants rate the appeal of a physically attractive man shown in a video either giving £30 to a beggar, giving him £1, or just passing him by. The women who watched the most generous video version rated the man as the most attractive. Similarly, research by Tim Phillips at the University of Nottingham found that more women than men rated altruistic behaviours, such as "regularly helps an elderly neighbour", as particularly attractive in a potential mate.

Psychologists believe there are two evolutionary reasons why women have come to see altruism as attractive. Whereas men are attracted to young women who appear fertile, women tend to be attracted to men with more status and resources. Consistent with this, altruistic behaviours involving giving are a clear sign that a man has ample resources at his disposal. The second reason for altruism's appeal has to do with gene quality. Acts of altruistic heroism by a man, be it donating blood or fending off a threat, are a sign that the man is fit and strong and therefore a good choice of mate.

What about contemporary forms of altruism – all those anonymous editors on Wikipedia and helpful amateur bloggers? These seem to be clear-cut examples of people helping others with no obvious benefit for themselves. The theory of altruism as a mating strategy won't wash,

How to make a toddler more altruistic

If you're comfortable with the idea of covert manipulation and the prospect of a more altruistic toddler sounds appealing, you could try placing two companionable dolls side by side in various places around the house. In 2009 Harriet Over and Malinda Carpenter at the Max Planck Institute split sixty eighteen-month-old infants into four groups. One of the groups viewed photos of household objects, all of which also featured two dolls standing together side by side in the background. The remaining groups looked at photos with household objects in the foreground, with either a doll on its own in the background; two dolls facing away from each other in the background; or just a pile of toy bricks in the background. The key finding was that afterwards, the infants who'd looked at the photos with the friendly dolls in the background were three times as likely to help an experimenter pick up some dropped sticks. Over and Carpenter said the effect had nothing to do with the children's mood (they had tested that), instead the mere sight of the two companionable dolls was enough to prompt more helpful behaviour.

because in many cases the contributions are anonymous. This is a phenomenon that researchers are only just beginning to investigate, and they think part of the (disappointing) answer may have to do with attention-seeking.

For example, Bernardo Huberman and colleagues at the Social Computing Lab in California analysed the viewing history of over 9 million videos posted on YouTube by 579,471 contributors. A striking feature of the data was that the more times a person's videos were watched, the more subsequent videos they tended to post, and vice versa. Another pattern to come out of this analysis was that prolific contributors appeared to be more concerned by how their current performance compared against their past performance, whereas newbies or infrequent contributors were more bothered by how their viewing statistics compared with other people's.

COOPERATION AND PUNISHMENT

Another aspect of helping behaviour that psychologists have investigated is the handling of cheats. If a group of people club together to achieve a shared objective, there's a temptation for a sneaky cheat to sit back and reap the rewards without contributing their fair share. Of course if everyone did this, the group effort would fall apart. So how is cheating deterred?

Just like our primate cousins and other animals, including dogs, humans have a strong sense of fairness. But that's not all. Crucially, unlike our furry friends, we also have a powerful drive to punish others when we feel they've been unfair. Psychologists have demonstrated this inclination with simple economic games such as the **Ultimatum Game** (see box on p.236). These show that people are willing to pay a price to punish cheats, even if it's too late to recoup their losses. Moreover, by comparing games with different rules, research has shown that the option to punish drives up cooperation, presumably because the threat of punishment acts as a deterrent to would-be cheats.

The story was made more complicated by a study published in 2008 by Martin Nowak and his co-workers at Harvard University. Using a game known as the **Prisoner's Dilemma**, their research suggested that reciprocity is more important than punishment when it comes to increasing gains. Consistent with past research, the introduction of the option to punish an unfair playing-partner drove up cooperation. However, the most successful players were those who refrained from punishing their partner, instead adopting a tit-for-tat strategy matching unfairness with a withdrawal of their own cooperation. According to David Rand, one of the co-authors of the research, "winners are those who can stay even-handed and not escalate conflicts."

These kinds of dynamics are played out today in real-life contexts such as the online marketplace eBay, where buyers and sellers depend to a large degree on trust. There's a temptation for sellers to take payment from buyers and withhold sending the purchased goods. However, this happens only rarely, probably because of the influence of fairness combined with a reputation based on a comprehensive feedback system. Indeed, research has shown that buyers are willing to pay more for goods from sellers with a good reputation.

One drawback of an early version of eBay's feedback system was that criticized sellers could retaliate by posting negative feedback about the disgruntled buyer, even if this was entirely unwarranted. In turn, this would deter unhappy buyers from criticizing unscrupulous sellers, thus undermining the whole system. To solve this problem, eBay consulted the behavioural economists Axel Ockenfelds at the University of Cologne and Ben Greiner at Harvard. They helped create eBay's current feedback system, in which buyers leave anonymous feedback and sellers have to post feedback about buyers before they can access feedback that's been left about them.

The economic games psychologists play

Real-life cooperative situations are so complicated that it can be difficult to isolate the precise psychological factors involved. To get around this problem psychologists and behavioural economists have devised a number of games:

❑ **The Ultimatum Game** Player A is given a set amount of money and must decide how much to share with Player B. Player B knows how much Player A started with and must decide whether to accept or decline the offer. If B chooses to reject A's offer, then neither party gets anything. People frequently choose to reject unfair offers, even though this means they lose out too.

❑ **The Prisoner's Dilemma** Another two-player game. In each round, both players must decide whether to "cooperate" or "defect". If they cooperate, they each make some kind of gain. If both defect, neither gets anything. If one player cooperates and the other defects, then only the defector gains. Martin Nowak's study (see p.235) introduced the option to pay a small fee to punish a defector. Although this option increased cooperation, the most successful players were those who refrained from dishing out punishment, responding instead by defecting themselves. The name of the game comes from the real-life situation in which two crime suspects have the option of betraying their partner, thus going free, or both staying silent so that both receive a light sentence.

❑ **The Public Goods Game** A group of players choose in private how much money to invest in the collective kitty. In each round, the rules dictate that the kitty gets multiplied and the proceeds divided equally among the players, regardless of their chosen investment. Each person's chosen investment is also revealed to the others. The group gains the most if every individual invests the maximum amount. However, a "freeloading" individual can boost his or her own profits by withholding investment while still cashing in on the returns. The ability to punish freeloaders has been shown to boost cooperation levels in this game.

Parapsychology

Almost as ubiquitous as religious belief are reports of paranormal experiences: ghostly sightings, weird coincidences, mind-reading and alien abduction. In some ways the two realms are related. A religious person who feels a presence in a room might interpret the sensation as a connection with God, whereas an atheist might see the same sensation as simply a spooky experience. Parapsychology investigates claims of psychic abilities and life after death, while anomalistic psychology studies bizarre experiences and beliefs, but both tend to be looked down upon by more mainstream fields of psychology. And yet there are many who believe in the paranormal (three out of four Americans according to one survey) and many who claim to have witnessed paranormal or inexplicable events, so it seems a glaring omission for psychology not to attempt to find out why.

Among the most famous experiments in parapsychology are those that involve the elaborate **Ganzfeld technique**, in which one person attempts to send mental images to a second person located in a sound-proof chamber, wearing translucent goggles and headphones playing white noise. The theory behind this procedure is that **extra-sensory perception** – if it exists – is a weak signal that is usually drowned out by the riot of sensory information that we're bombarded with most of our waking lives. The task of the "receiver" is to select from four images the one that most closely resembles the image or video viewed by the "sender". In 2001, Daryl Bem at Cornell University combined the results from lots of Ganzfeld studies (a process known as a "meta-analysis") and concluded that overall, these experiments have shown that the receiver selects the correct image more often than you'd expect by chance, indicating that there is a real paranormal effect. However, many sceptical parapsychologists think that this effect only emerges because of flaws in the design of the experiment, such as "sensory leakage" from the sender to the receiver (i.e. information is somehow being communicated via conventional means) and poor randomization of the stimuli, so that clues are discernible from the order the material is presented in.

Another popular focus of parapsychology research is **psychokinesis** – the purported ability of some people to influence physical matter with their minds. This skill was made famous in the 1970s by the Israeli illusionist Uri Geller, with his dramatic bending of spoons and speeding-up of watches. In parapsychology, tests for the existence of psychokinesis take place in highly controlled circumstances, and usually involve a person attempting to use mind-power alone to bias the output of an electronic random-number generator. If the pattern of numbers produced under the deliberate influence of a person's thoughts is different from the pattern produced without human interference, this is taken as evidence for psychokinesis. There was a fair degree of hullabaloo in 2006 when Holger Bosch at the University Hospital of Freiburg and his colleagues combined the results from over three hundred experiments

Uri Geller bending a spoon by gently rubbing it – one of his best-known routines. Geller has frequently claimed psychic abilities, but there is no evidence that he is anything other than an illusionist.

and concluded that there was evidence for a tiny but significant distorting effect of people's thoughts on random-number output. Critics said that if you combine enough studies, you'll be bound to uncover an effect and that it's the size of that effect that's more important. They further dismissed the average size of the effect observed in the meta-analysis as meaningless. However, Dean Radin at the Institute of Noetic Sciences, a believer in psychokinesis, countered that the energy within a single atomic isotope is similarly small, but our understanding of that energy eventually ushered in the atomic age.

Probably the most consistent finding to come out of parapsychology research is that believers in paranormal effects tend to report positive results, whereas sceptics tend to report negative results. Richard Wiseman, a sceptic, and Marilyn Schlitz, a believer, tried to get to the bottom of this in 2005. Both had previously investigated the idea that people can feel when they were being stared at – with Wiseman finding no evidence that this "sixth sense" really exists and Schlitz finding evidence that it does. The pair of them ran some tests together, taking turns at doing the meeting and greeting of participants and other duties including the actual staring. In this case, no evidence for the sixth sense was found, consistent with Wiseman's earlier work. Most importantly, the pair showed that collaboration between sceptics and believers is possible.

ANOMALISTIC PSYCHOLOGY

For a glimpse of the kind of insights that come from anomalistic psychology, read the following and decide whether it matches you or not: "You have a need for other people to like and admire you, and yet you tend to be critical of yourself. While you have some personality weaknesses you are generally able to compensate for them. You have considerable unused capacity that you have not turned to your advantage. At times you have serious doubts whether you have made the right decision or done the right thing." If it sounds like you, join the gang. Back in the 1940s the psychologist Bertram Forer showed that most people identify with these lines (extracted by him from a newspaper astrology column), and more recent research shows that they still do today. Sometimes called **Barnum statements** (in reference to the American showman), they match the kind of generalized material used by mediums and astrologers to convince the gullible that they have psychic insight into their personalities.

Other anomalistic psychology research focuses on people's misunderstanding of probability, tricks of memory and perception, and uncovering earthly explanations for outlandish experiences. An example of the latter is **sleep paralysis**, a common nocturnal experience in which awareness returns before conscious control of the body is regained (about half of us have the experience at least once in our lifetimes). The phenomenon involves a feeling of being unable to move, difficulty in breathing and is often accompanied by multi-sensory hallucinations, including a perception of nearby movement.

> "After well over a hundred years of systematic research into allegedly paranormal phenomena, I do not get the sense that ultimate proof of the paranormal is anywhere nearer than it was at the outset."
>
> Chris French, Professor of Anomalistic Psychology

The earthly explanation for sleep paralysis is that it results from wakefulness returning while REM-based dream sleep is still ongoing – hence the muscle paralysis and hallucinations. However, people's interpretations of the cause of the experience tend to vary in line with their cultural background. For example, the Japanese call it kanashibari and, according to tradition, it is attributable the actions of a Buddhist god. Medieval Europe blamed the experience on seductive demons – the female succubus and male incubus. Contemporary Westerners (especially in the US), meanwhile, often interpret the experience as an alien abduction.

16 Dangerous mobs vs. wise crowds

Influential studies by Solomon Asch, Stanley Milgram and Philip Zimbardo – three of the most famous in psychology's short history – are mostly interpreted as telling a bleak story about groups and the willingness of individuals to shun personal responsibility and abuse power. However, there has been a shift in recent years towards a more nuanced view. One by one, these classic experiments, with their dark messages, have been revisited and reinterpreted. An iconoclastic band of social psychologists has conducted new research showing the ability of groups to resist tyranny, and for shared identity to foster cooperation between individuals. There's been a similar revision of attitudes about crowd behaviour, which has traditionally been seen as volatile and dangerous – especially in the face of an emergency. The new message from psychology is that not all crowds are potential mobs. Sometimes groups can bring out the best in us.

Tyranny and the abuse of power

Perhaps the most famous and dramatic example of a group situation apparently causing good people to do bad things is the **Stanford Prison Experiment** of 1971. Philip Zimbardo recruited twenty-four young men and allocated half of them to play the role of guards and half to play the role of prisoners. Zimbardo went to extreme lengths to make the prison situation feel authentic, even recruiting the local police to "arrest" the prisoner participants on the day that the experiment began. The guards were dressed in khaki uniforms and mirror sunglasses; the prisoners in

What kind of a person applies for a prison study?

Philip Zimbardo has argued that his Stanford Prison Experiment showed "the evil that good people can be readily induced into doing to other good people", and in recent years he has explained the Iraqi prisoner abuse at Abu Ghraib in similar terms. But what if the participants in his experiment weren't "good people"? Perhaps the idea of participating in a prison experiment, or working at an interrogation facility, appeals to a certain type of character. Thomas Carnahan and Sam McFarland suggested this might be the case in a 2007 study in which they posted recruitment adverts in several campus newspapers, just as Zimbardo had done. One advert invited male participants for "a psychological study of prison life"; the other invited participants for "a psychological study". Again, just as Zimbardo had done, Carnahan and McFarland omitted all participants with mental health problems or a criminal or anti-social background. Crucially, when the pair compared the remaining 30 applicants to the "study of prison life" with the 61 volunteers for the "psychological study", they found the former scored significantly higher on measures of aggression, authoritarianism, Machiavellianism, social dominance, and lower on measures of altruism and empathy.

Contrary to Zimbardo's situationist perspective, the finding is compatible with a more interactionist view of human behaviour – one that acknowledges that people's personalities affect the situations they find themselves in. Moreover, like-minded individuals are likely to seek out similar situations. Carnahan and McFarland concluded that, whether in Zimbardo's study or in Abu Ghraib, similar characters may have "mutually weakened each other's constraints against abuse and reinforced in each other their willingness to engage in it".

knee-length smocks with no underwear, their ankles chained together. The experiment was due to last two weeks, but was abandoned after just six days. Several of the prisoners had breakdowns and many of the guards had become sadistic and cruel, even ordering the prisoners to clean out the toilets with their bare hands.

Zimbardo's interpretation of the experiment was that it shows how evil resides in the situation, not in individuals. If you create the circumstances where there is an enormous power differential between groups, he argued, and if you allocate people to roles that are traditionally seen as dominant or submissive, then they are likely to lose their individuality and become consumed by those roles. In a case of life apparently imitating the science, Zimbardo's explanation seemed to be borne out by the horrors that took place at the Abu Ghraib prison camp in Iraq in 2004, when American guards abused their prisoners in sickening

US Army reservist Charles Graner, the ringleader of the Abu Ghraib prisoner abuse, posing with the corpse of a detainee, Manadel al-Jamadi, who had arrived at the prison in good health. Graner, who had a history of violence and racism, was found guilty of five different charges of prisoner abuse and was sentenced to ten years in prison.

fashion. Zimbardo subsequently acted as an expert defence-witness for one of the guards, re-asserting his theoretical position that the abuses occurred because of the situation that the US authorities had created – a case of "bad barrels, not bad apples".

ZIMBARDO CHALLENGED

Zimbardo's study provided a striking counterpoint to the prevailing view of that time which saw the roots of tyranny and abuse as residing in the disposition of specific individuals, and for years his message went largely unchallenged. In 2001, however, that all changed when the two British psychologists Stephen Reicher at the University of St. Andrews and Alexander Haslam at the University of Exeter decided, with the help of the BBC, to recreate the prison study – as far as this was ethically possible.

Reicher and Haslam were concerned that Zimbardo's study failed to recognize that groups can come together not only to abuse power, but sometimes to resist tyranny. The kind of group dynamics that emerge depends largely on the extent to which individuals within a group identify with a shared cause. In the Stanford experiment, Reicher and Haslam pointed out that Zimbardo had played a key role in his own study. He'd been the "prison superintendent" and he provided the prison guards with a leader and a purpose with which they could identify. In fact, at one stage Zimbardo even instructed the guards: "You can create in the prisoners … a notion of arbitrariness, that their life is totally controlled by us, by the system, you, me – and they'll have no privacy … We're going to take away their individuality in various ways. In general what all this leads to is a sense of powerlessness."

In what became known as the **BBC Prison Study**, Reicher and Haslam allocated participants to the role of guards and prisoners, but rather than providing leadership to the guards, they sat back to see what would happen. In striking contrast to Zimbardo's study, the guards in the BBC Prison study failed to establish a group identity. This time, it was the prisoners who formed a cohesive, shared identity, which led them to organize themselves effectively and gave them social power, to the extent that they rebelled and overthrew the established regime.

A self-governing "commune" then emerged for a short time. This fell apart when a minority of participants refused to go along with the commune's self-imposed rules and the law-abiding majority lacked the will to discipline them. In the end, the recalcitrant minority attempted to establish a hard-line tyrannical system, far more extreme than the original guard-prisoner setup. At this point the experiment was brought to a premature conclusion.

Reicher and Haslam interpreted their study in line with "social identity theory", according to which power resides in the ability of a group to establish a sense of shared identity. This can be harnessed for negative, abusive ends (as happened with the guards in Zimbardo's study) or it can be harnessed for the common good, as when the prisoners overthrew the guards in the BBC study. By this account, there is nothing natural or inevitable about the corruption of individuals by a group mentality. It is only when people fail to unite according to fair, democratic values that a vacuum is created within which tyranny can emerge.

CONFORMITY

The groundwork for Zimbardo's perspective on group tyranny was actually laid some years earlier by the Polish-born social psychologist **Solomon Asch**. In the 1950s at Swarthmore College, Asch had groups of between six and nine people match the length of a target line with one of three comparison lines, with each person stating their verdict publicly. Crucially, all bar one of the group members were actually accomplices working for Asch, and on twelve of eighteen trials they were instructed to unanimously match the target line with the wrong comparison-line. Asch's finding was that in about a third of the misleading trials, participants chose to go along with the majority view, even though their own eyes told them it was wrong.

As with Zimbardo, people have traditionally seen Asch's work as showing how easily individual will is surrendered to the group mentality, even one that's patently in error. But again, some psychologists have dissented from the conventional interpretation. According to two such voices – Ronald Friend, now Emeritus Professor at Stony Brook and Yvonne Rafferty at Pace University in New York – Asch himself actually saw his work as demonstrating the power of independence. A closer look at the statistics helps show why. For example, while it's true that 76 percent of participants yielded to the majority view at least once, 95 percent stayed independent at least once. Or put another way, just 5 percent of participants were always swayed by the erroneous majority, while 24 percent were always true to their own opinion. "The facts that were being judged were, under the circumstances, the most decisive", Asch wrote.

In another retrospective analysis, Bert Hodges at Gordon College and Anne Geyer at Florida State University highlighted in 2006 that the majority of Asch's participants were sometimes yielding and sometimes independent, which makes perfect sense given that they were attempting to balance the demands of an extremely awkward situation in which everyone else appeared to be consistently wrong. Theirs is a more nuanced picture than the mindless-conformity myth found in many textbooks.

OBEDIENCE

If there was room for interpretation in Asch's data, the same surely can't be said for the obedience experiments of **Stanley Milgram** conducted at Yale in the 1960s. Inspired by Asch, Milgram invited participants to the university to take part in what they were told was a study of the effects of punishment on learning. Their task was to apply electric shocks to another participant, the "learner" (actually an actor), whenever he got answers wrong. This he kept doing, so the participants were instructed to continue cranking up the shocks in fifteen-volt increments. At 300 volts the learner pounded the wall in protest, at 315 volts he fell silent. Despite this, 26 out of 40 participants continued to obey the experimenter, a stern man in a grey lab coat, and applied shocks right up to the highest level of 450 volts. This took them past the level labelled as "Danger: Severe Shock".

Not long before Milgram conducted these rather alarming experiments, the Nazi war-criminal Adolf Eichmann had been on trial for his role in the Holocaust. The historian and philosopher Hannah Arendt witnessed the proceedings and wrote in the *New Yorker* that, far from appearing as a sadistic monster, Eichmann seemed to be an ordinary man. The fact that such an unremarkable man could, through blind obedience to authority, be capable of such crimes was famously described by Arendt as "the banality of evil". Just as Zimbardo's study had parallels in Abu Ghraib, Milgram's work had its real-world parallels in the evil of Nazi Germany.

However, there are variants of Milgram's classic paradigm which tend to get overlooked and which do resurrect some belief in the good of humanity. In follow-up experiments, Milgram contrived a situation in which participants witnessed another participant – actually an actor – resist the order to apply ever-higher electric shocks. With this role-model, participants were far less likely to obey the experimenter. It was a similar story in variations of Asch's experiments. Once again, all it took was a single rebellious ally to inspire far greater autonomy in participants. Just as Reicher and Haslam found in their prison study, the right kind of example, it seems, can inspire virtuous resistance rather than tyranny.

Hannah Arendt reported on the 1961 trial of Adolf Eichmann, one of the main Nazi organizers of the Holocaust. She claimed that Eichmann was more of a careerist than an anti-Semite, a position that has been challenged by later historians.

The bystander effect

It's 1964 in the Kew Gardens district of New York, and Kitty Genovese, a 28-year-old bar manager, is returning home after work. A man fatally attacks her outside a large apartment block. There are 38 witnesses in the block, or so the traditional account goes, yet not one of them does anything to help. The incident provokes moral outrage and inspires the psychologists Bibb Latane and John Darley to propose and test the "bystander effect" – the idea that people's sense of responsibility is diluted when they are in a group. If there had been just one witness to Genovese's murder, their theory suggests, they would probably have intervened in some way. Yet tragically, the abundance of witnesses left everyone thinking that someone else can deal with it. Many of us have encountered a less dramatic equivalent on a busy shopping street. A person falls and the majority walk on by, reassuring themselves that someone else is surely bound to help out.

But the traditional version of the Kitty Genovese tragedy has been challenged. Research by local historian Joseph De May, much of it based on transcripts of the trial of Genovese's killer Winston Mosely, suggests there weren't 38 witnesses after all. In fact, probably only one person saw

Virtual Milgram

A problem for contemporary psychologists wanting to investigate obedience, conformity and the abuse of power is that many of the classic studies can't be repeated. By today's standards they are judged unethical. However, that hasn't stopped researchers from improvising. In 2006, Mel Slater at UCL created a virtual reality version of Milgram's classic study. Participants donned a virtual-reality headset and were instructed to apply shocks to a computerized woman whenever she answered memory questions incorrectly. Although obviously unreal, the woman showed distress at the shocks and protested that she wanted to stop. It may sound daft, but in fact the study provided some hope that immersive technology could provide a way to replicate unethical studies. Out of 34 participants, six chose to withdraw from the study before it was due to finish, six more said they had considered withdrawing because they felt uncomfortable, and physiological measures suggested the participants had found the experience stressful.

Another way that contemporary psychologists have re-examined Milgram's work is by focusing on the 150-volt level. Jerry Burger at Santa Clara University noticed that this was something of a point of no return. In Milgram's original work, if a participant continued beyond the 150-volt level – when the actor playing the role of learner first said they wanted the experiment to stop – it was highly likely that they would go all the way. Indeed, 79 percent of participants who passed the 150-volt point went on to administer the top 450-volt shock. Burger carried out a replication of Milgram's study, but stopped proceedings immediately after participants refused or accepted the instruction to go beyond the 150-volt level. He found that 70 percent were willing to go beyond 150 volts, a proportion only slightly lower than Milgram's 82.5 percent. For Burger, this suggests that, under lab conditions, people's obedience to authority today is little changed from the 1960s.

the final fatal attack, which took place inside Genovese's own apartment block, out of view of the vast majority of the "witnesses" who were resident in the Mowbray apartment-block across the street. And contrary to the notion that nobody did anything to help, one of the Mowbray witnesses claims to have shouted at Mosely, scaring him off from his initial attack, and another, a fifteen-year-old at the time, says that his father called the police.

Regardless of exactly who did and didn't do what on the night that Genovese was murdered, the bystander effect itself has been supported by ample research – being in a group really does seem to dilute people's sense of individual responsibility. However, social psychologists like Rachel Manning at the University of the West of England worry that the notoriety of the mythical version of the Kitty Genovese story has reinforced the already powerful notion that crowds are inherently dangerous and bad, suppressing interest in research on the potentially positive aspects of group behaviour.

Bucking this trend is Mark Levine, a social psychologist at Lancaster University. He's used CCTV footage and a cleverly contrived lab situation to show that people in a larger group are actually more likely to help a victim, not less, if they and the other group members all belong to the same social category as the victim. So, for example, the more people a bystander female is with, the more likely she is to intervene and help another woman being assaulted – as long, that is, as her companions are female too. Levine calls this the "responsive bystander effect" and it reinforces the importance of shared social identity. Again, the message seems to be that people bonded by a common identity can sometimes act more altruistically than they otherwise would.

Panic

Surging, screaming, stampeding and everyone for themselves: this is what many people think of when they imagine large crowds of people in an emergency situation. It's certainly the view that was held for much of the twentieth century by advocates of the popular **panic** model of crowd responses to emergencies. Traditional media reports of disasters have tended to reinforce this perspective. Consider coverage of the infamous stampede at the 1979 Who concert in Cincinnati, which left several people dead. "Crowds capable of developing own personalities, says expert" was the headline in *The Cincinnati Enquirer*. The ensuing report noted that people were "horrified and disgusted" by the news that eleven people had been "trampled to death". A *Time* magazine article, "The Stampede to Tragedy", reported that one Cincinnati editor had compared children in the audience to "animals".

It's because of the influence of the **panic model** that emergency exits are often designed to be as wide as possible, and safety stewards sometimes use codes in a fire evacuation so that the crowd doesn't realize what's happening and run amok. However, new research is once again contradicting the traditional view. John Drury at Sussex University argues that the historical record shows that panic is actually extraordinarily rare and that people often stop to help each other. Drury's theory is that helping behaviour is more likely to emerge when people in an emergency feel a sense of shared identity (this is the same model used by

During a football match at Sheffield's Hillsborough Stadium in 1989, ninety-six Liverpool supporters died after being crushed against a pitch-side barrier. Many fans went to the assistance of the injured. Police control of the event was heavily criticized, as was *The Sun* newspaper for its negative and inaccurate reporting of the Liverpool fans' behaviour.

Reicher and Haslam to interpret their prison findings; see p.243). In 2009, Drury interviewed 21 people who'd been caught up in real-life emergencies, including the crush at Sheffield's Hillsborough football stadium, the Harrods bomb of 1983, and the overcrowding at the Fatboy Slim party on Brighton beach in 2002. He found that the same twelve participants who said the crowd in each case was united with a sense of a shared fate also tended to be the ones to report that they'd seen and experienced people helping others, including strangers, and that they'd seen signs of orderliness, such as people queuing to escape. The lesson seems to be that a collective mentality can, in the right context, be a force for good.

MASS HYSTERIA

Mass hysteria or mass psychogenic illness can last for days, weeks or even months at a time. It's defined by the exhibition of odd behaviour and/or physical or psychological symptoms, such as dizziness or nausea, in more than one person and in the absence of any identifiable organic cause. There are some striking historical examples. In 1374 along the river Rhine and at Strasbourg in 1518, hundreds of people were overcome by a kind of dancing plague – many of them literally danced and danced for days on end until they dropped down dead. Another famous example is the fits that afflicted girls during the Salem Witch Trials of the seventeenth century. A local doctor was unable to explain the fits experienced by two girls who'd been experimenting with fortune telling, and so he blamed the supernatural, claiming the girls had been "bewitched". Soon other girls and young women were experiencing the same fits, as hysteria spread through the community. A more recent manifestation was the emergence of "railway spine" in Britain in the nineteenth century – passengers reported feeling faint and suffering back pain. Experts at the time blamed the effect of 30mph speeds on the body, but in fact the symptoms were purely psychological.

The catalyst for mass hysteria is often prolonged stress, and the manifestation is usually influenced by the beliefs of the day. For example, in the case of the dancing plague in Strasbourg, the local population had endured months of famine, and they had a long-held belief in the power of saints and devils to unleash dancing curses.

Outbreaks of mass hysteria still occur to this day, often in schools, where the presence of large groups of people in relatively confined areas provides a fertile breeding-ground for a psychological contagion to spread, especially during stressful periods like exam time. In a typical case in 2007, for example, staff at a specialist science-college in South Yorkshire feared a gas leak when over thirty pupils and a teaching assistant suddenly fell ill. It all started when three children complained of feeling queasy during a class screening of a biology video. As more and more children reported similar symptoms, the emergency services were called and the school was abandoned. However, no gas leak or other environmental cause was found, and of the 32 pupils taken to hospital, all were discharged after four hours.

The wisdom of the crowd

Before closing this chapter, let's take a brief digression away from tyranny and conformity to look at one of the clearest and most intriguing examples of the positive side of group psychology – a phenomenon known as "the wisdom of the crowd". This is the finding that if you average the verdict of a group of people, their combined estimate will be more accurate than even the most expert individual. Francis Galton found this out in 1906 at the West of England Fat Stock and Poultry exhibition, when he averaged the estimates made by 787 people in a competition to guess the weight of an ox. The group's averaged guess was 1,197 pounds, just one pound below the ox's actual weight. Moreover, the crowd's joint estimate

The wisdom of the crowd in one person

Amazingly, we can use the principles of the "wisdom of the crowd" phenomenon to improve the accuracy of our own judgements, even when we're on our own. Stefan Herzog and Ralph Hertwig demonstrated this in a study published in 2009 in which they asked participants to estimate historical dates, such as the year that electricity was discovered. Crucially, half the participants were coached to make an initial estimate, then pause to consider how it might be wrong, before using this new perspective to make a new estimate. Herzog and Hertwig call this solo technique "dialectical boot-strapping". The control participants simply made two best guesses for each question. It turned out that the average of each dialectical boot-strapper's two guesses was, on average, 4.1 percent more accurate than their initial estimate. By contrast, the average of each control participant's two estimates was, on average, just 0.3 percent more accurate than their initial estimate. "Part of the wisdom of the many resides in an individual mind", was Herzog and Hertwig's conclusion. "Dialectical boot-strapping is a simple mental tool that fosters accuracy by leveraging people's capacity to construct conflicting realities." However, the pair also pointed out that their dialectical boot-strapping technique is no match for harnessing the wisdom of others. If a boot-strapping participant's initial estimate was averaged with the estimate of another participant, this improved accuracy by about twice as much as averaging that first participant's own initial and second guesses.

was more accurate than the competition winner and more accurate than cattle experts at the exhibition.

There's no magic or mystery to the "wisdom of the crowd" phenomenon. Individuals are rarely one hundred percent accurate, even if they are well-informed and expert in the question at hand. By averaging the estimates made by a crowd, the random error introduced in people's verdicts – sometimes in one direction, sometimes in the other – tends to cancel out, thereby homing in on the actual answer. The phenomenon only works, however, when certain conditions are met. Thus the group must be diverse, with individuals having unique insights into the problem at hand – obviously, if everyone brings the same information to the table, the averaged estimate will be no better than any individual's best guess. Group members must also be independent, in the sense that their own judgement is free from contamination or influence by the other group members. Again, this makes sense – if one individual in a crowd persuades all the others of the superiority of his insight, then this will spoil the balancing influence of the other estimates.

Part V

Psychology at large

17 The psychology of crime

People are appalled and fascinated by crime in equal measure. Most of us aspire to live in a safe, crime-free society, yet we're gripped by books and films about murderers, bank-robbers and sadists. In real life and in fiction, such tales often involve forensic psychologists who are responsible for assessing and treating criminals with mental-health problems. Sometimes they also advise the police as criminal profilers and hunters (as in the British TV series *Cracker*), an activity that particularly captures the public imagination. Psychologists also research many issues related to criminal behaviour and the criminal-justice system. Are jurors influenced by a defendant's choice of clothes? What makes a person make a false confession? Can the police be trained to tell whether a suspect is lying? How accurate is eyewitness memory?

A life of crime

Whether it's two minutes in an illegal parking spot or a mildly exaggerated insurance claim, many of us will have decided momentarily that the advantages to rule-breaking outweigh the potential costs. However, these minor transgressions aside, the majority of us live according to the rule of law most of the time, with due consideration of other people's interests as well as our own. It's actually a tiny proportion of persistent offenders who commit nearly all crimes, especially the most serious ones.

The psychologists Terrie Moffit and Avshalom Caspi, of the University of Otago in New Zealand, have established that this criminal minority can be divided into two distinct subgroups, based on their research following the lives of a large sample of people born in Dunedin in 1972.

Of those people with a criminal record, one subgroup had only begun to display criminal behaviour in adolescence (largely driven by peer pressure and teenage rebelliousness) and had grown out of it by early adulthood. In contrast, a second, far smaller, delinquent subgroup first displayed signs of criminal behaviour in early childhood, sometimes from as young as two or three. Their criminal tendencies worsened in adolescence and continued throughout adult life. Moffitt and Caspi call this type of offender **life-course persistent**.

Do broken windows really encourage crime?

The "broken window" theory of crime reduction argues that by clearing up signs of social disorder, such as litter, graffiti and broken windows, you help prevent the spread of undesirable behaviour. The idea was given a high profile by Malcolm Gladwell in his best-selling book *The Tipping Point*, in which he attributed the dramatic fall in crime in New York in the 1990s to the zero-tolerance approach of the police at that time. In 2008, the theory received the backing of a team of Dutch psychologists led by Kees Keizer, after they contrived a series of scenarios in which signs of orderliness were varied and the effect on passers-by was observed and measured. For example, Keizer's team found that bicycle owners in an alley were more than twice as likely to drop litter – a flyer attached by researchers to their handle bars – if the walls were covered in graffiti. In another scenario, passers-by were more likely to steal a money-containing envelope protruding from a postbox if litter was on the ground, or graffiti was on the postbox.

Their research has shown that individuals in the life-course persistent category are three times more likely to be convicted after the age of 26 than average, and five times more likely to be convicted after that age for a violent crime. Longitudinal research conducted in London by David Farrington has uncovered similar patterns. He began tracking 411 eight-year-old boys living in inner-city South London in 1961 and subsequently found that just seven percent of the sample were responsible for half of all the convictions received by the entire group, with those convicted at a younger age tending to have the most convictions and the longest criminal careers.

Moffitt and Caspi also found that life-course persistent offenders typically have an underactive version of the MAOA gene. This affects the production of a protein that breaks down neurotransmitters in the brain. Such individuals also tend to have a history of having been abused or neglected in early childhood, and it's this combination of early trauma with their genetic vulnerability that seems to set them on a path of criminality. Intriguing new research suggests, however, that these same individuals may thrive in more supportive conditions – an idea popularized in a 2009 article for *The Atlantic* by David Dobbs. Brain-imaging research has further shown that they are easily emotionally aroused, often seeing threats where none exist.

Findings like these have led to calls for early intervention programmes to "nip criminality in the bud". The idea is that by providing early support to parents and their children, the toxic combination of early trauma and genetic vulnerability can be avoided. A meta-analysis by David Farrington of intervention studies, including tests of parenting programmes, found that on average, offending rates were reduced by one third. Some experts have even advocated intervening before children are born. In the 1990s, David Olds at the University of Colorado carried out research involving "at-risk" mothers receiving supportive nurse-visits during pregnancy and for the first two years of their child's life. He found that by the time the children were aged fifteen, they'd clocked up only half as many arrests as a control group and received one fifth as many convictions.

These results sound promising, but such interventions aren't without their critics. Although the majority of adult offenders will have exhibited conduct problems in childhood (i.e. extreme disobedience or antisocial behaviour), it's also true that most children with such problems won't end up as persistent offenders. Some have argued that targeting at-risk parents and their children stigmatizes them, and is reminiscent of the film *Minority Report*, in which the authorities arrest people in anticipation of crimes they have yet to commit.

There is another complication, which is that among those children with conduct problems who are destined to live a life of crime, there are in fact two further subgroups. The majority, as we've heard, show exaggerated emotional reactivity. There's also a minority who show callousness, for example displaying cruelty to animals, and a lack of emotion. They seem to be psychopaths in the making and don't respond to the threat of punishment. However, the situation is not completely hopeless, because there is some evidence that the behaviour of these children can be improved through interventions that focus on reward rather than punishment.

Eyewitness memory

As well as the profound question of why some people turn to crime and how to stop this from happening, psychologists are also involved in several more specific, practical lines of research. Perhaps the most influential of these relates to the unreliability of eyewitness memory. The pioneer in this field is Elizabeth Loftus. She's shown, for example, that even the way that witnesses are questioned can affect their memory of an incident. Asked to estimate the speed that two cars were going when they "smashed" into each other, people will typically provide a faster estimate than if you asked them how fast the cars were going when they "hit" each other.

Loftus has also shown how easy it is to implant "false" memories in people's minds. In one of her most famous studies, she created in participants an entirely fabricated memory for a time when, as a child, they'd supposedly become lost in a shopping mall. The participants were presented with information about their past, provided by their friends and relatives, with the shopping-mall incident mixed in among truthful accounts of other events. For each event, the participants were asked to provide as many extra details as they could. Two weeks later, Loftus again asked the participants about the shopping-mall incident, by which time many of them said that they could recall the (entirely fictitious) event – in fact many of them embellished the story with fabricated details.

In subsequent variations of this seminal work, Loftus and her colleagues have successfully implanted **false memories** of all manner of wild and exotic incidents, from drowning to being licked by Pluto the dog at Disneyland. When sceptical critics continued to argue that perhaps these incidents really had occurred, Loftus and her team came up with the perfect riposte, implanting in participants the false childhood memory of having met Bugs Bunny at Disneyland – a truly impossible occurrence given that Bugs is a Warner Bros character.

The notion of false memories has proven to be controversial because of the claims made by some therapists that they are able to help clients recover long-suppressed memories of child abuse. Loftus's research shows how cautious we need to be when judging the veracity of these accounts. It would be all too easy for a therapist to implant memories of abuse through the power of suggestion, even without intending to do so. Indeed, a 2007 study by Elke Geraerts at the Erasmus University of Rotterdam found that memories of child abuse recovered during therapy were dramatically less likely to be corroborated by third parties,

Elizabeth Loftus's research on the reliability of memory has led her to testify or act as consultant for some of the world's most high-profile court cases, including the trial of Michael Jackson and the Bosnian war trials at The Hague. Currently Distinguished Professor at the University of California, Irvine, Loftus has received death threats as well as prestigious awards for her work.

or other evidence, than were memories of abuse recovered outside of therapy, or abuse memories that had never been forgotten. The American Psychological Association's consensus statement on this issue is that: "most people who were sexually abused as children remember all or part of what happened to them, although they may not fully understand or disclose it".

According to surveys conducted by Svein Magnussen at the University of Oslo, there continues to be a large gap between lay beliefs about memory and the facts established by psychology research. For example, Magnussen has found that a significant portion of judges and jurors erroneously believe that children are better at remembering than adults; that memory starts to decline from the age of forty (the reality is that episodic memory doesn't start to decline until approximately the age of sixty); and that a person's confidence and the details they give are signs of accuracy. A majority of people also fail to realize that most forgetting occurs immediately after an event, and think that memories for dramatic events

Criminal profiling

While fictional criminal psychologists usually get their man (or woman), real life has thrown up some disastrous mistakes. In London, in the early 1990s, the hunt for the killer of Rachel Nickell involved an elaborate but ill-judged undercover operation to entrap the chief suspect Colin Stagg. Later acquitted in court, Stagg had fitted the profile of a sexual deviant and fantasist drawn up by Paul Britton, a forensic psychologist who later wrote about the case, and others he'd worked on, in *The Jigsaw Man* (1998).

A US profiling case that went badly wrong took place in 2002 when police were advised that the Beltway sniper, who had shot and killed ten people in Washington DC, was probably a lone white man. The advice threw the hunt for the killer temporarily off course. In the end the culprit, John Allen Muhammad, turned out to be black and had been operating with a young accomplice who was also black.

Despite these high-profile errors, there is an intuitive logic to criminal profiling. There's no doubt that a criminal's *modus operandi* can provide the police with useful clues to direct their search. While the movies highlight criminal idiosyncrasies such as unusual means of entry, a taste for kitsch jewellery or gruesome murder-rituals, in reality the most reliable clues can be something as banal as where a crime occurred.

In a recent analysis of solved Northamptonshire burglaries, Lucy Markson at the Institute of Criminology showed that two burglaries by the same person (known as "linked crimes") were more likely to have occurred closer together geographically than two burglaries by two different people. Timing was found to be another important factor – linked crimes tended to occur closer together in time as well as geographical distance. David Canter, the first British psychologist to be consulted by the police and the founder of the International Academy for Investigative Psychology, says that this is the way forward for criminal profiling – finding patterns in large data-sets of criminal behaviour and using these to help narrow the hunt for the perpetrators of new crimes.

are more accurate. These misconceptions have serious consequences for justice. According to one estimate, 76 percent of wrongful convictions have been caused by misplaced trust in dubious eyewitness testimony.

The reality when it comes to memories for dramatic events – so-called **flashbulb memories** – is that they are extremely persistent, but not particularly accurate. This was borne out by research on people's memories for the 9/11 terror attacks. In 2003 a study found that 73 percent of 569 college students recalled watching the first plane hitting the north tower of the World Trade Center on TV the day that it happened. The reality is that the video footage of this event wasn't shown until 12 September.

Lie detection

Most of us are poor lie detectors. In a meta-analysis of 206 studies involving over twenty-four thousand people acting as lie detectors, Charles Bond Jr and Bella DePaulo at Harvard University found that, on average, people were able to correctly identify just 47 percent of lies as lies and 61 percent of truths as truths. There's some evidence that police officers fare better, but not hugely. Using clips of real suspect-interviews in a 2006 study, Albert Vrij at the University of Portsmouth found that police officers correctly identified truthful utterances 70 percent of the time and lies on 73 percent of occasions. Seven out of ten might not sound too bad, but extrapolated to real life, it means a lot of innocent people being wrongly perceived as liars.

Part of the reason we're so poor at detecting lies is that the folk wisdom on this issue is so deeply ingrained. We grow up learning from our parents and from literature and films that liars fidget and avoid eye-contact. Even influential police-training manuals such as *Criminal Interrogation and Confessions* (1986) propagate this myth, highlighting shifts in posture or nervous gestures as signs of lying. In fact these signs are most likely to reflect nerves, maybe because of the situation or simply the person's disposition. An innocent person who fears being falsely accused is just as likely to fidget with anxiety as a lying criminal. In fact, the experienced criminal might well have learned to keep still and maintain eye-contact, just so as to come across as telling the truth.

The latest findings in criminal neuroscience

In 2009 in Italy, Abdelmalek Bayout had his murder sentence reduced by a year on appeal after his defence persuaded the judge that he had violent genes, including a low-activity version of the MAOA gene (see p.255). In the same year, in the USA, fMRI brain-imaging evidence was admitted in court for the first time, as the defence attorneys of serial killer Brian Dugan attempted to provide evidence that their client had the brain of a psychopath and could not therefore control his violent nature. In 2010, a lawyer in Brooklyn successfully sought to present fMRI evidence to show that a key witness in a civil employer-retaliation suit was telling the truth. The evidence was disallowed on the basis that it's up to the jury, not a fancy brain scanner, to determine who's telling lies, but it's surely just a matter of time before fMRI-based lie detection reaches the courts.

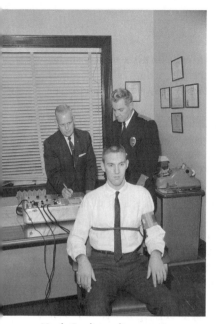

North Carolina police operating a polygraph test in 1962.

The **polygraph test**, still widely used in America, faces the same problem. The squiggly lines produced by measures of heart rate, breathing, and sweatiness are merely signs of stress – so again, the nervous innocent could end up being categorized as a liar. And cunning criminals may well be able to trick the system – by such ploys as biting their tongue during the control questions (for example, "is your name Jack?") they can distort the assessment.

What we do know for sure about lying is that it's more mentally demanding than telling the truth. This should mean that if the mental demands of a situation are ratcheted up, liars will struggle more than truth-tellers. That's exactly what Vrij found in a 2007 study in which he used the device of asking people to tell their stories backwards – a task that is known to be cognitively tricky.

Vrij invited students take part in a mock theft, half of whom later acted as liars. The demands of telling their story backwards exposed significantly more differences between the liars and truth-tellers than did the task of telling their story forwards. In the reverse-story condition, the liars gave fewer auditory details, gave less context, hesitated more, spoke more slowly, moved their feet more and blinked more. By contrast, among the students who told their stories forwards, the liars differed from the truth-tellers only in the fact that they moved their hands and fingers less, probably because of a deliberate effort to appear calm. Most importantly, when police watched video clips of the students, they successfully identified far more of the lying students based on the backward story-telling compared with the traditional forward story-telling.

An issue that's generated a great deal of excitement in recent years involves using brain imaging to determine whether someone is lying. In fact, companies such as No Lie MRI have started springing up in America, claiming to offer just such a service. Although there is research that shows that certain brain areas are more active when people lie than when they tell the truth, most of this research has averaged brain activity across groups of liars compared with groups of truth-tellers. Testing individual criminals could be much trickier. What's more, there's no single "neural signature" for lying: rather, the network of areas associated with lying tends to reflect increased mental effort. This means a crafty criminal could spoil their brain scan simply by performing mental arithmetic during the comparison truth-condition, so as to conceal their extra effort while lying.

Finally, critics of research in this area have pointed out that being told to lie about something as mundane as a playing card in your hand – a popular test in this field – is hardly comparable to lying about a murder so as to avoid a lifetime in prison, or, for that matter, telling the truth in the knowledge that if you're not believed, you could spend years behind bars. Also, the studies have involved drug-free, healthy participants – who knows if the results would be the same with drug-addled psychopaths?

False confessions

Ask most people if they'd ever consider making a false confession and they'll probably say the chances are remote. It's perhaps for this reason that psychologists have found that confessions exert a powerful influence on the decision-making of juries, leading them to assume that the confessor must be guilty. Unfortunately, false confessions are more common than we like to think. The Innocence Project – an American organization that works to exonerate the falsely accused using DNA evidence – reports that of the more than 200 people who have so far been exonerated, about 25 percent made false confessions or self-incriminating statements.

Saul Kassin at Williams College has conducted countless studies showing the power of confessions to sway juror judgement. In a 1997 study with Katherine Neumann, for example, he measured how much a mock jury was swayed by a confession, compared with how much they were swayed by an eyewitness identification or a character testimony. The confession was by far the most influential. He's also shown how a confession can contaminate other forms of evidence. For example, on being told that a suspect has confessed, witnesses become more confident in their own incriminating evidence. On the other hand, providers of alibis who are told that the suspect has now confessed suddenly lose faith in their own memory. "Well, if he's confessed," they seem to be saying to themselves, "I must have made a mistake about what the time was when I saw him."

Avoiding death row

Make sure you come across as sorry and sincere. Based on his interviews with eighty jurors who had played a part in real-life murder cases, Michael Antonio found that defendants who were perceived by jurors to be sorry and sincere were more likely to be sentenced to life imprisonment than to be sentenced to death. On the other hand, defendants who appeared bored or who looked frightening were more likely to be given the death penalty. That's despite jurors being instructed to make their decision based only on the legal facts of the case.

So why do people make false confessions? One problem is that innocent people often turn down their legal rights – to a legal representative or to remain silent – for fear that assuming these rights will make them look guilty. The police can also be persuasive. They might tell a suspect that their punishment will be far less severe if they confess. Another factor is the power of suggestion. As Elizabeth Loftus's work has shown, it is very easy for people to come to believe in entirely fabricated memories, and crucially, in many jurisdictions, the law only requires the police to provide a tape of the confession, not the interrogation that led to it. Saul Kassin, among others, is campaigning for this to be changed.

Other psychologists have looked at the type of interrogations that are most likely to lead to a false confession. In an experiment in which students were tricked into thinking that a computer they were working on had crashed, Jessica Flaver at Simon Fraser University found that so-called "minimizing" remarks were more likely to provoke the students into falsely confessing that they'd caused the crash. This included remarks that downplayed the "crime", such as "don't worry, it was just an accident" or "this programme seems not to be working lately".

18 Business Psychology

Despite the best efforts of *The Idler* – the periodical which aims "to return dignity to the art of loafing, to make idling into something to aspire towards rather than reject" – the stark reality for most of us is that we will spend a sizeable chunk of our lives working for someone else in return for a wage. And these employers want their bang for a buck. They want us to be as productive as possible. To help achieve this, many corporations, especially in rich, Western countries, hire organizational psychologists. Indeed, business is one of the areas of "real life" in which psychologists enjoy most influence. Consultant psychologists provide advice and tools for improving productivity, shaping organizational structure and selecting personnel.

The right mix of the right stuff

This last task is particularly important, given that research shows that the most productive individuals are disproportionately responsible for a huge amount of output. According to a respected review by the organizational psychologists Frank Schmidt and John Hunter, published in 1998, a superior skilled worker – which in statistical terms means one whose average output is one standard deviation above the staff average – will be 96 percent more productive than a poor worker – one whose average output is one standard deviation below the staff average. In plain English, this means finding the right person for the right job has profound financial consequences for businesses.

The good news for business is that – despite the controversies associated with intelligence- and personality-testing – the link between scores on properly validated tests and subsequent work-performance is extremely strong. All the evidence shows that IQ tests provide a powerful indicator of how well a person will perform on the job. When it comes to personality, organizations that use tests which tap into the five-factor

A 1950s personnel "officer" interviewing a prospective candidate for a job at a New Jersey pharmaceutical firm. Sometime during the 1960s, US personnel management was renamed human resources.

model of personality (see p.177) find that those who score high on conscientiousness and low on neuroticism tend to perform best at work.

The bad news is that there's a mismatch between what works in recruitment and what's popular. The most widely used personality measure is the **Myers-Briggs Type Indicator** developed by two amateur psychologists – Katherine Briggs and her daughter Isabelle Myers – in the middle of the last century. The test is used by many of the world's largest companies and was taken by around 200,000 people in Europe alone in 2009. It's a crude unreliable test that shoehorns people into one of sixteen personality types. The test has proved so popular largely due to aggressive marketing and appealing packaging – not a good evidence base. It gets worse. In France, it's reported that fifty percent of companies analyse job candidates' handwriting style – a process known as **graphology** – despite there being not one iota of scientific support for the practice.

Another hurdle confronting successful personnel recruitment is deliberate **fakery**. When it comes to personality scales, it's pretty easy for most candidates to feign their answers to make themselves sound appealing. However, in 2008, Jacob Hirsh and Jordan Peterson at the University of Toronto published a new-style test that pitched appealing answers against each other, such as: "I rarely get irritated" versus "I am full of ideas". This way test respondents were forced to sacrifice some positive attributes at the expense of others. The new test was found to predict accurately later school-performance, even when student participants were asked to fake their answers deliberately to create the best possible impression.

Of course, psychologists don't only concern themselves with how companies can recruit the best people: they also sometimes take the side of the nervous candidate. In this regard, there are some intriguing research-findings which show, for example, that it can make a difference **where you sit** in a group interview. In a 2006 study, Priya Raghubir and Ana Valenzuela analysed episodes from the TV quiz show *The Weakest Link*, which features eight contestants standing in a semi-circle, with one player – "the weakest link" – voted off each round by the other players. Those occupying the central positions were far less vulnerable to being voted off. In another experiment, 111 students were shown different versions of a group photo featuring five candidates for a business internship arranged in different positions. The student participants knew the candidates had similar abilities, but, when asked to play the role of staff recruiter, they still tended to choose the central candidate in the photos they were shown.

The 360-degree evaluation

One of the most popular tools used by occupational psychologists is the 360-degree evaluation. This involves gathering feedback about an employee from his or her manager, subordinates, peers and sometimes customers too, and comparing that feedback with how the employee sees him or herself. This can reveal "blind spots" – something other people know about a person, but which that person or her immediate superiors didn't realize.

For 360-degree evaluations to be beneficial, it is vital that they are executed appropriately. A poorly executed evaluation can damage staff morale and cripple an employee's self-esteem. It should be decided at the outset whether the exercise is for personal development or is being used as a means of appraisal, and coaches should be on hand to guide an employee through their feedback and how to respond to it. Ideally, the exercise shouldn't only be performed on one person, because this can create the sense that they are somehow a problem that's being investigated.

It's also important to choose the right people to provide feedback. Factors such as the time that participants have known the target can affect the quality of the feedback: research suggests the optimum time is one to three years – not too short for first impressions to dominate, and not too long for over-familiarity to skew the results.

It's also important that the right questions are asked. Ideally these should be customized and relate to an organization's overarching goals. It's also vital that those providing feedback are trained in how to provide constructive information. For obvious reasons, feedback tends to be more useful when participants are told that their answers will be anonymous.

The order that candidates are called to interview could also make a difference. In 2005, Wandi de Bruin at the University of Technology in Holland reviewed Eurovision Song Contest scores and scores given in European and World Figure-Skating Championships. The pattern was always the same – the later that a performer appeared, the higher the score she or he tended to receive. De Bruin surmised that perhaps there is no benchmark for the earlier candidates to be compared against, and it's therefore easier for later candidates to stand out. Taken together, these research findings suggest that you should try to sit in the middle during a group interview, and for one-on-one interviews, that you should try to be one of the last to be called.

In the office

Once the interviews are complete and the candidates selected, the focus for psychologists shifts to **optimizing performance**. For years, the most important factor in this regard was considered to be **job satisfaction**. Time and again, studies have found that staff who are more content also tend to be more productive. For this reason, a great deal of effort has been expended on finding out how to improve employees' job satisfaction.

A study published in 2005 by Professor Francis Green at the University of Kent used data recorded by the long-running British Household Panel Survey and others like it to find out why job satisfaction had tumbled in Britain during the 1990s. His findings pointed to people's loss of freedom to use their own initiative at work, combined with employees feeling that they were expected to work harder than they wanted to.

Other psychologists have tested ways to boost job satisfaction. To take just one example, in 2008 a Canadian programme called "Spirit at Work" was shown to reduce absenteeism and staff turnover. The programme derives from a movement within Positive Psychology (see p.349) that argues for the importance of employees finding meaning in work, forging connections with their colleagues and feeling that their work has a larger purpose. In their study of the programme, Val Kinjerski, director of the business consultancy Kaizen Solutions for Human Services, and Berna Skrypnek of the University of Alberta, Edmonton, provided the programme to 24 staff at a residential-care unit. Exercises focused on ways to live more purposefully and spiritually, on workplace community and inspired leadership, and how to

BUSINESS PSYCHOLOGY

Job satisfaction? A crowded open-plan office at Canoga Park, California in 1963.

foster a sense of meaning in one's work. Over the ensuing months, staff who completed the programme reported more job satisfaction, more focus on residents and improved teamwork and were less likely to take sick leave or leave their post than a control group of 34 staff at a similar unit who didn't take part.

Not everyone is convinced by the established job satisfaction–performance link. The psychologist Nathan Bowling at Wright State University muddied the water somewhat in 2007 when he looked at the combined results from several meta-analyses (studies that combine data from numerous prior investigations).

Bowling's combined data set involved thousands of staff at dozens of predominantly US organizations. The usual link between satisfaction and performance was found, but importantly, this association all but disappeared once staff personality (especially conscientiousness) was taken into account, along with organizational self-esteem – the extent to which employees feel that they matter to their employer. The implication is that rather than satisfaction causing improved productivity, it's more accurate to think of conscientious staff with high organizational self-esteem as being both more satisfied and more productive. Bowling concluded that it would be a mistake for businesses to focus exclusively on job satisfaction without bearing this in mind. Other obstacles to success at work are boredom and procrastination. Writing in 2007, the

267

Hawthorne experiments

Probably the most famous studies ever conducted in business psychology were at the Hawthorne works of the Western Electric Company in Chicago in the late 1920s and early 1930s. Initiated by Australian psychologist George Elton John Mayo, the studies involved making changes to factory working-conditions, including payment and supervision, and observing the effects on staff output. The participants were largely female staff working on telephone relays. The main finding was that the observed changes in productivity came about not because of the modifications put in place, but simply because the participants were the focus of increased attention – a phenomenon that's since come to be known as the "Hawthorne Effect", and which is often frequently invoked to explain the outcomes of other psychology studies.

However, in 2008 Mecca Chiesa at the University of Kent and Sandy Hobbs at the University of West of Scotland strongly criticized the popular use in psychology of this term. They reviewed over two hundred books published between 1953 and 2003, and found that the use of the term "Hawthorne Effect" had become so broad and varied as to be virtually meaningless. Sometimes the term was used in its original sense, but elsewhere it referred to the effects of anything from a warm climate to concern or friendly supervision. And while the Hawthorne Effect originally referred to effects on improved productivity, many authors have since used it to refer to all manner of outcomes, including feelings of pride and job satisfaction.

psychologist Sandi Mann warned of signs that boredom at work was on the increase, perhaps because so many tasks in the modern office are becoming automated. Mann cited a 2004 survey by the business consultancy DDI, which found that a third of Britons reported feeling bored for much of the day, and a *Washington Post* survey which found that 55 percent of US employees were "not engaged" at work.

There's some evidence that boredom is more common in people who are overly focused on their own moods and who have trouble sustaining attention to the task at hand. The opposite of boredom is the idea of **flow**, developed by psychologist Mihály Csíkszentmihály. The joyful, timeless sensation of flow occurs when you're absorbed in a challenging task that stretches your abilities, but doesn't exceed them. Another antidote to boredom is **mindfulness** – savouring the present moment, absorbing the colours and sounds around you and letting thoughts trickle through your mind without passing judgement on them.

Everyone has been guilty of **procrastination** at one time or another, but the habit is particularly thought to occur when a person perceives a task to be beyond their capabilities. The character traits of extroversion and perfectionism are also associated with an increased tendency to put off arduous tasks.

There's no easy fix for procrastination, although psychologists recommend getting into the habit of starting your working day with those tasks that seem most daunting. It's also worth remembering that procrastination isn't always a bad thing – as mentioned in Chapter 12, an incubation period is vital to creativity. It's likely that you're mulling over the solution to a problem even when you're not directly dealing with it. In fact, forgiving yourself could be the key. A team of Canadian psychologists at Carleton University led by Michael Wohl demonstrated this in a 2010 study. They found that those under-graduates who forgave themselves for procrastinating before their first mid-term exams subsequently procrastinated less prior to the second round of mid-terms, and performed better – possibly as a result of not procrastinating so much.

Working together

Once the most capable people have been recruited and the right working-conditions created, the next challenge for the psychologist is how to get people to work together effectively. A hugely popular group exercise in business is brainstorming, in which team members sit around a table bouncing ideas off each other. **Brainstorming** can be enjoyable, but unfortunately it doesn't work as well as most people think it does. Time and again research has shown that people think of more new ideas on their own than they do in a group. Two weaknesses of brainstorming are: **social loafing**, in which unforthcoming team members keep quiet while others bandy ideas around, and **evaluation apprehension**, in which people fear having their ideas shot down by more dominant team members. Psychologists have dubbed the false belief that people are more creative in groups the "illusion of group productivity".

Another reason that groups can work poorly is that team members tend to spend most of the time talking about information that they share with each other, rather than learning anything new. At its worst, group decision-making can lead to the feared phenomenon known as **groupthink**, which has been blamed for all manner of calamities, from the Challenger space-shuttle disaster to the decisions that led to the Iraq war. Groupthink occurs when team members get hooked on shoring up a consensus view and no longer consider other perspectives. It's particularly likely to emerge in groups made up of like-minded members who lack diversity, and when the group leader makes their own position known early on.

> "Though we are often taught to think of ourselves as inherently selfish, the longing to act meaningfully in our work seems just as stubborn a part of our make-up as our appetite for status or money."
>
> Alain De Botton,
> *The Pleasures and Sorrows of Work* (2009)

An alternative approach to traditional brainstorming is **brainwriting**. Group members write ideas on slips of paper in silence before passing the slips between each other, reading others' ideas and inserting their own. Ink colour indicates who owns which ideas, and when a paper slip has four ideas on it, it is placed in the centre of the table for all to see. This is repeated up to 25 times. Next, group members withdraw to the corners of the room and recall as many of the ideas generated so far as possible – the rationale being that this encourages attention to the ideas generated. The final stage involves group members working alone for fifteen minutes in an attempt to generate yet more ideas. Unlike brainstorming, brainwriting has been shown by business psychologist Peter Heslin to boost creativity compared with the performance achieved by the same individuals working on their own.

NEGATIVE BEHAVIOUR

Even with the most effective decision-making systems in place, there's always one scourge of the workplace that risks derailing a successful organization – **bullying**. Every organization should have a pro-active, anti-bullying protocol in place. Never mind the obvious harm caused by being the direct victim of bullying at work, research published in 2009 by psychologists at the University of Florida showed that merely witnessing bullying can stunt a person's creativity, impair their mental performance and make them less likely to be civil themselves.

Related to this, in 2007 Kathi Miner-Rubino at Texas A&M University and Lilia Cortina at the University of Michigan reported evidence that witnessing **misogynism** in the workplace is harmful not only to female staff, but to men too. University employees of both sexes who said they had witnessed either the sexual harassment of female staff, or uncivil, rude or condescending behaviour towards them, tended to report lower psychological wellbeing and job satisfaction. In turn, lower psychological wellbeing was associated with greater burn-out and increased thoughts about quitting. Miner-Rubino and Cortina surmised that these negative effects could arise from feeling that one is working for an unjust organization, and by feelings of empathy or fear.

Leadership

"Leaders are dealers in hope," said Napoleon Bonaparte, and indeed a key leadership role is to provide staff with a **vision** for where their organization is headed and what its goals and values are. Just as importantly, people want their leaders to have **integrity** and to refrain from abusing their power, for example by displaying favouritism. The best leaders also make the **right decisions** at the right times and are **competent** – that is, they've demonstrated their talent for whatever it is that the organization does, be it selling, publishing, teaching or whatever. It's a tall order. According to a 2005 paper by Robert Hogan and colleagues, countless surveys show that 65 to 75 percent of employees think the worst thing about their job is their immediate boss.

Disturbingly, there's some evidence that the kind of character traits that suit leadership overlap with those found in **psychopaths**. In a 2005 study, Belinda Board and Katarina Fritzon at the University of Surrey found that a sample of senior British managers and chief executives averaged higher scores on self-reported measures of histrionic, narcissistic and compulsive personality than did two samples of former and current patients at Broadmoor, the high-security psychiatric hospital! These personality dimensions reflect characteristics such as superficial charm, perfectionism, and a lack of empathy. However, unlike the Broadmoor patients, the business managers scored significantly lower on measures of aggression, impulsivity and mistrust.

The worst kinds of leaders are **bullies**. Preliminary research suggests that this behaviour can emerge when managers doubt their own competence. In 2009, Nathanael Fast at Marshall School of Business published results from a survey of ninety employees and found particularly high rates of self-reported aggression in workers who claimed to be in positions of power and who also described themselves as chronic worriers about what other people thought of them. A second study with 98 participants further showed that those who were primed to think about a

Space psychology

Work psychologists don't just provide advice to office-based organizations. Perhaps the most dramatic example of this is space travel. NASA classifies psychosocial issues as one of the most serious threats to a successful mission, and employs two aerospace psychologists to help recruit and support astronauts. The psychologists help find those rare individuals who are brave and ambitious, and yet are capable of coping with the monotony of long-distance space travel. Fortnightly psychological sessions with on-board astronauts ensure they are sleeping well and getting on with their fellow crew-members. Psychologists also oversee supportive interventions, including the sending of care packages containing gifts for the astronauts, such as a favourite T-shirt or drawings from their children.

Beyond NASA, other psychologists and psychiatrists have also conducted research on psychosocial issues in space. Nick Kanas at the University of California, for example, has uncovered an effect known as "displacement", in which during times of stress astronauts take out their frustration on ground control. James Cartreine at Harvard Medical School is developing a multimedia "Virtual Space Station" featuring videos, animations and interactive questionnaires to help astronauts cope with their own psychological and social issues onboard.

An unprecedented psychological challenge will be the first Mars mission, currently slated for the 2030s. To help plan for this, psychologists are heavily involved in a 520-day mock Mars mission, "launched" in June 2010, involving three Russians, one Chinese man, one Frenchman, and one Italian-Colombian, all locked in a simulation spacecraft. When it comes to the real mission – a two- to three-year round trip – there will be no more care packages and no chance to jump on the next shuttle home. Any contact with earth will suffer delays of twenty to thirty minutes in each direction.

Nick Kanas wonders about the psychological effects of losing sight of the earth. "No one in the history of humans has ever, ever perceived the Earth as an insignificant dot in space," he has said. "The sense of everything that is dear to you being so distant – we don't know what that means psychologically for people. It may mean nothing, it may mean an awful lot."

Aerospace psychologists were consulted in 2010 when a group of Chilean miners were trapped underground for many months with only very limited means of communication with the outside world.

time they'd been in a position of power, and to think about a time they'd felt incompetent, then went on to choose a particularly loud noise for students to be blasted by when answering incorrectly in a hypothetical quiz (this was used as a laboratory measure of aggressiveness).

Rather than listing those character traits that make an ideal leader, an alternative view of leadership was provided by Stephen Reicher and colleagues in 2007. They said that the most important thing is for followers or employees to **identify** with their leader, to feel that he or she is one of them. George W. Bush's cowboy hat and Yasser Arafat's head-scarf are both examples of leaders attempting to show their followers that they are just like them. Similarly, Reicher argued that effective leaders foster a sense of **shared identity** among their followers, transforming a disconnected crowd into a cohesive group. Consider how President Obama was careful to repeat "Yes WE can", not "Yes I can" in his campaign to become president.

On a less serious note, it seems that would-be leaders are more likely to succeed if they have **hair** and are tall. The United States hasn't had a bald President since Dwight D. Eisenhower, and in the UK, the only two Conservative party leaders since the early 1920s to have failed to become Prime Minister, William Hague and Iain Duncan Smith, were both bald. Regarding height, in 2004 Timothy Judge and Daniel Cable reviewed the results from 45 studies containing relevant data and found that taller people, especially if male, were more likely to find their way into leadership roles and to earn bigger salaries.

19 Money and shopping

Some say that money makes the world go round. Never mind the planet's rotation, what's certain is that money makes our heads spin. Among our financial confusions, most of us think that money will make us happier than it really does; we treat equal amounts of money as having a different value based on where the money came from (a habit known as "mental accounting"); most of us fail to save adequately for the future; and ironically, most of us think we're far more financially savvy than we really are. Behavioural economists and economic psychologists – who plough the same research fields but originate in different disciplines – investigate our relationship with money, both in terms of our financial decisions and the links between wealth, poverty and wellbeing. Consumer and marketing psychologists investigate the science of persuasion and the factors that influence our buying habits.

Money and happiness

Presumably the many people who play national lotteries around the world all think that winning huge sums of money will make them happier. Research suggests otherwise. While the gross domestic product of the USA, the UK and other developed nations has soared over the last fifty years, genuine progress in terms of happiness and wellbeing has flatlined. One probable reason for this is that it's our relative rather than our absolute wealth that has the potential to inspire happiness or discontent, so if everyone's average wealth has risen, none of us feel any better off. Another possibility is that increased national wealth tends to go hand in hand with social ills that undermine happiness, such as more divorce and inequality.

In 2009, in one of the first studies of its kind, Lara Ankin conducted a scientific comparison of lay beliefs about the relationship between money and happiness with the reality of that relationship. Ankin surveyed hundreds of Americans on different income-levels about their happiness and asked them to estimate the average happiness of people on other income levels. The participants were fairly accurate when estimating the happiness of wealthier people, but massively underestimated the happiness of people on lower than average wage-levels. There's little doubt that real poverty is miserable, but the research suggested that we overestimate the emotional impact of having less money than average. A 2010 survey of US workers by Daniel Kahneman found that a higher salary was associated with more happiness, but only up to an annual salary of $75,000, beyond which more money made no difference.

Related to the question of the link between money and happiness is materialism. The assumption is that people want more money in order to be able to buy more stuff. However, research by Tim Kasser at Knox College has shown that materialistic people, from children to pensioners, are less satisfied with life, lack vitality and suffer more anxiety, depression and addiction problems than do people who aren't materialistic.

It gets worse. Kathleen Vohs, in a paper published in 2006, showed that the mere thought of money makes us more selfish. She showed that participants who performed anagram tasks involving money-related words subsequently spent less time helping another participant (actually an actor) who was confused by the task. Other experiments

Looking happy enough, Nigel Page and his partner Justine celebrate his £56 million win on the Euro Lottery in February 2010.

by the same team showed that the more money participants were left with after a game of Monopoly, the less likely they were to help pick up pencils dropped by a passer-by, and that participants primed with money-related sentences subsequently opted to donate less money to charity than did control participants. Vohs thinks that reminders of money have this effect because money allows us to achieve goals without the help of others.

More recent research has reinforced the idea that money can reduce our enjoyment of life. Jordi Quoidbach at the University of Liège led a 2010 study in which being wealthier or being presented with the mere sight of money led people to spend less time savouring a chunk of chocolate and reduced their enjoyment of it. Quoidbach's team concluded "our findings provide evidence for the provocative and intuitively appealing – yet previously untested – notion that having access to the best things in life may actually undermine one's ability to reap enjoyment from life's small pleasures".

Mental accounting

Imagine that you earn a modest Christmas bonus of a few hundred pounds. You wouldn't normally consider spending that kind of money on a meal out, but – bonus in hand – you suggest to your partner that you dine out together at an exclusive restaurant. "After all," you reason to yourself, "this is money that I wasn't expecting to have." It's almost as if you're suggesting that the money contained in the bonus is somehow less valuable than the money that you earn week in, week out.

People often take a similar attitude with money saved in sales, money received as a birthday gift, or money represented in store-card loyalty points. Instead of recognizing the face value of the money, our judgement is skewed by its provenance. The ten pounds off that dress, or the twenty-pound birthday gift, are seen as fun money, unconstrained by our usual frugal consciences. The five-pound time-limited voucher earned through the loyalty-card, on the other hand, is seen as extra precious – we'll go to great lengths to make sure we don't miss the chance to cash in this well-earned "free" money.

This idea of carving up our money into pots of contrasting value is known as **mental accounting**. It can provoke us into some particularly irrational financial decisions. One costly example is when people leave a savings account untouched while paying off a loan. Invariably, the interest charged on the loan will far exceed the interest earned on the savings, yet people will have locked the savings money tight in a "mental safe" as secure as if it were built of steel. The consequence, of course, is that they lose money each month, rather than simply paying off the loan (or a portion of it) and starting from scratch.

The problem with saving

When we are in the enviable position of being able to put money by, most of us don't save enough. We place more value on money in our hand today than the prospect of the same or a greater amount available at some point in the future. In fact, the more distant the date, the less value we place on the money – a phenomenon known as **parabolic discounting**. This aversion to saving probably played a part in the global financial crisis that occurred at the end of the first decade of the twenty-first century (see p.280). In the UK between 2000 and 2002, the average amount of household income saved fell to 5.9 percent from an average of 9 percent between 1990 and 1999.

Clues as to how to save more effectively were uncovered in a 2007 study by Anna Rabinovich and Paul Webley. Using data collected over several years as part of the Dutch DNB Household Survey, they identified 1360 people who said they planned to save over the next two years and did, and 89 people who similarly said they planned to save over that period, but failed.

A key difference between the successful and failed savers was that the former tended to say that the future was more important to them – what the researchers called their "time horizon" was projected further forward. The successful savers also used techniques to control their saving, including setting up the automatic transfer of funds into a savings account each month. This and other techniques used by successful savers all helped to make the savings process more automatic and therefore less dependent on will power.

Overconfidence

Most of us are poor financial decision-makers, and yet most of us are also over-confident about our monetary know-how – a bad combination! A powerful source of evidence for our overconfidence comes from the stock market. People who trade stocks and shares usually make many more transactions than they ought to (called "churning"), because they think they know what they're doing when they don't. To take one example, research conducted by Terrance Odean at the University of California at Berkeley looked at all the trades made by 37,000 people between 1991 and 1997 and found that the more trades a person made, the more money they tended to lose. Men were particularly prone to this mistake, making 45 percent more trades than women on average.

The UK's Office of Fair Trading (OFT) published an eye-opening report in the summer of 2009. They asked a team of psychologists, led by Stephen Lea at the University of Exeter, to look into the psychology of scams. Perhaps the most surprising finding was that people with more background experience in finance actually tended to be more prone to financial scams – another powerful example of overconfidence at play. Consistent with this, scam victims tended to spend more time considering a would-be scam, not less, as you might expect, and it's probable that the time spent considering the scam made them even more overconfident. Non-victims tended to simply delete or dispose of scam material without giving it any consideration.

When faced with a suspicious financial proposal, it's best to focus on what you have to lose, not just on what you might gain. According to the OFT report, each year in the UK 3.2 million adults (around one in fifteen people) collectively lose around £3.5 billion to mass-marketed scams.

Spend now, pay later – the lure of the credit card.

Related to financial overconfidence is unrealistic optimism. A good example of this is the way that so many people continue using credit cards even though they have such high interest-rates. In 2007, Sha Yang at New York University surveyed nearly three hundred credit-card users and found that those who said they intended to pay off their balance each month, but actually didn't, tended to use cards with higher interest rates. It's as if their unrealistic optimism was leading them to choose a card that wasn't in their best interest – it's likely they would have been better off with a card with a higher annual fee, but lower interest-rate charges.

Another way that credit cards expose our financial irrationality is with the minimum monthly payment. Research in 2008 by Neil Stewart at the University of Warwick focused on credit-card users who pay off some, but not all, of their balance each month. Crucially, the amount they chose to pay off was related to the credit card's set minimum payment. This is an example of anchoring (see Chapter 5). It's as if knowledge of the minimum required payment had the effect of dragging down people's choice of how much to pay off. Stewart has created an online tool to help people to choose how much to pay off (www.stewart.psych. warwick.ac.uk/decisiontool/).

Shopping

It's common for people to set off for the shops knowing what they want to buy, only to arrive back home with something the shop wanted them to buy. One reason is the **zero-price effect** – the lure of anything that's free. The behavioural economist Dan Ariely of MIT's Sloan School of Management showed this in an experiment in which he gave people a choice between a Hershey's Kiss chocolate for one cent and a more luxurious Lindt truffle for 15 cents. In this case, 73 percent chose the truffle. Next, Ariely reduced the price of both options by one cent, so that the Hershey Kiss was free and the Lindt truffle was 14 cents. The difference in price between the options had of course remained the same, but now 69 percent of customers opted for the free Hershey Kiss, so swayed were they by the appeal of something for nothing.

Shops exploit the zero-price effect when they package up products with the offer of an extra item for free. You might arrive at the shop hoping to buy your favoured brand of shampoo, but you end up buying not one, but two bottles of an inferior product because the shop bundled it with a third, free bottle. Luxury items like televisions and DVD players are also often bundled together with "free" gifts, such as DVDs, to enhance their appeal and sway people's product choices. The lure of something for nothing is so great that Ariely has even shown that given the choice of a free Amazon voucher valued at $10 or a $20 voucher available for a fee of $7, most people opt for the free voucher. Of course, if they'd overcome the lure of the free and gone for the second option they'd have ended up three dollars better off.

Another trap that awaits shoppers is the **decoy effect**. Imagine purchasing a bicycle for the first time. If you're like most people, you'll make your choice through a process of comparison. The store manager

Can psychology explain the global financial crisis?

The global financial system was founded on the principles of traditional economics, which characterize humans as rational agents who always make decisions in their own best interest. However, the work of economic psychologists has shown that human financial decision-making is far from rational. We're overconfident, myopic and prone to numerous biases. In 2009, the MIT behavioural economist Dan Ariely published a supplementary chapter to his best-selling 2008 book *Predictably Irrational*, in which he argued that many of the events that led to the global financial crisis are understandable in light of these psychological findings.

For example, the deregulated financial system allowed for people to make their own decisions about how large a mortgage to borrow. When confronted with this decision, Ariely's research has shown that, thanks to our short-sightedness and unrealistic optimism, most people generally look to borrow as much they can, rather than the "optimum" amount. Perhaps it's no wonder that the sub-prime mortgage bubble burst.

Ariely also points to the role played by the vast multi-million dollar rewards that were made available to bankers. If doctors' or teachers' judgements were subject to such huge financial influence, it wouldn't be surprising if they were tempted not to make optimum decisions. Yet this is exactly the situation that confronted bankers.

In fact, Ariely's research has undermined the very notion that large bonuses are a good idea in business. When participants in India were offered the chance to win five months' pay on challenging tests of memory and concentration (low wages made this a feasible research strategy), their performance was actually worse compared with other participants who were offered more modest rewards.

knows this, so there's a particularly shiny model on display for £2000 or more. Although there's a bike for just £150, the presence of that pricier, snazzy model suggests you really ought to plump for something more in the middle, and you end up walking away with a £500 bike. If you're honest, you've no idea how much you ought to have spent, but the clever decoy dragged up your naïve estimate of the value of a decent bike.

From megapixels to megabytes, the modern technology consumer is confronted by a bewildering array of data on what the latest gadgets can and can't do. According to a 2008 study, the dazzle of these **specifications** is another factor that can sway consumer judgement. In a 2008 study, Christopher Hsee at the University of Chicago got people to choose

Banking jargon such as "widows and orphans" (unsuspecting investors), "yard" (a billion) and "stick" (a million) also helped shield bankers from the reality of the consequences of their decisions. In another study, Ariely looked at student cheating in a simple quiz in which they reported back their own performance. Crucially, the students cheated far more when they were paid in tokens that they had to exchange for cash, compared with when they were paid in cash directly. It's as if the extra symbolic step helped introduce moral fuzziness, which encouraged cheating. Ariely draws an analogy with bankers: in their case it was the jargon and complex financial procedures that created the moral fuzziness.

In many areas of social life, from driving regulations to drug laws, human foibles are taken into account. Speed limits are imposed, substances banned. Ariely argues for a similar approach to finance. He believes "that relying too heavily on our capacity for rationality when we design our policies and institutions, coupled with a belief in the completeness of economics, can lead us to expose ourselves to substantial risks".

Can psychology help us find a way out of the mess we're in? According to the economic psychologist Stephen Lea of the University of Exeter, saving is obviously important, but if everyone saves the economy will never recover. The key, he says, is for wealthy and comfortably-off people unaffected by the recession – and there are many of them – to be given the confidence to spend, especially in ways that leave money in the economy, for example by hiring the services of the less well-paid.

between two digital cameras – one boasted better resolution, the other more vividness. In the absence of detailed technical specifications, but with the evidence of sample photos, most people favoured the camera with superior vividness. However, after people were given the detailed specs on megapixel resolution, as well as sample photos, most chose the model with superior resolution.

Hsee said people should make sure they try out products where possible, rather than relying on specifications. Also he advised against spending too much time comparing models. After all, your real-life use of a product will usually be in isolation, not side-by-side with its rivals.

20 Politics and persuasion

From the facial appearance of candidates to the location of the polling booth, psychologists are uncovering the numerous intriguing factors at play when we decide how to vote. Other lines of research have uncovered systematic differences in the personality traits of people who subscribe to liberal values compared with those who subscribe to more conservative values. Meanwhile, politicians are increasingly recognizing that psychological findings can be harnessed to persuade voters and inform political policy. Persuasion and influence are key to politics, not only in relation to voting, but also when it comes to some of the most pressing issues of the day, such as encouraging people to behave in more environmentally friendly ways.

Voting intentions

Most people probably like to think that they vote in a considered fashion, and in their country's best interest – well, at least in their own best interest. So you wouldn't think the location of a polling station would make much difference. However, that's exactly what Jonah Berger at the University of Pennsylvania found when he analysed votes cast in an election in Arizona in 2000. People who voted in polling stations located in schools were significantly more likely to have voted in favour of a tax increase to fund schooling than were people who voted in churches and other locations.

Other research has examined the effects of candidate personality and appearance. Unsurprisingly perhaps, voters are more likely to go for politicians who are attractive and who are perceived as having a personality similar to their own. They are also influenced not so much by how competent candidates are, but rather by how competent they look. John Antonakis and Olaf Dalgas at the University of

Lausanne presented Swiss undergraduates with photographs of pairs of competing candidates from the 2002 French parliamentary elections. They had no idea who these candidates were, but their task was to indicate which candidate in each pair they felt was the most competent based on appearance. For about 70 percent of the pairs, the candidate rated as looking most competent was the candidate who had actually won the election in real life. The disconcerting implication is that the real-life voters must also have based their choice of candidate on looks – at least in part.

As if the arbitrary influence of polling-station location and candidate appearance were not worrying enough, the position of candidates' names on a ballot paper has also been shown to influence voting behaviour. Studies involving voters with some knowledge of the candidates have revealed an advantage to being listed higher up the ballot paper. The reason is that weighing up the options takes mental effort. By the time voters reach the bottom of the ballot paper their mental resources are running low, which means the candidates in these positions don't get full consideration.

Research presented by Andy Johnson of Coventry University at the British Psychological Society's annual conference in 2010 found a further influence of ballot-paper position when participants were asked to vote

Political adverts

Political parties spend fortunes on carefully choreographed adverts with dramatic music and strategically placed children and animals. But do these Hollywood-style tactics really make much difference? The evidence suggests that they do. In 1998, against the backdrop of the Democratic nomination for Governor of Massachusetts, Ted Brader at the University of Michigan recruited 286 volunteers, ostensibly to participate in research into TV news. Participants watched a real news-programme, which included a commercial break into which Brader had embedded various versions of a carefully-designed political advert, either in favour of or in opposition to one of the competing candidates.

Brader found that participants who watched a version of the positive advert enhanced by uplifting music and images of children were more interested in the election and more likely to vote than those participants who saw the same advert with the same script but without the music (and now set outside a local government building). Viewers of the enhanced, positive advert were also more likely to vote based on their pre-existing preferences. Responses to the negative advert were also affected by the additional music and imagery. Those participants who saw the version with tense discordant music and black-and-white images were more likely to choose their favoured candidate on the basis of topical issues rather than their entrenched beliefs.

for fictional political parties about which they knew nothing. In this case, voters showed a bias against the top and bottom positions on a vertical ballot-paper of six parties. The effect disappeared when the study was repeated with real, well-known UK parties, which suggests it may be the less knowledgeable voters who are more susceptible to the effects of ballot-paper position. The obvious solution to these kinds of biases is to rotate candidate position on ballot papers in random fashion, but of course this would incur practical and financial costs.

Even if, by some means, we were able to avoid the influence of all these extraneous factors on our political decision-making, it's still quite likely that we'd fail to make a coolly rational judgement. Drew Westen showed this in a brain imaging study in which he presented partisan participants with contradictory statements or actions by their favoured candidates during the 2004 US presidential election. Not only did the participants fail to acknowledge the contradictions, but the information they were presented with activated areas of their brains associated with emotion rather than areas associated with cold reasoning. It's as if they were suppressing and rationalizing the information that threatened their preconceived view. What's more, this was followed by activity in reward-related brain areas, almost as if there was some satisfaction derived from successfully resolving the awkward conflict in their minds.

Conservatives vs. liberals

Another strand of research in political psychology has focused on the personality traits and situational factors associated with different political orientations. Broadly speaking, political ideology can be divided into a resistance to change or the pursuit of change – conservatism versus liberalism. It's tempting to believe that how people position themselves on this political continuum is based on reason alone, but there's mounting evidence that our political persuasion is primarily rooted in our psychological make-up.

Several studies by John Jost at New York University have shown that self-declared political conservatives show more positive implicit (subconscious) attitudes towards conformity, stability and hierarchy than do self-declared liberals. Either their chosen political orientation has become ingrained or their political persuasion was motivated by deeply held, non-conscious attitudes. Similar research has shown that conservatives have stronger implicit preferences for dominant social groups such as – in the US – white people over black people and heterosexuals over homosexuals.

Turning to the Big Five personality factors (see p.177), Jost has also uncovered evidence that conservatives tend to score higher on Conscientiousness, whereas liberals tend to score higher on Openness to Experience. Consistent with this, there's evidence that conservatives are less creative than liberals. Stephen Dollinger at Southern Illinois University asked over four hundred students, who had been categorized as conservative or liberal according to their views on issues such as gay rights and immigration, to complete a half-finished drawing and take twenty photos on the theme "Who are you?". The efforts of the more conservative students were consistently rated as less creative by the judges.

Further research by Jost has found that conservative values appear to be motivated by an exaggerated fear of uncertainty and threat, including death. There's also evidence that people who hold conservative values are more sensitive to interpersonal disgust, as measured by things like a dislike of sitting on a seat left warm by someone else or an aversion to wearing second-hand clothes. In a 2007 investigation involving Canadian students, Gordon Hodson of Brock University found that those who scored higher on interpersonal disgust tended to hold more right-wing authoritarian beliefs, had a less-than-human perception of immigrants and more negative attitudes to marginalized groups such as the poor.

Sometimes circumstances can interact with people's psychological motives, shifting their position on the ideological spectrum. For example, there's evidence that terrorism can increase the appeal of conservatism. The Republican President George W. Bush grew in popularity after the 9/11 terror attacks, and research by Jost with people in or near the World Trade Center at the time of the attacks found that 38 percent reported becoming more conservative during the ensuing eighteen months, compared with just 12 percent saying they'd become more liberal. Similar results have been replicated in the laboratory. In 2009, Paul Nail at the University of Arkansas showed that asking liberal students to think about their own death led them to express their opinions with more conviction – a characteristic usually associated with conservatism – and to show more sympathy for homophobia. There's less research on situational factors that can induce liberalism, but travel and education have both been cited as catalysts for a more liberal political view.

The science of persuasion

Politicians are wising up to psychology. Several psychologists and behavioural economists acted as advisors to Barack Obama during his campaign to become US President. One of Obama's first appointments was behavioural economist Cass R. Sunstein, who was put in charge of the Office of Information and Regulatory Affairs. Sunstein is the co-author with Richard H. Thaler of *Nudge* (2008), a highly influential book about how psychologically inspired political interventions can influence people to make decisions that are better for themselves and for society – an approach that the authors dub **libertarian paternalism**. For example, they suggest that governments should exploit the fact that people often stick with whatever is their default choice. If you want more people to donate their organs or to sign up to private pension plans, the thinking goes, all you need to do is to make these options the **default**, so

> "Nudges are not mandates. Putting the fruit at eye level counts as a nudge. Banning junk food does not."
>
> From *Nudge* (2008)

that people have to opt out rather than opt in. Sunstein and Thaler's ideas have already had an impact in the UK, with 10 Downing Street recently establishing a "Nudge Unit", which receives advice from Thaler. Moreover, early in 2010, leaked emails from David Cameron's strategy director Steve Hilton found him extolling the usefulness of psychology. "Here are some great examples," he wrote to Conservative colleagues, "of how harnessing the insights of behavioural economics and social psychology can help you achieve your policy goals in a more effective and light-touch way..." It's not just a UK and US fad. In 2009, the French set up a dedicated strategy unit to advise the prime minister on the implications of findings in psychology and neuroscience.

Another important factor in persuasion research relates to **social norms** – the overpowering tendency to follow

Richard H. Thaler, co-author of *Nudge* and a government advisor.

the crowd, to behave in a way that is thought of as "normal". A good example of this comes from the research of Robert Cialdini, Professor of Psychology and Marketing at Arizona State University and author of the hugely successful *Influence: The Psychology of Persuasion* (1984). Cialdini investigated to what extent hotel guests place their towels straight into the laundry after use or reuse them. The standard persuasion tactic that a hotel uses is to leave a card imploring guests to consider the environment and reuse towels as much as possible. Far more effective than this, as Cialdini's research showed, is a message stating that most guests reuse their towels at least once during their stay. This social-norms message made Cialdini's participants 26 times more likely to reuse their towels than those guests subjected to the standard environmental message.

According to a *Time* magazine article published in April 2009, President Obama's team of psychologist advisors recommended exploiting this very effect in the run-up to the 2008 presidential election. Their advice was that by spreading the word that a record voter-turnout was

Persuading people to go green

Although it seems that a lot of people recognize the human contribution to climate change, and wish to make their behaviour more environmentally friendly, many of them don't. So what stops them? The psychologists Gerald Gardner, Professor Emeritus at the University of Michigan-Dearborn, and Paul Stern, Director of the Committee on the Human Dimensions of Global Climate Change at the National Research Council, think they know the answer. The problem, as they see it, is a lack of clear information on ways in which individuals can reduce their energy consumption.

According to Gardner and Stern, people end up doing things that are highly visible and make them feel good – such as turning off lights and turning down the thermostat – when actually these kinds of activities are relatively ineffective. In a 2008 article in *Environment Magazine*, Gardner and Stern outlined some of the most effective actions people can take to help limit the man-made contributions to climate change (see http://tinyurl.com/5jd6f7).

In general, they felt that a few, costly actions were more effective than engaging in numerous modifications or curtailments of existing activities. For example, it's better to invest in modern insulation and a more efficient heating-system than it is to try to remember to turn the thermostat down a notch each day. They also argued that this approach is psychologically advantageous because "curtailment actions must be repeated continuously over time to achieve their effect, whereas efficiency-boosting actions, taken infrequently or only once, have lasting effects with little need for continuing attention and effort".

Psychological factors were also highlighted in a report published by the British government in 2009 about how to encourage people to move to a lower-carbon economy. One approach, favoured by psychologist Patrick Devine-Wright of Manchester University (a consultant on the report) was for "smart metering". This would make people's energy use more visible to them and enable it to be compared against typical consumption-patterns. Research has shown that the installation of such meters can reduce people's energy use by up to ten percent. A similar ploy has also been shown to increase household recycling. Providing feedback to a person on how much their household has recycled compared to the average for their street generally leads the whole street to end up recycling more.

expected, Obama's camp could actually influence more people to turn out to vote, creating a self-fulfilling prophecy.

Another psychological effect politicians might benefit from is **framing** – how to phrase things in such a way that it either increases the appeal of your ideas and policies, or reduces the appeal of those of your opponents. This tactic was clearly in use during the British General Election campaign of 2010, when the Conservative party repeatedly branded Labour's planned increase in National Insurance as a "jobs tax". This was an especially canny move, because research consistently shows that people are swayed more by negative than by positive information – an effect known as the **negativity bias**.

Politicians would also do well to remember that the easier a message is to process, the more likely people will think it true and agree with it. This is called the **fluency effect**, and can be achieved through such superficial means as an easy-to-read font, or through repetition. While people sense the ease with which they've processed the message, they're not so good at identifying why it was easy to process, assuming that it must be because of its truth or familiarity. The implications for politicians are manifold – for example, in the writing of political slogans and manifestos. Finally, when on the defensive, it's unwise for politicians to repeat any allegations made against them. The more times people hear it, the easier it is to process and believe it.

21 Psychology at school

Spelling out his future government's priorities in 1996, the would-be UK prime minister Tony Blair famously put it like this: "Education, education, education." Ever the shrewd politician, Blair was addressing the anxieties of millions of parents who, understandably enough, want their children to have the best schooling possible. Inevitably, debates over what works best in education are both intense and rife. Psychologists make an important contribution, from the question of whether children should be placed in streamed classes, to how best to boost their academic performance with praise and discipline.

Educational psychologists usually train first as teachers before beginning postgraduate studies in educational psychology. Once qualified, they spend much of their time assessing and helping children with special educational needs, and they advise teachers and policymakers on the optimum conditions for learning. Researchers in educational psychology test different teaching approaches and styles, and they study the factors – such as working memory and self-discipline – associated with children's success at school.

Teachers

Parents often deliberate anxiously over which school to send their child to. But the evidence suggests that teachers matter far more than schools, and in fact there's often more variation in quality between teachers at the same school than between teachers at different schools, which seemingly undermines the efforts some parents make to find a school with the best teachers.

A non-profit movement in the United States, called Teach for America, recruits graduate students to teach in poor areas, and they've kept meticulous records of the relative success of their different recruits as measured by pupil grade-achievement. The organization has noticed that factors

you might think would be important, such as a teacher having past experience of teaching in a poor area, matter little when it comes to effectively predicting success. Instead, they've found that a teacher having **perseverance** is key – in life in general and in relation to teaching.

This observation was supported scientifically by a study published late in 2009 by positive psychologist Angela Duckworth and her colleagues at the University of Pennsylvania. They followed the progress of nearly four hundred novice teachers enrolled in the Teach for America programme and found that it was those who'd scored highly on **grit** and **life satisfaction** who tended to have the most teaching success in terms of their pupils' later grade-achievement. Duckworth and her colleagues speculated that grittier teachers are likely to try harder and maintain effort in the face of setbacks. Life satisfaction, meanwhile, could manifest as energy and zest that enthuses pupils.

PRAISE

A perennial question for teachers is how much to praise pupils who strive and excel, and how much to admonish those who misbehave or don't make an effort. A British study, the results of which were presented at a conference in 2006, suggests that it's praise that pays.

Educational psychologist Jeremy Swinson of Liverpool John Moores University and his co-workers devised a three-hour training package that encouraged teachers to focus on praising pupils. Before the training, nineteen participating teachers spent, on average, 54 percent of class time praising pupils, compared with 46 percent of the time scolding them. After the training, a shift occurred, with the result that they averaged 85 percent of the time praising versus 15 percent scolding. Most importantly, 94 percent of the pupils were deemed obedient after the training, compared with 78 percent before.

Swinson built on these findings with colleague Brian Apter in 2008. In the largest study of its kind, Swinson and Apter's team observed pupil behaviour in 141 schools located across the UK, and found that they spent an average of 85 percent of the time on task – a higher rate than found in related studies published in 1987, 1992 and 2005. Importantly for the issue of praise, teachers' verbal behaviours were also analysed, and it was found that they were providing positive verbal feedback three times as often as in earlier studies. Moreover, amounts of positive and neutral verbal feedback – the latter is another sign of pupil engagement – were positively linked with pupils' spending more time on task.

However, it's important to realize that not all praise is equal. The Stanford University psychologist Carol Dweck has published numerous studies showing that pupils fare better if they have a mindset that sees success as related to effort rather than innate ability. Those who tie success to intelligence and who see intelligence as fixed are demoralized by failure, whereas those who recognize the importance of effort and the power to learn are often galvanized by failure to try even harder. This has implications for how we praise children. Teachers and parents who respond to a child's success by telling them how clever they are risk fostering a fixed mindset in that child. By contrast, praising a child for their effort and for the strategies they use to succeed helps to foster a malleable, effort-based mindset. Importantly, Dweck's research has shown that pupils who view success as tied to effort subsequently outperform their "intelligence as fixed" peers, even when they are matched for academic achievement at the start of the study.

More controversial than verbal praise is the use of bribes to motivate pupils. Although there's evidence that cash and other rewards can boost student performance, there's also a downside. For example, a meta-analysis of 128 studies published in 1999 by Edward Deci at the University of Rochester concluded that external rewards undermine intrinsic motivation and that this is particularly the case for children. What typically happens is that the positive effects of external rewards diminishes over time, and then, when the rewards are stopped, pupil motivation dissolves. Using material rewards also risks the morally dubious situation whereby less capable kids miss out on rewards even if they've worked hard.

Class size and streaming

Politicians and school leaders are often heard pledging to reduce class sizes as if it's a given that to do so is beneficial. A large-scale American study published by psychologists in 2005, provided robust evidence that class size really is important. Jeremy Finn at the University of Buffalo followed 4,948 kindergarten pupils over time to see which of them went on to graduate from high school 13 years later. He found that of those children who spent their first four years of school in a small class (between 13 and 17 pupils), 88 percent graduated from high school, compared with 76 percent of children who were in a large class (of between 22 and 26 students). The difference grew to 18 percent when only children from lower-income families were considered. Deeper analysis showed that it wasn't purely academic performance that led the pupils in smaller classes to be more likely to stay on – other factors such as motivation played a role too.

Another contentious topic in schooling is the question of whether or not to stream children according to ability – putting high achievers all together in one class and underachievers all together in another. A common criticism of streaming is that it stigmatizes and demoral-izes children placed in lower-ability streams. However, this concern may be misplaced. A Singaporean study published in 2005 followed hundreds of pupils for three years after they were separated into a lower and upper stream on the basis of public examinations taken before starting secondary school. While at the start of the study the lower-stream students had lower academic confidence than the upper-stream students, this had actually reversed by the end of the study. Academic self-esteem had dropped across the entire sample – no surprise given that adolescence can be a difficult time – but after three years the lower-stream students had more **academic confidence** than the upper-stream students. Liu Woon Chia at the National Institute of Singapore, who conducted the study, surmised that the lower-stream students enjoyed a "big fish in a small pond" effect, whereas the upper-stream students had faced stiffer competition and more pressure. The Singaporean system also allows lower-stream children limited opportunities for jumping up to the top stream, which may have had a motivating effect.

Lessons from educational psychology

❑ **The importance of testing** Once a pupil has successfully recalled an item of information in a test, thus suggesting they've learned it, this shouldn't be regarded as the end point. Neither should they simply revise what they've already learned. Instead, further studying *and* repeated testing of the same material will help consolidate the earlier learning, leading to deeper memorization. (see also p.88 on the importance of spacing in study).

❑ **Concrete examples aren't always helpful** Common sense tells us that successful teaching depends on an ability to invoke interesting concrete examples to explain abstract concepts. In fact, such examples can be counter-productive, at least when it comes to maths. Jennifer Kaminski at Ohio State University showed this in a 2008 study in which students learned the rules governing mathematical relations between three items in a group. Students taught with the help of pizza and tennis-ball metaphors were able to learn the rules, but were unable to transfer them to a novel real-life situation. By contrast, students taught using abstract symbols not only mastered the mathematical relations but were able to transfer what they'd learned to a new context.

❑ **Museum visits really are beneficial** Class trips to the local museum seem like a good idea, but do pupils really learn much? According to Julien Gross at the University of Otago, the answer depends on how the children are tested. He published a study in 2009 involving pupils who visited the Royal Albatross Centre in Dunedin. Confronted afterwards with a standard comprehension test, the children didn't seem to have remembered much. However, when they were simply asked to freely recall as much as they could from the day, it was clear that they'd retained a huge amount. This was especially the case if they were allowed to use drawings to help convey what they'd remembered.

IT'S NOT ONLY ABOUT IQ

Of course, academic success doesn't just rest on external factors, such as teachers and class size, it also depends on a child's own traits. Intelligence is the most obvious factor linked to school success, and unsurprisingly many studies have shown that IQ-test performance is an accurate predictor of later grade-achievement – although not the only relevant factor. Recently, for example, there's been a surge of interest and evidence pointing to the role of **working memory** – a child's capacity for holding and manipulating information mid-task.

❑ **Look away from me when I'm talking to you** When children avert their gaze, adults often assume they aren't concentrating. In fact, gaze aversion is a useful strategy used by adults as well as children to help block out unwanted visual stimulation when thinking hard about something. Gwyneth Doherty-Sneddon at the University of Stirling has shown that gaze aversion in response to tough questions is a skill that increases with age – it's used less by five-year-olds than eight-year-olds, the latter doing it as much as adults. What's more, Doherty-Sneddon has shown that teaching five-year-olds to look away when thinking improves their performance on difficult maths and verbal questions.

❑ **Let children gesture** On a related note, teachers used to tell children to sit on their hands, to deter them from fidgeting. However, research by Karen Pine at the University of Hertfordshire and others has shown that children's gestures help them think and learn. For example, one study showed that children were able to name twice as many pictures when their hands were free to gesture, compared with when their hands were constrained by mittens velcroed to a table (see also Chapter 9 on language).

❑ **Hollywood films can help students** There's usually an audible sigh of relief when a teacher tells pupils their double-history lesson is going to be taken up with watching *Elizabeth I* or some other popular historical film. Psychology research suggests such films really can help pupils understand related material in a text book, with one caveat – the teacher must point out in advance where the film deviates from the true historical record. Andrew Butler demonstrated this in a 2009 study in which pupils' recall of textbook facts was boosted by an accompanying, related and accurate film clip. A clip with an inaccuracy could provoke mistakes in later testing, but this problem was eradicated if the teacher pointed out any inaccuracies in advance.

In one study conducted by Tracy and Ross Alloway at the Universities of Stirling and Edinburgh, for example, two hundred children had their IQ and working memory tested at age five and were then followed up at age eleven. Working memory at age five was the strongest predictor of the children's reading, spelling and maths performance at age eleven, accounting for between ten and twenty percent of the variation in their performance – even more than IQ. Alloway said that working memory has this predictive power because it measures a child's capability for learning, whereas IQ tests are more focused on what a child already knows. The encouraging thing about this line of work is that preliminary research suggests that working-memory capacity may be amenable to training.

Another pupil trait that's been found to predict academic success accurately is **self-discipline**. Angela Duckworth, working with Martin Seligman, asked 140 children (average age thirteen), their parents and teachers to rate their self-discipline one autumn and then looked to see how well they did in their exams at the end of the year. The children with more self-discipline scored higher grades and were more likely to get into High School. A follow-up study was similar, but recorded pupils' IQ scores in the autumn as well as their self-discipline – the latter was found to account for twice as much of the variation in their subsequent academic performance as IQ. Consistent with this, when Walter Mischel tracked down the kids

School shootings

A tragic reason for psychologists' involvement in schools in recent years has been the occurrence of school shootings in which one or more pupils have gone on the rampage against their teachers and classmates. These include the Columbine High School massacre in 1999 and the Virginia Tech Massacre of 2007 – the latter leaving 32 people dead. Such events aren't confined to the US. In Winnenden in Germany in 2009, for example, Tim Kretschmer killed fifteen people including pupils and teachers. The challenge for psychologists is to discern identifiable patterns in these incidents even though they remain, thankfully, relatively rare.

Despite the scant evidence-base, the psychologists Traci Wike and Mark Fraser at the University of North Carolina, writing in 2009, said there were some clear lessons to be learned from past incidents. For example, in nearly all previous school-shootings, the killers lacked attachment to their school, suggesting schools should have procedures in place for increasing pupil attachment and sense of belonging.

Another finding is that 71 percent of attackers have experienced bullying and harassment, suggesting that it's vital for schools to have resources available to help troubled and rejected students. Other recommendations proposed by Wike and Fraser include reducing levels of social aggression, for example through conflict-resolution programmes; breaking down codes of silence, in which pupils have an implicit agreement not to share information with teachers and parents; and bolstering communication between school and community agencies, thus allowing the rapid review of pupils whose essays and compositions betray signs of mental distress.

Other experts have accused the media of irresponsible coverage of school shootings. Forensic psychiatrist Park Dietz at the UCLA School of Medicine, for example, has advised the media not to broadcast images of school-shooting perpetrators and not to represent them as anti-heroes in a way that could incite copycat incidents.

whose self-control he'd tested in the 1960s (see p.113), he found that those who were more skilled at deferring gratification were more academically successful and had fewer behavioural problems a decade later.

Whereas IQ has always been considered largely immutable, self-discipline shares with working memory the distinct possibility that it is amenable to training. For that reason, these new findings are optimistic, suggesting that children can be taught the skills they need to help them excel in academic work.

Learning difficulties

One of the most common learning difficulties that educational psychologists deal with is **dyslexia**, from the Greek meaning "difficulty with words". It's a controversial topic because in some countries a diagnosis of dyslexia can unlock resources and extra teaching provision that would otherwise be unavailable or punitively expensive.

The conventional view is that dyslexia manifests as a reading ability lower than you'd expect based on a child's general intelligence. This reading deficit has been traced to a problem handling the building blocks of sound from which words are formed, known as **phonemes.** Whereas a confident reader can use letter-to-sound conversion rules to read a nonsense word like "challyhoo", a child with dyslexia is likely to struggle.

Critics of the concept of dyslexia point out that poor readers with low general intelligence also struggle with phonemes. They also benefit from the same kind of phonological training as do children diagnosed with dyslexia. By this account, some children, smart and not so smart, have reading difficulties and we should help them all.

Some psychologists have focused on other problems that often seem to go hand in hand with dyslexia, including postural instability and difficulty telling left from right. For example, the Dore treatment approach (named after paint-tycoon Wynford Dore who funded the programme) is based on the idea that the root cause of dyslexia lies in irregular function of the **cerebellum** – the cauliflower-like structure at the back of the brain that's known to be involved in learning and movement. Clients on the Dore programme undertake physical exercises designed to improve their co-ordination and cerebellar functioning, with the effect, it is claimed, of aiding reading ability. But just because dyslexia sometimes coincides with movement problems doesn't mean those problems cause dyslexia – as several critics in mainstream psychology have pointed out.

The psychologist Maggie Snowling at the University of York is one of the world's leading authorities on dyslexia. In 2008, she reaffirmed that the most effective interventions for dyslexia target readers' difficulties with phonemes, including providing training in letter knowledge and how to make links between letters and sounds.

Less well known than dyslexia is **dyscalculia** – from the Greek to "count badly". Children with this diagnosis have mathematical skills that are far weaker than you'd expect based on their overall intelligence. They display problems with both arithmetical processing and arithmetic facts, such as learning multiplication tables. In severe cases, such children find even basic numerical challenges difficult, such as being able to say whether the answer to $3 + 4$ is in the region of 30 to 40.

Dyscalculia often coincides with other learning problems, including ADHD (see p.320) and, in about forty percent of cases, dyslexia. Psychologists have attempted to find out whether these other conditions are the root cause of the number difficulties, but the results are extremely inconsistent. Babies and even some animals show basic numerical skills in terms of distinguishing between quantities, which points to there being a core numerical system in the brain. Increasingly, the consensus view is that dyscalculia probably reflects a problem with this core system.

Supporting this idea, research has shown that children with dyscalculia lack a fundamental numerical ability known as **subitising** – this is the ability to glance at a group of items of four or less and know in an instant, without counting, how many items there are. Children with dyscalculia will often resort to counting to three or four instead of being able to recognize these quantities on sight.

Recently, psychologists have turned their attention to finding where in the brain the core number-system resides. The intra-parietal sulcus, towards the back of the head, is a prime candidate. For example, a 2007 study found that the application of **transcranial magnetic stimulation** to this area – a technique that involves placing a magnet near the skull, thereby temporarily affecting neuronal activity underneath – disrupted people's performance in a task that depended on their sense of numerical magnitude. What's more, brain-imaging studies have found that children with dyscalculia have abnormal functioning in this same neural region.

22 Sport

It's taken a while for psychological science to catch up with sport. The US Olympic Team didn't take a psychologist with them until 1988, and the British Psychological Society didn't create a full Division of Sports Psychology until 2004. But today, psychology and sport have become inseparable. By the time of the London Olympics in 2012, most international athletes will have worked with a sports psychologist at some stage in their career. In fact, as competing athletes reach ever-greater heights of physical readiness, it's often the mental arena in which winners and losers are made. Today, sports psychologists provide advice on – among other things – mental attitude, team cohesion, visualization techniques, and coping with injuries and setbacks.

Thinking like a winner

How do elite athletes cope with the intense pressure they are put under? Is it possible to think like a winner? A great deal of research in sports psychology has attempted to answer these kinds of questions by conducting extensive interviews with top-class sportsmen and women.

In one study published in 2005, Stephen Bull and his colleagues at the England and Wales Cricket Board interviewed twelve top English cricketers, uncovering evidence of what they called **tough attitudes** and **tough thinking**. Taking risks, going the extra mile, belief in quality preparation and having a "never say die" mindset were all examples of tough attitudes. For instance, one cricketer recalled his early career attitude: "You can throw whatever stones you want at me," he used to say to himself, "but I am not going off this course. It might take me ten or fifteen years, but I will get there. I will play for

> "It's a funny thing, the more I practise the luckier I get."
>
> Credited to Arnold Palmer (among others)

England." Tough thinking, meanwhile, was characterized by astute decision-making at critical moments in a match, honest self-appraisal and overcoming self-doubt.

In another study, Maurizio Bertollo of the Gabriele d'Annunzio University of Chieti-Pescara interviewed thirteen members of Italy's 2004 Olympic pentathlon squad about their thought processes during the shooting event. Several of the athletes said that when they stopped concentrating on making the best possible shot and focused instead on not making a bad shot, this often had the opposite effect and resulted in them doing just that. Bertollo said this was an example of the "ironic effects" that can be caused by how an athlete is thinking.

This tallies with other research which indicates that thinking too much about an already mastered technique can be counter-productive. In a 2008 study, Daniel Gucciardi asked twenty experienced golfers to perform putts in one of three ways. In the first – designed to make them conscious of elements of their technique – they had to focus on the words "arms", "weight" and "head"; in the second they simply focused on

Why your team should wear red

Teams or individuals who wear red seem to be at an advantage. Psychologists have looked at past records in English football and found that teams who wear red do better than average. Other researchers have focused on taekwondo contests in which one competitor wears red while the other wears blue. If the fight is one-sided, colours don't make any difference. But in closely-fought bouts, the combatant wearing red is significantly more likely to win. In a striking demonstration of this effect, Norbert Hagemann at the University of Münster asked experienced referees to score taekwondo contestants seen in a series of video clips. When Hagemann used digital trickery to switch the colours worn by the fighters, he found that the referees scored the same fighter's performance more generously when he wore red than when he wore white.

Why does Tiger Woods always wear a red shirt on the final day of tournaments? Perhaps he's been reading up on the research. Red is also associated with dominance in the animal kingdom – male Mandrill monkeys, for example, get redder when they're angry and the reddest individual in a face-off tends to win. It's an association we've inherited and still subscribe to, albeit subconsciously. In a revealing study conducted by Anthony Little and Russell Hill, participants were presented with pairs of circles or squares, one red, one blue, and had to say which shape was more dominant and aggressive, and which would win in a physical competition. The participants overwhelmingly chose the red shape.

Tiger Woods celebrates as he holes a putt during the final round of the 2005 Buick Invitational in San Diego.

three irrelevant words; and in the third on a single word that encapsulated the entirety of their movement, for example "smooth".

At first, Gucciardi kept the atmosphere casual. However, when he raised the stakes by offering cash rewards, the performance of the participants in the first category suffered, whereas the performance of the golfers in the latter two categories actually improved slightly. This suggests that **anxiety** harms performance not because it is distracting per se, as some have argued, but because it causes performers to focus too much on actions that should be automatic.

One way that elite athletes attempt to overcome the curse of anxiety, also known as "the yips", is to make **practice** sessions as much like the real event as possible. This is of course easier said than done. Filming your technique can help recreate the excessive self-focus that occurs during competition. Raising the stakes through informal league tables or by performing in front of an audience are other obvious strategies. Ironically, having recreated the tension of a real competition during practice time, the pentathletes interviewed by Maurizio Bertollo said that during actual competition they then tried to recreate the relaxed feeling of gentle practice.

THE MYTH OF THE HOT STREAK

One of the most widespread beliefs among sports fans is that players go through periods of being "on form", also known as "hot streaks". Stated simply, most fans think that if a basketball player was successful with his last two basket attempts, or if a soccer striker scored with his last two shots at goal, then their chances of scoring on their next attempt is raised compared with if they'd just had two misses.

In fact, when researchers looked at the historical record, they mostly found no evidence for hot streaks whatsoever. A player is just as likely to make the basket after two preceding misses than after two preceding scores. Thomas Gilovich of Cornell University was the first to show this, in a 1985 study in which he looked in detail at the scoring records of nine members of the 1980–81 Philadelphia 76ers.

Similar findings have emerged for golf, with players on the PGA tour just as likely to score par or better after scoring above par on the preceding hole than after scoring below par. And it also applies to tennis, darts, bowling and other sports. Why do we continue to believe in hot streaks when the idea appears to have no basis in reality? Psychologists think it probably has to do with our misunderstanding of randomness. We expect hits and misses to alternate more evenly than they do, so that

How to save a penalty

The penalty shoot-out, used to settle drawn matches in international football competitions, must be one of the most nerve-wracking situations in sport. It's a tense one-on-one situation in which a player must get the ball past the opposition's goalkeeper with one kick from the penalty spot.

According to sports psychologist Geir Jordet of the Norwegian School of Sports Sciences, one possible key to success is for the player taking the kick to take his time. In 2009, Jordet analysed all previous penalty shoot-outs in major international competitions and found that players who rushed to take a penalty were at a distinct disadvantage. Those who took less than 200 milliseconds to respond to the ref's whistle scored, on average, just under 57 percent of the time. By contrast, those who took more than a second to respond averaged a success rate of eighty percent. Jordet thinks that a penalty taken too quickly could be a sign of "self-regulatory breakdown", in which intense stress causes the player to want to escape the situation as quickly as possible. Other research has shown that players who fixate on the goalie are less likely to score. The trick is to ignore the goalie and focus instead on where you want the ball to go.

What about psychology-inspired advice for goalkeepers? Apparently they should try staying in the middle of the goal more often, rather than jumping. In 2007, Michael Bar-Eli from Ben-Gurion University of the Negev watched hours of archival footage and noticed that goalkeepers saved many more penalties when they stayed in the middle of the goal, rather than jumping to the left or right. Despite this apparent advantage, Bar-Eli found that most often – 93.7 percent of when a string of hits or misses occurs, we attribute this to an athlete being on or off form, rather than recognizing that the pattern is most likely down to chance.

The power of the mind

Another line of research in sports psychology has looked at mental practice – where a sportsperson imagines performing sporting techniques without making any actual physical movement. Neuroscience has shown that there is extensive overlap in the areas of the brain responsible for performing an action and imagining that same action. Consistent with this, psychology studies have shown that **mental rehearsal** really does benefit subsequent physical performance. However, in a 1994 meta-analysis of the literature on this topic, James Driskell warned that the effects

the time in fact – keepers chose to jump rather than stay in the middle. He thinks this reluctance not to jump may be a sporting manifestation of the "omission bias" – that is, failure feels worse after doing nothing than after doing the wrong thing.

Manchester United goalkeeper Edwin van der Sar saves a penalty from Chelsea's Nicolas Anelka during their 2008 Champions League final.

can be short-lived. They recommended completing mental rehearsal every one to two weeks. They also found that mental practice produces diminishing returns the more you do it, and suggested that sessions of twenty minutes gave the best results.

Exactly how you should go about visualizing a given technique depends on your skill level. In a 2008 study, Sian Beilock at the University of Chicago tested the putting accuracy of novice and experienced golfers after they had performed one of two visualization practice sessions – either imagining performing a putt as quickly as possible or imagining performing a putt at leisure. The outcome depended on experience: the novice golfers benefited most from the slow visualization task whereas the experienced golfers benefited most from the quick version. This corresponds with the research showing that experienced athletes can benefit from executing moves quickly, because it stops them from thinking too much about actions which have become automatic. Novices, by contrast, typically benefit from taking their time and thinking about actions which are not yet familiar.

Believe it or not, there's also research suggesting that the mere thought of performing exercises can increase muscle power. Vitoth Ranganathan of the Cleveland Clinic Foundation led a twelve-week study in which, for fifteen minutes five times a week, participants imagined pushing their little finger against a resisting force with all their might. Amazingly, the mental training increased the participants' little-finger strength by forty percent compared with before the training, whereas no change in strength was observed among a control group who didn't do the mental training. A comparison group who used actual physical exercises to train their little finger exhibited increased strength of 53 percent. Ranganathan said that the mental training (like the physical training) had increased the size of the signal sent from the brain to the muscles, thus increasing muscle strength when an actual movement was performed.

Finally, imagine you could take an inert substance, which, because you believed it was something more potent, actually ended up enhancing your performance. Would there be anything wrong with doing that? This isn't a hypothetical question. The placebo effect occurs when inert substances lead to real physical changes based on a person's belief in the power of what they've taken. The effect is usually associated with medicine (see p.313), but it can also be exploited in sport.

In a 2007 study, for example, Fabrizio Benedetti and colleagues at the University of Turin Medical School and the National Institute of Neuroscience gave athletes injections of morphine during training to increase their endurance (the controlled use of morphine during training is legal). When it came to the day of the real event, the researchers replaced the morphine with salt solution without telling the athletes. The result? Compared with a control group, the athletes showed enhanced endurance just as if they'd been given a real dose of morphine that day.

In another Benedetti study, published in 2008, weightlifters in training were tricked into thinking they'd been given a high dose of caffeine prior to each lift. The participants subsequently worked their muscles harder than if they hadn't had the placebo, although their feelings of muscle fatigue were unchanged. Next, to make the placebo even more convincing, the researchers surreptitiously reduced the weight being lifted, so that it felt lighter than usual, thus creating the illusion that the effect of the placebo had kicked in. Afterwards the weight was returned to normal and the placebo re-administered. This time the participants worked their muscles harder and reported less muscle fatigue than if the placebo hadn't been given.

23 Bodily health

Illness isn't always something that just happens to us. The choices we make, the ways we conduct our lives, the beliefs we hold, all have profound consequences for the health of our bodies. Smoking, excess drinking and over-eating are obvious examples of behaviours that have a direct effect on our health, and which in many instances, we have a strong degree of control over. For these reasons, health psychologists play an increasingly central role in health care. They want to know why we adopt certain behaviours to excess, even when we know them to be harmful, and they investigate ways to get us to reduce or cease these behaviours once we've started them.

But health psychology isn't only about trying to control excess consumption. With illnesses such as breast cancer and testicular cancer, where early detection can vastly improve survival rates, self-checking becomes vitally important. Health psychologists investigate ways of encouraging people to follow such procedures, and they explore the reasons that deter many people from doing so.

Psychological factors also come into play in the event of a global pandemic, such as the swine flu of 2009 when millions of people needed to adopt stricter hygiene in order to help halt the virus's spread. The psycholinguist Brigitte Nerlich has argued that, in such circumstances, apocalyptic metaphors of the kind favoured by tabloid newspapers may grab people's attention, but actually end up inhibiting behavioural change. The message that "we're all going to die" paralyses people, whereas calm advice on how to control the threat is far more constructive.

Psychologists can also play a part once an illness has been diagnosed, by working in palliative care with patients and their families, for example, or by helping people adjust to the life changes imposed by a chronic illness or disability. They have helped inform labelling practice on drug packaging and have devised easy-to-use scheduling sheets to help patients keep track of which drugs they need to take and when.

Central to health psychology is recognizing that the mind and body are deeply entwined. Our mood, our stress levels, our loneliness can all affect our health. Physical wounds literally take longer to heal when we're stressed. In turn, it almost goes without saying that our health can affect our mental wellbeing. A heart attack can trigger a bout of serious depression; obesity can crush a person's self-esteem.

Explaining and influencing behaviour

Psychologists have spent years creating models to help understand why we choose to behave the way we do in relation to our health. One of the best known and influential is **The Theory of Planned Behaviour**, developed by Professor Icek Ajzen of the University of Massachusetts. This proposes that whether or not we choose to behave in a certain way depends on our attitudes and beliefs about that behaviour. These include what we think the likely outcome of it will be, whether we believe other people (especially those close to us) engage in it, and whether we think we're actually capable of behaving that way.

The benefit of this model is that it provides an immediate guide as to how to influence people's health-related behaviours. For example, it suggests that persuading a smoker that most people don't smoke is likely to deter him or her from continuing to light up. Similarly, highlighting the positive outcomes likely to emerge from stopping – such as living longer, feeling fitter, saving money and not having smelly clothes – may also help someone decide. Finally, it can help if the person can be persuaded that it is well within their ability to stop smoking. This might involve telling them about other people's successes, or offering them aids, such as nicotine patches or gum.

Other findings in relation to behavioural change are not so obvious. Consider health-promotion campaigns that use dramatic imagery to highlight the dangers of drink-driving. A 2010 study by Steffen Nestler of Johannes Gutenberg-University, Mainz found that for a portion of the population these kinds of campaigns can backfire. People who are what is known as **cognitively avoidant** respond to threats by distracting themselves or denying that the threat is relevant to them. When Nestler gave participants a scare story about a fictional illness related to the consumption of caffeine, those with a high score for cognitive avoidance rated the threat from the illness as less severe after reading the scare story than they did after reading a milder, low-key version.

Bedside manner

Traditionally, doctors were expected to assume a "paternalistic" approach to patients. They were seen as the authoritative expert who would make your symptoms go away. Today, the ideal doctor-patient relationship is expected to be far more egalitarian. They are the experts in diagnosis and treatment, but the patient is the expert on symptoms and concerns. There's also a greater emphasis on involving patients in decision-making – a laudable aim, although many studies show patients prefer their doctor to take ultimate responsibility for medical decisions.

Patients do, however, want plenty of information, and countless surveys have shown that doctors tend to underestimate this. There's also often a mismatch between the kind of technical information the doctor provides – for example, about the disease stage and category – and the practical information that a patient seeks (such as degrees of pain and the chances of recovery). Thanks to the amount of health information available on the Internet, how doctors and patients communicate has become a pressing issue, and new research is needed to find out the best way forward.

Striking the right balance in communication isn't an easy task for doctors. If they are over-dependent on medical jargon, patients can find it difficult to understand. Conversely, if they are too colloquial – for example asking patients to "wee" for a urine sample – they can be seen as patronizing. A study published in the early-1990s, by Jan Hadlow at the Polytechnic of East London and Marian Pitts at the University of Zimbabwe, found that it was the language of psychology-related conditions, words such as "depression" and "migraine", that tended to cause the most confusion between doctors and patients – presumably because many such terms have everyday meanings alongside their medical usage.

Related to this, there's evidence that the warnings on cigarette packs could actually encourage some people to smoke. Jochim Hansen at Basle University found that smokers who saw their habit as important to their self-esteem (for example, they agreed with statements such as "smoking allows me to feel valued by others") were made to feel more positive about smoking by death-related warnings on packs than by neutral warnings (such as "smoking makes you unattractive"). Hansen argued that this was because thoughts of death can make us seek ways to boost our self-esteem (an effect explained by Terror management theory, see p.227), and for some smokers that's exactly what the act of smoking provides.

Bedside manner is about more than just improving patient satisfaction, and there's evidence that a doctor's interpersonal style can have a real effect on patient-health outcomes. In 1989, Sherrie Kaplan, now at the University of California, Irvine, and her colleagues reported that chronically ill patients with doctors who provided more than the usual information, showed emotion and allowed ample time for questions, subsequently showed better outcomes in terms of blood pressure, blood-sugar levels and other markers. More recently, a team led by David Rakel at the University of Wisconsin School of Medicine and Public Health found that patients who rated their doctors as highly empathic and attentive recovered from the common cold a day earlier than patients with a more remote doctor – an effect similar to that of the most promising anti-viral drugs.

Exercise, obesity and self-control

One of the most pressing threats to health at the start of the twenty-first century is obesity. In 2007 a UK government report warned that nearly sixty percent of the country's population would be obese by 2050, if nothing was done to halt current trends. And obesity isn't just a problem for the rich countries of the West – the World Health Organization has warned that "overweight and obesity are dramatically on the rise in low- and middle-income countries".

Stated simply, obesity is a problem that arises when a person's energy intake consistently exceeds the energy they burn up. A popular belief is that in rich countries, tasty, fatty food is now in far greater abundance than in previous eras, and it's this ease of access which leads so many people to become overweight. In fact, there's evidence in Britain that while obesity has risen, average energy-intake since the 1970s has fallen. This suggests that it's the second half of the equation – a failure to burn up enough energy through exercise – that is the greater problem. This makes sense when you consider the rise of the motor car, the ubiquity of lifts and escalators, and how many daily tasks – such as washing the dishes – have become mechanized.

Successful obesity interventions, such as the UK's MEND ("mind, exercise, nutrition, do it") programme, target both eating behaviours and encourage more exercise. The MEND programme, devised for children by psychologist Paul Chadwick and paediatric dietician Paul Sacher, uses enjoyable activities to teach them about healthy eating and ways to exercise. Particular care is taken to help children who may be daunted by exercise, for example by not making the activities competitive. When it comes to adults, there's evidence that setting a specific time and place to exercise – for example, committing to going running on Monday and Thursday evenings after work – is more likely to be successful than making a loose promise to go running more. Formally, this is known as making "if-then" implementation plans, such as "if it is a Friday morning, then I will eat some fruit". A study published in 2010 by Thomas Webb at Manchester University showed that such plans could be used to break the usual link between being in a bad mood and behaving more recklessly, for example by making the plan "if I am in a bad mood, I will take deep breaths".

Whether it's forcing yourself to pound the pavements in the December drizzle or preventing yourself from reaching for one last cookie, the crucial factor in your success or failure is self-control. The psychologist Roy Baumeister at Florida State University has conducted years of fascinating research showing that self-control is a finite resource. The more you use it up in one situation, the less you'll have left over in another. In a study published in 1998, Baumeister and his colleagues asked a group of participants to resist a plate of cookies and eat the radishes on offer instead. Compared with a control group who got to eat the cookies, these abstemious participants persisted for far less time at a puzzle, presented a few minutes later, which unbeknown to them was unsolvable. Similar findings have been observed for other acts of self-restraint, such as suppressing laughter (while watching a comedy film), and for different lab measures of self-control such as the Stroop test. This latter task requires

Man's best friend?

There's a long history of research showing the health benefits of owning a dog. One typical study published in 1995 found that dog owners were 8.6 times more likely to still be alive one year after a heart attack than non-owners. One possible explanation is that the benefits arise from the amelioration of depression and loneliness: dogs can provide companionship and they also act as a talking point. A study comparing walkers with and without a dog found that canine accompaniment prompted far more chance conversational encounters. Dogs have also been shown to have some specific health uses, as in the recent case of a dog that continually sniffed a mole on its owner's skin which turned out to be malignant.

Other investigations suggest that dogs can be trained to use human facial expressions and postures to help predict the imminent onset of an epileptic fit, and that their keen sense of smell can detect hypoglycaemia in diabetics. Dogs have also been used in "pet therapy" to improve outcomes for elderly inpatients. An Italian study published in 2010, for example, found that ten elderly inpatients (with conditions including dementia and psychosis) showed larger reductions in depression after six weeks of dog visits than did a control group. Most of them also said that their quality of life had improved.

participants to name a colour word – for example "blue" – while ignoring the distraction of the ink colour it is written in. The lesson from these studies is to watch out for those moments – perhaps after a particularly testing day at work – when self-control levels are likely to be running low.

This may well be easier said than done. Research by Northwestern University psychologist Loran Nordgren shows how poor we are at predicting our future levels of impulse control – a phenomenon he's called the **restraint bias**. In one scenario, Nordgren and his colleagues offered students arriving at or leaving a cafeteria a choice of snack bar to take away, with the promise that they could keep the bar and get a cash reward if they returned it uneaten a week later. The key finding was that students who had already eaten at the cafeteria, were more likely to over-estimate their future self-restraint. They tended to choose their favourite snack bar rather than a less tempting option, and to eat the bar before the week was up, thus failing to earn the cash reward.

The message from this experiment and others like it was that when we're in a "cool" state – that is when satiated – we tend to overestimate our ability to control our visceral drives when we're in a hot state (hungry, tired or lustful). For example, the person who goes shopping *after* lunch is more likely to buy chocolates thinking they'll be able to resist them until the weekend, when the likelihood is they'll end up eating them that night.

On a more hopeful note, research shows that many of us are more physically active than we think, and would benefit if only we perceived that activity as physical exercise. In a 2007 study, Alia Crum and Ellen Langer told hotel cleaners that the work they performed on a daily basis counted as exercise and meant that they effectively led an active

Improving hospitals

While billions of dollars are spent on the latest breakthrough drugs and hi-tech medical equipment, psychology research has confirmed that the simple fact of a hospital's architectural design and layout can have a profound effect on patient recovery. A patient who has a window with a view is likely to recover more quickly than one who doesn't. Large, old-fashioned hospitals, with maze-like corridors, are easy to get lost in, causing potential stress to patients, which in turn can affect their immune system and speed of recovery. A light-filled environment with an intuitive layout and clear signage can have the reverse effect, fostering an atmosphere of care and wellbeing. Research has also highlighted that fewer falls and medication errors occur in private rooms than in public wards, and that single-sex wards are more conducive to recovery than mixed wards. Providing patients with access to quiet areas and to the outdoors, especially to gardens, can also aid their recovery. A US pioneer in this field is Dr John Zeisel, co-founder of Hearthstone, an organization which provides residential care for people with Alzheimer's disease. The design of Hearthstone's six residences are informed by psychological findings, such as that people with Alzheimer's display less anxiety when they are surrounded by their own possessions.

Introducing artwork into hospitals – something the UK charity Paintings in Hospitals has been doing since 1959 – can also benefit patients and improve the overall environment. Indeed, in 2004 the Chelsea and Westminster Hospital, London, published "A Study of the Effects of Visual and Performing Arts in Healthcare", which concluded that art in healthcare facilities can reduce levels of patient anxiety and depression, boost staff morale and even reduce the use of some medications. Chelsea and Westminster Hospital, which opened in 1993, has made both the visual and the performing arts an integral part of its healthcare philosophy. In 2006, Zeisel told *The Psychologist* magazine that there is an almost spiritual component to the way art contributes to our health and wellbeing: "It touches our brains in a way that wakes us up."

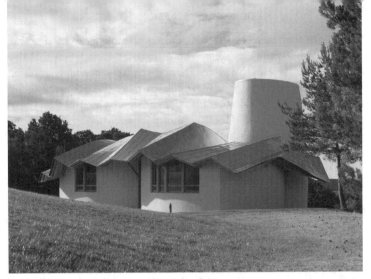

Maggie's Centre at Ninewells Hospital, Dundee in Scotland, designed by Frank Gehry. Maggie Keswick Jencks, with her husband Charles, thought up the idea of drop-in centres for cancer sufferers during the late stages of her own cancer. Both of them believed that a beautiful environment could raise the spirits to a profound extent, and all the centres are designed to the highest standards.

life, easily fulfilling government recommendations. A month later these cleaners showed health benefits in terms of their weight, body-mass index, body-fat, waist-to-hip ratio and blood pressure, compared to other cleaners at the same hotel who hadn't been given the earlier information.

What was going on here? The cleaners showing the health benefits hadn't changed their diets, smoked less or started exercising in their spare time. The researchers' conclusion was that, in the same way that some medicines work because patients believe in their healing power, so the benefit of exercise can also be related to the level of confidence in its effectiveness – otherwise known as the placebo effect.

THE POWER OF BELIEF

Whenever drugs companies test the efficacy of a new compound, they have to demonstrate that its benefits exceed those obtained with a drug-free sugar pill. The reason for this is that the mere act of taking a pill tends to have a significant benefit of its own, even if there's no active ingredient. This phenomenon, the **placebo effect**, is one of the most important in psychology.

The idea that mere beliefs can lead to physiological changes and reduce disease symptoms seems almost magical. Expectation that the treatment will be effective is crucial, and can influence how powerful the effect is. For example, four sugar pills are more effective than two for treating gastric ulcers; saltwater injections are more powerful than sugar pills (presumably because the injection paraphernalia creates a more powerful expectation of relief); and pink sugar pills are more effective as a stimulant than green ones.

Some instances of the placebo effect are truly astonishing. Consider research by Cynthia McRae of the University of Denver, which compared the effects of a radical new treatment for Parkinson's – implanting embryonic dopamine neurons into the brain – against a "sham surgery" control condition. The sham surgery was just like the real thing, except that the needles were empty and didn't pierce the brain. This meant that there wasn't any way for the patients to know which group they were in. When the patients were followed up several times over the following year, both groups showed significant benefits. Remarkably, the strongest predictor of quality-of-life improvements wasn't the group a person was in, but the group they thought they were in. That is, those patients who thought they'd had the treatment – even if they hadn't – tended to show the greater improvements in their quality of life.

> "All bow before the might of the placebo effect, it is the coolest, strangest thing in medicine."
>
> Dr Ben Goldacre

Unfortunately, the placebo effect has an evil twin known as the **nocebo effect**. This is the phenomenon whereby the expectation that something is harmful, even if it isn't, can actually lead to negative effects. Some experts believe the nocebo effect could explain why some people report experiencing headaches after exposure to electrical devices like mobile phones. Lab studies under controlled conditions haven't been able to recreate the symptoms that many people insist are caused by mobiles. This suggests that it could be the mere belief that phones are harmful which causes some people to experience negative symptoms after using them.

Part VI

Psychological problems

24 Developmental conditions

Given the dizzying complexity of the human brain, it's little wonder that things often go wrong in the course of neural development. When the brain is damaged before birth, for example through lack of oxygen, this can give rise to conditions like cerebral palsy, which is associated with motor-control problems. Other developmental conditions, such as Down's Syndrome, have direct genetic causes. This chapter will focus on three developmental conditions that continue to attract a great deal of attention from psychologists – autism, ADHD and Tourette's – not least because of their profound effects on behaviour. The exact causes of these conditions remains unknown, although genetic influences clearly play a role. Dyslexia and dyscalculia, which have specific implications for education, are dealt with in Chapter 21.

Autism

Mention autism and people often think of Dustin Hoffman's character Raymond Babbitt in the 1988 multi-Oscar winning film *Rain Man* (see p.319), or, more recently, of Lisbeth Salander, the heroine of Stieg Larsson's best-selling *Millennium* trilogy. In fact, these characters only give a partial view of the condition. Babbitt was actually an **autistic savant**, meaning that he displayed not only the social and communication problems associated with autism, the narrow interests and repetitive behaviour, but also exceptional skills, such as an encyclopaedic memory and the ability to calculate the day of the week for any given date. Similarly, Salander is portrayed as a genius computer-hacker. In reality, however, only a minority of people with autism – around one in ten – have these kind of savant skills.

Autism is not something you either have or you don't. It's more like a **spectrum** of varying degrees of severity. People who display many of the characteristics of autism in mild form, but without any speech- or language-delay and who have normal or above-average IQ, are usually diagnosed with **Asperger's Syndrome**.

Simon Baron-Cohen, Director of the Autism Research Centre at the University of Cambridge, has defined autism according to two traits: empathizing and systematizing. People with autism tend to score very poorly on tests of **empathizing** – for example, they find it difficult to tell a person's emotions from their facial expression, especially their eyes, and they struggle to imagine being in another person's shoes. By contrast, they score strongly on **systematizing**. This is the ability to break a system down so as to understand the rules governing the way the parts work together. So, to resort to stereotypes, a typical person with autism probably wouldn't make an ideal therapist, but they might excel at engineering.

This idea that people with autism are particularly attentive to detail has been explained by the **Weak Central Coherence Theory**, proposed by Professor Uta Frith in the 1980s. Frith suggested that underlying many of the outward manifestations of autism is a perceptual bias towards detail, paired with a deficit for the bigger picture. More recently, the theory has been refined, and the current view is that autism might be more accurately described as a deficit when switching from processing at the local level to processing at the bigger-picture level. Frith's work has also shown that while people with autism struggle to understand other people's perspectives, they do have sound morals and, in contrast to psychopaths, are moved by other people's emotions.

Autism is around four times more common in men than women, a fact that underlies another recent theory which sees the condition as an "extreme" form of the male brain. According to Baron-Cohen, in surveys men tend to score more highly on systematizing, while women tend to score higher on empathizing. For example, the former are more likely to agree with statements like "I have my clothes organized carefully according to type", while the latter are more likely to agree with statements like "I prefer to speak to people in person rather than emailing". Consistent with the extreme male-brain theory, a 2009 study led by Baron-Cohen found that the more testosterone there is in the womb during pregnancy, the more likely a child is to show autistic-like traits when they're older, between the ages of six and ten.

Understandably, the small minority of people with autism who also have exceptional "savant" talents tend to generate a lot of interest. Two of the most famous are **Temple Grandin** and **Stephen Wiltshire**. Grandin, a professor of animal science at Colorado State University, has designed humane livestock-facilities by drawing on her ability to identify details which can cause animals distress. In 2010, her life story was turned into an HBO feature-length biopic. Wiltshire, a celebrated British artist, started producing accurate and photo-realistic depictions of buildings and cityscapes from the age of eight. Many of his works are produced from memory, and in 2006 he was appointed MBE for his services to art.

Some experts have suggested that these kind of talents lie within us all. In 2006, Allan Snyder, director of the Centre for the Mind at the University of Sydney, showed a way to improve people's ability to count large numbers of discrete objects in an instant – in this case 50 to 150 blobs on a computer screen. Snyder found that by applying transcranial magnetic stimulation (TMS) to their left temporal lobe, he was able to significantly improve participants' performance. Before TMS, one participant had twenty guesses with twenty different displays and was always more than

Dustin Hoffman and Tom Cruise in the Oscar-winning film *Rain Man*. The inspiration for the autistic savant character in the film was Kim Peek, who died in December 2009, aged 58. Nicknamed "Kim-puter" by his friends, Peek was a non-autistic savant born with brain abnormalities including a malformed cerebellum and an absent corpus callosum (the thick bundle of nerve fibres that joins the two hemispheres). Peek struggled with abstract and conceptual thinking, but his savant skills were astonishing, and included an encyclopaedic knowledge of history, literature, classical music, US zip codes and travel routes.

five away from the true figure. After TMS, she made six out of twenty guesses that were within five blobs of the true figure. Snyder's team think that by temporarily inhibiting activity in the temporal lobe, the TMS made the participants' brains act more like an autistic brain, focusing on the raw data and ignoring the distraction of random patterns.

ADHD

ADHD stands for "attention deficit hyperactivity disorder", a developmental condition that, as the name suggests, is characterized by an inability to concentrate, poor impulse-control and excessive energy. It's very much a **syndrome** – some children show only the attentional aspect, others just the hyperactive element. Although it begins in childhood, it can persist into adulthood, causing problems throughout life.

Autistic Pride

Every year on 18 June, people on the autistic spectrum congregate to celebrate Autistic Pride day. The movement was founded by Amy Roberts and Gareth Nelson, both of whom have been diagnosed with Asperger's Syndrome. The idea of the movement is to celebrate the strengths of autism and to challenge the notion that the condition is a disease that needs curing. Roberts, Nelson and their followers prefer to see autism as a form of "neurodiversity", as distinct from non-autistic "neurotypicals". Rather than pursuing cures for the condition, they would like society to be more sensitive to the autistic way of thinking and behaving. For example, people on the autism spectrum are typically thought of as being antisocial. However, the emergence of virtual worlds such as Second Life and technologies like email and instant messaging has shown that people with autism can be highly sociable, it's just that they don't like face-to-face contact.

The Autistic Pride movement also opposes the development of pre-natal screening for autism, which may one day become available. Supporters of the movement point out that if screening had existed in the past, then geniuses like Albert Einstein and Michelangelo – who today would probably be diagnosed as autistic – would have been lost to the world.

The Pride movement is not without opponents. The parents of some children with severe autism say their plight is often unbearable and that treatments should be welcomed. These critics point out that the bulk of the Autistic Pride movement is made up of "highly functioning" people with Asperger's Syndrome, for whom the strengths of their condition outweigh the costs.

ADHD is a **controversial** diagnosis because it's made largely on the basis of parents' and teachers' reports of a child's behaviour, and it is often difficult to draw the line between naughtiness and genuine disorder. This controversy is compounded by the fact that drugs like **Ritalin** – paradoxically, a psychostimulant – are often part of the treatment plan. Prevalence rates and prescription rates for ADHD have spiralled in recent decades, and there's a concern that some frazzled parents are seeking medical help to control unruly children who don't really have anything wrong with them.

A longitudinal study published in 2007 cast doubt on the long-term superiority of drugs like Ritalin compared with **psychological interventions**. Around five hundred children with ADHD were followed over three years. Although the children treated with Ritalin showed early advantages compared with their peers on behavioural-treatment programmes, these advantages had disappeared by the end of the trial period. There was also some evidence that the drugs had interfered with the children's growth.

The current consensus is that drugs should never be the first resort for children with ADHD, and should never be prescribed to preschool children. When drugs do need to be prescribed, they should be part of a holistic approach that involves psychological interventions, including social-skills training and psycho-educational classes for parents.

Tourette's Syndrome

First described by French neurologist Gilles de la Tourette in 1885, Tourette's Syndrome usually emerges at around the age of seven and is characterized by involuntary verbal and physical tics, the latter involving the limbs and head. The stereotype of a Tourette's sufferer is of someone repeatedly shouting out obscenities. This is called **coprolalia** and is only exhibited by about one third of people with Tourette's.

Although Tourette's Syndrome often co-occurs with other emotional and behavioural problems, including ADHD, some intriguing recent research suggests it may also be associated with certain cognitive advantages. For example, in 2006 Sven Mueller and his colleagues at the University of Nottingham documented the way children with Tourette's had superior mental control when tested in an eye movement task. The rules of the task were switched every two trials, so that instead of looking at a target, the participants now had to look away from it. Each time the rule changed, all the participants' responses slowed down as they adjusted to the new rule, but the responses of the children with Tourette's slowed down less than those of the children without Tourette's.

Some genetic conditions

There are a plethora of genetic disorders which affect children's psychological and physical development. Some (like Down's Syndrome) are relatively common, others are less well known.

❑ **Down's Syndrome** is the most common cause of learning disability in children. Caused by an extra chromosome 21 – hence the formal name "trisomy-21" – the condition results in numerous physical and mental impairments, including low intelligence and increased risk of Alzheimer's Disease.

❑ **Williams Syndrome** is caused by the absence of a gene on chromosome 7 and is characterized by visuospatial problems, including difficulty with drawing and solving puzzles. By contrast, language skills and face processing usually remain relatively intact. Children with the condition are often energetic and talk in a precocious manner.

❑ **Turner Syndrome** only affects girls and is caused by an abnormality on one of the X chromosomes, or when one of the X chromosomes is missing altogether. As well as physical complications such as infertility, the condition is also associated with cognitive problems, including memory impairment and attention deficits.

❑ **Prada Willi Syndrome** is caused by an abnormality on chromosome 15 and is associated with learning disabilities, an insatiable appetite and obsessive behaviour such as hoarding.

❑ **22q11.2 deletion Syndrome** is one of the most common forms of learning disability. Caused by abnormalities on chromosome 22, children with this condition typically exhibit a delay in early cognitive, motor and language development, with an average IQ of 70–85. They have particular difficulty performing visuospatial and numerical tasks, with comparatively stronger verbal-test performance.

This finding was followed by another in 2010 by Carmelo Mario Vicario at the Sapienza University of Rome, which showed that children with Tourette's were better at a task related to time processing. The kids had to observe how long a circle appeared on-screen and then hold down the space-bar key for the same length of time. For durations longer than a second, there was no difference in performance between the Tourette's children and controls. However, for sub-second durations, the children with Tourette's were more accurate. The researchers aren't certain why children with Tourette's show these advantages, but one possibility is that their constant need to suppress their tics has left them with stronger powers of control over other brain processes.

25 Depression and anxiety

Sadness and dark moods, nerves and jitters. We all know what these feel like. But sometimes a line is crossed and lives are tainted by such extremes of negative thinking and dread that something seems to be seriously wrong. This is when people are likely to be diagnosed with depression or anxiety, or both – the two conditions frequently co-occur. Awareness of these complaints and the misery they can bring has increased hugely in recent decades. Where Victorian society, at least in the West, referred coyly to nervous trouble and people were expected to display a "stiff upper lip", today the stigma of mental illness is gradually fading. But there's a worrying aspect to this increased awareness, with ever more states of mind becoming medicalized, and rates of antidepressant use soaring.

Depression

This is how the bestselling author Marian Keyes described her experience of the illness on her blog in 2010: "Although I'm blessed enough to have a roof over my head, I still feel like I'm living in hell. I can't eat, I can't sleep, I can't write, I can't read, I can't talk to people. The worst thing is that I feel it will never end." Fellow sufferer, the American novelist William Styron talked about his depression as a "gray drizzle of horror" and "a storm of murk". Others believe such attempts at description are in vain. The developmental biologist Lewis Wolpert, author of the semi-autobiographical *Malignant Sadness: The Anatomy of Depression* (1999) has said that if you can describe your severe depression, you've never really had it, adding that during his bout of the illness all he wanted to do was to kill himself.

From the perspective of a formal psychiatric **diagnosis**, you're depressed if, for two weeks or more, you've been feeling in low mood and/or you've lost interest and enjoyment in usual activities, plus you've experienced four or more of the following: significant weight gain or loss; difficulty sleeping or sleeping too much; lethargy; feeling worthless or guilty; indecisiveness or distractibility; physical slowing or agitation (for example, pacing up and down); persistent thoughts of death or suicide. Bereavement is the one caveat – if these symptoms appear after loss of a loved one, then diagnosis of depression is made only if they persist for more than two months.

> "...there fell upon me without any warning, just as if it came out of darkness, a horrible fear of my own existence."
>
> William James,
> *Varieties of Religious Experience* (1902)

The figures vary from one study to another, but roughly speaking it's estimated that between four and ten percent of us can expect to meet these criteria for major depression at some point in our lifetimes. Women are about twice as prone to the illness as men – quite why remains something of a mystery.

Although it's a "mental" illness, there's increasing recognition that depression is also associated with **poor physical health**. A 2007 study by the World Health Organization measured the health of over two hundred thousand people across sixty countries and found that depression was associated with poorer physical health than physical conditions like angina and diabetes. Based on this, the study's lead author Saba Moussavi said that doctors should be taught not to ignore the effect that depression can have on physical health.

WHAT CAUSES DEPRESSION?

Depression is usually triggered by what the formal jargon describes rather unfeelingly as one or more significant **life events** such as bereavement, divorce or redundancy. Indeed, in a classic study involving interviews with 458 women in South London, the sociologist George Brown and the psychologist Terri Harris found that of the 37 in their sample who had experienced depression over the previous year, almost 90 percent had lived through a personal trauma. Exposure to neglect or abuse in childhood can also increase a person's risk of developing depression later in life. An earlier bout of depression is yet a further risk-factor – someone who's had the illness once is left much more vulnerable to experiencing it again.

While extreme strife can tip some people into a period of depression, others are more resilient. **Genetic factors** probably play a role here,

Suicide

Somewhere in the world a person kills themselves every forty seconds. That's according to the World Health Organization, which also warns that suicide rates have increased by sixty percent worldwide over the last 45 years. Perhaps the most shocking statistic is that among young people, suicide is the second leading cause of death after traffic accidents.

Depression is obviously a major risk factor for suicide. Less expected is the extraordinarily high suicide-rate among people with an eating disorder – fifty to sixty times higher than in the "general population". Why might this be? Experts don't know for certain, but one possible reason could be that people with eating disorders are more used to pain and discomfort. This might make it easier for them to overcome the deterrents to self-annihilation that lead many people to pull back from the brink. After all, suicide requires not just the motivation to end one's life, but also the ability to carry out the fatal act. Research shows that people who are used to pain and violence, such as soldiers, and those who have ready access to the means of killing themselves, including doctors and farmers, are also at greater risk of suicide.

Other clues as to the difference between those who think about suicide and the minority who actually kill themselves were suggested by a huge community survey carried out by Kate Fairweather at the Australian National University. She and her team identified 522 people who said they had thought about killing themselves during the previous year. The ten percent of this subgroup who had also actually made a suicide attempt were more likely to suffer from serious ill-health, be unemployed and have poor relationships with friends and family than those who didn't act on their suicidal thoughts. However, rates of depression or anxiety were actually no greater among the suicide attempters than among the contemplators of suicide.

because depression is known to run in families. Among identical twins, for example, if one of the pair has depression, there's a fifty percent chance that the other twin will too.

Depression has also been shown to snowball through the generations. A study led by Myrna Weissman at Columbia University, published in 2005, focused on 47 people recruited in 1982 and continued with their children and grandchildren. The researchers were looking for signs of childhood anxiety in the grandchildren, because it is known to be a precursor of depression later in life. Among the 161 grandchildren, those with a parent and a grandparent who had suffered depression were five times more likely to experience anxiety than grandchildren with a depressed grandparent, but not a depressed parent.

Longitudinal research in New Zealand has identified a **specific gene** which, combined with traumatic life-events, increases the likelihood that a person will develop depression later in life. Avshalom Caspi at Duke University and his colleagues followed 1032 people from Dunedin from the age of three until their twenty-sixth birthday and paid particular attention to which forms of the 5-HTT transporter gene they had – long or short. This gene is known to be involved in the transmission of the brain-chemical serotonin, and the long form is more efficient at doing its job.

For the small proportion of participants who experienced a bout of depression without any personal trauma, it made no difference what form of the 5-HTT gene they had. However, among those participants who had suffered a personal trauma, having one or two short forms of the 5-HTT transporter gene was associated with an increased risk of developing depression, compared with having two long forms. The result appeared to be a clear case of how a person's genetic disposition interacting with their life circumstances can influence their risk of mental illness.

This result from New Zealand and the fact that most modern anti-depressants target the serotonin system have led to the popular theory that depression somehow reflects a **chemical imbalance** in the brain, and in particular a deficit in serotonin activity. However, critics of this idea suggest it's little more than "biobabble" – a myth deliberately propagated by drug companies to help boost sales of antidepressants.

These critics point to the fact that paracetemol's effectiveness at alleviating headaches doesn't mean that headaches are caused by lack of paracetemol. They also point out that attempts to induce depression by lowering serotonin levels have failed, and conversely, that directly boosting serotonin levels using high doses of tryptophan (the amino acid processed by the body to make serotonin) has failed to alleviate depression. In any case – so the argument goes – who is to say what the "right" chemical balance is? Critical psychiatrists, such as Joanna Moncrieff, claim that antidepressants exert their effects not by correcting an imbalance but merely through non-specific effects such as sedation or stimulation.

DOES DEPRESSION HAVE AN UPSIDE?

Another area of controversy concerns the **evolutionary roots** of depression. Paul Andrews, an evolutionary psychologist at Virginia Commonwealth University, and Anderson Thompson, a psychiatrist based in Charlottesville, argue that depression is akin to fever, in the sense that it feels awful but it serves a useful purpose. Specifically, they say, the excessive rumination and withdrawal associated with depression can help a person find a solution to their problems. In support of their claims, there's research showing that low mood can harness a highly analytical mode of thought, and that people with depression have increased sensitivity to other people's emotions. Inducing low mood in research participants has also been shown to boost their performance on memory tests and other tasks.

On a related theme, there's also evidence for what's become known as **depressive realism**. Imagine you have to judge whether a switch controls a light or not. Sometimes flicking the switch seems to turn the light on and off, but other times it has no effect. In such a scenario,

Bipolar disorder

Far rarer than typical or "unipolar" depression, bipolar disorder is associated not only with extreme lows of mood, but also periods, lasting days to months, of intense exhilaration, energy and activity known as mania. This state may sound appealing, but it can cause problems such as chronic insomnia and social inappropriateness, and in fact occasionally manifests as excess irritability rather than as a hyper-positive mood. Mania can also sometimes cross over into psychosis when the surge of self-esteem overflows into delusional beliefs of invulnerability and omnipotence (see Chapter 26).

Anecdotal evidence suggests that bipolar disorder is experienced more often by musicians, artists, writers and actors than the general population, and may even fuel bouts of intense creativity. Historically, composers like Tchaikovsky and Handel are known to have experienced extreme mood swings. Modern-day celebrities diagnosed with the condition include the British writer and actor Stephen Fry and the US film star and novelist Carrie Fisher.

The actor, writer and general wit, Stephen Fry. In 2006, Fry spoke about his and others' struggles with bipolar disorder in a TV documentary, *Stephen Fry: The Secret Life of the Manic-Depressive.*

non-depressed people tend to overestimate how much influence they really have over the light – a kind of illusion of control that also applies to their feelings of control in life in general. By contrast, people with depression are far more accurate at judging how much control they have over the light and over life too.

There are also reports of links between depression, especially bipolar or **manic depression** (characterized by extreme highs and lows of mood) and **creativity**. The clinical psychologist Kay Redfield Jamison and the psychiatrist Nancy Andreasen have both made studies of artists and writers and found exceptionally high rates of depression among their ranks.

Others have warned against championing the so-called "upsides" of depression. Writing for the *World of Psychology* blog in 2010, the psychiatrist Ronald Pies said that in nearly thirty years of meeting patients with depression, he'd "almost never" encountered one who said that their major depressive episode had had a net benefit. He challenges the depression creativity link, arguing that most artists blame their symptoms for stalling their creativity. We should accept ordinary sadness and sorrow as part of the human condition, he wrote, but the idea that severe clinical depression can help solve life's problems is a "destructive myth".

Anxiety

In small doses, anxiety is a good thing. It steels the mind and body for a challenge, whether it be a public presentation, an important game of darts or a job interview. Even a generally anxious disposition has its benefits – a 2006 study by William Lee at the Institute of Psychiatry followed the fate of thousands of people born in 1946, and found that those who were more anxious were less likely to have died of accidental causes before the age of twenty-five.

It's only when anxiety becomes excessive and prolonged that it becomes a problem. Unfortunately, it seems that this is often the case, since anxiety is the most common of all mental disorders. Nervous excitement gives way to sustained tension and fear: the stomach keeps turning, the heart races, the hands shake and the dread just won't go away.

Anxiety comes in numerous varieties. **Generalized anxiety disorder** is a continuous sense of nervous apprehension about all manner of things: loved ones, work, being late, losing weight, running out of money – the list goes on. There are also forms of anxiety with a specific focus, the most common of which is **social anxiety** – worrying about making conversation, making a fool of oneself, being disliked, blushing, speaking in public and so on.

Another form of anxiety is **panic disorder**. This is characterized by a feeling of losing control, and a fear that one is about to faint or even die. Typically it's not tied to a particular situation. Rather it's a sensation that can arise anytime, anywhere, and is often triggered by a bodily sensation – a shortness of breath, perhaps, or a skipped heartbeat.

Then there are the **specific phobias,** the most common of which include fear of flying (aviophobia), enclosed spaces (claustrophobia), heights (acrophobia), spiders (arachnophobia), sharp objects (aichmophobia) and snakes (ophidiophobia). The list is virtually unlimited – pluck almost any object from your imagination and the chances are that someone, somewhere will have an exaggerated fear of it.

Obsessive compulsive disorder (OCD) is also categorized as a form of anxiety. Obsessions are persistent, unwanted thoughts about such things as cleanliness or safety, which are only relieved by performing

Footballer David Beckham's OCD takes the form of having to arrange everything in a straight line or everything in pairs. "I'll go into a hotel room and before I can relax, I have to move all the leaflets and all the books and put them in a drawer."

certain compulsive actions, such as hand-washing or the checking of gas hobs. In 2008, Mary Robertson and Andrea Cavanna described an extreme case of OCD in which a British boy became distressed because he thought the 9/11 terrorist attacks were his fault. He'd failed to walk on a particular white mark on the road – one of his compulsive rituals – and shortly afterwards had heard the news from the US. Fortunately, the boy's psychologists were able to persuade him that he wasn't responsible, partly by explaining that because of the time difference between the US and the UK, he'd missed his ritual after the attacks had taken place.

Another form of anxiety is **post-traumatic stress disorder** (PTSD), which usually arises after someone has been in a terrifying, life-threatening situation. Car crashes, rape, natural disasters, physical assault – all these kinds of experience can leave people at risk of developing the condition. Typical symptoms, including flashbacks to the traumatic event and a desperate desire to avoid reminders of what happened, have in fact been reported since at least ancient Egyptian times. During World War I the condition was known as shell-shock, and it remains as much of a threat to combat troops today as ever.

Civilians caught up in war are, of course, also particularly prone, although surprisingly this is less often researched. The clinical psychologists Howard Johnson and Andrew Thompson at the University of Sheffield drew attention to that imbalance in 2008, publishing a review of the few studies that have looked at rates of PTSD and its duration among civilian survivors of war and torture. Rates of PTSD varied hugely from six percent to more than ninety percent, probably reflecting the different questionnaires used, language problems, and the diversity of experiences the survivors had lived through. Unsurprisingly perhaps, women and the elderly were found to be at increased risk, though that may have been because of the kinds of traumas they'd suffered, rather than any inherent vulnerability.

Several forms of psychological therapy have been found to be effective for treating PTSD, including cognitive behavioural therapy (see p.348) and eye-movement desensitization and re-processing – an evidence-based, but still controversial treatment that involves the traumatized client recalling and holding in mind a painful memory, while simultaneously tracking with their eyes the horizontal movements of a therapist's finger. People with PTSD often have only a fragmented, toxic memory of what happened to them, and part of the aim of both these therapeutic approaches is to help those with PTSD to process and manage their memories better (see also Chapter 4).

A more surprising therapeutic approach was reported in 2009. Emily Holmes at the University of Oxford and her collaborators showed that ten minutes spent playing the computer-based game Tetris led participants to experience fewer flashbacks to a disturbing film clip they had seen earlier, compared with participants who had spent the same time sitting quietly. Holmes' team called their approach a "cognitive vaccine", which they suggested may have occupied the "sensory-perceptual" system, thereby preventing the memory of the traumatic scenes from getting lodged there.

It's easy to forget that the majority of people who survive traumatic experiences actually don't go on to develop PTSD. In fact, a curious occurrence in large-scale disasters is that people living in the most devastated regions are actually the least concerned by the ongoing risks, a phenomenon that's been dubbed "psychological typhoon eye". This was documented in interviews carried out by Shu Li of the Institute of Psychology, Beijing with survivors of the 2008 Wenchuan Earthquake, which killed over 68,000 people. Li's team weren't sure why the effect occurred, but it may be related to cognitive dissonance (see p.27), leading people to justify their decision to stay in a dangerous location by downplaying the ongoing risks.

THE BIO-PSYCHO-SOCIAL APPROACH

As with other mental disorders, psychologists have attempted to understand anxiety on several levels, including the biological, behavioural and cognitive. From a **biological perspective**, attention has focused on the peripheral nervous system, with its two balanced elements – the sympathetic and parasympathetic. The first cranks the body up for action, the second calms things down. Stated crudely, people with anxiety disorders are thought to have some kind of dysfunction in the balance between these two systems. Among the chief culprits for triggering this imbalance are the amygdala – the two almond-shaped brain structures that are known to be involved in emotional learning, including the acquisition of fears.

Behaviourally-minded psychologists focus on the circumstances under which an anxious person linked a particular situation with an unpleasant outcome, thereby coming to fear that situation. An example might be someone with social phobia who was left tongue-tied in a tutorial or laughed at when giving a presentation, and who therefore now associates these situations with public humiliation.

What is normal?

Just when does shyness become social phobia? When does sadness become depression? These aren't easy questions to answer, and a great deal of controversy exists in psychology about where the dividing lines should be, or if they should exist at all. There can be little doubt that contemporary social values influence psychiatric diagnoses – as can be seen by the fact that the American Psychiatric Association only removed homosexuality from its list of mental disorders in 1973. The critical psychiatrist Thomas Szasz has taken this argument to extremes. The author of *The Myth of Mental Illness* (1961), Szasz proposed that even the most serious conditions, such as schizophrenia, are socially constructed – a way for society to label and control awkward behaviour.

Another influential figure in the critical-psychiatry camp is the psychologist David Rosenhan. He conducted a study in the early 1970s in which he and several others gained admission to psychiatric hospitals merely by telling staff they could hear voices saying words like "empty" and "thud". Staff failed to realize the experimenters were frauds and in fact began interpreting much of their behaviour in pathological terms. Even after the impostors told staff they were feeling better, the diagnoses were difficult to get reversed and some of them took up to 52 days to be discharged. Published in *Science* in 1973 as "On Being Sane in Insane Places", Rosenhan's study has become a classic for those wishing to argue that psychiatric diagnoses are unscientific.

Another criticism of psychiatric diagnoses is that they are too strongly influenced by pharmaceutical companies, or "Big Pharma" as the industry has been nicknamed. Part of the reason for this suspicion is that the industry has a clear vested interest in the creation of new

The cognitive approach, on the other hand, considers the thought processes that underlie anxiety. The person with panic disorder, for example, might misinterpret benign bodily symptoms in catastrophic terms, such as mistaking indigestion as a sign of an impending heart attack. The nervous flier will listen intently to every whir and click of the aircraft, convinced that innocent sounds are an indication of malfunction and danger.

The reality, of course, is that all these elements – biological, behavioural and cognitive – are involved at once. The woman with social phobia thinks to herself that she is boring her friend (cognitive); this mental-health diagnoses that they can claim to have treatments for. These suspicions have been kindled by the number of disorders listed by psychiatry's diagnostic bible – the *Diagnostic and Statistical Manual of Mental Disorders* – which has spiralled with each successive edition (182 in the second edition published in 1968, 297 in the fourth edition published in 1997).

Drugs companies have also been known to re-brand old drugs as a treatment for a different mental disorder from the one they were originally intended for, thus opening their products up to new markets. Famous antidepressants like Prozac and Paxil have since been marketed as effective treatments for social anxiety. "You're not shy, you're sick!" was the catchphrase of one associated marketing drive.

Work is currently underway on the fifth edition of the *Diagnostic and Statistical Manual*, and there have already been noisy claims that board members have conflicts of interest by virtue of their ties with the pharmaceutical industry. Drug companies and critics alike will be watching keenly to see if new diagnostic categories such as "hyper-sexuality" and "binge-eating disorder" make the final cut.

A related area of controversy concerns whether mental illnesses should be seen as akin to "real" physical illnesses. It's not just drug companies that have championed the idea that mental illnesses have physical causes. Charities like the National Alliance for The Mentally Ill have campaigned for mental illnesses to be seen as brain diseases, because they feel that this will help reduce stigma and get people the treatment they need. In fact, there's evidence suggesting that the "medical model" approach increases stigma by encouraging the belief that a patient is stuck with their problems for good.

makes her nervous, her heart races (biological); she forgets what she was saying, and she leaves the scene feeling that she made a fool of herself, vowing to avoid such situations ever again (behavioural). And, of course, complementing this triangle of factors are the combined influences of a person's upbringing, social situation and genetic inheritance.

26 Schizo- phrenia

One of the most devastating of mental illnesses is schizophrenia, a partly inherited condition that's associated with delusions and hallucinations (particularly hearing voices), disordered thinking, a flattening of the emotions and a loss of motivation. In the psychiatric jargon, the delusions and hallucinations are known as positive symptoms, whereas the loss of emotion and motivation are known as negative symptoms. Schizophrenia usually begins in adolescence or early adulthood. For some people it can manifest itself as a one-off episode of psychosis – a loose term used to describe the symptom of being disconnected from reality, including having delusions and hallucinations. For others, it is a life-long illness with an undulating course of recovery and relapse.

Losing touch with reality

For a glimpse of what it's like to be psychotic, there are few people better to ask than Peter Chadwick, a clinical psychologist and psychosis expert who experienced his own psychotic episode in the late 1970s, leading him to be diagnosed with paranoid schizophrenia. In books and articles, Chadwick has recalled his youthful social awkwardness, poor emotional control and the toll of endless bullying for being a transvestite. In his early thirties, recently fired from a casual filing-job for which he was over-qualified, he suddenly saw personal meaning everywhere.

The DJ on the radio mocked him; the intensity of the rain on the windowpane waxed and waned in rhythm with the drama of his diary writing; and he noticed phrases from private letters he'd written to friends and relatives quoted on television and by passers-by. "From a meaningless life, a relationship with the world was reconstructed by me that was spectacularly meaningful and portentous even if it was horrific" Chadwick writes in a candid 2007 article. Recalling how his mental crisis deepened, Chadwick continues: "it was as if I was not 'thinking the delusion,' the delusion was 'thinking me!' I was totally enslaved by the belief system." Days later, Chadwick threw himself under a bus on New King's Road in what he thought at the time was a hugely symbolic act that would see Jesus return to the world. He survived, was hospitalized and administered anti-psychotic medication, which he has taken ever since.

An influential theory for the delusions associated with schizophrenia is the **aberrant salience framework** developed by the psychiatrist Shitij Kapur. It's an approach that marries the psychological observation that patients seem to find meaning everywhere with the neurobiological observation that patients have an abundance of the brain-chemical dopamine. This is a neurotransmitter that's known to be involved when we find something rewarding or meaningful. In an interview for *The Psychologist*, Professor Kapur suggested that if you tested patients with schizophrenia before they were ill, you'd probably find that they tended to jump to conclusions. When you add to this "a biochemical fuel – excess dopamine," he explained, "you inflame this way of thinking".

The drugs used to treat schizophrenia work by blocking the action of **dopamine** in the brain. According to Kapur's account, they "douse the flames". Thus, when Kapur asked patients on anti-psychotic medication what effects their drugs had, they tended to say that their outlandish beliefs – such as that the FBI were chasing them – were still there, it's just that they don't care so much any more.

In 2008, Jonathan Roiser at UCL and colleagues provided direct support for the aberrant salience theory. In a learning task, completed by medicated patients with schizophrenia and by a healthy control group, the participants had to press a button as fast as possible in response to the appearance of a black square on a computer screen. Crucially, speedy performance on some trials earned participants a financial reward, while performance on other trials did not. The learning aspect of the task was based on the fact that certain images – an image of a chair, for example – preceding the black square, predicted the likelihood that fast performance on an upcoming trial would be rewarded financially. Other images, meanwhile, were irrelevant. Those participants who responded faster after a predic-

> "The Voices swirled around me, teaching me their Wisdom ... They told me their secrets and insights, piece by piece. Slowly, I was beginning to make sense of it all. It was no delusion, I knew – in contrast to what the doctors said."
>
> Erin Stefanidis

tive image would be showing evidence of "adaptive salience"; those who speeded up after an irrelevant image would be showing "aberrant salience" – that is, seeing meaning where there was none.

Although there was no overall difference in performance between the patients and the controls, those patients who were still experiencing delusions showed more evidence of aberrant salience than those who were in remission. Moreover, among the healthy controls, those who reported having more schizophrenia-like experiences in their everyday lives (for example, having unusual thoughts or sensations) tended to show more aberrant salience in the task than the controls reporting fewer schizophrenia-like experiences.

In keeping with this latter result, there's been a growing recognition in recent years that many people – not just those with a diagnosis of schizophrenia – hold **outlandish beliefs** and have **unusual experiences**, such as hearing voices. According to statistics, ten percent of us will have some kind of psychotic experience once or more in our lifetimes, three percent of us will seek and receive treatment as a result, while just one percent will end up with a diagnosis of schizophrenia or a related condition. What seems key to schizophrenia is that the heard voices and beliefs are distressing. Many self-proclaimed "psychic" mediums are happy to hear voices that they say are from the dead. Spiritual leaders feel blessed that they can hear God. The patient with schizophrenia, by contrast, will describe frightening voices that are mocking and unwanted.

WHAT CAUSES SCHIZOPHRENIA?

Schizophrenia was first documented in the 1890s by the German psychiatrist Emile Kraeplin, who called it **dementia praecox**, literally "precocious madness", referring to the fact that the illness tends to strike in adolescence and early adulthood. In 1908 the Swiss psychiatrist **Eugen Bleuler** coined the term "schizophrenia", which literally means fractured mind – thus fuelling the widespread misuse of schizophrenia to denote split personality.

The early decades of the twentieth century witnessed the rise of psychoanalysis, and it was from this school that the first explicit theories of the causes of schizophrenia emerged. The analyst Frieda Fromm-Reichmann, for example, blamed mothers of a certain disposition for inducing schizophrenia in their children, calling them "schizophrenogenic". We know today that a history of trauma plays an important role in schizophrenia, so it's conceivable in some circumstances that an abusive mother could be responsible for such a trauma. However, many patients with schizophrenia have loving mothers, and it is now known that there is a large genetic component to the illness.

Hundreds of studies, many of them conducted in Denmark because of that country's extensive medical and adoption records, have shown that if one identical twin has the illness, then the other twin (who shares all the same genes) has approximately a fifty percent chance of having the same diagnosis – dramatically higher than the one percent risk in the general population. This remains true even if the twins are raised apart in separate homes, thus showing the important role played by genes. Also, the close relatives of patients with schizophrenia often have a mild, sub-clinical version of the illness known as **schizotypy**, which is characterized by unconventional beliefs and experiences, such as believing they can read minds or feeling that part of their body is unreal. Of course, having said all this, if the identical twin of a patient with schizophrenia has only a fifty percent chance of having schizophrenia, this means that the environment must play a big role too.

This is borne out by research which shows that a history of **childhood abuse** is found in the

"I will write a lot because I feel that I am going to be destroyed. I do not want destruction..." The brilliant dancer and choreographer Vaslav Nijinsky (1890–1950) suffered a mental breakdown that ended his career in 1917. Diagnosed as schizophrenic, Nijinsky was unsuccessfully treated by Eugen Bleuler in Zurich and sent to a sanatorium in nearby Kreuzlingen. His diary, written between January and March 1919, is an extraordinary record of mental disintegration.

majority of patients with schizophrenia. The clear implication is that when a genetic vulnerability is combined with an early traumatic experience, the outcome, in many cases, is schizophrenia. This idea of

Schizophrenia and creativity

From an evolutionary perspective, you'd think that schizophrenia would be a disadvantage. This is borne out by the fact that people diagnosed with schizophrenia tend to have fewer children than average. It is, therefore, an enduring mystery why schizophrenia remains stubbornly prevalent at around one percent of the population in most cultures of the world. How come the genes responsible for predisposing people towards schizophrenia haven't become progressively rarer? One theory proposed by Daniel Nettle at Newcastle University is that the relevant genes manifest in some people as an embryonic, harmless form of schizophrenia called schizotypy – a condition associated with enhanced artistic creativity. In turn, Nettle predicts that these creative types may have more children than average, thus propagating their schizophrenia-related genes. What evidence does Nettle have for this? In research published in 2005, Nettle and his colleague Helen Keenoo surveyed hundreds of people, including poets and artists, and found that those who reported having more unusual thoughts and experiences – questions included: "Do you believe in telepathy?", "Does your mood go up and down easily?", and "Does a passing thought ever seem so real it frightens you?" – also tended to be more creative and to have had more sexual partners. Further support came in a 2006 survey, also conducted by Nettle, of hundreds of patients with schizophrenia, plus non-schizophrenic poets, artists, mathematicians and other healthy controls. The creative types reported just as many bizarre, psychotic-like experiences as the patients. However, unlike the patients, they didn't score highly on "introvertive anhedonia", which manifests as a lack of emotion and motivation. Curiously, the mathematicians had fewer unusual experiences than the other controls did, yet they scored highly on "introvertive anhedonia" – the opposite pattern to the artists and poets.

vulnerability reacting to stress is corroborated by research conducted in Southeast London by James Kirkbride at the University of Cambridge, which revealed that rates of psychosis are higher in poorer, more crime-ridden neighbourhoods.

A history of emotional or physical trauma could also be the key ingredient that makes unusual experiences pathological. In 2005, Maarten Bak interviewed thousands of people – none of whom had had a psychotic experience – to find out whether they'd been abused in childhood. Three years later, the same participants were contacted again. By this time, a minority had had a psychotic experience. Crucially, whether or not they'd found that experience distressing depended largely on their childhood history. Among the sixteen people who reported having had one or more non-distressing psychotic experiences since the first interview, just one had been traumatized as a child. In contrast, among the 21 people who reported having had one or more distressing psychotic experiences, nine had experienced a childhood trauma. The people who said they'd been traumatized also tended to report having less control over their psychotic experiences.

Schizophrenia and violence

You've probably seen a headline "Paranoid Schizophrenic Stabs Stranger at Bus-stop" or something similar. An unfortunate consequence of journalists' love of these kinds of stories is that they give a distorted impression of the links between psychosis and violence. In fact, the overwhelming majority of murders and violent acts are committed by people who are not psychotic or mentally ill. There's also evidence that murders by people with a serious mental illness have fallen since the 1970s (to around twenty per year in the UK), while murders in general have increased.

A 2009 study, led by psychologist Martin Grann at Stockholm University, goes further. Grann and his colleagues analysed Swedish crime records and found that among people with schizophrenia but without a related alcohol problem, rates of violent crime were no higher than among the general population. The study's lead author Niklas Langstrom concluded: "...the idea that people with schizophrenia are generally more violent than those without is not true".

Of course, these kinds of statistics and claims are of little consolation to the relatives of people attacked by a person with a serious mental illness, especially if there's reason to believe that the attack wouldn't have happened had the patient been on medication. Relevant to this argument is an analysis of international crime data by Matthew Large, an independent clinician, and Olav Nielssen of St Vincent's Hospital in Sydney. Their data-crunching suggested that the risk of murder by a person experiencing a first episode of psychosis is twenty times higher before treatment than afterwards. Large believes that psychotic patients receiving treatment are barely more dangerous than the average healthy person, but he said that untreated first-episode psychosis is "a singularly dangerous condition".

Research, such as that conducted by Large and Nielssen, has led to calls for laws to be introduced to compel people with a diagnosis of schizophrenia to take anti-psychotic medication. However, many other experts

Does cannabis cause schizophrenia?

This has proved a tricky question to answer. There are certainly reasons to think it might. An authoritative meta-analysis published in 2007 by Theresa Moore of the University of Bristol combined the results from eleven longitudinal studies, and concluded that heavy users of cannabis were between fifty and two hundred percent more at risk of developing psychosis than non-users. Among users in general (light and heavy), the increased risk was forty percent. If we assume that the link is causal – that smoking cannabis brings on psychosis in people who wouldn't otherwise have developed it – this would equate to 800 extra cases of psychosis in 15 to 34-year-olds every year in the UK. So, what's the caveat? The problem with research of this kind is that it's very difficult to know whether the cannabis users in these studies would have developed psychosis anyway even if they hadn't taken cannabis. In fact, there's evidence that people who exhibit very mild psychotic-like symptoms are more likely than average to begin smoking cannabis, perhaps as a form of self-medication. Another problem is that the intoxication associated with taking cannabis can bring on acute psychotic-like symptoms. This can make it difficult to establish whether cannabis really triggers long-lasting psychosis beyond the period of intoxication.

and mental health campaigners oppose this idea. They point to the statistics showing how rare it is for a mentally ill person to harm other people, and they question the morality of imposing drugs that often have serious, unpleasant side-effects. In all this debate about schizophrenia and violence, it's also worth remembering one sad, undisputed fact that often goes overlooked, which is that someone with a diagnosis of schizophrenia is at increased risk of being a victim of violence. For further information on the issues surrounding mental illness and psychosis, the British Psychological Society produced a free booklet, which although published over ten years ago, remains useful (tinyurl.com/lt4xnl).

27 Therapy & positive psychology

To many people, psychology is synonymous with psychotherapy. As previous chapters have shown, psychologists are in fact involved in a huge variety of activities outside of psychotherapy. But it's also true that many psychologists do act as therapists and many conduct research into the effectiveness of therapy. In fact, clinical psychology is the largest professional grouping in the British Psychological Society and the second largest – after independent practitioners – in the American Psychological Association.

More often than not psychotherapy is beneficial. That's the good news. The bad news is that it is a highly fragmented field. There are literally hundreds of different therapeutic approaches, many of them lacking scientific credibility, and it is still permissible in some countries for anyone to call themselves a psychotherapist. This makes it difficult to identify a qualified therapist for specific needs. Also, in many developing countries there is a dire shortage of mental-health professionals. In Ghana alone, there are only five psychiatrists for a population of 22 million, and no clinical psychologists working in public health.

Types of therapy

Before the twentieth century, the treatment of people with mental illness was frequently inhumane. In the Middle Ages, superstition was rife, and people with mental problems were often considered to be possessed or guilty of some moral transgression for which they were being punished. From the early nineteenth century, the situation improved marginally as hundreds of asylums were built to house "the insane". Although the idea

Sigmund Freud (1856–1939)

The grandfather of psychoanalysis began his career as a scientist and medic with a leaning towards neuroscience. His interest in psychology was triggered by his work under the French neurologist Jean-Martin Charcot at the Salpêtrière Hospital in Paris, where he encountered patients diagnosed with hysteria – physical ailments with no apparent organic cause. Freud's most famous works include *The Interpretation of Dreams* (1899) and *Introduction to Psychoanalysis* (1920), the latter presented as a series of lectures. Mention of Freud today often provokes sniggers from many quarters because of his belief in libidinous desire as the primary human motive underlying all others, and his numerous sex-themed theories including penis envy, the castration complex and the Oedipus complex (in which he argued that children have lustful desires for their opposite-sex parent and, out of

Challenged on the symbolism of his own heavy smoking, Freud is alleged to have remarked "sometimes a cigar is just a cigar."

jealousy, fantasize about the death of their same-sex parent). However, his recognition of the powerful effect of non-conscious processes on our attitudes and behaviour was accurate, and his influence on the field of psychotherapy is immeasurable. Moreover, while many contemporary psychologists consider Freud's theories as largely unscientific, on the basic that they are unfalsifiable, there has been a trend in recent years to claim support for his theories in modern neuroscience. For example, it's been suggested that the neuropsychological condition of anosognosia – in which the paralysed patient denies their disability – is a manifestation of a classic Freudian defence mechanism in which the psychologically unpalatable is swept under the proverbial carpet.

was to provide a place of refuge, the conditions in many of these asylums was grim, and treatment often extremely primitive, including ice baths, straitjackets, isolation and blood letting.

In the West, the birth of psychotherapy – literally "healing the mind" – is popularly traced to Sigmund Freud's psychoanalysis, which he developed at the end of the nineteenth century. Freud, in turn, was inspired by his mentor, the neurologist **Jean-Martin Charcot**. The latter had a particular interest in those patients at the Salpêtrière Hospital in Paris who displayed neurological symptoms (such as paralysis) without seeming to have anything physically wrong with them. Whereas other medics tended to dismiss such patients as malingerers, Charcot took them seriously and attempted to treat their "hysteria" with hypnosis.

Western psychotherapy's roots actually go back even further than Freud and Charcot. For example, in the late eighteenth century, another physician based at the Salpêtrière, **Philippe Pinel**, was interested in the psychological causes of mental illness, such as bereavement and stress. His approach to treatment was founded on kindness and discussing patients' problems with them – a revolutionary idea at the time. Today Pinel is considered by many to be the "father of modern psychiatry".

In recent decades a division has emerged between so-called "empirically supported" therapeutic approaches, such as Cognitive Behavioural Therapy (see p.348), and other approaches. Indeed, some psychologists like David Barlow, founder and Director Emeritus of the Center for Anxiety and Related Disorders at Boston University, have called for a distinction to be made between evidence-based psychological treatments for treating psychopathology, and psychotherapy, which he says is for personal growth, happiness and improving relationships. Speaking in 2006 at a conference of the Division of Clinical Psychology in the UK, Barlow described psychotherapy as a "noble undertaking", but warned that "it's harmful to confuse it with what psychologists do in a health setting".

PSYCHODYNAMIC THERAPIES

Psychoanalysis, the most famous approach to psychotherapy, is based on the idea that psychological problems are largely caused by unresolved mental and emotional conflicts, many of which bubble away beneath the level of conscious awareness. These unconscious processes are considered to be dynamic, and any therapeutic approach that attempts to resolve or modify these processes is a form of psychodynamic therapy.

One key psychoanalytic technique is **free association.** This involves the analysand – the formal term for a person undergoing psychoanalysis – uttering thoughts aloud as they spontaneously come to mind. Meanwhile, the analyst provides **interpretations** of these utterances to try to help uncover any underlying mental conflicts, so that they can be worked through and resolved. Traditionally, this exercise was performed with the analysand prostrate on a couch to aid the flow of ideas – hence the mythical symbolism of the psychoanalyst and his or her couch.

Psychoanalysis has inspired countless other schools of **psychodynamic therapy**, from Jungian variants (named after Freud's student Carl Jung) to the more contemporary **interpersonal therapy**. A technique pioneered by Jung was word association. Similar to free association, this involves the analyst saying a word to which the analysand must immediately offer the first thoughts that come to mind. One of the first interpersonal therapists was the US psychoanalyst Harry Stack Sullivan. His approach was based on the idea that psychological problems often arise from a person having dysfunctional interpersonal relations. The interpersonal therapist typically uses their own interactions with the analysand to identify the problematic ways in which the latter relates to others.

A theme common to all psychodynamic therapies is the idea of transference and counter-transference. **Transference** is when the dynamics

What works?

Psychotherapy can be highly effective. Over thirty years of research has shown that about eighty percent of clients are in a better state following therapy than if they hadn't had any. For forty percent of clients, therapeutic progress occurs in a sudden burst between one particular session and another. Unfortunately, there is also evidence that around five to ten percent of clients are worse off for having therapy (see p.348). Partly because of the risk of harm, advocates of the **empirically-supported therapies movement** believe there is an onus on the different therapeutic schools to conduct research to demonstrate their effectiveness, and that those lacking evidence should be avoided.

Which forms of therapy work better and indeed which work at all is a political hot potato in the world of psychology and psychotherapy. To be told that a therapeutic approach that you have spent years delivering is substandard or ineffective must be hard to swallow, although continuing to practise a harmful therapy is, surely, insupportable. Perhaps because of this, the field of research into psychotherapy effectiveness is plagued by what's known as "allegiance effects" – the tendency for psychologists of a particular therapeutic orientation to find supporting evidence for their own particular brand of psychotherapy.

Another criticism is that there is a world of difference between the "manualized" therapy used in research, which is conducted with carefully selected clients, and the messiness of therapy in the real and attachment styles of previous relationships are played out in other, newer relationships, including the relationship with the therapist. For example, a client whose father was absent or aloof in their childhood, who then proceeds to behave in a filial fashion towards his therapist may be considered to be exhibiting transference. **Counter-transference** is simply the label given for when these kinds of processes affect the therapist's behaviour toward the client. A key part of many forms of psychodynamic therapy is interpreting and identifying issues of transference that may be affecting a client's current relationships.

HUMANISTIC-ORIENTED THERAPIES

In psychoanalysis and other psychodynamic therapies, the therapist usually plays what's called a **directive** role, overtly assisting the analysand in resolving and interpreting their issues. In contrast, the psychologist Carl Rogers (1902–87) pioneered a more **person-centred** approach to

world, where clients may be more complicated and unpredictable. Related to this is the claim that some forms of therapy are more amenable to research and measurement, especially those, like CBT, which are more technical. That's probably the reason why CBT (and its offshoots like DBT) have gained more research support than probably any other therapeutic approach.

One curious finding that emerges from many comparisons of effectiveness is that outcomes are often fairly equivalent regardless of the particular therapy that's used. In fact, this occurs so frequently that it's been given a name – the **Dodo bird verdict**, after the Dodo in *Alice in Wonderland*, who organizes a race in which everyone wins. The phenomenon has led to the claim that what makes therapy effective is not the particular approach that's used, but rather key **common factors**, including the quality of the relationship between the therapist and client – what's usually called the **therapeutic alliance**.

Other important factors for success (or otherwise) include the motivation of the client, what their expectations are, and how much support they have outside therapy. Other research has focused on the therapist. Irrespective of their chosen therapeutic orientation, a minority of therapists are unusually effective – dubbed "super shrinks" in the research literature – while others are particularly poor. Unfortunately, quite what these super shrinks have going for them remains rather elusive, with obvious explanations such as years of experience or professional status proving to be relatively irrelevant.

therapy. Rogers was influenced in part by the work of Abraham Maslow (1908–70), the founder of humanistic psychology – so-called because of its emphasis on each person's individuality and capacity for goodness. In anticipation of the Positive Psychology movement that emerged at the end of the twentieth century, Maslow studied high achievers and creative geniuses, with the aim of finding out how we can all realize our true potential.

Today most psychologists refer to people undergoing therapy as clients, rather than patients or analysands, a convention started by Rogers which helps reduce stigma and promotes greater equality between the therapist and client. Following the humanistic tradition, the Rogerian therapist plays a passive, listening role and the emphasis is on providing an empathic ear. Clients are viewed with so-called **unconditional positive regard**, which means caring for and respecting them irrespective of what they say and do. Rogers challenged the notion of the therapist as "expert", and argued instead that therapy was about providing a safe environment for clients to work through their problems in the way they feel is best. The Rogerian approach underlies modern-day "counselling", in which a client talks through their problems with a receptive stranger.

BEHAVIOURAL AND COGNITIVE APPROACHES

Behavioural therapy is based on the idea that many mental problems, particularly phobias, are learned and can therefore be unlearned. Behavioural therapy is rooted in the learning theories of Ivan Pavlov, John Watson and B.F. Skinner (see p.14). The "mother of behavioural therapy", Mary Cover Jones, is said to have been inspired by hearing Watson talk about his research with Little Albert (see p.110). Jones's most famous work is her treatment of a three-year-old called Peter, who had a fear of rabbits. By consistently presenting Peter with a rabbit and at the same time offering him his favourite candy, Jones was able to get Peter to unlearn his fear.

Another way fears can be unlearned is through gradual **exposure** to incrementally increasing intensities of the fear-inducing situation. For example, imagine that a client has developed a fear of crossing bridges. The therapist might begin by teaching relaxation techniques while standing near or on a small footbridge over a gentle stream. As the client's confidence increases, the sessions could graduate to progressively larger, busier and more challenging bridges. A related approach is **flooding**, which is akin to dropping the client in at the deep end – that is, subjecting them to an extreme form of what they most fear. It's a risky strategy, but the idea is that by surviving exposure to their worst nightmare, the client learns that there is nothing to be afraid of.

As well as the unlearning of fears, other behavioural techniques include **aversion therapy**, in which an unwanted behaviour – such as excess drinking – is repeatedly paired with a punishment of some kind. This is the rationale behind the drug disulfiram (also known as Antabuse), which induces nausea whenever alcohol is consumed. Some institutions employ behavioural principles on a large scale by using **token economies**, in which tokens are exchanged for privileges, as a way to encourage good behaviour and deter unwanted behaviour.

Cognitive therapy focuses on irrational and negatively distorted thoughts, in line with the view of Epictetus, the Greek Stoic, that "Men are disturbed not by things, but by the view which they take of them." By this account, a person's fear of, say, bridges is caused by their beliefs about bridges, such as that they might collapse or that one could easily fall off them. The cognitive approach to therapy was developed by the US psychiatrist Aaron Beck and by the US psychologist Albert Ellis. Both had trained as psychoanalysts, but became disillusioned by the analytical approach, especially its lack of scientific rigour.

Ellis's technique was known as **Rational Emotive Therapy**, part of which involves identifying an activating event ("A") behind a client's problems, the emotional consequence of that event ("C"), together with the client's beliefs ("B") linking the two – known as the ABC model. For example, a woman with obsessive-compulsive disorder may recall her habitual act of locking and unlocking the door three times when leaving the house (A), the anxiety relief that act brings (C), because she believes that performing such a ritual will prevent something bad from happening (B). Beck's approach was called **Cognitive Restructuring**, and involves encouraging the client to think about their thinking, in order to identify the systematic distortions and biases in their attitudes to themselves, the world and the future. For example, a client might reveal that they have a habit of thinking negatively – perceiving unfortunate circumstances as evidence for their own inadequacies, seeing lack of opportunity and fairness in the world, and assuming that bad things are going to continue happening to them.

In practice, one way irrational thoughts are identified is with the help of written thought-records. The client thinks back to situations that have caused problems and tries to identify **hot thoughts** that precipitated discomfort. An example might be a man with a social anxiety about parties, who tends to think that everyone at the party is looking at him or thinks he's boring. The therapist will then help him question the grounds for these thoughts and find new ways of seeing things in a more positive light. Is it really his responsibility to be entertaining? Would the person who asked for his phone number have done so if they thought him boring? And so on. The therapist might also encourage the client to try to shift his thinking and attentional focus – for example by considering more what he thinks of the other guests, rather than what they may or may not think about him.

By the 1990s, behavioural and cognitive therapies were being routinely merged to form **Cognitive Behavioural Therapy**, frequently abbreviated

When therapy causes harm

Finding out whether a treatment has caused harm is a methodological minefield. If a client deteriorates, it doesn't mean the therapy was to blame – decline may have happened further and faster without therapy. Similarly, improvement isn't necessarily a sign that therapy hasn't been harmful because the client could have recovered more quickly or smoothly without therapy. Whatever the reason, most experts agree that five to ten percent of clients get worse after therapy. Some approaches are more suspect than others, and Scott Lilienfeld, a professor of psychology at Emory University, has called for a list of potentially harmful therapies to be drawn up – a kind of negative complement to the list of empirically supported treatments. Candidates for the harmful list, according to Lilienfeld, represent the "dark underbelly" of psychotherapy and include recovered-memory techniques, boot camps for conduct disorder, and critical incident stress debriefing.

One way that therapeutic harm can be averted is for clients to fill out questionnaires after each session. The psychologist Michael Lambert at Brigham Young University is a pioneer in this area. He sees providing feedback on a session by session basis as the equivalent to a medical doctor checking a patient's blood pressure: "It's simply a mental health vital sign – it says whether it's going in the right direction or not." This is important not least because clients who fare worse than average in early sessions are at particular risk of ending therapy in a deteriorated state (whereas early progress shown by clients tends to be maintained). Raising the alarm about clients who are off-track can cue the therapist to change tack or intensity, and get the client back on course.

to CBT. Proponents of CBT recognize that thoughts and behaviour can influence each other in self-propagating ways that affect a client's problematic experiences. For instance, imagine that a client's fear of driving is sustained by the belief that they aren't competent enough to drive on busy roads. This leads them to avoid busy roads by taking back-street routes. This behaviour in turn means that they never get to experience driving in heavy traffic, further undermining their confidence and sustaining their distorted belief in their own driving incompetence.

The intuitive logic of CBT has made it particularly amenable to delivery in groups and via computer and self-help manuals, making it cost-effective and practical, especially for those unable to reach (or not wishing to see) a therapist. The systematic nature of CBT and its easily identifiable aims have also made it amenable to scientific tests of its efficacy. Far more than psychodynamic therapies, which are traditionally delivered over longer timescales and far vaguer in their aims. Considerable scientific evidence has accumulated that CBT is highly effective for many clients, either on its own or together with pharmacological treatments. However, CBT isn't suitable for everyone, and psychoanalytic and other therapies continue to play an important role.

The last decade has seen the emergence of a so-called third generation, or third wave, of cognitive-behavioural therapies. In **Mindfulness-Based Cognitive therapy** clients are taught how to meditate and are encouraged to pay attention, in non-judgemental fashion, to their inner thoughts and experiences. **Acceptance and Commitment Therapy** follows a similar approach and includes a commitment to changing one's behaviour, while Marsha Linehan's **Dialectical Behavioural Therapy** (DBT) similarly draws on the Buddhist principles of mindfulness, acceptance and self-observation and also teaches emotional coping skills. DBT has shown particular promise for treating borderline personality disorder – a condition associated with emotional turmoil and problematic relationships.

Positive Psychology – a new approach

Notwithstanding the humanistic psychology movement that emerged in the 1960s, it's arguable that psychology for most of its history has displayed a bias towards people's mental problems and distress. In 1998, in his address as President of the American Psychological

The Dalai Lama and Martin Seligman (right) share the stage at a conference on "The Mind and Its Potential" held in Sydney, Australia in 2009.

Association, Martin Seligman of the University of Pennsylvania attempted to change that. He called on his colleagues to expand their focus to include people's strengths, to study the positives – such as how to nurture talent – and not just the negatives. The Positive Psychology movement was born.

The Journal of Positive Psychology published its first issue in 2006 and the International Positive Psychology Association was formed in 2007. Other key players include Mihály Csíkszentmihály at Claremont Graduate University, who conceived the idea of flow (see p.268), Barbara Fredrickson at the University of Michigan, and Alex Linley, founding director of the Centre for Applied Positive Psychology in the UK.

Central to Positive Psychology is the idea that positive emotions are more than just the absence of negativity – they have active, functional benefits. According to Fredrickson's **Broaden-and-Build Theory**, whereas negative emotions like fear cause us to narrow our focus and prepare our bodies for fight or flight, positive emotions such as joy widen our focus and prompt us to engage in activities – such as sport and art, that trigger a cascade of long-term positive benefits – improving our health and broadening our social networks.

Fredrickson has demonstrated aspects of the "broaden" part of her theory in the laboratory. For example, after watching joy-inducing video clips featuring playful penguins, students are more likely to categorize arrays of shapes according to their overall arrangement rather than according to the similarity of each individual shape, thus suggesting that they are thinking about the big picture. Other research has shown that watching comedy video-clips, as opposed to clips about maths, improves people's performance at a lab test of creativity (the Dunker test, see p.199), and that being in a positive mood leads people to be more sociable.

The "build" part of Fredrickson's theory refers to the idea that the experience of positive emotions helps us deal with negative emotions during times of turmoil – providing what Fredrickson calls "psychological resilience". In one test of this idea, Fredrickson re-interviewed a sample of non-bereaved undergraduates after the 9/11 terrorist attacks, who she had originally tested at the start of 2001. She found that those who scored high on psychological resilience at the start of 2001 (i.e. they tended to agree with statements like "I quickly get over and recover from being startled") were half as likely to be feeling depressed after the attacks compared with those low in resilience. Most importantly for the broaden-and-build theory, the protection these students had from negative emotions was mediated by their experience of post-9/11 positive emotions such as gratitude and optimism. "Amidst the emotional turmoil generated by the September 11th terrorist attacks," Fredrickson wrote in a journal report of the findings, "subtle and fleeting experiences of gratitude, interest, love, and other positive emotions appeared to hold depressive symptoms at bay and fuel postcrisis growth."

> "You've got to accentuate the positive / Eliminate the negative / Latch on to the affirmative / Don't mess with Mister In-Between."
>
> Song by Harold Arlen and Johnny Mercer

POSITIVE PSYCHOLOGY AND REAL LIFE

Recent years have seen positive psychologists publish findings relevant to many aspects of life, including personal relationships, therapy, trauma and business. In a 2007 paper, Gary Lewandowski and Nicole Bizzoco at Monmouth University surveyed 155 young people who'd recently ended a relationship (in 25 percent of cases, it was the other partner who'd initiated the break-up). Crucially, 58 percent of those surveyed said they experienced multiple positive emotions after the break-up, such as feeling energized and hopeful, while 71 percent said they'd experienced growth – measured by their agreement with statements like "I've learned a lot about myself". The key predictor of positive outcomes was the quality of the prior relationship. As you'd expect, if the old relationship was an emotional dead-end then the break-up tended to bring benefits. In their write-up of the research, Lewandowski and Bizzoco suggested that rather than seeing the potential negative consequences of breaking up as a reason to stay in a bad relationship, "people could use the present results as a motivation for leaving the bad relationship. In fact...leaving a bad relationship is likely to result in personal growth and positive emotions."

In relation to therapy, research has shown that when therapists focus on their clients' strengths and not just their problems, outcomes improve. In a 2008 study, Christoph Fluckiger instructed trainee therapists to chat about a client's strengths with a colleague for a few minutes before each of that client's first five sessions. Outcomes after twenty sessions were improved compared with comparable therapist-client pairs previously treated at the same clinic.

More controversial is the idea that traumatic experiences, including being unwell, can have a positive side-effect. Following the *Herald of Free Enterprise* disaster, in which a car ferry capsized with the loss of 193 lives, research revealed that 43 percent of the survivors felt their view of life had changed for the better. In a separate 2006 study on character strengths, involving over two thousand people filling in an on-line form, participants were asked if they'd ever suffered any physical or psychological illness. Christopher Peterson, who conducted the study, found that those 422 people who answered yes tended to score themselves more highly on appreciation of beauty, curiosity, fairness, humour and several other positive attributes. Though far from conclusive, Peterson said the findings suggested that many people can be strengthened by the experience of being ill.

These findings were backed up by a 2010 study by Mark Seery at the University of Buffalo, in which over two thousand people were repeatedly surveyed over several years. As you might expect, those people who experienced a high number of major adverse life-events, for example losing their job or falling ill, subsequently reported more negative psychological outcomes, such as signs of stress and low life-satisfaction. In line with positive psychology, however, Seery's study also found that those people who experienced some adverse events were happier and psychologically healthier at the end of the study than those people who'd suffered no adverse events.

What about positive psychology in the workplace? A 2002 survey by the Corporate Leadership Council involving over 19,000 employees from 80 companies across 7 industries in 29 countries found that productivity was on average between 21 and 36 percent higher when managers focused on staff strengths. According to Alex Linley, our strengths are not merely those things we're good at, they're activities that energize us the more we do them – rather like the way driving causes the alternator to charge a car battery. The trick for a fulfilling life, he says, is to discover your unrealized strengths, marshal the strengths you do know about, manage your weaknesses and keep your "learned behaviours" in check – they're the things you're good at but which you don't find energizing.

All this emphasis on positivity is not without its critics. For example, in her 2009 book, *Bright-sided: How the Relentless Promotion of Positive Thinking Has Undermined America,* Barbara Ehrenreich blamed too much optimism for the banking crisis (see also Chapter 19) and other evils. Ehrenreich, a former cancer patient, challenged claims that a positive attitude is health-giving, and she warned that pressuring patients to see the sunny side of their ill health can be cruel, especially if they deteriorate and blame themselves for not being positive enough.

Recent research also suggests that thinking positively as a way to combat negative emotions doesn't work for everyone. In a paper published in 2009, Weiting Ng and Ed Diener of the University of Illinois at Urbana-Champaign asked 68 students to imagine being rejected from eight graduate schools, to report how that made them feel, and then to say what mental strategies they'd used to cope with the imaginary news. The key finding was that students who scored high on the personality dimension of neuroticism (see Chapter 11) tended to experience more negative emotion, even if they employed effective coping strategies such as thinking about how they could learn from the experience. It was a similar story in follow-up studies in which students were coached how to use positive thinking coping strategies and asked to recall a real-life bad event that they'd experienced. For students high in neuroticism, the positive thinking didn't prevent the imaginary or remembered bad news from making them feel miserable.

If this seems like a downbeat note to end on, perhaps we should heed the advice of the child psychotherapist and essayist Adam Phillips, who has argued that happiness is an unwise aspiration. In an essay for the *Guardian* newspaper published in 2010, he pointed out that happiness for many people can be prompted by immoral acts or desires. On the other hand, he argued, unhappiness, or more specifically frustration – can motivate us to correct injustices and losses. "What we are lacking when we are unhappy is not always happiness, any more than what an alcoholic is lacking is a drink", he wrote. "And proposing a right to the pursuit of happiness may seduce us, by a kind of word-magic, into thinking that happiness is just the thing."

Part VII

Resources

Books, magazines & multimedia

Hopefully, by this stage, your appetite for psychology has been whetted. If so, the following list of books, magazines, TV and radio shows, blogs and Twitter feeds should give you plenty to feast on. I've avoided textbooks and focused instead on popular science and fiction, with the emphasis on more recent publications.

Books

POPULAR SCIENCE

Dan Ariely *Predictably Irrational*
HarperCollins, 2008
Cheeky and revealing experiments described with wit by one of the world's leading behavioural economists. Also look out for his 2010 book, *The Upside of Irrationality*.

Ludy T. Benjamin Jr. *A Brief History of Modern Psychology*
Blackwell Publishing, 2007
The author has a passion for psychology's history and it shines through in this slim, entertaining volume.

Mick Cooper *Essential Research Findings in Counselling and Psychotherapy*
Sage, 2008
The many mixed and contradictory findings in the field of therapeutic research are laid out and explained with great clarity.

Antonio Damasio *The Feeling of What Happens, Body and Emotion in the Making of Consciousness*
William Heinemann, 1999
Emotion expert Damasio uses neurological case studies as inspiration for his "embodied" theory of consciousness. Poetic and thought-provoking.

Noah Goldstein, Steve J. Martin & Robert B. Cialdini *Yes! 50 Secrets from the Science of Persuasion*
Profile Books, 2007
An accessible and entertaining account of psychological principles that can be used as practical tools of persuasion – from the "foot in the door effect" to the "scarcity principle".

Alison Gopnik *The Philosophical Baby: What Children's Minds Tell Us About Truth, Love and the Meaning of Life*
Bodley Head, 2009
Drawing on her own and others' research, Gopnik, a developmental psychologist, tackles the question of what it's like to be a baby or young child. An engaging mix of psychology, philosophy and personal reflection.

Stephen Murdoch *How Psychology Hijacked Intelligence*
Gerald Duckworth & Co Ltd, 2009
A no-holds-barred historical account of the shadier side of intelligence testing.

David G. Myers *Intuition: Its Powers and Perils*
Yale University Press, 2004
A spate of books on human judgement and decision-making have been published over the last few years. Myers' effort was one of the first and, arguably, one of the most readable and comprehensive.

Daniel Nettle *Personality*
Oxford University Press, 2007
Nettle uses anonymous real-life stories to explain the science behind the Big Five theory of personality in this lively introduction to the field.

Steven Pinker *The Blank Slate: The Modern Denial of Human Nature*
Penguin, 2003
A detailed and eloquent mix of evolutionary psychology, anthropology and the politics of the nature–nurture debate. Pinker has a depth of knowledge and clarity of thought unsurpassed by any other psychologist writing for a general audience.

Matt Ridley *Nature via Nurture*
Harper Perennial, 2004
After reading this excellent introduction to behavioural genetics, you'll wince any time someone says there's a specific gene "for" a particular trait or condition.

Oliver Sacks *The Man Who Mistook His Wife for a Hat*
Summit Books, 1985
A collection of neuropsychological case studies described with feeling and erudition by British neurologist Sacks.

Tom Stafford and Matt Webb *Mind Hacks: Tips and Tools for Using Your Brain*
O'Reilly, 2005
Discover how your mind works through self-experimentation. The "hacks" are illusions and other phenomena that exploit the brain's engineering to entertaining and educational effect.

James Surowiecki *The Wisdom of Crowds, Why the Many Are Smarter Than the Few*
Abacus, 2005
The rise of social-networking websites has made research into collective intelligence more relevant than ever. This fascinating account is brought to life with real-life anecdotes.

Richard Thaler and Cass Sunstein *Nudge: Improving Decisions About Health, Wealth, and Happiness*
Yale University Press, 2008
The book that captured the imagination of world leaders. It outlines the approach of "libertarian paternalism", advocating policies or "nudges" designed to encourage people to make better decisions.

Richard Wiseman *59 Seconds: Think a Little, Change a Lot*
Macmillan, 2009
Evidence-based self-help for those short on time. Wiseman, a magician and professor of the Public Understanding of Psychology, debunks myths and ploughs research literature for the methods and means of improving your life.

FICTION

Sebastian Faulks *Human Traces* and *Engleby*
Vintage, 2006 & 2008
Human Traces provides a fictionalized account of the origins of psychiatry told through the lives of two boyhood friends: an English psychiatrist and a French neurologist. The later novel, *Engleby*, is a first-person confessional thriller set in 1970s Britain and written from the perspective of a character who is certainly odd and possibly dangerous. Faulks' meticulous research is on display in both novels.

Liz Jensen *The Rapture*
Bloomsbury, 2009
An apocalyptic eco-thriller laced with psychology. Wheelchair-bound art therapist Gabrielle Fox takes on the case of a troubled teenager who has premonitions of natural disasters.

Philippa Perry & Junko Graat *Couch Tales*
Palgrave Macmillan, 2010
A year-long journey of psychoanalysis explored through the medium of a graphic novel. Perry, a psychotherapist, provides explanatory footnotes throughout.

Jed Rubenfeld *The Interpretation of Murder*
Headline Review, 2007
A gripping crime thriller set in New York and featuring psychoanalysts Sigmund Freud, Carl Jung, Abraham Brill and Sándor Ferenczi. Inspired by Freud's only lecture visit to the US in 1909.

Magazines

New Scientist www.newscientist.com
A weekly science magazine that frequently features psychology-related cover articles and news.

Scientific American Mind www.scientificamerican.com/sciammind
A bi-monthly covering the whole breadth of psychology and neuroscience, with regular columns from such heavyweight contributors as Vilayanur Ramachandran.

The Psychologist www.thepsychologist.org.uk
Published monthly by the British Psychological Society, *The Psychologist* is a mix of features, interviews, job ads, reviews, news and research updates with a section on the history of the discipline.

Psychologies www.psychologies.co.uk
A women's glossy monthly with a focus on psychological issues. Less scientific than the other magazines and with more of a self-help theme.

Blogs & Twitter feeds

The BPS Research Digest www.researchdigest.org.uk/blog
Plain-English reports on the latest research findings in psychology, chosen and written by Christian Jarrett, the author of this book.

Mind Hacks www.mindhacks.com
A cornucopia of psychology and neuroscience curiosities, principally written by Vaughan Bell, a clinical neuropsychologist based in Colombia.

The Frontal Cortex www.wired.com/wiredscience/frontal-cortex
Fascinating postings from Jonah Lehrer, author of *How We Decide* and *Proust Was a Neuroscientist*.

PsyBlog www.spring.org.uk
A popular blog written by Jeremy Dean, with posts arranged according to themes and in "top ten" lists. More of a self-help vibe than the other blogs listed.

Neurophilosophy scienceblogs.com/neurophilosophy
Longer psychology and neuroscience postings, often with a historical bent. Written by neurobiologist-turned-science writer Mo Costandi.

For a comprehensive list of psychologists who tweet, see tinyurl.com/psychologistswhotweet. The list includes autism expert @UtaFrith, behavioural economist @DanAriely, developmental psychologist @cfernyhough, cognitive psychologist @Mark_Changizi and Christian Jarrett @researchdigest. The last provides links to the latest psychology-related newspaper articles, TV and radio shows and public lectures.

Films, TV, radio & podcasts

Inception (2010) Littered with Jungian references, Christopher Nolan's film features a dream device that allows its users to enter and manipulate another person's subconscious.

The Machinist (2004) A paranoid insomniac, played by a skeletal Christian Bale, battles his inner demons in this psychological thriller directed by Brad Anderson.

One Flew Over the Cuckoo's Nest (1975) Miloš Forman's anti-psychiatry movie starring Jack Nicholson as the incorrigible Randle McMurphy is set almost entirely within a repressive mental institution.

In Treatment This multi-award-winning HBO drama stars Gabriel Byrne as the psychoanalyst Dr Paul Weston. Each episode eavesdrops on a single therapy session with one of Weston's clients.

Lie to Me Fox drama series focused on the escapades of psychologist Dr Cal Lightman, the head of The Lightman Group, which provides lie-detection advice and other investigative services to the FBI. The real-life psychologist and emotion expert Paul Ekman is a consultant to the show.

All in the Mind; Mind Changers; Case Study Three psychology-themed radio series broadcast by BBC Radio 4 and presented by Claudia Hammond. Most episodes can be listened to again or downloaded via the Radio 4 website www.bbc.co.uk/radio4.

All in the Mind A psychology-themed radio series broadcast by ABC radio in Australia and presented by Natasha Mitchell. www.abc.net.au/rn/allinthemind/default.htm.

Neuropod Hosted by the journal *Nature*, this is a monthly podcast featuring psychology and neuroscience, presented by Kerri Smith. www.nature.com/neurosci/neuropod.

This Week in the History of Psychology For several years until 2009, Christopher D. Green, professor of psychology at York University in Toronto, provided a weekly history of psychology podcast. The archive is online at www.yorku.ca/christo/podcasts.

Vocational guidance

To find out about careers or qualifications in psychology, contact your national psychological society. The American Psychological Association (www.apa.org) is the world's largest with 150,000 members, followed by the British Psychological Society (www.bps.org.uk), which has close to 50,000 members. There are also equivalent organizations in Canada (www.cpa.ca), Australia (www.psychology.org.au), New Zealand (www.psychology.org.nz) and South Africa (www.psyssa.com).

You couldn't make it up

Neuropsychological conditions and delusions make regular appearances in fiction and on screen. Capgras syndrome, in which a patient believes that friends and relatives have been replaced by impostors, seems a particular favourite. Richard Powers' 2006 novel *The Echo Maker*, for example, has 27-year-old Mark Schluter emerge from a car crash-induced coma only to find that his sister, his dog and even his home appear to be impostors or replicas.

Other recent novels inspired by neuropsychological conditions include Mark Haddon's *The Curious Incident of the Dog in the Night-Time* (autism); Jonathan Franzen's *The Corrections* (depression, paranoia, Parkinson's, dementia – not all in the same character); and Ian McEwan's *Enduring Love* (de Clérambault's syndrome – the delusional belief that another person is in love with you). Examples aren't restricted to contemporary fiction. Heinrich Heine's poem "Der Doppelgänger" (set to music by Schubert), Edgar Allan Poe's short story *William Wilson* (1839) and Dostoevsky's novella *The Double* (1846) all feature characters who believe they have a double, a condition known as heutoscopy.

In the movies, Stanley Kubrick's 1964 satire *Dr Strangelove* (loosely based on Peter George's novel *Red Alert*) features the eponymous and deranged German-American nuclear scientist struggling to stop his hand from performing the Nazi salute in what appears to be a case of Anarchic Hand Syndrome. In the 1999 film *Fight Club*, adapted from a Chuck Palahniuk novel, the character played by Edward Norton suffers from a dissociation of identity (also known as multiple personality disorder). Issues of fragmented identity also crop up in Philip K. Dick's sci-fi novel *A Scanner Darkly* (1977), along with characters with delusional parasitosis (the belief that you are infected with parasites). The novel was adapted into feature-length animation film in 2006. In the same year the South Korean movie *I'm a Cyborg, But That's OK* featured a central character so deluded that she licks batteries for sustenance and cuts her wrists as a way to plug herself into the mains.

While live theatre has never shied away from extreme emotions, recent years have seen an increasing fascination with neuropsychological conditions. In 2008 the clinical neuropsychologist Vaughan Bell acted as consultant on a play, *Reminiscence*, based on the recollections of Mrs O'Connor. She was an 88-year-old nursing home resident, first described by Oliver Sacks, whose epileptic seizures triggered vivid childhood memories. Paul Broks is another neuropsychologist who has worked in the theatre, collaborating with director Mick Gordon on the play *On Ego* (2005), which explored the nature of personal identity. In 2008, their second collaboration, *On Emotion*, featured a cognitive behavioural therapist, his daughter, autistic son, and a puppeteer patient, and asked the question: "are we the puppets of our emotions?"

Index

Picture credits

Front cover: © 3D Stock Illustrations/Alamy
Back cover: Phrenological Head: © Classic Image/Alamy; Crowd: Gianni Murtore/Alamy;
William James: © Getty Images
Inside front cover: © Simon Fraser/Science Photo Library
Author photo: © Christian Jarrett

© Bettmann/Corbis 8, 15, 24, 44,106,116, 167, 187, 193, 195, 278, 337, 342; © Corbis 69, 245; ©
Helen King/Corbis 4; © Michael Nicholson/Corbis10; © Jose Luis Pelaez, Inc./Blend Images/
Corbis 27; © Bernard Bisson/Sygma/Corbis 30; © Antar Dayal/Illustration Works/Corbis 58;
© Edith Held/Corbis 66; © Corbis Sygma 81; © Peter Turnley/Corbis 82; © Jon Feingersh/
Blend Images/Corbis 90; © Reuters/Corbis 95; © Hulton-Deutsch Collection/Corbis 97; ©
Isabel Ellsen/Corbis 101; © LWA-Dann Tardif/Corbis 108; © Diane Kosup/Corbis 115; © Jutta
Klee/Corbis 121; © Clarissa Leahy/Corbis 125; © Tom & Dee Ann McCarthy/Corbis 128; © Iris
Images/Corbis 136; © Anna Peisl/Corbis 140; © George Shelley/Corbis 149; © Ondrea Barbe/
Corbis 152; © James Leynse/Corbis 159; © Wolfgang Flamisch/Corbis 161; © Karen Kas-
mauski/Science Faction/Corbis 172; © John Springer Collection/Corbis 178; © John Springer
Collection/Corbis 183; © Basta/dpa/Corbis 201; © Lawrence Manning/Corbis 203; © Hulton-
Deutsch Collection/Corbis 205; © Karen Huntt/Corbis 209; © Christy Bowe/Corbis 217 ©
Richard T. Nowitz/Corbis 224; © Joel Stettenheim/Corbis 232; © Ina Fassbender/Reuters/
Corbis 238; © ABC News/Charles Fredrick/Handout/Reuters/Corbis 242; © Handout/Reuters/
Corbis 248; © Ashley Cooper/Corbis 254; © Charles E. Rotkin/Corbis 264; © Andy Rain/epa/
Corbis 275; © Ralf-Finn Hestoft/Corbis 287; © ERproductions Ltd/Blend Images/Corbis 291;
© Tim Tadder/Corbis 301; © Kai Pfaffenbach/Reuters/Corbis 303; © Keith Hunter/Arcaid/
Corbis 313; © Frank Trapper/Corbis 327; © Ben Radford/Corbis 329; Getty Images 46, 53, 181,
188, 267, 350; AFP/Getty Images 218, 283; Time & Life Pictures/Getty Images 309; © Link Hall
35, 38, 39, 42, 68; Diana Jarvis © Rough Guides 77, 78; Moviestore Collection 227, 319; Collection
of Jack and Beverly Wilgus 41; © Lewis Bush 123; © RIA Novosti/Alamy 120; © Premaphotos/
Alamy 157; Photo Researchers/Science Photo Library 134; Peter Thompson/University of York
145; Hoang Xuan Pham/University Communications 257; diagram on p.190 reproduced by
kind permission of Dr John Raven.